WHEN THE
WHISTLE BLOWS

The Story of the Footballers'
Battalion in the Great War

ANDREW RIDDOCH & JOHN KEMP

WHEN THE WHISTLE BLOWS

The Story of the Footballers'
Battalion in the Great War

FOREWORD BY RICHARD HOLMES

Haynes Publishing

Dedication

To L/Sgt Archie Strike F/311
Compositor, Linesman and Soldier
Killed in Action 13 November 1916

© Andrew Riddoch 2011

First hardback edition published in 2008
This paperback edition published, with minor amendments, in November 2011

A catalogue record for this book is available from the British Library

ISBN 978 0 85733 103 8

Library of Congress catalog card no 2011926163

Published by Haynes Publishing,
Sparkford, Yeovil, Somerset BA22 7JJ, UK
Tel: 01963 442030 Fax: 01963 440001
Int. tel: +44 1963 442030 Int. fax: +44 1963 440001
E-mail: sales@haynes.co.uk
Website: www.haynes.co.uk

Haynes North America Inc.,
861 Lawrence Drive, Newbury Park,
California 91320, USA

Designed and typeset by Dominic Stickland
Printed and bound in the USA by Odcombe Press LP,
1299 Bridgestone Parkway, La Vergne, TN 37086

CONTENTS

ACKNOWLEDGEMENTS

When the Whistle Blows owes much to many people. We are greatly indebted to the staff of the following institutions for their friendly and professional assistance: the British Newspaper Library, the British Red Cross Archives, the Brotherton Library at the University of Leeds, the Imperial War Museum, the National Archives and the National Army Museum.

Various club historians and supporters have also contributed much to *When the Whistle Blows* in the way of information and photographs. We are particularly grateful to: Tim Carder (Brighton & Hove Albion Collectors' and Historians' Society), Stuart Basson (Chesterfield Town), Alan Futter (Croydon Common), Stephen Jenkins (Leyton Orient), Roger Wash (Luton Town), Gary James (Manchester City), Dave Sullivan (Millwall), Ken Smales (Nottingham Forest), Frank Grande (Northampton Town), Peter Hall (Plymouth Argyle), David Downs (Reading), Duncan Holley and Gary Chalk (Southampton), Bob Goodwin and Andy Porter (Spurs), Trefor Jones (Watford), and John Northcutt (West Ham). Special mention must be made of Mike Davage (Norwich City) for his boundless enthusiasm for the book, and his unerring ability to root out obscure biographical information.

Other individuals have helped in a variety of ways. We would like to thank: Graham Adams, Ben Armstrong, Chris Baker and numerous members of the Great War Forum (http://www.1914-1918.invisionzone.com/forums/), Chris Bailey, David Barber (Football Association), Stephen Beeby, Dr John Bourne, Steve Bramley, Philippa Brazier, Lee Cognetta, Roger Cook, Andrew Cowie (Colorsport), Alan Clark, Peter Cluness, Graeme Cooper of Corporate Battlefields, Jason Crimp, Terry Denham, Joe Devereux,

Roy Evans, Roy Eve, Charles Fair, Dick Flory, Gerald Gliddon, Andrew Graham, John Hamblin, Michael Harrison, Brian Hill, Ian Hook (Essex Regimental Museum), Peter Jackson, Mark Johnston, Jane Jones, Peter Kemp, Angela Knox, Abby Koerner, H.G.M. Leighton, Chris Leonard and Isobel Black, Doug Lewis, Calista Lucy (Dulwich School), Stuart McLaren, Simon May (St Paul's School), Martin Middlebrook, Simon Moody (NAM), Mick Mills, Ian Nannestad (*Soccer History* magazine), Chris Noble, Paul Nixon, Mike O'Reilly (Scottish Rugby Union), Max Poilu, Chris Preston, Patrick Quirke, Terry Reeves, Alex Reid, Pamela Riddoch, D.J. Royle, Patrick Schallert, Douglas Scott, Andrew Seeley and Lorraine Payne, René Senteur, Jack Sheldon, John Sinkins, Guy Smith, Phil Stant, Ingo Steinmeyer, Michael Thierens, Ian Thomson, Tim Thurlow, Phil Vasili, Alan Wakefield (IWM), Michael and Karen Warmoth, Glyn Warwick, Finbarr Whooley (Horniman Museum), Hayley Wilding (Bank of England Archives), Jackie Withers (Commonwealth War Graves Commission) and Dr Michael Worms (St Paul's Church, Mill Hill). For those individuals, who have been inadvertently omitted from the above list, we offer our sincerest apologies.

It has been a particular pleasure to make contact with families of some of the brave men who served with the 17th Middlesex, several of whom got in touch after the publication of the hardback edition in November 2008 with additional information about their relatives. Our thanks go to Terry Andrews, Alex Barker, William Barnfather, Kym Baskerville, Betty Carter, Rupert Casey, Alan Childs, Wendi Friend, Geoffrey Grainger, John Hickmott, Joan Harmston, Michael Horniman, Anne Jenkins, Geoff Kentfield, Steve Key, Zoe Linkson, John Luvian-Wade, Lorne Maclaine, Patrick and John McCormick, John and Sandra Matthews, Vicky Moore, Bill Reed, Lauretta Rolph-Dickinson, Julia and Stephen Rhys, Bern Stacey, Kyle Tallett, Mike Websell and Sarah Woodcock.

Michael McCarthy, Steven Broomfield, Jeremy Elms and Ian Riddoch read much of the draft manuscript and offered many helpful and valuable suggestions. Mark Hughes, Jonathan Falconer and the team at Haynes were always accessible, and we are grateful for the opportunity to make some minor amendments to this edition. We remain particularly indebted to the late

Professor Richard Holmes for contributing a foreword. Having a foreword written by such a respected historian and battlefield guide meant a great deal to two first-time authors.

Extracts from the papers of Capt J.G. Howard and papers relating to Capt A.M.C. McReady-Diarmid are quoted courtesy of the Council of the National Army Museum, London. We are grateful to Richard Davies (Liddle Collection), Brotherton Library, University of Leeds, for permission to quote from the papers of Pte Wilf Nixon and papers relating to Pte Fred Hodges. The extract from J.L. Wade's letter in Chapter 12 is quoted by kind permission of the Governors of Dulwich College. We have been unable to trace the copyright holders of the papers of Maj W.G. Bailey and Lt Col R.S.S.H. Stafford, which are held by the Imperial War Museum. The authors and the Imperial War Museum would, therefore, be grateful for any information, which might help to trace the copyright holders of these papers. The authors would also be pleased to hear from other copyright holders, who remain unknown to us, so that due acknowledgement might be made in any future edition.

Lastly, our greatest debt is owed to our long-suffering families. Accordingly, we thank Lisa, Elizabeth, Oliver and Isabel; and Angela, Jack and Adam for their patience, love and support.

AGWR
JMK

FOREWORD

Few aspects of the British army of the First World War have the extraordinary poignancy of the pals' battalions. These were part of Lord Kitchener's 'New Armies', wartime volunteers who responded in unprecedented numbers to the call to arms. Some battalions – like the Accrington Pals and the Sheffield City Battalion – were recruited in specific areas, and owed much of their character to this fact. Others, such as the Public Schools and Sportsmen's battalions, were raised from particular interest groups.

What was known formally as 17th (Service) Battalion (1st Football) The Middlesex Regiment was not unique: 23rd Middlesex later rejoiced in the title 2nd Football Battalion, and Sir George McCrae not only formed 16th Battalion The Royal Scots largely from players and supporters of Heart of Midlothian FC, but proceeded to command it in the field. Yet there was something distinctive about 17th Middlesex. In 1914 there were growing complaints that English professional footballers were setting a bad example by playing on, attracting large crowds of young men of military age: 'All they seem to care about is football,' complained a recruiting officer. In December 1914 the flamboyant politician William Joynson-Hicks was asked to form 'a footballers' battalion of Kitchener's army' and at a public meeting on 15 December Fred 'Spider' Parker, captain of Clapton Orient, became the first man to volunteer for the new battalion. Recruiting soon took off, although it was clear from the start that this would be no walk-over, but 'a game of games against one of the finest teams in the world'.

Like so many other pals' battalions, 17th Middlesex first saw serious action on the Somme in 1916, losing over 500 officers and men between 24 July and 11 August, with another 300 casualties at Redan Ridge that autumn, and 462 at Oppy the following spring. The battalion helped check the German counterattack at Cambrai in November 1917, and one of its company commanders, Captain Allastair McReady-Diarmid, earned a posthumous Victoria Cross: an official report credited him with killing or wounding 94 Germans before being felled in the moment of victory.

Love of the game shone out even in the darkest moments. Just before he died, Private William Jonas told his boyhood friend Sergeant-Major Richard McFadden, who played for the same club: 'Goodbye, Mac. Best of luck . . . and best regards to the lads at Orient.' The chain of medical evacuation was, thought one soldier, 'worse than a whole season of cup ties', and another reported, in 1917 that: 'We have a big match on. We are still unbeaten . . .'

'The spirit of the professional players, amateurs and "club enthusiasts" within the ranks of the battalion made a lasting impression on everyone who encountered it,' write the authors. In their skilful interweaving of the story of professional football in Britain they have produced not only a beautifully researched history of a fine battalion, but a lasting tribute to men who remained true to their salt when the whistle blew, not on manicured greensward, but in a muddy trench.

Richard Holmes

A BRIEF NOTE ON BRITISH MILITARY ORGANISATION MID-1916

The following table provides a simplified overview of the theoretical fighting strength (in terms of infantry only) of a British Army on the Western Front in mid-1916. By the end of the year, General Headquarters (GHQ) was responsible for five such armies in France and Flanders.

Formation	Approximate infantry strength	Additional units	Usually commanded by
Army (usually 3–4 corps, but variable)	108,000–192,000	Army HQ plus other supporting arms and ancillary services	General
Corps (usually 3–4 divisions, but variable)	36,000–48,000	Corps HQ Heavy artillery Cyclist company Cavalry regiment Tunnelling companies plus other supporting arms and ancillary services	Lieutenant-General
Division (in the region of 18,000 men, consisting of 3 infantry brigades plus divisional troops.	12,000	Divisional HQ Signal company Field artillery (64 guns grouped in 16 batteries) Trench mortar batteries (3) Pioneer battalion Engineer units (3) Field ambulances (3) Transport Mobile veterinary services Sanitary section	Major-General
Brigade (4 battalions)[i]	4,000	Brigade HQ Trench mortar battery Machine gun company	Brigadier-General
Battalion (e.g. the 17th Middlesex)	1,000[ii]	Battalion HQ	Lieutenant-Colonel
-Company (4 platoons)	240		Major/Captain
-Platoon (4 sections)	60		Lieutenant/ 2nd Lieutenant
-Section	15		Corporal/ Lance-Corporal

[i] In 1918, the number of battalions in a brigade would be reduced to three.
[ii] The fighting strength of infantry battalions was frequently well short of this figure due to factors such as battle losses, training courses, sickness and home leave. As the war progressed, it became common practice to leave a cadre of men out of the line before an attack, in order to facilitate the re-building of battalions in the event of heavy casualties.

PROLOGUE

FA Cup Final, 25 April 1914
Burnley v Liverpool
Venue: Crystal Palace

At 2.55 p.m. King George V, wearing a dark-grey lounge suit and bowler hat, with a red rose in the buttonhole of his overcoat, left Buckingham Palace by motor car. Cheering crowds lined his route to Sydenham, hoping to catch a glimpse of their monarch on his way to the match. On his arrival at Crystal Palace, the King was met by Lord Derby outside the entrance to the Royal Pavilion. The President of the Football Association (FA), Lord Kinnaird, an Old Etonian and himself a holder of five FA Cup winners' medals, then presented senior officials of the FA – Charles Clegg (Chairman), Charles Crump (Vice-Chairman) and Frederick Wall (Secretary) – to the King. As the King was conducted to his seat, he was accorded an enthusiastic reception by a boisterous crowd in the region of 72,000, half of whom were estimated to have made the trip to London from their native Lancashire. In keeping with such a carnival atmosphere, the respective bands of the Irish Guards and the King's Liverpool Regiment struck up the National Anthem.

Both clubs had struggled in the Football League, and there had been little interest in proceedings outside the Lancashire working classes. True to form the first half was a disjointed affair, with each team primarily seeking to deny attacking opportunities to the other. Beneath the dazzling sunshine, on a dusty pitch, Liverpool initially looked the better side. Sewell, the Burnley goalkeeper, twice spilled the ball at the feet of Liverpool forwards, but at half time, the game remained goalless.

Ten minutes after the interval, Nesbitt, the Burnley outside-right, centred the ball. After taking a slight deflection it fell invitingly for Freeman, who struck a volley past an unsighted Campbell in the Liverpool goal. The game thereafter noticeably improved. Mosscrop and Lindley both missed chances to extend Burnley's lead, while an inspired Sewell made some exhilarating saves to deny Liverpool an equalising goal. It was still 1–0, when H.S. Bamlett, the referee from Durham, blew the final whistle. Burnley had won the FA Cup for the first time in their history.[1]

After presenting the Cup to Boyle, the Burnley captain, the King left the stadium. Some observers noted that unlike Ferguson, the stand-in Liverpool captain, who seemed to have been somewhat overawed by meeting the King, Boyle had displayed a quiet dignity more reminiscent of a cricketer or a golfer than a professional footballer. It had been a truly momentous day for association football. As far back as 1892, the then Prince of Wales, the future Edward VII, had accepted an invitation to become the first royal patron of the FA, but this was the first occasion on which a reigning monarch had elected to attend the FA Cup Final and honour the winners by presenting the Cup. The people's game had been given formal recognition by the highest authority in the land.

The largely good-natured crowds, several of whom were wearing gaudy paper hats and carrying ribbon-decked sticks, began to disperse. The King and his entourage had witnessed a clean, hard-fought contest, which had undoubtedly challenged the notion that a 'true' sportsman should, as a matter of principle, ignore games played by those unable to play without being paid for their services. It would have been quite inconceivable to the spectators making their way home that association football would very soon, like the British Empire itself, be facing a crisis of a quite unprecedented magnitude.

1. At the time of writing, this remains the only occasion on which Burnley have won the FA Cup.

CHAPTER 1

THE GREATER GAME

Why is it only soccer that is attacked? Why not golf, hockey and other outdoor sports? What about closing music-halls, theatres and dancing rooms?
L/Cpl Lionel Hayburn, 31st Signal Company, Indian Army

The exact origins of football in the British Isles are obscure, although it is known that Romans brought with them a ball game called *Harpastum*. What is certain is that various forms of the game were being played in different parts of England from the Middle Ages onwards. The rules of these generally rough games were very much dependent on the locality, where they took place. Teams often consisted of large numbers of players. Goals might be marked by wooden posts in the same field, or by prominent local landmarks, such as a stream or a town wall, situated several miles apart. Such games were usually played on market days, fairs or holidays, and were predominantly associated with the lower classes of society. The authorities largely viewed such games as a rowdy free-for-all, frequently giving rise to injury, property damage and civil disorder.

By the beginning of the 19th century the traditional forms of the game had gone into decline in the wake of the Industrial Revolution, which had undermined many rural traditions, and had left little time for the working classes to indulge in leisure pursuits. Football was also adversely affected by various legislation, such as a series of Inclosure Acts between 1750 and 1860, which resulted in the enclosure of vast amounts of common land, traditionally used for local sports and pastimes, and the Highways Act 1835, which prohibited the playing of football on highways. Were it not for the rising popularity of the game in a number of English public schools, it is likely that the football would be of little interest to anyone now, other than social historians.

Similarly rough forms of the game had long been played at

public schools, such as Eton, Harrow and Charterhouse. Over time schools began to develop their own sets of rules with the result that there were several different variants of the game. At a time when the public schools were preparing their pupils to meet the administrative and military needs of the British Empire, football and organised sport generally were increasingly seen as fulfilling a vital role in a schoolboy's moral, social and physical development, and were used as such to promote values of participation, unselfishness and fair play.

The significant variations in the rules of the various games inevitably led to difficulties when former pupils wanted to play the game at university and beyond. This resulted in several attempts to codify the rules, most notably in the formation of the Football Association by a number of Metropolitan clubs in 1863. The position of the FA, as a fledgling governing body of the game, was further strengthened by the introduction of the FA Challenge Cup, entered by just 15 clubs in its inaugural competition in 1871/2, which soon began to attract entrants from a wider geographical and social background.

Within a few years the ascendancy of southern teams derived from former public school players, such as Old Etonians, Old Carthusians and Wanderers, began to be challenged by new clubs from the textile towns of Lancashire, several of which were rumoured to be engaged in the illegal payment of players by the late 1870s. In 1882, Blackburn Rovers reached the FA Cup Final where they were defeated by Old Etonians. This would be the last occasion on which an 'Old Boys' team would win the FA Cup. The following year, in a competition entered by 84 clubs, the winners were Blackburn Olympic. With rumours of professionalism rife many amateur clubs were less than impressed. The idea of paying players to participate in sport was abhorrent to many of the upper and middle classes in late-Victorian England. With professionals striving to win at all costs, there was every chance that the true spirit of the game would be lost. In some quarters professionalism was seen as a threat to the well being of society itself, with its emphasis on financial reward and spectatorship, as opposed to the values of sportsmanship and participation in physical activity.

Matters finally came to a head in January 1884 when a London club, Upton Park, lodged an official complaint that the Preston North End side, against which it had played in an FA Cup tie, was essentially a professional one. By now several northern clubs were making little or no attempt to conceal the fact that they were paying their players. Thirty-one leading clubs threatened to split from the FA and set up a rival British Football Association. Recognising that such a split would be disastrous for the game, the FA took the momentous decision to legalise professionalism in July 1885.

In order to manage the impact of professionalism on the game, stringent conditions were attached. Initially, clubs were only allowed to pay players, who had been either born, or had lived for a period of two years, within a 6-mile radius of the ground. Professional players were also subject to an annual registration requirement and along with ex-professionals were prevented from serving on FA committees. Despite such 'safeguards' the decision to legalise professionalism met with much opposition in the traditional amateur strongholds of the game, namely London and the south-east, Sheffield and Birmingham. The animosity would continue to simmer through the game in the years leading up to the First World War, as the game's amateur administrators strove to limit the growing commercialisation of football and the perceived erosion of true sporting ideals.

Following the legalisation of professionalism, football clubs were not slow in recognising the commercial opportunities afforded by the growing popularity of the game. Timber terracing was erected and embankments of earth created in order to ensure a better view of the field of play. The most important consequence of professionalism was the founding of the Football League by six clubs apiece from Lancashire and the Midlands in 1888, which maximised potential revenue by ensuring regular fixtures between clubs on pre-arranged dates.[1] During the inaugural season, the 12 clubs attracted a total of around 600,000 spectators to League fixtures. The league model was subsequently embraced at all levels of the game, providing a sound platform for its expansion. Four years later the First Division was expanded to 16 clubs and a 12-club Second Division established, but professional football was still very much a northern phenomenon, with not one of the 28 League clubs from south of Birmingham. In 1894 the Southern League was set up, consisting initially of nine clubs in its First Division and seven in the Second. The Southern League was to prove vital for the development of professional football in southern England.

The beginning of the 20th century saw the game continuing to grow in popularity, but the residual tension surrounding professionalism surfaced again when the local football associations of Surrey and Middlesex, comprised largely of Old Boys' amateur teams, refused to acknowledge a FA resolution that they should admit local professional clubs as members. The result was an acrimonious split. Upwards of 500 amateur clubs, principally from London and the south-east, broke away from the FA in 1907 to set up the Amateur Football Defence Federation, later renamed the Amateur Football Association (AFA).

Recognition of the AFA as a governing body was not slow in coming from the organisations that shared its amateur ideals, such as the Hockey Association and the Rugby Football Union, but it was less successful in securing recognition from other bodies, most notably the Fédération Internationale de Football Association (FIFA) and the Scottish, Welsh and Irish Football Associations. It was soon evident that a split was in the best interests of neither faction, but there was no reconciliation until January 1914, when the AFA returned to the fold as a FA-affiliated society. The split had many repercussions, most notably that several public schools began to switch from football to rugby. Despite the reconciliation, amateur hostility towards professional football remained. Within only a few months the uneasy peace would be shattered by the outbreak of the First World War, which would provide critics of the professional game with a perfect opportunity to settle old scores.

On 28 June 1914 Archduke Franz Ferdinand, heir to the throne of the Austro-Hungarian Empire, and his morganatic wife Sophia, while on a state visit to Sarajevo, capital of the recently annexed Austrian province of Bosnia-Herzegovina, were shot by a young Serbian nationalist, Gavrilo Princip. Stepping forward from the crowd, after the Archduke's driver had taken a wrong turning into a side street, Princip managed to fire two shots before he was seized. The Archduke and his wife died within minutes.

Encouraged by Germany, Austria sought revenge, issuing a

harsh ultimatum to Serbia. Despite a conciliatory Serbian response, Austria declared war on 28 July. The fragile peace that had existed in Europe for a number of years began to unravel. On 31 July Russia having made it clear that she would not stand aside in the event of an Austrian invasion of Serbia, ordered a partial mobilisation of her armed forces. When Russia refused to countermand this order, Germany duly declared war on 1 August. That same day France, Russia's ally since 1894, issued mobilisation orders. On 3 August Germany declared war on France, following her refusal to give a guarantee of neutrality in the event of a Russo-German conflict. The next day German cavalry crossed the Belgian frontier. Belgium resisted the German advance and appealed for assistance.

In an effort to avoid a war on two fronts with France and Russia, German military planners had formulated a plan to defeat the French in six weeks, which would allow the victorious German armies to be transported across her vast rail network to the Eastern Front in time to meet the expected Russian onslaught. The Schlieffen Plan, as it was called after its chief architect Count Alfred von Schlieffen, involved German armies driving through Belgium and Luxembourg into northern France, bypassing the more strongly fortified Franco-German frontier. Time was of the essence. According to military estimates, Russia would not be ready to launch an invasion of Germany until at least six weeks after mobilisation. Operations in France had to be brought to a successful conclusion within that time frame.

The problem was that Prussia, the dominant German state prior to unification in 1871, along with Britain, Russia, France and Austria, had been a signatory to the Treaty of London in 1839, which had stipulated that Belgium should remain a neutral and independent state in perpetuity. Only a few days earlier the British government had sought assurances from France and Germany that they would respect Belgian neutrality. France had answered in the affirmative, but tellingly there had been no response from Germany. The British Ambassador in Berlin was duly instructed to inform the German government that, unless it undertook to withdraw its troops from Belgium by 11 p.m. (GMT), Britain would have no choice, but to declare war. Later that evening, as

German troops continued their advance through Belgium, Britain declared war on Germany, and an angry mob assembled outside the British Embassy in Berlin.

The general feeling in Britain was that the forthcoming conflict would be a brief affair. Such a view was not shared by the newly appointed Secretary of State for War, Field Marshal Earl Kitchener of Khartoum. It was Kitchener's belief that the war might last some three years and that some 70 divisions would be required. Parliament was duly asked to sanction an additional 500,000 men for the Army. On 7 August, the day on which advance parties of the British Expeditionary Force (BEF) crossed the Channel, the press published Kitchener's appeal for the first 100,000 volunteers, aged 19 to 30, to serve as regular soldiers 'for a period of 3 years or until the war is concluded'. In terms of numbers, the British army was ill prepared for a continental war. In August 1914 the total strength of its army was only 733,514 officers and men.[2] Of this figure, less than a quarter of a million were regulars, and half of these troops were scattered across the empire. In contrast, Germany was able to muster some 3.8 million men on mobilisation. France, Russia and Austria-Hungary could each put similarly impressive numbers of men into the field.

As a result of mobilisation, large numbers of sportsmen, who were either territorials or army reservists, were called up, including Ronald Poulton Palmer, the England rugby captain, and Sir Archibald White, the Yorkshire cricket captain, who left the dressing room in the middle of a Roses match. Among their number were footballers from several clubs, including three Nottingham Forest players: John Bell, William Fiske and Robert Firth. All three men had seen prior service with the regular army. They were seen off at the railway station by the club secretary, R.J. Master, who wished them 'Godspeed', and presented them with gifts of sweets and tobacco.

Over the next few days, as the first men to answer Kitchener's call flooded into the recruiting offices, several club secretaries were alarmed to discover that their football grounds had been commandeered for use by the War Office. Territorial soldiers practised their drill on the pitch at Goodison Park, and Hyde Road, Manchester City's ground at that time, became a stable for over

300 horses. Otherwise it was very much a case of 'business as usual', the prevailing doctrine of the day. Several sides started their pre-season training, and the traditional cricket match between Chelsea and Tottenham Hotspur took place at Fulham Cricket Ground. After a delayed start on account of the weather, Vivian Woodward, the celebrated Chelsea and England amateur, dispatched the Spurs bowlers to all corners of the ground, bringing up his century with a majestic six that landed on the pavilion roof. The game ended in a resounding victory for Chelsea, the Pensioners posting a score of 173 all out (Woodward 110 not out), in response to a Spurs total of 90 all out.

With the start of the new football season only a few weeks away, there were already questions being asked about whether it was appropriate for a football season to commence at such a time. The FA secretary, Frederick Wall, had no such doubts, believing that it was in the greater interests of the country that the football season should start as planned. The game would provide a pastime for those without military training, and those individuals for whom the government was unable to find profitable employment. Futhermore, the usual pre-season matches would generate a significant amount of money. In the current climate, Wall was sure that the clubs would donate this money to the various War Relief Funds.

On 15 August it was widely reported in the press that the Rugby Football Union, having already offered to place Twickenham at the disposal of the War Office, had circulated a notice to all rugby clubs: 'The Rugby Union are glad to know that a large number of their players have already volunteered for service. They express a hope that all Rugby players will join some force in their own town or county.'[3] By the end of the month leading rugby clubs, such as Blackheath and London Scottish, were announcing that they were cancelling their fixtures for the forthcoming season, due to shortages of players. These enlistments were not just confined to the ex-public school players. Nine months previously, in South Wales, the Senghenydd rugby team had been virtually wiped out in a horrific mining disaster that had left 439 men dead. Within days of Kitchener's call for men, 11 players of the new team had enlisted.

The nation's amateur footballers were also perceived to be 'doing their bit'. The various amateur leagues, such as the Isthmian and Spartan Leagues, had intended, like the Football and Southern Leagues, to start their season as normal. Throughout August amateur players, particularly those of the upper and middle classes, were queuing up outside the recruiting offices. Within a matter of weeks no less than 16 players of Dulwich Wood FC would have answered their nation's call. It was not long before several amateur sides were announcing their intention of scratching their fixtures for the season. Quite simply, they had run out of players.[4]

The Corinthians, the famous club set up by N. Lane 'Pa' Jackson, an assistant secretary of the FA and a vociferous opponent of professionalism, for the finest ex-public school and university players in 1882, set a particularly stirring example. Fourteen members of the club had left for a tour of Argentina in July. On learning of the outbreak of war at the Brazilian port of Pernambuco, the Corinthians had duly cancelled their tour and 'caught the first vessel back', eight players enlisting soon after disembarkation. While players from professional clubs were not enlisting at the same rate as their amateur counterparts, many were, in fact, doing so. The professional football club with the finest record in the country was Southern League club, Croydon Common.[5] Within a few weeks of the outbreak of hostilities, no less than 13 of its players would have responded to the nation's call to arms.[6]

On Saturday 22 August, the day before the BEF would fight its first battle of the war around the Belgian town of Mons, professional football clubs of all sizes participated in a programme of matches to raise money for the Prince of Wales's National Relief Fund. At White Hart Lane, where Tottenham Hotspur played Arsenal, the extraordinary sum of £365 was raised. In Lincoln, nearly 6,000 spectators turned up to watch Lincoln City, generating £27 10s 10d for the fund[7]. By the end of the month such pre-season matches had raised a total of £7,025, which was donated to an assortment of charities and relief funds.There was no doubt that football was raising significant sums of money for a worthwhile cause, but there was an increasingly prevalent view that the continuance of organised sport was wholly inappropriate during wartime. Even the game of cricket, which was nearing the end of its season, did not escape censure. Sir George Pragnell, a vice-president of the AFA, went so far to recommend that cricketers should be pelted with turf from the ground and that every footballer, unmarried and able-bodied, should be treated like a football and kicked. On 27 August the venerable W.G. Grace added his voice to the debate:

> There are many cricketers who are already doing their duty, but there are many more who do not seem to realise that in all probability they will have to serve either at home or abroad before the war is brought to a conclusion. The fighting on the continent is very severe, and will be probably be prolonged. I think that the time has arrived when the county cricket season should be closed, for it is not fitting at a time like the present that able-bodied men should play day after day and pleasure-seekers look on.[8]

Two days later, Field Marshal Lord Roberts of Kandahar spoke for many of the middle and upper classes when he addressed a New Army battalion of the Royal Fusiliers: 'I respect and honour you more than I can say. My feeling towards you is one of intense admiration. How very different is your action to that of the men, who can still go on with their cricket and football, as if the very existence of our nation were not at stake'.[9]

One did not need to be as well informed as Lord Roberts to know that the war was not exactly proceeding to plan for the Allied powers. On the Eastern Front, although Russia had surprised everyone with the speed of her mobilisation, her plans for a great sweep into Germany were going disastrously awry in the forests of East Prussia. On the Western Front, pre-war French plans for the liberation of Alsace-Lorraine and a swift advance to the Rhine lay in tatters. Further north, heavily outnumbered British and French forces were in full retreat, as German troops having swept aside Belgian resistance, drove southwards towards Paris.

On 31 August the Management Committee of the Football League met in London. The decision was made that 'the great Winter game should pursue its usual course', although the committee did recommend that each club should arrange military drill for its players and provide them with the facility of a miniature rifle range.[10] The committee concluded its lengthy public statement with the words:

Every club should do all in its power to assist the war funds. Every player should especially train to be of national service – at least, in national defence – and while we unreservedly authorise the due fulfilment of the League programme, we must accept to the full every obligation that we can individually and collectively discharge for our beloved country and our comrades in arms who in this fight for righteousness and justice at the risk of their lives have answered to duty's call.[11]

That same day the Consultative Committee of the FA also held a meeting at the offices in Russell Square. The following resolution was unanimously passed in the hope that such a stance might alleviate the growing criticism of plans to start the football season as normal:

The Football Association earnestly appeals to the patriotism of all who are interested in the game to help in all possible ways in support of the Nation in the present serious crisis, and particularly to those who are able, to render personal service in the Army and Navy, which are so gallantly upholding our national honour. To those who are unable to render personal service the Association would appeal for their generous support of the funds for the relief and assistance of those who are engaged in serving the country. The Football Association will contribute £1,000 to the Prince of Wales's War Fund, and will be prepared to assist the authorities in any direction that they may desire.[12]

Speaking in support of this resolution, the chairman, Charles Clegg, said that 'It has been suggested that all games should be stopped. Having regard to the great anxieties which all must feel during the continuance of war I think total suspension would be mischievous rather than good.'[13] The FA also urged football clubs to release professional players from their contractual obligations for the war's duration. A War Sub-Committee was set up to liaise with the appropriate authorities. Within a few days a series of proposals would be submitted by the War Sub-Committee to the War Office for consideration: clubs were to be advised to place their grounds at the disposal of the War Office on non-match days; and to arrange for local public figures to address players and spectators; and County Football Associations were to be instructed to work closely with local recruiting officers.

On 2 September the day after the first fixtures of the new season had taken place, Frederick Wall took issue with recent claims made by Dr Thomas Fry, the Dean of Lincoln and a former headmaster of two leading public schools, Oundle and Berkhamsted. Dr Fry had expressed many of the prejudices against the professional game, writing that the continuance of football was 'due not merely to the apathy of the onlookers, but to the bookmakers, the betters, and the men who have money invested in football gambling'.[14] Unimpressed with such allegations, Wall called upon the Dean to produce some justification for his assertions, warning him that if he were unable to do so, 'you will know what is due from you both as a gentleman and a Christian Minister'.[15]

No apology was forthcoming. Instead the Dean went even further in his reply to Wall's letter, asserting that football coupons and betting were largely responsible for not just the present apathy, but for many of the professional game's less savoury aspects as well: 'True sport is killed by it. The not infrequent ill-treatment of referees is caused by it. There is no local patriotism at all in it, where players are practically bought and sold. Professional football becomes merely a business, not a sport.'[16] The Dean's demands were threefold: first, that the FA should support a Bill to stop the coupon system; second, that the FA should cancel players' contracts with immediate effect so 'that those who are willing (and I am told many are willing) may go immediately to the front'; third, that only men over 40 should continue to be admitted to football matches. The Dean neglected to adduce any evidence to support his initial assertion that the gambling industry was behind the continuance of football.

Wall responded immediately, pointing out that the FA supported such a Bill, which had been recently introduced into the House of

Commons by William Hayes Fisher MP, president of Fulham FC. Wall also took the opportunity to remind him that contracts of employment were legally binding on both clubs and players and repeated his request for the Dean to provide some justification for his original statement, along with the names of any players who were being prevented from enlisting by their clubs. In the event no details were provided; once more the Dean's reply was couched in the most general of terms. The Dean also announced his intention of declining to enter into any further correspondence on the matter. A further letter from Wall provoked no response and there the exchange ended.

On 4 September, the same day on which the recruiting proposals of its War Sub-Committee were approved, the FA placed 'its whole organisation and influence at the service of the War Office'. All affiliated clubs were sent copies of posters to be displayed prominently around their grounds: 'Recruits for the Army are at the moment most urgently needed. Players and spectators who are physically fit, and otherwise able, are urged to join the Army at once.'[17] The next day, when Aston Villa played Sunderland, recruiting officers paraded around Villa Park in search of men, while a band played the French and Russian national anthems. The results were encouraging, several supporters stepping forward. By now many clubs were taking steps to implement drilling and shooting practice for their players. The first club to organise military training was Brighton & Hove Albion under the guidance of one of their players, Charlie Webb, who had seen previous service with the Essex Regiment. At the instigation of their chairman, Capt Henry Wells-Holland, Clapton Orient were another club taking the lead.[18] A rifle club was set up next to the ground in Homerton, and supporters were invited to join the players in learning to march and shoot. Such patriotic measures did little to placate those who believed that the football season should never have started in the first place.

One of the most formidable opponents of football to emerge at this time was the noted philanthropist, F.N. Charrington, who had renounced 'a colossal fortune because he did not believe in being a partner in a brewery' and had devoted himself to advancing the causes of Christianity and Temperance in London's East End.[19]

During the latter quarter of the 19th century, Charrington had conducted a vociferous crusade against music halls, which had twice resulted in his arrest for harassment. For many people, music halls were perceived to foster alcoholism, absenteeism and moral corruption, thus resulting in poverty for many of their patrons. In Charrington's eyes, the dangers of professional football, with its many links to the brewing industry, were no different from those engendered by the music halls. The present debate surrounding the playing of football was too good an opportunity to miss. A few weeks earlier Charrington had paid a visit to Frederick Wall and written a letter to the *Morning Post*, contending that it would be 'a national shame and disgrace to our country if we have our best athletes charging one another on the football field, instead of charging the Germans on the battlefield'.[20] He had demanded that the FA immediately release all professionals from their contracts and band them together as 'footballer battalions', which could be named after various football clubs, and used to facilitate recruiting. The failure of the FA to adopt his proposals immediately had filled Charrington with feelings of 'shame and indignation'. He fired off telegrams to the King respectfully suggesting that His Majesty should withdraw his patronage of the FA, and to Lord Kinnaird that he should resign as president of the FA in view of that body's 'unpatriotic decision' to proceed with the football season.

The responses to these telegrams were disappointing for Charrington. Lord Stamfordham, Private Secretary to King George V, replied:

The question raised in your telegram to the King of the 1st September has received the careful consideration and respect, which is due to anyone speaking with your great experience and authority. I gather that the Football Association are in direct communication with the War Office, and that a general desire has been expressed by the association to assist in obtaining recruits for the army.

I understand that there may be difficulties in giving up all the matches of professional football clubs in view of contracts which have been made with players. But the doings of the association will be carefully followed, having regard to the King's position as its patron.[21]

Lord Kinnaird's reply was more dismissive in its tone:

> I have not yet had full details of the action of the Football Association Council on Monday last, but I hardly expect that they would do anything unpatriotic. The notices I have seen in the papers rather indicate that they want to encourage recruiting for the Army and to help in many ways.
>
> Giving up football entirely is not so simple as you think. Contracts have been made which can be enforced in a Court of Law, and you could not advocate the breaking of contracts.[22]

As a postscript to his letter, Lord Kinnaird added that 'the reasons for continuing some football are too long for a letter'. Undeterred, Charrington would continue his crusade against football over the next few months, dispatching telegrams to a wide range of public figures, including Admiral John Jellicoe and every Field Marshal in the British army. His tactics, although effective, were at times disingenuous. One of his anti-football pamphlets contained a photograph showing hordes of fit young men at a football match. Readers could not help but be shocked by the fact that not a single man was in uniform. The absence of khaki was hardly surprising, given that the photograph had been taken at the Scotland *v* England match in April 1914, several months before the outbreak of hostilities.[23]

On 5 September the French counterattacked the advancing Germans, north-east of Paris. The ensuing 'Miracle of the Marne' would put an end to German hopes of a swift, decisive victory. That same afternoon Charrington attended Fulham's match against Clapton Orient, where he was given permission to address the spectators, provided that he spoke only of the need for recruits, and that he did not seek to denigrate the game of football. Although Charrington had refused to give such an undertaking to the club secretary, Phil Kelso, he was nonetheless allowed to take his seat in the stand.

During the half time interval, Charrington stood up to speak: 'I come here to protest against this football . . .'[24] The chairman of Fulham, W.G. Allen, tapped him on the shoulder and requested him not to speak. Charrington merely repeated his sentence, whereupon pandamonium ensued. After an unsightly scuffle he was summarily ejected from the ground in front of around 12,000 spectators. Charrington immediately lodged a summons for assault against the Fulham chairman and secretary. The hearing took place at the West London Police Court a few weeks later, Charrington's allegation that he had been subjected to 'grossly unnecessary violence' foundered once it was established that, 'His tall silk hat remained on his head, he did not lose possession of his cigar, and never lost his foothold.'[25] Both defendants were discharged and Charrington ended up having to pay two guineas in costs.

On 8 September Frederick Wall sent copies of the various documents, which had been circulated to football clubs, to the War Office. He took this opportunity to seek official sanction for the continuance of football: 'I am also instructed to say that The Football Association is prepared to request all its Members to stop the playing of matches if the War Office is of the opinion that such a course would assist them in their duties.'[26] While demonstrating gratitude for the FA's efforts to date, the War Office reply fell short of a wholehearted endorsement of the decision to continue with the football season:

> The question of whether the playing of matches should be entirely stopped is more a matter for the discretion of the Association, but the [Army] Council quite realise the difficulties involved in taking such an extreme step, and they would deprecate anything being done which does not appear to be called for by the present situation. Should your Association decide to continue the playing of matches, the [Army] Council trust that arrangements will be made so as not to interfere with the facilities at present afforded to the recruiting authorities.[27]

The publication of this correspondence did little to stifle criticism of football. The adverse publicity and the numbers of young men enlisting in the army caused attendances to plummet. The average Saturday gate receipts for First Division matches in the Football League fell from £735 the previous season to £414. With several smaller clubs close to collapse, the Football League hurriedly 'encouraged' players to accept wage cuts with the resulting monies being placed in a relief fund to assist clubs struggling to meet their bills. On 9 October the Football League stipulated that each of its clubs should contribute 2.5 per cent of its gross gate receipts to the relief fund.[28]

On 12 October the FA Council adopted a more aggressive stance in its efforts to defend the game, pointing out that other sports and pastimes were not being subjected to the same degree of scrutiny: 'Football, which is essentially the pastime of the masses, is the only sport which is being attacked. It is producing more men for the Army, and money for relief, than all the others. Other sports and the places of entertainment, are being carried on as usual.'[29]

Undeterred by the criticism, the FA proceeded with plans for the 1914–15 FA Cup, provoking a celebrated *Punch* cartoon on 21 October entitled 'THE GREATER GAME'. It featured a shame-faced professional footballer being told by Mr Punch that 'No doubt you can make money in this field, my friend, but there's only one field today where you can get honour.' In retrospect it might have been better for everyone if the War Office had asked the FA to suspend the season with immediate effect. It would have spared the image of the game untold damage over the coming months, particularly as it was becoming increasingly clear that the war would almost certainly not 'be over by Christmas'.

After their advance had been brought to a peremptory halt on the Marne, the Germans had retreated 40 miles to the River Aisne. On the high ground along the northern banks of the river the Germans dug trenches, sited machine-guns and positioned artillery. Over the next few days French and British forces strove in vain to dislodge the Germans from their positions. The resulting deadlock was indicative of what was to follow. A new form of warfare was beginning to assert itself, in which, as Field-Marshal Sir John French, the Commander-in-Chief of the BEF, told the King: 'The spade will be as great a necessity as the rifle and the heaviest types and calibres of artillery will be brought up on either side.'[30]

By the end of September the stalemate on the Aisne had led to both sides moving troops northwards in an attempt to outflank the opposing armies, in what was erroneously termed by journalists as 'The Race to the Sea'. The respective lines of trenches snaked steadily northwards, but still neither side was able to gain a decisive advantage. By early October the BEF had redeployed around the Belgian town of Ypres. On 18 October British troops advanced eastwards in the direction of Menin, hoping to turn the German flank, but they soon ran into a mass of German troops intent on pushing forward to secure the Channel Ports. The fierce encounters that followed would later be known as 'The First Battle of Ypres'.

The next couple of weeks saw relentless German attacks gradually pushing the heavily outnumbered BEF back towards Ypres. On 31 October, a day of supreme crisis for the BEF, the creaking British line came perilously close to breaking at Gheluvelt, a few miles east of Ypres; the situation stabilised only through a desperate counterattack mounted by a depleted battalion of the Worcestershire Regiment. Although it would be some time before the heroic exploits of the 2nd Worcesters were widely known in Britain, the gravity of the situation was óbvious. With recruitment numbers significantly down on previous weeks, it was inevitable that the continuance of professional football would be subjected to fresh scrutiny.[31] On 7 November a letter from the historian A.F. Pollard was published in *The Times*: 'Every club that employs a professional football player is bribing a needed recruit to refrain from enlistment, and every spectator who pays his gate money is contributing so much towards a German victory'.[32] Four days later the BEF only just survived another day of crisis when the Germans made an all-out attempt to break through the British lines around Ypres.

Over preceding weeks the FA had continually sought to defend its position on the grounds that the War Office had not requested that the football season be suspended. Now, even the validity of this defence was called into question, when a private letter from Harold Tennant, Under Secretary of State for War and the Prime Minister's brother-in-law, to Thomas Forsyth, the chairman of Airdrieonians FC, was published in the Press:

No objection is taken by the military authorities to occasional recreation. It is considered, however, that professional football does not come within that category, and that it can only be admitted on grounds of contract or employment. It is much more desirable that professional footballers should find employment in His Majesty's forces than in their old occupation. With regard to the question of breach of contract, it is considered that this is a time when all should be prepared to make sacrifices.[33]

The publication of Harold Tennant's comments led to renewed negotiations between the War Office and Frederick Wall with a view to securing more recruits at football matches. On 19 November the Poet Laureate, Robert Bridges, joined the debate: 'I certainly voice the feeling of the country in declaring that it is high time that professional football should be discontinued . . . It is high time that our footballers let the world see what they are really made of and that they do not deserve the execration that is falling upon them.'[34] The position of the FA was growing more untenable by the day. Attention now turned to the recruiting measures that were to be put in place that weekend. Posters urging good sportsmen to enlist were to be prominently exhibited at football grounds. Various dignitaries would address the spectators at half-time. If feasible, military bands were to be in attendance, the plan being that newly enlisted recruits would march behind the band to the local recruiting office at the end of the match.

On Saturday, 21 November prominent public men rose to address the crowds during the half-time interval at football grounds in London and the provinces. At Stamford Bridge, where Chelsea were playing Notts County, Col Charles Burn MP made an emotionally charged appeal for recruits:

I want you to understand that I am a sportsman as well as a soldier. I believe in football. I believe in your games being carried on as usual. I have come here to ask if there is any young man who has no encumbrances to join the forces. I don't say come. I say, 'Come for God's Sake. You are wanted.' I have given my son. He enlisted at the start of the war. He is now dead. I have given my house up as a shelter for the care of wounded officers. I say to you young men that if I had 12 sons I would give them all, as well as my own life, for my country and my King.[35]

Not a man was induced to enlist. Press reports claimed that the attendance was 30,000; the FA maintained that the number of spectators was less than half this figure, and that there were 6,702 servicemen, 783 boys and additionally several ladies present. Recruiting efforts were similarly unsuccessful at other football grounds that Saturday: six recruits at the Cardiff City *v* Bristol Rovers match, one at the Arsenal, and not a single man enlisting at the grounds of Nottingham Forest and Brighton & Hove Albion.[36]

After Brighton & Hove Albion's 4–1 victory over Croydon Common at the Goldstone Ground, a recruiting officer fumed that: 'Such a crowd is a disgrace to the country at such a time as the present. All they seem to care about is football and home comforts while our brave soldiers are experiencing so much discomfort and hardship to protect the country.'[37] The results were 'grievously disappointing'. As *The Times* put it: 'There is apparently something about the professional match spectator which makes a recruiting appeal a failure.'[38] Only at Goodison Park, where a significant proportion of the crowd were soldiers and convalescent Belgian officers and men, had there been some success. Scores of men were reported to have enlisted, even though the half-time military parade had been cancelled on account of dense fog.

The day's efforts were nothing short of disaster for the image of football. The critics had been right all along. Charrington described the results as a 'direct slap in the face of the War Office'. Once again comparisons were drawn with more patriotic sports, *The Times* noting that, 'This failure contrasts strongly with the wholesale volunteering which has distinguished the performers and devotees of other forms of sport. Rugby Union clubs, cricket elevens and rowing clubs throughout the kingdom have poured men into the ranks.'[39] Such newspaper reports predictably fuelled another wave of hostile letters to the newspapers, including one from an 'Old "Soccer" Back', undoubtedly of the amateur persuasion:

The worst foe to recruiting is the professional footballer. Every Saturday, dozens of fit, active young men go forth to a spectacular combat for money. Hundreds of young men also fit and well pay to look on. They are absolutely obsessed all the week with these matches. It would be stopped but for two reasons: (1) The pretended one – sanctity of contract. This is, of course, all nonsense; if the players and the Association agree to cancel their contracts of course they are cancelled. I hope that this absurd reason will never again be put forward by anyone. (2) Money.[40]

There is little doubt that money was, to some extent, behind the decision of the football authorities to proceed with the football season. At that time around 100 football clubs were limited companies. Although there was not much opportunity for club directors to profit directly from their involvement with the game with dividends capped by the FA at 5 per cent, there were certainly opportunities for individuals to make money indirectly from the game, particularly through building and catering contracts. Of particular concern to club directors was the fact that many of them had entered contracts and given personal guarantees to banks, covering liabilities in excess of £500,000. According to FA estimates, only £80,000 of these liabilities had been paid back during the close season.

The debate was followed closely by soldiers in France. Countless letters from Tommies appeared in the press in support of the game. Harry Allwood, a Birmingham referee serving in France with the Coldstream Guards, wrote home that: 'If football does not appeal to the imagination of certain gentry at home, it has a great fascination for the gallant fellows at the front; they do not want it stopped.'[41] Other letters, mainly from officers, expressed nothing but disgust at the fact that professional football was still being played while the British Empire was in such dire straits. The widely reported response to the recruiting measures on the 21st was all too much for one 'Yeoman' of the Yorkshire Hussars, prompting a letter to the *Saturday Review*:

Last Saturday I began work at four in the morning, and did not go off duty till seven on Sunday morning. I find that while I was at work hundreds of thousands of able-bodied young roughs were watching hirelings playing football. As a result of stirring appeals, one of these brave fellows enlisted. I can assure you that we don't like the job of defending these miserable curs.[42]

The renewed furore led to discussion in the House of Commons. One MP suggested that railway companies should charge individuals travelling to football matches twice the normal fares. Another MP proposed a tax on all spectators not in uniform. On 26 November Sir John Lonsdale, Unionist MP for Mid-Armagh, asked the Prime Minister in the House of Commons whether he would 'introduce legislation taking powers to suppress all professional football matches during the continuance of the War?'[43] Asquith stated that he did not believe that there was any need for such legislation, given the fact that FA was currently liaising with the War Office on the issue of recruiting. Lonsdale, who had apparently not read beyond *The Times* headline 'ONE RECRUIT AT ARSENAL MATCH', then asked whether Asquith was aware that only one recruit had been obtained at the football grounds the previous Saturday, despite 'the most strenuous efforts'. Asquith replied: 'I saw that in the papers; but, on the other hand, I am glad to say that in Scotland there was a very different response'.[44]

The response had indeed been different in Scotland, where a similarly vitriolic debate had been raging since the outbreak of war. The previous afternoon 11 Heart of Midlothian footballers, stung by a recent suggestion that their club should adopt a nom de plume of 'The White Feathers of Midlothian', had enlisted in a battalion being raised by Sir George McCrae, a former Liberal Member of Parliament for East Edinburgh. Hearts supporters and members of at least 75 Scottish professional and amateur football clubs lost little time in following their lead. Scottish footballers, at least, had answered the critics.[45]

South of the border the hostility towards professional football was growing by the day, particularly in London and the south-east. At a meeting on 27 November the Council of the Newspapers Proprietors' Federation, which represented the London daily press, resolved to publish nothing more than the results of football matches, in anything other than the sporting newspapers. The next morning, when one newspaper made its announcement that it would no longer be featuring match reports, it did not escape one reader's attention that on the same page of this 'conscientious journal', there appeared 'three whole columns of racing news, half a column of amateur football and nearly a column of billiards'.[46] That same morning a robust defence of the football appeared in

The Times, influential members of the FA Council having obviously sought to bring certain facts to the newspaper's attention:

It is claimed by members of the Council of the Football Association that upwards of 100,000 recruits for the Army have been secured from the ranks of Association Football, and that this total exceeds by far the combined recruits who have enlisted from all other branches of sport.[47] All professional players of the leading clubs, in addition to the ordinary football training, undergo military drill on certain days of the week, and rifle ranges have been constructed on most grounds for daily practice. The fitness of this body of men for home defence or active service is unquestioned.

The number of professional football players has been much exaggerated. A member of the Council of the Football Association states that the number registered with the Association this season is less than 5,000. Not less than 2,000 are serving in various branches of his Majesty's forces. There are in this country 2,000 players earning their living by the game. The number of first-class players is put at 1,500, more than two thirds of whom are married. The total number of unmarried men who depend on the game for a livelihood is reckoned at 600. There are, roughly, 3,000,000 unmarried men of military age, of whom over 2,000 000 have not undertaken service of any kind. People interested in football say they cannot understand why the 600 football players who might enlist should be singled out for special condemnation.

A football official in London believes that the professional clubs would welcome the compulsory stopping of football. The average decrease in the drawings at matches throughout the country this season is 50 per cent, while the wages to be paid under contract, from which the clubs are unable to escape, amount to £272,000. Football must continue until it is prohibited by an Act of Parliament.

No football club has refused permission to any player who is desirous to enlist. The breaking of a contract is exclusively the right of a player. These contracts are usually binding for a year.[48]

Such reasoned arguments made little impression on the game's detractors, not least *The Times* itself, which would subsequently declare in an editorial that: '... it is not football that we need to abolish now, but professional football – just as we should need to abolish any other game that hired large numbers of able-bodied young men from their country's service.'[49] Something clearly had to be done. Reacting to public pressure, the War Office instigated a fresh round of discussions with the FA. While there was no suggestion that football should be stopped in its entirety, Harold Tennant, Under Secretary of State for War, maintained that the time had come for some account to be taken of public opinion. He suggested that international matches and the FA Cup should be cancelled. During the course of these discussions, the suggestion was also made that a footballers' battalion be formed. Proposals for such a unit had been made on several occasions over the preceding months, most notably by F. N. Charrington back in August, but had for some reason not found favour in military quarters. No doubt the success of McCrae's Battalion in Scotland had convinced the War Office that an English footballers' battalion might be the solution to everyone's problems.

Within only a few days of McCrae's Battalion being raised, William Joynson-Hicks, Unionist MP for Brentford, paid a visit to the War Office. The exact reason for his visit is unknown, but it was to discuss a matter entirely unconnected with football. Popularly known as 'Jix', Joynson-Hicks was a controversial figure in British politics. He was born plain William Hicks in Canonbury on 23 June 1865, and was educated at Merchant Taylors. In 1895, by then a successful solicitor, he married Grace Joynson, the daughter of a wealthy Manchester silk manufacturer, thereafter adopting the name 'Joynson-Hicks'. Joining the Conservative Party, he unsuccessfully stood for Parliament in the elections of 1900 and 1906. Following Winston Churchill's defection to the Liberals, Joynson-Hicks contested his Manchester North-West seat in a 1908 by-election, and won an astonishing victory. Losing this seat two years later, Joynson-Hicks was subsequently elected as MP for Brentford in March 1911, and began to use his considerable oratory skills to attack the government over its failure to invest in an air force. On the outbreak of hostilities in August 1914, Joynson-Hicks had thrown himself wholeheartedly in the war effort. Before long he was at the head of a movement to supply the Belgian Red Cross with ambulances. He was also serving on various committees to facilitate recruiting. During the course of his visit to the War Office, it was suggested that if he was looking to assist further with the war effort he might concern himself with the raising of an English footballers' battalion. A man of energy and initiative, Joynson-Hicks lost little time in setting about the task.

On 5 December, two days after the four National Football Associations had decided that international matches, but not Cup Ties, would be stopped,[50] a letter was sent out from the FA to the secretaries of the 11 professional clubs in London, inviting them to send representatives to a meeting on 8 December to discuss 'the formation of a Footballer's Battalion of Kitchener's Army'. Chaired by Joynson-Hicks, the meeting took place at the FA offices in Russell Square. Every professional club in London sent delegates.[51] Other attendees included Lord Kinnaird, Frederick Wall and Capt Thomas Whiffen, Chief Recruiting Officer for London. After much discussion, a resolution was passed: 'That this meeting with the directors of London Professional Football Clubs heartily favours the project of the formation of a Footballers' Battalion'.[52] An executive committee was duly formed. In addition to recruiting, the committee would be responsible for accommodating, feeding, clothing and equipping the battalion, until such time as it could be taken over by the military authorities.[53] Frederick Wall agreed to act as its honorary secretary, and Sir Henry Eggar, a former solicitor to the Government of India, assumed the post of treasurer.[54] It was decided to invite all the professional players in London to a meeting to be held on 15 December at Fulham Town Hall, which would be made available for the occasion by one of the committee members, Henry Norris, Mayor of Fulham and Arsenal chairman.

Norris was an entrepreneurial property developer, who had amassed a considerable fortune from developing vast tracts of West London during the last decade of the 19th century. As chairman of Fulham FC, Norris had guided the club to successive Southern League championships in 1905/6 and 1906/7, and then to a place in the Football League. In 1910 he became a director of Woolwich Arsenal, while still retaining his position on the Fulham board. After unsuccessfully trying to merge the two clubs, Norris was eventually forced to sever his connections with Fulham. He had then instigated the Arsenal's relocation from Woolwich to

Highbury in 1913, a move that had been vehemently opposed by the other north London clubs.

Over the next few days further details emerged about the proposed Footballers' Battalion. Its strength was to be 1,350 men. Its ranks were to be open to all those interested in the amateur or professional game, as well as their friends: 'The Footballers' Battalion wants players, officials and club enthusiasts. Are YOU fit and free?' Applications for membership were to be made at the FA Offices in Russell Square, or at West Africa House in Kingsway, Holborn. Given the small stature of many footballers, it was decided to dispense with the usual height requirements. Players were to be given leave to play for their clubs in league and cup matches for the rest of the season, while the battalion underwent military training.[55] Battalion HQ was to be situated at Richmond Athletic Ground. This latest addition to Kitchener's New Armies would officially be known as the 17th (Service) Battalion (Football), Middlesex Regiment.[56]

The Duke of Cambridge's Own (Middlesex Regiment) was the local regiment in Joynson-Hicks's parliamentary constituency. It had been formed in 1881 as a result of reforms introduced by Edward Cardwell, Secretary of State for War, the purpose of which was to develop local connections in order to facilitate recruiting. The result of these reforms was that the 57th (West Middlesex) Regiment of Foot and the 77th (East Middlesex) Regiment of Foot, which had been providing each other with drafts since 1873, now became the 1st and 2nd Battalions of the Duke of Cambridge's Own (Middlesex Regiment) respectively. Both regiments had long and distinguished records of service with the British Army. One battle during the Peninsular War would prove to have lasting significance for the officers and men of the Middlesex Regiment.

On 16 May 1811, as part of a force of 1,800 defending a ridge near the village of Albuhera, the 57th Regiment of Foot had stood its ground against a superior French force of 8,000 under Marshal Soult. Under heavy fire, their commanding officer, Col William Inglis, lying mortally wounded in front of the line, had continually rallied the thinning ranks, 'Die hard, 57th! Die hard!'[57] At a roll call that evening only seven officers and 150 other ranks remained. The Battle of Albuhera was subsequently commemorated in the design of the cap badge of the 57th, and later that of the Middlesex Regiment. Of greater significance, perhaps, was the fact that the officers and men of the Middlesex Regiment would forever be the 'Die-Hards'.[58]

1. The 12 clubs were: Accrington, Aston Villa, Blackburn Rovers, Bolton Wanderers, Burnley, Derby County, Everton, Notts County, Preston North End, Stoke, West Bromwich Albion, and Wolverhampton Wanderers.
2. The breakdown of the British army in August 1914 was as follows: Regular Army (247,432), the Reserve (145,347), the Special Reserve (63,933) and the Territorial Force (268,777).
3. BNL: *The Times*, 15 August 1914.
4. Around 1,500 amateur clubs in the Greater London area announced their intention to suspend fixtures for the season. The so-called 'Old Boy' sides were particularly hard hit by the rush to enlist. By early September it was reported that, 'Only five players out of four XIs remain' at Old Haberdashers FC.
5. Nicknamed the Robins on account of their claret shirts, Croydon Common were the first professional football club in Croydon. Founded in 1897, the club played in various local leagues before joining the Southern League for the 1907/08 season. Beset by financial troubles, the club folded in 1917 and its ground in Selhurst, known as the Nest, was subsequently taken over by local rivals Crystal Palace. For a detailed history of the club, see Alan Futter, *Who Killed the Cock Robins? – The History of Croydon Common F.C. 1897–1917*.
6. By 14 September around 50 players from Football League clubs were reported to be serving in a branch of the forces. By way of comparison, Southern League clubs had 73 players in the forces. BNL: *Athletic News*, 14 September 1914.
7. Money was reckoned in pounds (£), shillings (s) and pence (d). A guinea was worth 21s.
8. BNL: *Sportsman*, 27 August 1914.
9. *Ibid.*, 31 August 1914.
10. *Ibid.*, 1 September 1914.
11. *Ibid.*
12. *Ibid.*
13. *Ibid.*
14. *Ibid.*, 7 September 1914.
15. *Ibid.*
16. *Ibid.*
17. *Ibid.*
18. For further details of Clapton Orient's contribution to the Footballers' Battalion, see Stephen Jenkins, *They took the Lead*.
19. BNL: *Sportsman*, 31 August 1914.
20. BNL: *Morning Post*, 29 August 1914.
21. BNL: *The Times*, 8 September 1914. Charrington wrote a letter to Lord Stamfordham a week later. It drew the following terse reply: 'Many thanks for your letter of the 14th September. I am afraid that it will not be possible for the King to take any action with regard to the affairs of the Football Association. Yours very truly, Stamfordham.'
22. BNL: *The Times*, 8 September 1914.
23. Charrington was also happy to reward footballers who answered their country's call. On hearing of Arthur Grimsdell's enlistment in the army, he sent the sum of £5 to the Tottenham Hotspur half-back, hoping to encourage other players to do likewise.
24. BNL: *Athletic News*, 7 September 1914.
25. *Ibid.*, 28 September 1914.
26. BNL: *Sportsman*, 14 September 1914.
27. *Ibid.*, 14 September 1914.
28. Eighteen football clubs would end up drawing money from this fund.
29. FA: Extract from Minutes of the FA Council meeting, 12 October 1914.
30. Holmes, R., *The Western Front* (London, BBC Worldwide, 1999), p. 46.
31. In October 1914 only 136,811 men enlisted in the army, compared with September's impressive total of 462,901.
32. BNL: *The Times*, 7 November 1914.
33. BNL: *Athletic News*, 16 November 1914.
34. BNL: ©*The Times*, NI Syndication Limited, 19 November 1914.
35. BNL: *The Times*, 23 November 1914.

36. At Nottingham Forest's match against Stockport County, it was reported that there were even motor cars waiting outside the ground to drive new recruits down to the recruiting office, displaying cards, which read: 'If you want to enlist, jump in.'

37. BNL: *The Times*, 23 November 1914.

38. *Ibid.*, 25 November 1914.

39. *Ibid.*, 23 November 1914.

40. *Ibid.*, 25 November 1914.

41. BNL: *Sportsman*, 13 November 1914.

42. BNL: *Athletic News*, 7 December 1914. The newspaper was less than impressed with such sentiments, commenting that, 'We revere the heroic British soldiers but there are black sheep, it seems, even in the ranks of the British. This letter is a fair specimen of the "arguments" that he and the hostile critics of the poor man's game employ. The arrogance of the man is appalling. He is the kind of "cur" who would be at home with a long whip superintending gangs of slaves on a plantation. His stamp is not required among the defenders of a free people.'

43. *Hansard* HC, vol 68, col 135, 26 November 1914.

44. *Ibid.*

45. Recruiting for McCrae's Battalion formally commenced at a grand public meeting in Usher Hall on 27 November. Jack Alexander has admirably chronicled their story in *McCrae's Battalion: The Story of the 16th Royal Scots*.

46. BNL: *Athletic News*, 14 December 1914.

47. This figure was probably based on reports of county football associations. By the end of November the Durham County FA reported that 2,572 players, 669 officials and 279 other members had enlisted from 380 clubs, an average of 9.26 men per club. Twenty-seven local referees had also joined the Colours. Clubs had also contributed the sum of £524 12s 10½ d to the relief funds.

48. © *The Times*, NI Syndication Limited, 28 November 1914.

49. *Ibid.*, 1 December 1914.

50. The conference had been convened at the request of the Scottish FA. There was much ill feeling in England when the SFA subsequently acted contrary to the resolution passed at the conference, and resolved to suspend International matches *and* Cup Ties on the grounds that it was honourably bound to do so, given the earlier decision of the FA Council to place itself 'unreservedly in the hands of the War Office'.

51. At a meeting on 30 November London's 11 professional football clubs had resolved that they were 'prepared to discontinue the game and close their grounds simultaneously with the closing of racecourses, golf links, theatres, music halls, picture palaces and kindred entertainments'.

52. BNL: *Sportsman*, 9 December 1914.

53. The War Office would formally take over control of the 17th Middlesex on 1 September 1915.

54. Four club directors were nominated to serve on the committee: W.C. Kirby (Chelsea), H.G. Norris (Arsenal), J.B. Skeggs (Millwall) and Capt H. Wells-Holland (Clapton Orient). In January 1915 T.A. Deacock (Tottenham) would also join.

55. Following press reports that the Hearts players would be allowed to play in club matches until the end of the season, the FA had intimated to the War Office on 30 November that 'a similar concession to professional football players in England generally would result in the immediate enlistment of the majority of them'. This was not to prove the case.

56. Forty-six battalions of the Middlesex were to serve during the First World War at home or overseas. Twenty-six would see service in the field.

57. These words would later be echoed by 2/Lt Rupert Hallowes of the 4th Battalion during the First World War. During desperate fighting at Hooge on 30 September 1915, while lying mortally wounded, he uttered his last words: 'Men, we can only die once; if we have to die, let us die like men – like Die-Hards.' 2/Lt Hallowes was awarded the Middlesex Regiment's first Victoria Cross of the Great War.

58. There are various cap badges in circulation purportedly worn by officers and men of the 17th Middlesex. These badges consist of a football and corner flags suspended from the usual regimental badge. Such badges do not feature in the standard reference works on the subject of military badges, nor do any such badges seem to appear in surviving photographs of the 17th Middlesex. The authors have uncovered no evidence to suggest that its officers and men were issued with anything other than the standard cap badge of the Middlesex Regiment.

CHAPTER 2

THE RAISING OF THE 17TH MIDDLESEX

Every man can help in keeping the Teutonic team as far away as possible from our goal area. Forwards are required as well as backs.

Athletic News

The meeting to raise the 17th Middlesex took place at Fulham Town Hall on 15 December. Present in the audience were several directors and officials from London's professional clubs, along with Harry Bradshaw, the secretary of the Southern League and a former manager of Fulham. The Football League was not represented in any official capacity. It had been thought that the smaller hall would be sufficient for the purposes of the meeting, but shortly before it was due to start at 3.30 p.m., a large group of professional players 'trooped in as one party', bringing the number of attendees to over 400.[1] The decision was made to move proceedings to the larger hall.

By the time the meeting was ready to start, William Joynson-Hicks occupied the chair on the platform, flanked by two political allies: Henry Norris and William Hayes Fisher, Unionist MP for Fulham. Also on the platform were the FA secretary Frederick Wall, Capt Henry Wells-Holland, the Clapton Orient chairman and a former mayor of Hackney, J.B. Skeggs, the Millwall chairman and Southern League treasurer, and two army officers, Col Charles Grantham and Capt Thomas Whiffen, chief recruiting officer for London. They were later joined by Lord Kinnaird, who was unable to be present at the start of the meeting.

In the opening speech, Joynson-Hicks stated that he believed that everyone was aware of the reasons for attending the meeting. He referred to the numerous attacks on footballers, clubs and spectators in the press before reminding everyone that the present was not the time to answer those critics. The recriminations should wait until the war was over. In his view, the game's most effective answer to the critics would be the formation of a footballers' battalion, or a footballers' brigade. To the sound of applause, he informed the audience that the War Office had recently given him official sanction to raise a battalion of footballers, which would be known as the '17th Service Battalion of the Middlesex Regiment, "the Die Hards"'. The London professional clubs had unanimously agreed to support the players in their endeavours, and to make more of an effort to assist recruiting at their respective grounds. The clubs wanted a battalion for themselves, consisting of footballers fighting alongside those with whom they fought at football. Footballers who enlisted in the battalion would be given leave on Saturdays to play their matches for the rest of the season, so that they might fulfil their contractual obligation contracts. Such an undertaking had been given by no less a personage than Lord Kitchener himself.

Joynson-Hicks reminded his audience this was a war of 'business, bitterness and danger'. Germany had treated the Belgians terribly. He went to great lengths to remind everyone that, if the Germans ever landed in Britain, everything would be far worse. Each man had to ask himself the question, 'Can I live as an Englishman without doing something against these barbarians?' He finished his speech with a final appeal for a battalion that would be a testament to the honour of footballers from Flanders to the centre of Berlin, not just in Great Britain. These words were loudly applauded.

It was then the turn of William Hayes Fisher MP to speak. A barrister by profession, Hayes Fisher had first entered parliament in 1885. Accorded a hearty reception by everyone present, he opened his speech by saying that, as president of Fulham FC, he was proud of being a profound believer in sport, particularly as he had participated in such activities during his youth.[2] To the sound of laughter, he admitted to being one of 'those very wicked individuals who did not object to looking on at football'. He appealed to footballers and their friends to raise sufficient numbers for a battalion. He stated that he could not necessarily concur with Joynson-Hicks' view that football should not respond to its critics until the war was over. These critics had perpetuated 'the worst nonsense that had ever been written'. Hayes Fisher illustrated his point by making reference to those who seemed to think that the 2,000 or so individuals who earned a living from the game were fit and ready to fight as soldiers immediately. 'If only they had crossed over [the Channel], those two thousand could have driven the Germans out of France and Belgium.' This wry observation was warmly received by the audience.

Not everyone present was a supporter of football. At this point, a member of the audience chose to interrupt, asking whether the number of registered professionals was not, in fact, 2,000, but over 4,000. It was explained that the majority of registered professionals earned only a few shillings for their efforts on a Saturday afternoon, relying on employment outside the game to earn a living. Hayes Fisher went on to refute the charges levelled against football. Turning on the game's critics, he challenged their belief that football was preventing thousands of young men from enlisting. Football's efforts to assist the recruitment drive had been a success. In London 8,700 amateur footballers had already enlisted. Attendances had fallen by 50 per cent. Many footballers and followers of the game were clearly 'playing the game elsewhere'.

Hayes Fisher told the audience that ultimately it was a question of conscience for every man, whether or not he should be fighting 'against the tyranny of an evil monarch'. He referred to Lord Kinnaird, who had recently lost his eldest son in the heavy fighting around Ypres, before going on to outline the particular difficulties facing professional footballers.[3] Unlike a clerk returning from the war with a shattered leg, a footballer's career would be over. He would no longer be able to earn a living from the game. Professional footballers ran the risk of being left without a living after the war. Notwithstanding this fact, Hayes Fisher was confident of securing some of the 'best men in the Kingdom to fight their country's battles'. Those present were told that they could enlist immediately at the meeting, or at the FA offices in Russell Square, which had been placed at the disposal of the battalion. The players were asked to become recruiting officers for their respective clubs. It was clear that the committee was seeking to extend recruiting beyond the players themselves. In essence, the footballers were being used to encourage the followers of their clubs to go to war.

Various questions were asked once Hayes Fisher had finished speaking. The only footballer to pose a question was Archie Needham, an exceptionally versatile player with Brighton & Hove Albion, who had played in every outfield position for the club during his four seasons at the Goldstone Ground. In response to a query about pay, the audience was told that recruits would be paid 7s per week. An additional allowance of 3s 6d was available for those resident in London, and further allowances were available in respect of wives and children. These payments were to be made in addition to their football wages. Until living quarters could be arranged for the battalion, a billeting allowance of 2s 9d would be available for each man. It was also stated incorrectly that the committee had agreed to provide the expenses of players travelling to and from games on Saturday afternoons. The reality of the situation was that the football clubs themselves would be responsible for bearing the cost of their players travelling between London and their respective clubs. Such additional expense would hardly be an attractive prospect for clubs outside London, many of whom were already experiencing financial difficulties.

It was then the turn of Lord Kinnaird to speak. Warmly cheered, he told the audience that the movement was a right one. He believed that large numbers of footballers would join the battalion, particularly now that their wages would be supplemented by the pay of a soldier until the end of the season. Footballers were to have the privilege of fighting side-by-side, like the bankers and insurance clerks, as 'pals'. He appealed to the footballers present to join up immediately, following the example of the 100,000 'connected with the grand game of football who were already serving their King and Country'. Once Kinnaird had finished speaking, Capt Whiffen appealed, as an old footballer himself, for men to come forward.

The first player to step up on to the recruiting platform was Fred 'Spider' Parker, the Clapton Orient captain, a married man with three children. A hugely popular figure at the club, his benefit match had seen the largest reserve attendance in the club's history, resulting in gate receipts of over £200. Within a couple of weeks Parker would receive a letter from an Orient supporter in the trenches, in which the writer told the Orient captain how proud he was that 'Spider' had been the first to come forward at the recruiting meeting. The Orient captain was followed by Archie Needham and Franklin 'Frank' Buckley, a forceful centre-half who had recently moved from Derby County to Bradford City for a transfer fee of £1,000. The 32-year-old Buckley had offered his services to the recruiting committee a few days earlier, as soon as he had heard of the plans for a footballers' battalion.[4]

Buckley had already seen service in the regular army. In February 1900, at the age of 18, he had enlisted in the King's Liverpool Regiment, the same regiment in which his father had been a musketry and gymnastics instructor.[5] Three years later, he had bought himself out of the army for the sum of £18, after an Aston Villa scout had spotted him playing in an army match. Unable to break into the Villa first team, Buckley's footballing career had taken off once after moving to Brighton & Hove Albion in 1905. Spells at Manchester Utd, Manchester City and Birmingham City had followed. In 1911, Buckley had signed for Derby County, where he had gone on to win a Second Division championship medal and an England cap in the side that had sensationally lost 3-0 to Ireland in February 1914.

Other players followed Parker, Needham and Buckley up on to the platform. Whenever there was a lull in players stepping forward, various individuals stood up to encourage other footballers to enlist, including Mr H. Glibbery, father of the Essex County goalkeeper, who told the audience of the excellent way in which his sons were treated by the army. By the time it was apparent that no one else was prepared to enlist that afternoon, a mere 35 people connected with the professional game were standing on the platform. Such a total was hardly likely to satisfy the critics, but as the *Sportsman* reminded its readers a few days later: 'It must not be overlooked that the intention was not to enlist players on the spot; the meeting was only called to put the proposal plainly before them, and it was an afterthought to ask for volunteers, this being possible, as the Town Hall is a recruiting station.'[6]

The Crystal Palace chairman, Sydney Bourne, then asked whether players who had already enlisted in other regiments would be permitted to transfer to the Footballers' Battalion. Ever since it had been reported that there was to be a 'pals' battalion of footballers, several footballers serving with other regiments had expressed a desire to serve alongside their fellow players. Joynson-Hicks replied that the final decision would have to be left to the War Office, but that the committee would do what it could in relation to this possibility.[7]

A motion of thanks was then proposed by Henry Norris to the chairman, Joynson-Hicks, and to all the speakers. The motion was seconded by Capt Wells-Holland, whose previous military service had ended in 1906 when he had resigned his commission in the 4th Volunteer Battalion of the Royal Fusiliers on being elected Mayor of Hackney. In seconding the motion of thanks, Capt Wells-Holland added that he hoped that Clapton Orient would have its own platoon in a battalion. In his view, a footballers' battalion would be 'a splendid answer to the unjust strictures in the press'. The vote of thanks was enthusiastically carried. In reply, Joynson-Hicks told the audience that no thanks were needed. Gesturing at the footballers behind him on the platform, he told the audience that 'these are the thanks, the expression of loyalty footballers have given to the King'. It was only left to announce that Hayes Fisher had offered to deal with any further queries, in relation to pay and allowances. The meeting concluded with a lusty rendition of the National Anthem. The Footballers' Battalion had its first 35 recruits:

Arsenal	Thomas Ratcliff (assistant trainer)
Bradford City	Frank Buckley
Brighton & Hove Albion	Archie Needham, Ralph Routledge, Frank Spencer, John Woodhouse
Chelsea	William Krug, David Girdwood, Edward Foord
Clapton Orient	Fred Parker, Jimmy Hugall, Nolan Evans, Harold Gibson, Bob Dalrymple, William Jonas, Edward King, Arthur Tilley, Richard McFadden, Thomas Pearson
Croydon Common	Ernie Williamson, Thomas Newton, Dick Upex, Cyril Smith, Albert Tomkins, Percy Barnfather

Crystal Palace	James Bowler, William Middleton
Luton Town	Hugh Roberts, Frank Lindley
Southend Utd	Frederick Robson
Tottenham Hotspur	George Bowler, William Oliver
Watford	Reg Williams, Alexander Stewart, Joe McLauchlan[8]

Over the next few days the 17th Middlesex Committee determined that the first battalion parade should take place outside West Africa House, Kingsway, on 4 January. Enlisted men were promised 1s for each extra recruit they could bring along. The most impressive contribution was from Brighton & Hove Albion; an astonishing 13 of the club's 17 registered professional players enlisted in the 17th Middlesex. The response of the Albion players was largely down to the efforts of Archie Needham, who did his utmost to ensure that the club was well represented in the ranks of the battalion. On one occasion he even managed to persuade three team-mates to visit West Africa House, while the team crossed London en route to a match.

On 4 January around 120 recruits turned up at West Africa House in anticipation of commencing their military service with the 17th Middlesex. Various photographs were taken to various cries of 'Goal!', 'Offside!', and 'Well tried'. The men were disappointed to discover that Richmond Athletic Ground had been deemed unsuitable by the authorities and that another headquarters had yet to be procured. Everyone was disheartened to be sent back home.[9]

That same day the 17th Middlesex Committee met at 42 Russell Square to discuss the selection of officers for the battalion. Col Charles Grantham had already been appointed as the commanding officer, and Col Henry Fenwick as his second-in-command. Both men were so-called 'dug outs' in that that they had retired from the Army several years previously. Capt Alexander Elphinstone, a Cambridge 'Double Blue', who had been wounded in France while serving with the East Surrey Regiment, was appointed adjutant.[10] Within a few days the Bishop of Birmingham, Dr Russell Wakefield, would be nominated by Joynson-Hicks as Honorary Chaplain of the 17th Middlesex.

Col Charles Grantham, known as 'Johnnie' to his friends, cut an impressive figure. A tall, strongly built man, he came from a military family; both his grandfathers had served in the Peninsular War, and a great-uncle had been present at the Siege of Cadiz. Born in 1857 at Trincomalee, Ceylon, Grantham had been commissioned into the 15th Regiment of Foot in 1878. Joining the Sind Horse, he had taken part in the Khelat Expedition, and had later seen action in China with the Poona Horse. After serving for a period as Commandant of the Governor's Body Guard in Bombay, he had commanded the 3rd Bombay Light Cavalry from 1903 until his retirement in 1909. Grantham was a holder of the Royal Humane Society's certificate for saving life in the Thames. He was a keen sportsman; in his youth he had played three-quarter back for Munster and had excelled as a runner, at one time being holder of the Indian mile record. On the outbreak of war Grantham had been appointed Chief Inspector of the Special Police for the Dittons, a district in the county of Surrey, before becoming a recruiting officer in London.

Col Henry Fenwick was born into a wealthy Northumberland family of brewers in 1863. Educated at Eton, he was commissioned into the Royal Horse Guards in 1885. By the outbreak of the Boer War, Fenwick was a brevet lieutenant-colonel, and second-in-command of his regiment. During the war in South Africa, he had seen plenty of action, and was awarded the Distinguished Service Order. Promoted to the rank of colonel in 1909, Fenwick had commanded the Royal Horse Guards until his retirement in 1911. Despite being a career soldier, Fenwick had sat from 1892 to 1895 as Liberal Member of Parliament for Houghton-le-Spring, in addition to maintaining a diverse range of business interests. In October 1914 he had been a member of the General Courts Martial, which had convicted Karl Lody, the first German spy to be executed in Britain during the Great War.

Finding experienced company and platoon commanders was proving a problem, given the rapid expansion of the New Armies.[11] Among the nominations was the 50-year-old Capt Wells-Holland, who had managed to conceal his true age from the authorities.[12] Having played football for Tottenham Town in his youth, Wells-Holland had been chairman of Clapton Orient since the reorganisation of the club in 1906, and had played a pivotal role in maintaining Orient's League status later that year. Wells-Holland was a former Superintendent of the Bill Office at the Bank of England. In the autumn of 1913, Wells-Holland, his own bank account having been closed a few years earlier owing to 'irregularities', had signed another clerk's name on one of his wife's cheques without the necessary authority. In the light of such a 'grave irregularity', the Bank of England had decided to dispense with his services on the grounds that he was not 'a fit person to be retained in the Bank'.[13]

Other names put forward, included Robert Foxcroft-Jones, who had served with Wells-Holland in the 4th Volunteer Battalion of the Royal Fusiliers, and William Scotland, a director of Crystal Palace and a Superintendent of Public Works, who had once been the holder of the world deep-sea 'Diving Duration Record'. Another nomination was 26-year-old Herbert Wall, the younger son of the FA secretary. Wall was an intrepid journalist, who had spent the first few months of the war reporting from the front with the Belgian Army. Previously, he had travelled extensively throughout Europe, Africa and the Americas. Wall would be the only one of these junior officers to proceed on active service with the 17th Middlesex.

The Footballers' Battalion had now attracted around 600 recruits. On Monday 11 January the first 250 lined up outside West Africa House, Holborn, including William Jonas, the Clapton Orient centre-forward, and the Millwall goalkeeper Joe Orme, both of whom had been sent off for fighting during Saturday's FA Cup match at New Cross. Having received their first pay, the men paraded in Keeley Street under the watchful eye of Col Grantham. The men then marched 'with swinging stride' through the streets of London to White City, where the 17th Middlesex were to be housed in the huge Machinery Hall. Proceedings were cheered by a large crowd, which had gathered to witness the first parade of the Footballers' Battalion. Not everyone was impressed. One onlooker, 'seeing them in their caps and sweaters, and with their hands in their pockets', remarked loudly that 'they were not the stuff of which soldiers are made'.[14] The remaining 350 recruits joined the first batch in White City the following day.

The majority of these early recruits were either local amateur players, or 'club enthusiasts', those of Clapton Orient and Chelsea being particularly well represented. The response of professional footballers had been disappointing. An unidentified officer of the 17th Middlesex told a journalist not long after the battalion arrived at White City:

We want more players and we must have them . . . I am much disappointed, and not a little disgusted, and shall feel like ceasing my active connection with the game when the war is over. The response has been good, but is by no means representative of the number of players there are about. I am convinced that a proportion of the first team men of the league clubs could join, and the example would mean a rush on the part of the lesser lights, and there would be no fears about the success of the battalion. I have spoken to several whom I thought I could influence by becoming attached to it, and they tell me they will wait until the end of the season and see. Well, I will not discuss what they might see then, but you know what my thoughts are.[15]

Notwithstanding the fact that there were several professional footballers 'hanging back', the same officer had nothing, but praise for those who had volunteered:

I am particularly proud of the men who have come forward. Some of them have been very queer people to manage on the field, and I had my doubts about them submitting to military rule. But the result of the very first day in camp was astonishing. I will give you an instance, as you know _____ has an extraordinary temperament, and the day after we came here, I had occasion to ask him to render me a little personal service. He saluted me as satisfactorily as one need wish for, carried out our mission and, when I offered to thank him, he interposed with a "No Thanks, Sir, delighted to serve you," saluted and went on with his business.[16]

Unlike many battalions of Kitchener's New Armies, the 17th Middlesex did not have to wait long for their khaki uniforms, which were issued within days of their arrival at White City. The days were spent practising drill and developing march discipline: 'Sometimes the men march from the White City to the West End, halting perhaps at the Marble Arch end of Hyde Park for quarter of an hour's rest prior to setting off on the return journey'. No. 1 Platoon, which was comprised entirely of professional players, was placed under the command of the newly commissioned 2/Lt Frank Buckley, who was reported to have 'put himself on the perfect understanding with the men of his platoon'.[17] Onlookers were impressed:

> The men have taken to drill like ducks take to water, and so far as the footballers' platoon is concerned it is probably in a more advanced stage of training than any other body of men with such a short actual experience of army life. This is due to two reasons, the intelligence of the men, added to their previous experience, and the smartness and painstaking work of the officers.[18]

Buckley was a man who stood no nonsense from anyone. Appearing once before an FA committee for striking an opponent during a match against Stockport County, a committee member recalled that Buckley 'frankly told us he had struck the man, and that he would do the same again if necessity arose. The other man he said used filthy language every time he came near an opponent, and as he persisted after being warned "he let him have it"'.[19] The remaining footballers were placed in No. 2 Platoon, where they were put through their paces by Lt William Scotland and the Brighton & Albion goalkeeper, Sgt George Wilcock, formerly of the Royal Field Artillery.[20]

Conditions at White City were far from comfortable. After a few days in the damp Machinery Hall, the battalion moved to another building, but these quarters were still cold and draughty. It was not long before recruits were reporting sick with bad colds and influenza. Although the footballers were said to be 'more than satisfied' with their food, the same could not be said of the straw mattresses on the low wooden beds, nor the 6 a.m. reveille, which was 'a bit trying'. Old soldiers were unimpressed with the grumbling. One former soldier told a visiting journalist that White City was a marked improvement on billeting arrangements during the Boer War: 'Of course wherever you go, you will find grumbles, but there's nothing to shout about here.'[21]

Even though the majority of recruits were in superb physical condition – the average chest measurement was 38in – many footballers found the regime of endless drill and physical exercise exhausting. Angus Seed, a Reading reserve and brother of future England international Jimmy, wrote to the club secretary that: 'We are all getting on fine here, and if they keep giving us the drills we had this morning, we will have muscles like stones. It would do some of the boys good to come down here, it would harden them a bit.'[22]

The physical exhaustion was compounded by the fact that many players were still turning out for their clubs. On 23 January no less than ten Brighton & Hove Albion players left White City to travel down to the Goldstone Ground for the match against Cardiff City. That same day a platoon of the 17th Middlesex, with six Orient players among their number, was addressed by the Mayor of Hackney in front of the Town Hall. During the half-time interval of Clapton Orient's match against Hull City, Capt Wells-Holland and Lt Buckley led the platoon around the ground to the accompaniment of a military band. At West Ham, various members of the Parliamentary Recruiting Committee made 'stirring addresses on three sides of the ground' during the half-time interval.

On the afternoon of 25 January around 200 officers and men of the 17th Middlesex marched from White City to the Park Cinema in Shepherds Bush to see a *Daily Express* film *Wake Up!*, which was based on a serial story written by one of the 17th Middlesex officers, Maj John Pretyman-Newman, Unionist MP for Enfield.[23] Once the 17th Middlesex had taken their seats, the remainder of the hall was filled with local Boy Scouts. Among the audience were William Joynson-Hicks, Maj Pretyman-Newman and Sir William Bull, Unionist MP for Hammersmith. All three men made speeches, Maj Pretyman-Newman telling the audience that, when the 17th Middlesex reached Berlin, he knew of a 'football ground not far from the Kaiser's palace, where they could have an exhibition match for the benefit of the Germans'.[24] Among the films that followed was a short film of the Footballers' Battalion 'getting ready for the final' by going through exercises at the

White City. Various exclamations were made as the men recognised themselves on the screen. Once the films had been screened, a Miss Bettie Leclair sung the popular sentimental song, *Your King and Country Want You*, the footballers and Boy Scouts enthusiastically joining in the chorus:

> Oh! We don't want to lose you
> But we think that you ought to go
> For your King and Country both need you so
> We shall want you and miss you
> But with all our might and main
> We shall cheer you, thank you, kiss you
> When you come home again[25]

With the ranks of the battalion still incomplete, the recruiting drive continued. Special posters continued to be displayed at grounds of London clubs, specifically aimed at the home supporters. A Millwall supporter would thus find himself being exhorted to 'Let the enemy hear the 'Lion's Roar', while home supporters arriving at Stamford Bridge were confronted with a poster, which asked the question: 'Do You want to be a Chelsea Die-Hard?' At several League and FA Cup matches over the coming weeks patriotic speeches would be made encouraging supporters to enlist in the 17th Middlesex.

One such event took place at The Nest after Croydon Common's 4–1 victory over Reading on 30 January. The Reading inside-left, Pte Walter 'Joe' Bailey who had recently enlisted in the battalion, was called upon to address the spectators. Nicknamed 'Bubbles', Bailey had started his career at Oxford City before moving to Nottingham Forest. Joining Reading in 1911, Bailey had lost little time in forging a highly effective partnership with fellow 17th Middlesex recruit Allen Foster. During the 1912/13 season, Bailey had gained two amateur international caps against Belgium and Holland, scoring twice on each occasion. A talented all-round sportsman, Bailey had also played cricket for Berkshire and hockey for Oxfordshire.

Observers noted that when Pte Bailey stepped up onto the platform in his uniform, a 'sporting allusion to the defeat of his side made him at once as popular': 'We shall die fighting – the same as we have at football today (Loud cheers, and cries of "Good old Bailey"). I hope on another occasion we shall be able to talk to some of you in barracks (Hear, Hear).'[26] Elsewhere that day a platoon of the 17th Middlesex marched around the pitch during Chelsea's Second Round FA Cup tie against Arsenal, a game won by the home side 1–0. The platoon received a rousing reception as they collected money on behalf of a fund to provide the 17th Middlesex with musical instruments for a band. A journalist present at Stamford Bridge that afternoon would later record his impressions of the soldier footballers that afternoon: 'They marched like "pals" steady and true, with their shoulders touching.'[27]

Recruiting for the 17th Middlesex was also taking place away from football grounds. On 1 February Joynson-Hicks addressed an audience in the Municipal Hall, Tottenham:

> I tell you whether the Censor likes it or not, that we are holding our own in Flanders and no more, and that unless we are able to send enormous reinforcements by April and May, we shall do no more than hold our own. Germany has Belgium and the North of France in a vice, and she will not give up until she is forced, step by step, by the lives of Englishmen and Frenchmen. I am inviting you to no picnic. It is no easy game against a second-rate team. It is a game of games against one of the finest teams in the world. It is a team worthy of Great Britain to fight.[28]

Another meeting took place at King's Hall Baths in Hackney on 17 February. In the absence of the Mayor of Hackney on account of illness, Capt Wells-Holland chaired the meeting with various speeches being made by Col Grantham, Albert Jessel KC and Horatio Bottomley, president of Clapton Orient.[29] On the same platform were Sgt Fred Parker and the famous Chelsea footballer forward Lt Vivian Woodward, who had recently been commissioned into the 17th Middlesex from the ranks of a territorial battalion, the 1/5th Londons.[30]

Known 'first and foremost as a gentleman', Vivian Woodward was an architect by profession. A creative player with excellent dribbling and passing skills, Woodward had remained an amateur throughout his career. After playing for local Essex sides, he had signed for Spurs in 1901. At White Hart Lane he had scored 96 goals in 193 appearances, including Spurs' first ever goal in the Football League, later becoming a director of the club. In 1909 Woodward had announced his retirement from football at the top level, but had then surprised everyone by signing for Chelsea. By the time of his enlistment in September 1914, he had made over 100 League and FA Cup appearances for the Pensioners. Although Woodward had never won a major domestic honour, he had scored a remarkable 29 goals in 23 appearances for England, in addition to gaining 44 amateur international caps.[31] He had also captained the Great Britain team to consecutive gold medals at the Olympics in 1908 and 1912.[32]

The meeting at King's Hall Baths secured a further 18 recruits, bringing the strength of the 17th Middlesex up to over 850 men. Virtually all of these men were from London and the south-east. Originally it had been envisaged that the 17th Middlesex would recruit players and supporters from clubs outside London as well. Shortly after the battalion's formation, Frederick Wall had written to all professional clubs south of the River Trent, asking them to set up recruiting committees, but there 'had been little or no response from the provinces'. Undeterred, Joynson-Hicks and Lord Kinnaird sent a letter to every professional footballer in England, who had yet to enlist: 'A large number of some of the finest players in the kingdom have already joined the Battalion, but we do not see your name amongst them . . . We do urge you as a patriot and a footballer to come to the help of the country in its hour of need.'[33] Results were similarly disappointing.

The problem was a financial one rather than a want of patriotism. As Walter Hart, the Birmingham City chairman, pointed out: 'If men from the Midlands joined the battalion, their expenses to and from London would have to be borne by their clubs, and money was very scarce with them all at present. For them to send twenty players to London each week was out of the question.'[34] Requests were subsequently made to the 17th Middlesex Recruiting Committee for assistance with rail fares, but these were turned down flat.

In a further effort to stimulate recruiting in the provinces,

Joynson-Hicks sent 2/Lt Arthur Tickler to Grimsby with the object of persuading local players and supporters to enlist in the 17th Middlesex. Second-Lieutenant Tickler was an ideal choice to secure recruits in this locality, his father being the local Member of Parliament.[35] Accompanied by club officials, 2/Lt Tickler visited Blundell Park on the morning of 24 February to interview the players of Grimsby Town, nearly all of whom were present. As soon as 2/Lt Tickler had explained that the players would be given the privilege of completing their engagements with their club, the Grimsby captain, Sid Wheelhouse and four other players, Frank Martin, Alf Gregson, David Kenney and David Chalmers, 'expressed their willingness to join at once'.[36]

The five Grimsby players left Blundell Park immediately to undergo their medical and necessary attestation procedures. They were joined soon after by Percy Summers, the goalkeeper, and Thomas McKenna, a full-back. An appeal for recruits was subsequently made by 2/Lt Tickler at the Prince of Wales Theatre for the club's supporters to follow the example of their players. The response was encouraging. By the time 2/Lt Tickler returned to London a few days later, another 25 recruits had been secured for the battalion.

On 10 March a 17th Middlesex team travelled to the Goldstone Ground to play Brighton & Hove Albion, with gate receipts going towards the battalion band fund. The crowd enjoyed the sight of 700 soldiers making their entrance into the ground, accompanied by a military band. The 17th Middlesex now had a march of its own, entitled *Play for Goal*, which had been dedicated to Col Grantham and the officers and men of the Footballers' Battalion by its composer, Richard Levett. During the half-time interval Col Grantham and William Joynson-Hicks made appeals for recruits. Brighton & Hove Albion won the game 2–0.

For several weeks there had been rumours circulating that the certain football clubs were actively discouraging their players from joining the 17th Middlesex. Some clubs were even alleged to have 'punished' players, who had chosen to enlist in the 17th Middlesex, by reducing their wages, or not selecting them for matches.[37] On 26 March Col Grantham, his eldest son having been killed in action a few weeks earlier, wrote a letter to the Management Committee of the Football League:[38]

As the Officer Commanding the Footballers' Battalion it is my duty to bring the following facts to your notice. You are aware that some little time ago there was much controversy in the papers with regard to the manner in which the professional football player had failed in his duty by not coming forward to serve this country in its time of stress. The laxity of the football professionals and their following amounted to almost a public scandal. Mr Joynson-Hicks M.P., therefore, raised the Footballers' Battalion, and public opinion died down under the belief that most, if not all, of the available professionals had joined the battalion.

This is not the case, as only 122 professionals have joined. I understand that there are forty League clubs and twenty in the Southern League, with an average of some thirty players fit to join the Colours, namely 1,800. These figures speak for themselves. I am also aware and have proof that in many cases directors and managers of clubs have not only given no assistance in getting his men to join but have done their best by their actions to prevent it.

I am taking the opportunity of your meeting on Monday to ask you gentlemen if you and your clubs have done everything in your power to point out to the men what their duty is. Your King and country call upon every man who is capable of bearing arms to come forward, and upon those that are unable, to use their best endeavours to see that those that can do so. It is no use mincing words. If men who are fit and are capable of doing so will not join, they and also those who try by their words and actions to prevent them will have to face the opinion of their fellow-men publicly. I will no longer be a party to shielding the want of patriotism of these men by allowing the public to think they have joined the Football Battalion.[39]

The letter was read out at a special general meeting of the Football League, held at the Connaught Rooms, Great Queen Street, on 29 March. An animated discussion ensued. Col Grantham's views were heartily endorsed by Capt Wells-Holland, but were rejected in their entirety by everyone else. One representative suggested that 'the letter was the outcome of pique owing to the fact that the Football Battalion not being the success anticipated'. Henry Norris disagreed, stating that the battalion, now some 1,200 strong had been a success, despite the fact that not many players from clubs outside London had joined the battalion. A resolution was passed re-affirming the 'importance of all professional players who can do so joining the Colours'. No action would ever be taken in response to Col Grantham's allegations, despite the subsequent publication of a letter from Joynson-Hicks in the *Sportsman*, which claimed that several unpatriotic team managers had given no help whatsoever in the formation of the 17th Middlesex, due to 'financial considerations'.[40]

Further adverse publicity for the game followed. On 3 April Middlesbrough were entertaining Oldham Athletic, the unlikely leaders of Football League Division One. Ten minutes after the interval, Oldham Athletic found themselves 4–1 down in a bad-tempered match. The Oldham Athletic full-back, William Cook, fouled a Middlesbrough player and was sent off. Inexplicably, Cook refused point-blank to leave the field of play, and the referee decided that he had no choice, but to abandon the match.[41]

Events at Ayrsome Park were soon overshadowed by the Good Friday match at Old Trafford, where Manchester Utd, facing the possibility of relegation after a poor season, beat Liverpool by two goals to nil in a strangely lifeless encounter. It was not long before rumours began to circulate that the match had been rigged. Bookmakers were reported to have paid out on a flurry of bets on Manchester Utd winning the match 2–0. Within a couple of weeks a notice would appear in the *Sporting Chronicle* offering a £50 reward for information about a match played in Manchester over the Easter weekend. After a protracted investigation by the Football League's commission of enquiry, several players would be given lifetime bans from the game.[42] Among their number was John 'Jackie' Sheldon, the Liverpool outside-right. Prior to moving to Merseyside in 1913, Sheldon had played for Manchester Utd. Within only a few weeks of the infamous Good Friday match, Sheldon would enlist in the Middlesex Regiment.

On 14 April a 17th Middlesex team played the Royal Naval Division at Crystal Palace watched by Frederick Wall and a large group of the battalion's officers. The match was refereed by Cpl Archie Strike, a compositor in civilian life with the company registration agent Richard Jordan & Son in Chancery Lane. The game ended in a resounding 8–0 victory for the 17th Middlesex. Pte Allen Foster scored a hat-trick; Pte Joe Bailey and Cpl Bob Dalrymple scored two apiece. Sgt James McCormick, who had joined the forward line shortly before the final whistle, scored the last goal.[i] Three days later, a 17th Middlesex team played Hampstead Town at the Avenue Ground in Cricklewood Lane, winning 3–1. Pte Henry Pennifer of QPR scored two of the battalion's goals, the other being scored by L/Cpl Charles Bell, who had moved from Arsenal to Chesterfield Town only a few months earlier.[ii]

For the previous few weeks the 17th Middlesex had been under orders to be ready to leave White City at short notice. On 24 April the battalion finally received orders to take up training in camp at the country residence of William Joynson-Hicks in Holmbury St Mary, near Dorking. The battalion now numbered some 1,400 men, but the War Office had recently sanctioned a further increase in strength to 1,600. Large crowds turned out to watch the officers and men of the battalion as they marched through the streets to Waterloo 'occasioning much enthusiasm'. There were some gaps in the ranks. Several recruits were turning out in matches for their respective clubs. At Millfields Road in Homerton, where Clapton Orient were playing Leicester Fosse in the club's last home match of the season, there was a military parade around the ground so that the supporters could give a rousing send-off to the Orient men in the battalion. The contribution of Clapton Orient to the 17th Middlesex had been truly remarkable, over 40 players, officials and staff having enlisted in the battalion.

That same day Chelsea played Sheffield Utd in the FA Cup Final in front of around 50,000 spectators. The game took place at Old Trafford as the usual venue, Crystal Palace, had been commandeered by the Admiralty. It had been widely reported that Lt Vivian Woodward of the 17th Middlesex was going to turn out for Chelsea, but when the game started, Woodward was not on

[i]The 17th Middlesex team: Pte Joe Webster (West Ham Utd), goalkeeper; Sgt Tommy Gibson (Nottingham Forest) and Pte Nolan Evans (Clapton Orient), backs; Sgt James McCormick (Plymouth Argyle), Capt Frank Buckley (Bradford City), Pte Billy Baker (Plymouth Argyle), halfbacks; Sgt Fred Parker (Clapton Orient) Cpl Bob Dalrymple (Clapton Orient), Pte Allen Foster (Reading), Pte Joe Bailey (Reading) and L/Cpl Percy Barnfather (Croydon Common), forwards.

[ii]The 17th Middlesex team: Pte Peter Roney (Bristol Rovers), goalkeeper; Pte George Robertson (formerly Birmingham City) and Pte Harry Reason (formerly Clapton Orient), backs; Pte William Ripley (Stoke City), Sgt Sam Morris (Bristol Rovers) and Pte Henry Hogarth (Burnley), halfbacks; Pte David Gray (St Mirren), Pte Charles Bell (Chesterfield), Pte Henry Pennifer (Queen's Park Rangers), Pte William Gerrish (formerly Aston Villa) and Pte Hugh Gallacher (Bristol Rovers), forwards.

the pitch, but in the stands. Having featured in only a few games for Chelsea that season, Woodward had characteristically declared that he had no wish to play if it meant taking the place of a player who had played all season for the club.

During the half-time interval, a number of soldiers, many of them Boer War veterans, walked around the perimeter of the pitch, holding out large khaki-coloured sheets, into which the crowd hurled pennies for the benefit of the Red Cross. There were so many soldiers in the crowd that the match was dubbed the 'The Khaki Cup Final'. With the country in the grip of such a terrible war, the pageantry of Cup Final day seemed strangely inappropriate.[43] The spectators appeared noticeably subdued. It was increasingly apparent that now was the time to stop. Lord Derby memorably captured this sentiment, as he addressed the players after Sheffield Utd had beaten Chelsea 3–0 to lift the Cup: 'You have played with one another and against one another for the cup; play with one another for England now.'[44]

Within a couple of months, the decision was finally made to suspend football by representatives of the Football League, the Scottish League, the Southern League and the Irish League at a conference in Blackpool. In July 1915 the FA issued its wartime regulations, concerning the playing of football:

The Council, having carefully considered the present and future prospects of the game, and recognising the paramount duty of every man to help carry on the war to a victorious issue at the earliest possible moment, and not to do anything that will in any degree postpone or hinder the desired result, resolve that for the present the following Regulations shall be observed:

- That no International matches, or the Challenge Cup and Amateur Cup matches of this Association be played during the next season.
- That Association, Leagues and Clubs be allowed to arrange matches without Cups, Medals, or other awards, to suit local conditions, provided that they do not interfere with the work of those engaged in war-work. Clubs may join any combination of clubs, which may be convenient to them.
- That matches be played on Saturday afternoons, and on early closing and other recognised holidays.

- That no remuneration shall be paid to players, nor shall there be any registration of players, but clubs and players shall be subject to the rules and conditions applicable to them on April 30th, 1915.
- Agreements with players for service after April 30th, 1915 shall be suspended until further order.'[45]

It was not quite the end of football. Over the next few months various regional competitions were set up to provide a welcome diversion for munitions workers and servicemen on leave, or recovering from wounds. The Football League oversaw the Lancashire Combination and the Midlands Combination, each competition consisting of a Principal Tournament and a Subsidiary Tournament for the participating clubs, 14 clubs in each section.[46] In the south-east, the London Combination was formed, consisting of Southern League teams based in and around the capital, as well as five southern clubs from the Football League.[47] The clubs were divided into two groups of seven, the members of each group playing only teams belonging to the other group, a total of 14 games. A Supplementary Competition was then arranged to fill up the remainder of the season. As Charles Clegg, FA chairman, would later comment: 'Thousands found their only recreation in football, played by professional footballers without reward.'[48]

1. BNL: *Sportsman*, 16 December 1914. All quotations used in relation to the meeting on 15 December 1914 are taken from this article. Interestingly, the service records of several footballers who enlisted at the meeting state that enlistment took place at Chelsea Town Hall. It can only be assumed that this was a clerical error, given that contemporary newspaper reports state that the meeting took place at Fulham Town Hall.
2. Hayes Fisher was one of the original directors of Fulham FC when the club became a limited company in 1903.
3. Capt Douglas Kinnaird, 1st Scots Guards, was killed in action on 24 October 1914. His grave can be found in Godezonne Farm Cemetery, a few miles south-west of Ypres.
4. Not long after the outbreak of war when someone had accused professional footballers of cowardice, Buckley had refuted the charge in a letter to the Birmingham newspapers.
5. At the time of his enlistment on 24 February 1900, Frank Buckley was already a member of the 1st Volunteer Battalion, Manchester Regiment.
6. The raising of the 17th Middlesex made little impression on F. N. Charrington. In February 1915 he protested directly to Herbert Asquith 'on behalf of many ministers of religion and the Mayors of numerous boroughs, condemning professional football and the playing of cup finals during the present crisis'. His campaign against football did not halt his advocacy of other causes. On 18 May 1915 Charrington rushed into the House of Commons and picked up the mace from the Speaker's table in protest at MPs frequenting the bar in the members' lobby. He was immediately arrested, but later released without charge.
7. Following the raising of the 17th Middlesex, the War Office received numerous such requests, including one from Elias 'Patsy' Hendren, the well-known Middlesex cricketer and Brentford forward, as to whether they might transfer to the battalion. The decision was subsequently taken by the War Office not to permit any such transfers.

8. The size of the Clapton Orient contingent resulted in many messages of congratulation being received by the club, including one from the president of Real Sociedad, the club having recently toured Spain: 'Hurrah for Clapton Orient and England's success.' Within a few days the Orient players would be joined by former full-back Harry 'Jumbo' Reason, who had left the club in 1910 after six years service with Orient.

9. The problem of finding suitable accommodation for the New Armies was particularly acute at this time. During the winter of 1914/15 around 800,000 troops had to be billeted in private houses.

10. Later Sir Alexander Elphinstone Logie of Glack, 10th Bt. In addition to Elphinstone, another five of the original officers of the 17th Middlesex were 'Double Blues'.

11. Finding experienced non-commissioned officers was also an acute problem. In the early days, practically all the battalion's NCOs were men who had shown 'proficiency in football', including many well-known referees. Among their number were a few footballers with previous military experience, such as James McCormick of Plymouth Argyle.

12. Henry (Wells) Holland was born on 8 June 1864 in Stroud, Gloucestershire. For the purposes of obtaining his commission, he gave his birth date as 8 June 1870. TNA: WO 339/ 581124.

13. BoE: Minutes of the Court of Directors: G4/136.

14. BNL: *Athletic News*, 18 January 1915.

15. *Ibid.*

16. *Ibid.*

17. *Ibid.*

18. BNL: *Football Post*, 23 January 1915.

19. BNL: *Sporting Chronicle*, 7 August 1916.

20. Lt Scotland subsequently assumed command of 'B' Company of the 23rd Middlesex in July 1915, where he sustained a serious head injury after a fall from a horse. After service with the Royal Engineers, he was invalided out of the army in August 1916: WO 339/ 23714.

21. BNL: *Oriental Notes: The Official Organ of the Clapton Orient Football Club Ltd*, 27 February 1915.

22. BNL: *Berkshire Chronicle*, 22 January 1915.

23. The making of *Wake Up!* had been sanctioned by the War Office, with a view to stimulating recruiting. The film told of a dream by Lord Pax, Secretary of State for War, showing how the country was invaded, and how 'England' finally woke up to defeat the enemy.

24. BNL: *West London Observer*, 29 January 1915.

25. Popular recruiting song written by Paul A. Rubens (1875–1917). When sung by a man, the word 'kiss' was replaced by the word 'bless'! At the time of writing, two versions of the song can be heard at: http://www.firstworldwar.com/audio/yourkingandcountrywantyou.htm

26. BNL: *Berkshire Chronicle*, 5 February 1915.

27. BNL: *Sporting Chronicle*, 20 September 1916.

28. BNL: *Scotsman*, 2 February 1915.

29. The financier, journalist and swindler, Horatio Bottomley, was Liberal MP for South Hackney from 1906, and an Independent from 1918 until his imprisonment for fraud in 1922.

30. One of Woodward's character references when applying for his commission was Frederick Wall, secretary of the FA. Woodward had originally enlisted on 8 September 1914.

31. There has been some dispute over the years about whether one of Woodward's goals, scored against Hungary in 1909, should have been classified as an own goal. His tally of 29 England goals was finally surpassed by Nat Lofthouse and Tom Finney in 1958.

32. The England team represented Great Britain at the Olympics in 1908 and 1912.

33. FA: Letter signed 'Kinnaird' and 'W. Joynson-Hicks', dated February 1915. Notepaper headed '17th (Service) Battalion Middlesex Regiment (Football)'.

34. This was a particular problem for Cardiff City, with three players in the battalion. Each time a player returned to Cardiff for a match, it cost the club 12s 9d in rail fares.

35. Thomas Tickler MP, a former Mayor of Grimsby Town, had founded T.G. Tickler Ltd, the famous jam-making firm that supplied vast quantities of jam, especially the ubiquitous 'plum-and-apple' variety, to the forces from its factories in Grimsby and Southall. In the early days of the war, these jam tins were frequently used by soldiers in France to make grenades.

36. BNL: *Athletic News*, 24 February 1915.

37. According to press reports, the FA, when asked to intervene in relation to the reduction of wages, had responded that 'arrangements must be made between players and their clubs, and it could not interfere'.

38. Lt Charles Grantham was killed in action on 3 March 1915 at the Battle of Shaiba, while serving with his father's regiment, the 33rd Queen Victoria's Own Light Cavalry (formerly 3rd Bombay Light Cavalry).

39. BNL: *Scotsman*, 30 March 1915.

40. The alleged 'unpatriotic' clubs do not appear to have ever been named.

41. The FA suspended William Cook for one year. The 4–1 score line was ordered to stand. Oldham Athletic subsequently missed out on the First Division Championship by a single point to Everton.

42. For detailed accounts of the scandal, see Inglis, S., *Soccer in the Dock: A History of British Football Scandals 1900–1965*, and Sharpe, G., *Free the Manchester One*.

43. In the weeks leading up to the Khaki Cup Final, football had continued to be vilified by F.N. Charrington and other detractors of the game. One newspaper had even featured a cartoon suggesting that Kaiser Wilhelm II was the most appropriate person to present the Cup, where the winning captain says, 'Thank you, sire,' and the Kaiser replies, 'On the contrary, thank you.'

44. Green, G., *History of the Football Association 1863–1953*, p. 266.

45. *History of The Football Association*, p. 292.

46. Some clubs initially declined to participate in the various wartime competitions. Clubs, such as Middlesbrough, Newcastle Utd and Sunderland, faced obvious logistical problems given their geographical location. Other clubs, like Blackburn Rovers, and several clubs situated in and around Birmingham, were more altruistic in their motives.

47. The Football League would have liked to oversee this competition, but the London clubs elected a Special Management Committee, which subsequently placed itself under the London FA, to which all participating clubs, with the exception of Watford, belonged.

48. BNL: *Athletic News*, 3 July 1916.

CHAPTER 3

SOLDIER FOOTBALLERS

*Firing on a range is about the only time one
has to coax a Tommy into doing anything*
2/Lt Cosmo Clark

On 26 April 1915 the 17th Middlesex suffered their first fatality, when 21-year-old L/Cpl Edward Frost, a shipping clerk, who had only enlisted in the battalion on 19 February, died of 'acute meningitis' at his home in Catford. That same day a 17th Middlesex team travelled up to London to play the 23rd Royal Fusiliers at Craven Cottage.[1] Gate receipts were split between the 17th Middlesex Band Fund and Benevolent Fund of the 23rd Royal Fusiliers (1st Sportsman's). The team of the 23rd Royal Fusiliers contained several notable sportsmen, including cricketers Patsy Hendren (Middlesex), Andrew Sandham (Surrey) and William Bates (Yorkshire). Their attack was led by Ebenezer Owers, who had featured in the Bristol City side that had lost to Manchester Utd in the 1909 FA Cup Final.

As soon as the game started, the 17th Middlesex team 'assumed the offensive' but were unable to find the net in the first half. Both Pte Allen Foster and L/Cpl Percy Barnfather missed chances, and Kirton, the opposition goalkeeper, 'time after time saved the shots rained on him in most capable fashion'.[1] Shortly after the interval, Barnfather crossed the ball, and Foster headed into the net to give the 17th Middlesex the lead. Having opened the scoring, the 17th Middlesex 'almost monopolised the attacking, but were swarming so closely around the goal that they rather thwarted one another . . . Kirton

[1] The 17th Middlesex team: Pte Joe Webster (West Ham Utd), goalkeeper; L/Cpl Ernest Coquet (Fulham) and Pte Nolan Evans (Clapton Orient), backs; Sgt James McCormick (c) (Plymouth Argyle), Sgt Joe Mercer (Nottingham Forest) and Pte Billy Baker (Plymouth Argyle), halfbacks; Sgt Fred Parker (Clapton Orient), Cpl Bob Dalrymple (Clapton Orient), Pte Allen Foster (Reading), Pte Joe Bailey (Reading) and L/Cpl Percy Barnfather (Croydon Common), forwards.

continued his excellent efforts between the uprights, two low saves from Parker and Mercer deserving special attention'. Seven minutes before the final whistle, the 17th Middlesex were awarded a penalty for handball, which Pte Foster converted to give the battalion a 2–0 victory. After the match, both teams were 'hospitably entertained' in the boardroom of Fulham FC. As a fund-raising fixture, the match was not a success. The move down to Holmbury had deprived the 17th Middlesex team of their support, and the fact that the game had been scheduled for a Monday afternoon meant that it ended up being watched by less than 1,000 spectators.

The camp of the 17th Middlesex was situated about a mile and half outside the picturesque village of Holmbury St Mary: 'The country around us is lovely, all round are small hills, little woods and banks covered with primroses, violets, bluebells etc.'[2] Joynson-Hicks had bought Holmbury House from E.F. Leveson-Gower in 1906.[3] It was perched high on the side of Holmbury Hill, the site of a former Iron Age hill fort, and enjoyed stunning views of the Sussex Weald.[4] Under the supervision of Grace Joynson-Hicks, a wing of the house was converted into a temporary hospital, and the 'excellent open-air swimming pool' was made available to the men. Military training soon started in earnest. Within a few days the tranquillity of the surrounding countryside was disturbed by soldiers of the 17th Middlesex digging trenches and undergoing route marches along the narrow country lanes.

During the first few days at Holmbury, several officers reported for duty with the battalion. Among their number were 2/Lt John Engleburtt, a banker's clerk in civilian life, and 2/Lt Albert 'Bertie' Wade, a former London Scottish scrum-half, who had represented Scotland against England in 1908. Educated at Dulwich College, Wade was a talented black-and-white cartoonist and had been studying art in Paris in the summer of 1914. Like many former public schoolboys imbued with a sense of duty, Wade had lost little time in answering his country's call. Within three days of Britain's declaration of war he had returned home and enlisted in the 1/13th Londons (The Kensingtons), where he had befriended a fellow recruit, John 'Cosmo' Clark, an 18-year-old art student. The two friends had subsequently undergone officer training together with the Inns of Court Officer Training Corps before applying together for commissions in the 17th Middlesex. First impressions of the 17th Middlesex were not exactly encouraging, 2/Lt Cosmo Clark wrote home that:

> The officers are a mixed crew, one or two quite hardened cockneys, but the majority seem very decent. I am sharing a tent with Wade and we're both very comfortable – the poor men sleep ten to a tent the same size . . .
>
> My platoon of sixty men are a mixed mob who haven't (through bad teaching) realised what is expected from them as soldiers. In fact, the whole battalion are the same – the majority of the junior officers let unforgivable little crimes slip by without saying anything. In consequence I find, and so do the other men from the Inns of Court, that we're considerably more efficient than the other subs and even some senior officers. My platoon sergeant is a man who went through the Boer War and seems pretty good. I was warned that he is inclined to forget his position and try to boss so am on my guard! . . . During a lecture by a sergeant major on musketry I spotted a man who was actually fitting a live cartridge into the chamber of his rifle! Men were all about him and his rifle was pointing into the midst of them.
>
> I have got a chap from my own platoon for my batman – he is quite a youth but seems very good. My beery voiced sergeant recommended him to me – said 'He's a good lad, strict teetotaller, and 'as been valet to Lord _____ !![5]

Even though the 17th Middlesex were now undergoing military training, football matches continued to be arranged against a range of clubs. The primary object of these games was to further the recruiting drive, with gate receipts being donated to an assortment of war charities. On 1 May a 17th Middlesex team visited The Nest, Selhurst, in order to play Croydon Common in front of 3,000 spectators.[ii] Five soldiers of 17th Middlesex donned their club's

[ii] The 17th Middlesex team: Pte Joe Webster (West Ham Utd), goalkeeper; L/Cpl Ernest Coquet (Fulham) and Pte Nolan Evans (Clapton Orient), backs; Sgt Joe Mercer (Nottingham Forest), Capt Frank Buckley (c) (Bradford City) and Sgt Tommy Gibson (Nottingham Forest), halfbacks; Sgt Fred Parker (Clapton Orient) Cpl Bob Dalrymple (Clapton Orient), Pte Allen Foster (Reading), Pte Joe Bailey (Reading) and Sgt Richard McFadden (Clapton Orient), forward

colours to play against the battalion team, including L/Cpl Percy Barnfather, a firm favourite of the Robins supporters.[6] The son of an umbrella maker, Barnfather was a skilful outside-right, who had started his career at Wallsend Park Villa in his native North-East before making his Football League debut with Barnsley in 1903.

The game was a good one. One of the Croydon Common players, Pte Charles Stewart had the satisfaction of scoring against his battalion to give the Robins a 1–0 lead. Despite mounting strong attacks, with 'Buckley feeding his forwards admirably', the 17th Middlesex were unable to reply before half-time.[7] After the interval, Croydon Common continued to exert pressure on the 17th Middlesex defence, but Capt Buckley and Pte Nolan Evans made sure that the Robins did not increase their lead. Sgt Joe Mercer then equalised for the battalion with a header from a corner: 'Play was faster after this, and of good quality, both teams striving strenuously for the winning goal, which eventually fell to the Battalion, Mercer heading into the net from another corner.' Both goalkeepers, Ptes Webster and Williamson, were forced to make several saves before the final whistle.

Over the next few weeks the 17th Middlesex underwent basic field training. There were numerous lectures on bayonet fighting and musketry, but the emphasis remained on drill and physical fitness. The last week of the month was 'very slack' owing to the battalion being given various vaccinations. Everyone was given 48 hours' leave in consequence. Most men stayed in the neighbourhood, which led to some friction with the locals. On 28 May, after dinner in the officers' mess, 2/Lt Cosmo Clark went for a cycle ride:

When I got to Cranleigh, there was great excitement. Half the town was running about, police whistles blowing and everyone shouting. On enquiring what was the matter I found that four of our Tommies had been breaking windows in the town and they were trying to find them. They eventually collared them and took them to the police station. I went there and got their names from the sergeant who it seems collared the man who had done all the damage. They had got him handcuffed and he seemed pretty miserable. Of course he had been drinking and gone potty. He's a great big Scotsman about six feet high and broad in proportion.[8]

By the beginning of June around 1,600 men had enlisted in the 17th Middlesex, but this number had been reduced by several desertions, with other recruits being struck off battalion strength on account of illness, debility or 'general inefficiency'. Although the majority of recruits were club supporters and amateur footballers, the battalion contained a significant number of professional players, predominantly from Southern League clubs. There were also several retired players in the ranks. Among their number was 46-year-old Charles Bunyan, who had given his age as 38 on enlistment, in order to secure his place in the Footballers' Battalion.

The illegitimate son of a straw plaiter, Charles Bunyan had been the Hyde goalkeeper in the team that had lost 26–0 to Preston North End in the record-breaking FA Cup match in 1887. After spells at Sheffield United and Derby County, Bunyan had moved to Chesterfield Town in 1892, where he had combined his football career with that of a publican, supplementing his income by selling home-made shinguards to local players. A strong-minded individual, Bunyan had frequently found himself at odds with authority throughout his career, being punished on one occasion for altering the transfer form of another player in order to secure financial benefit for himself.

After a series of run-ins with the club's directors, Bunyan's time at Chesterfield had come to an abrupt end as a result of his habit of wandering up the field to involve himself in his team's attacks. When Chesterfield conceded a goal during one game, Bunyan could still be seen in the opposition's half, remonstrating with his forwards.[9] It was the last straw for the club's directors, who promptly sacked him. After spells at several clubs, including Walsall, New Brompton and Newcastle Utd, Bunyan moved into coaching with Brimington Athletic in 1908. Two years later, he became one of the first Englishmen to coach overseas, when he was appointed as the football and cricket coach of Racing Club de Bruxelles in Belgium, later assisting with the organisation of the 1912 Stockholm Olympics. After the German invasion of Belgium in August 1914, Bunyan escaped back to England, disguising himself and his family as refugees. His three sons, Ernest, Cyril and Maurice, who were all accomplished sportsmen, enlisted in the army within 30 hours of their arrival back in England.[10] It was not long before their father followed their example, enlisting at West Africa House on 12 March 1915. Promoted to a lance-corporal three months later, Bunyan would be discharged from the army on account of 'debility' in the spring of 1916.

Charles Bunyan was not the only recruit to conceal his age from the authorities. On 4 June Pte Sidney Prince succumbed to 'cerebro-spinal fever' at the Royal Herbert Hospital in Woolwich. His death certificate records that he was 20 years old at the time of his death, but Prince had been born 'Sidney Print' in Warwick in 1897.[11] Like thousands of boys up and down the country, Print had added a couple of years to his age when presenting himself at the recruiting office. Four days later, the battalion lost another recruit, Pte William Bell-Wedge, a 23-year-old fireman on the Great Western Railway, who succumbed to 'cerebro-spinal meningitis'.[12]

During the first week of July the 17th Middlesex left Holmbury and proceeded to Clipstone Camp, near Mansfield. Second Lieutenant Cosmo Clark described Mansfield to his brother, as 'a typical Midland town: smoky, fairly small and noisy with kids and trams'.[13] The Holmbury camp would now be taken over by the 23rd Middlesex (2nd Football), which had been raised by Joynson-Hicks in London on 29 June 1915. Clipstone was one of several camps that had sprung up across Britain to accommodate the men of Kitchener's New Armies. It consisted of a mass of army huts and could accommodate more than 30,000 men. The 17th Middlesex were joining the 33rd Division, which was largely composed of 'pals' battalions of the Middlesex Regiment, Royal Fusiliers, Essex Regiment and the King's Royal Rifle Corps. The 17th Middlesex formed part of the 100th Brigade, the other units being the 16th Middlesex (Public Schools), 13th Essex (West Ham) and the 16th King's Royal Rifle Corps (Church Lads Brigade).[14] At Clipstone the 17th Middlesex began to undertake training exercises at brigade level. On 26 July 2/Lt Clark wrote home: 'This morning we had a very stiff time. Started at 8.30 and got back at 3 p.m. with no rations. 16 miles with battalion drill and a big attack in the middle.'[15]

The 17th Middlesex were at Clipstone for no more than a few weeks. At the beginning of August, the 33rd Division began to entrain for Perham Down on Salisbury Plain, where a vast tract of land had been purchased for the purposes of military training at the end of the 19th century. The 17th Middlesex moved on 5 August. Second-Lieutenant Cosmo Clark wrote home:

Reveille was at four 'o'clock on Thursday morning and we had a five-mile march to Warsop station to entrain – it was 8.30 before we started in the train and we didn't get out until five in the afternoon. The camp fortunately is only about a mile and a half from Tidworth station and so we were soon in huts. After tea began the endless job of unloading the battalion's kit from the motor transport wagons of the A.S.C . . . The place is ideal for a battalion training but is fearfully lonely.[16]

It was only during their time at Perham Down that many men had their first experience of firing rifles on the long ranges. On 22 August 2/Lt Clark wrote home:

For the past four days I have been in charge of 'C' Company again and so have been very busy. We have been doing our firing at the long ranges. This is the first time any of the men had fired with ball cartridges (except old soldiers). It was a great business getting them all through the course. Anyhow, we got though without any casualties and did second best out of the battalion so I'm rather bucked. It's most extraordinary how nervous a lot of the men are when firing. Quite ten of the whole two hundred and forty had to be coaxed and assured that everything was quite safe and that there was nothing to be afraid about in firing a rifle . . . Firing on a range is about the only time one has to coax a Tommy into doing anything.[17]

Interspersed with the military training were several football matches. On 4 September a 17th Middlesex team played Reading at Elm Park in front of over 3,000 spectators, including 200 wounded soldiers who were admitted free of charge.[18] Capt Buckley was expected to play, but he had sustained an injury in training. Pte Ben Butler, a former Reading player, jumped at the chance to play against his old club.[iii] The 17th Middlesex dominated the game, but their forwards, 'whose passing and general combination was delightful to watch', were unable to find the net until five minutes before the final whistle, when Cpl Jack Cock gave the battalion a hard-fought 1–0 victory.[19]

On 2 October a 17th Middlesex team played a match against Cardiff City at Ninian Park. Although selected, Lt Vivian Woodward was unavailable to play. His place was taken by Pte George Pyke, a young centre-forward from the north-east, who had been signed by Newcastle Utd in 1913. The game ended in a 1–0 victory for the battalion, Pte Pyke scoring the winning goal.[iv] Elsewhere that day the band of the 17th Middlesex took part in a recruiting rally in Birmingham. The following Saturday, a 17th Middlesex team lost 3–2 to Luton Town.[v]

During their time at Perham Down, the 17th Middlesex underwent the final stages of the military training. On 14 October the battalion participated in a live training exercise on the edge of Salisbury Plain, proceedings being watched by Brig Gen Wellesley Paget. As part of the exercise, which involved all three brigades of the 33rd Division, the 17th Middlesex assaulted practice trenches near the village of Shipton Bellinger, with 'prisoners' being sent back to Kimpton Church.

Two days later, a 17th Middlesex team drew against Birmingham City at St Andrews in front of 15,000 spectators. This game was followed by a 3–2 defeat against Reading at Elm Park on 23 October. Several Reading players in the battalion turned out for their club, which made all the difference. Cpl Fred Bartholomew

[iii]The 17th Middlesex team: Pte Tommy Lonsdale (Southend Utd) goalkeeper; Sgt Tommy Gibson (Nottingham Forest) and Sgt Joe Mercer (Nottingham Forest), backs; Pte Ben Butler (Queen's Park Rangers), Pte Jack Borthwick (Millwall) and Pte Frank Martin (Grimsby Town), halfbacks; Pte Jackie Sheldon (Liverpool) Pte Alf Gregson (Grimsby Town), Cpl Jack Cock (Huddersfield Town), Sgt Norman Wood (Stockport County) and Sgt Percy Barnfather (Croydon Common), forwards.

[iv]The 17th Middlesex team: Pte John Stephenson (Cardiff City), goalkeeper; Sgt Tommy Gibson (Nottingham Forest) and Pte Sid Wheelhouse (Grimsby Town), backs; Pte William Booth (Brighton & Hove Albion), Capt Frank Buckley (Bradford City) and Pte Frank Martin (Grimsby Town) halfbacks; Pte Jackie Sheldon (Liverpool), Pte George Beech (Brighton & Hove Albion), L/Cpl Jack Cock (Huddersfield Town), Pte George Pyke (Newcastle Utd) and Sgt Percy Barnfather (Croydon Common), forwards.

[v]In the last week of September 1915, a 17th Middlesex team beat Bath City 3–2. The team was: Pte Peter Roney (Bristol Rovers), goalkeeper; Pte Frank Spencer (Brighton & Hove Albion) and Sgt Tommy Gibson (Nottingham Forest), backs; Pte Jack Borthwick (Millwall), Capt Frank Buckley (Bradford City) and L/Cpl Ben Butler (Queen's Park Rangers) halfbacks; Pte Alf Gregson (Grimsby Town), Pte George Beech (Brighton & Hove Albion), Lt Vivian Woodward (Chelsea), Sgt Norman Wood (Stockport County) and Pte Hunter (Gainsborough Trinity), forwards. The battalion's goals were scored by Gregson, Buckley and Beech.

played a fine game, and Reading's second goal was scored by the club's former centre-half, Cpl Terence 'Ted' Hanney. A former soldier with the 1st Royal Berkshires, Hanney had helped the Southern League club win the Second Division in the 1910/11 season. Hanney had also been a member of the Great Britain team at the Stockholm Olympics in 1912, although he had missed the final on account of injury. Having made more than 100 appearances for Reading, Hanney had moved to Manchester City in 1913 for a transfer fee of £1,250.

On 30 October a 17th Middlesex side paid a second visit to St Andrews. With the ranks of the 23rd Middlesex (2nd Football) almost complete, the primary object of the fixture was to obtain recruits for a reserve battalion for the two Footballers' Battalions.[20] Shortly before kick-off it transpired that Birmingham City were two players short, so the 17th Middlesex lent them: Pte Ben Butler of Queen's Park Rangers and Sgt Norman Wood of Stockport County.[vi] The game kicked off at 3 p.m. in front of 10,000 spectators. Midway through the first half Birmingham City took the lead, against the run of play, but Pte Tommy Barber, who had scored the winning goal for Aston Villa in the 1913 FA Cup Final, equalised 10 minutes before the break. During the interval, recruiting speeches brought in over 100 recruits. In the second half Birmingham scored again, but two goals from Pte Jackie Sheldon, by all accounts the best player on the pitch, gave the 17th Middlesex victory. An obviously 'off-colour' Lt Vivian Woodward, was reported to be have 'missed several excellent opportunities of scoring' on a rare appearance for the battalion football team.[21]

That same day another 17th Middlesex team visited the Dell to play Southampton. Played on a greasy surface, the game ended in a 4–2 defeat for the 17th Middlesex, the battalion's goals being scored by Pte Hugh Roberts of Luton Town, and former England international Pte John 'Tim' Coleman of

[vi]The 17th Middlesex team: Pte Tommy Lonsdale (Southend Utd) goalkeeper; Pte Sid Wheelhouse (Grimsby Town) and Pte Fred Bullock (Huddersfield Town), backs; Pte William Booth (Brighton & Hove Albion), Capt Frank Buckley (Bradford City) and Pte Frank Martin (Grimsby Town) halfbacks; Pte Jackie Sheldon (Liverpool), Pte George Pyke (Newcastle Utd), Lt Vivian Woodward (Chelsea), Pte Tommy Barber (Aston Villa) and Sgt Percy Barnfather (Croydon Common), forwards.

Nottingham Forest.[vii] For part of the match, the 17th Middlesex had played with ten men, as L/Sgt Walter Tull had been forced to leave the field after being badly winded.

At the beginning of the 21st century, the story of Walter Tull is perhaps the most well known of all the footballers in the 17th Middlesex. At a time of deep-rooted prejudice against non-Whites, Tull, the grandson of a slave, was of mixed-ethnicity. Originally from Barbados, Tull's father, Daniel, came to England in 1876. Settling in Folkestone, Daniel Tull married a local girl, Alice Palmer, and worked as a joiner to support his wife and five children. After Alice's death in 1895, Daniel married Clara Palmer, his wife's niece, only to succumb to heart disease in 1897, by which time another child had been born. Walter's stepmother was unable to support the family, and so Walter and his brother Edward were placed in a Methodist-run Children's Home and Orphanage in East London.[22] During his time at this institution, Tull received a decent education and played left-back for the orphanage football team.

After serving an apprenticeship as a printer, Tull started playing for Clapton, a London amateur club. Following a series of impressive displays as an inside-left, the skilful 'dusky forward' was signed by Tottenham Hotspur in July 1909, having already accompanied the club on a South American tour a couple of months earlier. 'Darkie' Tull played in six out of the first seven matches of the 1909/10 season, but was unable to keep his place in the first team. Part of the problem was a perceived lack of pace, but it has been suggested that racial abuse from hostile crowds had undermined Tull's confidence. Against Bristol City in October 1909, Tull was reportedly taunted by a section of the crowd in 'language lower than Billingsgate'.[23] By the time he moved to Northampton Town in the autumn of 1911, Tull had made only 12 League and FA Cup appearances for Spurs.

At Northampton Town, Tull resurrected his career as a half-back

[vii]The 17th Middlesex team: Pte John Stephenson (Cardiff City), goalkeeper; Pte Alf West (Notts County) and Pte William Stephenson (formerly of Hull City), backs; Pte George Scott (Clapton Orient) Pte Fred Keenor (Cardiff City) and Pte Walter Tull (Northampton Town) halfbacks; Pte Hugh Roberts (Luton Town), Pte William Jonas (Clapton Orient), Pte Joe McLauchlan (Watford), Pte Tim Coleman (Nottingham Forest) and Pte Fred Whittaker (Millwall), forwards.

and went on to make over 100 appearances for the club.[24] On 21 December 1914 Walter Tull had enlisted in the 17th Middlesex. The fact, that he was soon promoted to the rank of lance-sergeant, suggests that his fellow footballers were happy to respect a man for his personal qualities, whatever the colour of his skin.

On 5 November the 17th Middlesex finally received orders 'to prepare forthwith for France'. Three days later Queen Mary inspected the 33rd Division, less its artillery and transport. King George V was a noticeable absentee. A few days earlier the King had been thrown from his horse during an inspection of the First Army in France and was still recovering from 'stiffness and bruises'. This was a cause of considerable disappointment to the officers and men of the 17th Middlesex, as King George V had 'graciously announced' his intention of inspecting the Footballers' Battalion several months earlier in response to a request from Joynson-Hicks.

Four days later the sister battalion of the 17th Middlesex, the 23rd Middlesex, marched through the streets of London as part of the Lord Mayor's Show. There was none of the pageantry traditionally associated with the event. Four captured German guns and a detachment of the Anti-Aircraft Corps formed part of the procession, and recruiting meetings were held at various points along the route. That same day a farewell message from the King was read out to the 17th Middlesex at Perham Down, as the officers and men made their final preparations for active service, many taking the opportunity to make their wills.

The 17th Middlesex were now under orders to move at 12 hours' notice. Second-Lieutenant Clark wrote of the ensuing chaos: 'We are still most frantically busy doing all manner of things – issuing deficiencies in men's kits and so on. You issue all the towels for instance that you've drawn from the quartermaster's stores and when you've given them all out someone has lost his, which he had previously, and then you have to send another indent to the quartermaster and so on!'[25]

At this late stage, there was a change in command. Col Grantham left the battalion, having recently received orders to assist with the raising of the 24th (Works) Battalion, the King's Liverpool Regiment.[26] On 10 November his former second-in-command, Col Henry Fenwick, assumed command of the 17th Middlesex. The following day the 35-year-old Maj Kenneth Maclaine of Lochbuie reported for duty, as the new second-in-command. A brave and fearless officer, Maj Maclaine of Lochbuie had experienced the traditional upbringing of a Highland laird, stalking and shooting his first stag by the age of 10. After service with the Imperial Yeomanry in South Africa, the 24th Maclaine of Lochbuie had succeeded to his father's estates in 1909, only to discover that they were heavily mortgaged. In an attempt to stave off the creditors, Lochbuie had decided to make use of his talents as a performer and musician, telling a journalist: 'Look at my position; I have been left poor with an embarrassed estate. What equipment have I to make my progress in the world? I could not even take up work in an office. I would not know what to do'.[27]

His decision had caused consternation in certain quarters of Highland society, who believed that a career on the stage was a wholly inappropriate course for a Scottish clan chief.[28] Many variety artistes had also resented the appearance of Lochbuie on the stage: 'Why should this Scots lord come in and do real professionals out of a living?' Unperturbed by the criticism, Lochbuie had undertaken successful tours of the United States and Australia, but his plans for a return visit to North America were thwarted by the outbreak of war. While serving with the 15th Hussars, Maclaine of Lochbuie had been awarded the Military Cross for bravery, near Ypres in May 1915. King George V had presented the award in person, only a few weeks before Lochbuie had reported for duty with the 17th Middlesex at Perham Down.

The 17th Middlesex were preparing for the Western Front, which was to be the primary theatre of operations for the British army during the First World War. Essentially the product of the fighting during the latter quarter of 1914, the front lines ran approximately 450 miles from the Flanders coast to the Swiss frontier. Despite major French offensives in May and September 1915, which had incurred heavy losses for small gains, the Germans were still firmly entrenched in France and Belgium. The rapidly expanding British army had also played a part in the fighting throughout 1915, launching attacks at Neuve Chapelle, Aubers Ridge, Festubert, and more recently at Loos, with equally disappointing results. On the Eastern Front an Austro-German offensive launched in May had driven the Russians back some 180 miles east of Warsaw

Results had been similarly disheartening in other theatres of operations, which had come into being as the fighting had spread across the globe. Having landed at Gallipoli in April, with the intention of knocking Turkey out of the war, Allied forces were now facing the possibility of a humiliating evacuation. Turkish forces were also putting British and Indian troops under mounting pressure in the Middle East. Italy had declared war on Austria-Hungary in May, but her forces had made little progess. In the Balkans, Bulgaria had entered the war on the side of the Central Powers, participating in the successful invasion of Serbia in October. Nonetheless, there was some cause for optimism. Despite the emergence of the submarine as potent weapon of war, the Allies had practical command of the sea and were enforcing a highly effective blockade against the Central Powers. Over the coming months, it was hoped that the Allies could utilise their greater resources, in terms of men and material, to gain a decisive advantage.

1. BNL: *Sportsman*, 27 April 1915.
2. Clark, C., *The Tin Trunk – Letters and Drawings 1914–1918*, p.18.
3. (Edward) Frederick Leveson-Gower (1819–1907).
4. When Joynson-Hicks was first being shown around the house, Leveson-Gower told him: 'Fire may rob you of your home, floods might destroy your garden, but nothing can ever steal away this view.'
5. PC: Letter to James Clark, 2 May 1915.
6. The other four soldiers who donned the colours of Croydon Common for this fixture were Pte Ernie Williamson, Pte Albert Tomkins, Pte Charles Stewart and Pte Cyril Smith.
7. BNL: *Sportsman*, 3 May 1915.
8. PC: Letter to James Clark, 30 May 1915.
9. In Bunyan's day goalkeepers were allowed to handle the ball anywhere in their own half. This rule was changed in 1912.
10. The three Bunyan brothers belonged to the Racing Club of Brussels and were members of the Anglo-Belge cricket team. The youngest son, Maurice, was also a fine lawn tennis player and a talented athlete. Six weeks before the outbreak of war, he had won a local championship at Cologne over 200m.
11. Sidney Print, a barman, is listed by the Commonwealth War Graves Commission (CWGC) as Pte Sidney Prince, the name under which he served. It is likely that he gave a false name on enlistment to conceal his true age.
12. Pte Bell-Wedge had only enlisted in the 17th Middlesex on 27 May 1915. His widow, Ada, would give birth to their son, William Henry, on 3 October 1915.
13. PC: Letter to Percy Clark, undated (c.July 1915).
14. The other infantry brigades in the 33rd Division were the 98th Brigade: 18th Royal Fusiliers (1st Public Schools), 19th Royal Fusiliers (2nd Public Schools), 20th Royal Fusiliers (3rd Public Schools), and 21st Royal Fusiliers (4th Public Schools); and the 101st Brigade: 17th Royal Fusiliers (Empire) 22nd Royal Fusiliers (Kensington), 23rd Royal Fusiliers (1st Sportsman's) and 24th Royal Fusiliers (2nd Sportsman's).

15. PC: Letter to James Clark, 26 July 1915.
16. *Ibid.*, undated (*c.*August 1915).
17. Clark, C., *The Tin Trunk*, p. 20.
18. Gate receipts for the match were £61 6s 10d.
19. BNL: *Berkshire Chronicle*, 10 September 1915. Reading players, Pte Joe Bailey, Cpl Fred Bartholomew, Pte Allen Foster and former Reading player Cpl Ted Hanney, turned out for the home side in this fixture.
20. Known as the 27th Middlesex, the reserve battalion, formed from depot companies of the 17th and 23rd Middlesex, became the 101st Training Reserve Battalion at Aldershot, part of 23rd Reserve Brigade in September 1916.
21. BNL; *Birmingham Daily Post*, 1 November 1915.
22. In November 1900, Edward was adopted by the Warnock family in Glasgow. Edward Warnock-Tull grew up to become a successful dentist, having taken over his adopted father's dental practice.
23. See Vasili, P., *Colouring Over the White Line: The History of Black Footballers in Great Britain*, p. 50.
24. The manager of Northampton Town at that time was Herbert Chapman, later of Huddersfield Town and Arsenal, one of the most successful managers in the history of English football.
25. Clark, C., *The Tin Trunk*, p. 21.
26. There appear to be no surviving records of this battalion. In *British Regiments 1914–1918*, Brig E.A. James suggests that this battalion may have later been renumbered as the 27th (Works) King's Liverpool Regiment. Col Grantham then took command of various forts and defences in the Thames Estuary.
27. *Daily Record and Mail*, 4 October 1913.
28. Such was the furore surrounding his choice of career that in 1913 Maclaine of Lochbuie was refused entrance to the Highland Gathering after the Oban Games.

CHAPTER 4

PLAYING THE GAME ELSEWHERE

I can honestly tell you it is all work and very little play
Pte Bob Whiting F/74 (Brighton & Hove Albion)

Around mid-day on 16 November 1915 the advance and transport parties of the 17th Middlesex, consisting of about 120 men and 2/Lt Rhodes Cobb, the transport officer, 2/Lt Archie Brown, 2/Lt Bertie Wade and 2/Lt William Hendry, departed Ludgershall Railway Station, arriving at Southampton around 2 hours later. That evening the transport party boarded SS *Bellerophon* and disembarked in Le Havre in the early hours of the following morning. During disembarkation, a couple of minor accidents occurred, both of which necessitated hospital treatment for the two soldiers concerned. Thus Pte Williams and Pte Newton, of Croydon Common, became the battalion's first casualties on active service. The following day the transport party was joined at Le Havre by the advance party, which had crossed the Channel on SS *Mona's Queen*.

The remainder of the 17th Middlesex had been left behind near Salisbury. On 17 November 'A' and 'B' Companies, under Col Henry Fenwick, and 'C' and 'D' Companies under Maj Maclaine of Lochbuie left in two parties 'to take part in the greatest war in the annals of history'[1]. After what the Battalion War Diary termed a 'long and tedious journey', both parties arrived at about 10 p.m. in Folkestone before marching down the steep road, known today as 'The Road of Remembrance', running down from the town to the harbour. Three hours later the men began to board SS *Princess Victoria*, formerly of the Larne and Stranraer Steamboat Company. There were reports of mines in the Channel. Earlier in the day the officers and men of the 13th Essex had witnessed the distressing sight of the hospital ship SS *Anglia* sinking after striking a mine, with a loss of around 150 lives.

Fortunately the crossing was uneventful. The 17th Middlesex disembarked at Boulogne 1½ hours later. Much to everyone's annoyance an administrative error ensured that the battalion was left waiting on the quayside in pouring rain for a couple of hours before orders were finally received to march to Ostrohove Camp. The camp was situated on the heights overlooking Boulogne, close to the Colonne de la Grande Armée, where Napoleon had once amassed a large army with the intention of invading England. Second-Lieutenant Cosmo Clark, who had visited Boulogne on a family trip before the war, wrote to his parents:

We are in what is known as a 'Rest Camp' and arrived here this morning at three o' clock feeling very tired and fed up. Tramping through the town where we disembarked in the early hours of the morning over frozen cobblestones and up that very steep hill! Do you remember it? It was very interesting seeing all the places that we visited a few years ago. All the place was in darkness and we had a guide with a lantern at the head of the column. Marching on the right hand side of the road seemed very strange and awkward.

We are in tents which strange to say I don't find cold. The men are twelve in a tent – we are five and are very cosy. We have all been trying our various stunts: primus stoves, tommy's cookers, café au lait, Oxo cubes, cocoa cubes and various concoctions – not because we needed them very badly, but just to pass the time away. Within the next day or two we are moving from here to somewhere a bit nearer the trenches. Everybody is excited and keen to get up at last to within sound of the guns.[2]

The following day the advance and transport parties rejoined the battalion, having undergone an uncomfortable train journey of nearly 24 hours from Le Havre, in what were described as 'cattle trucks', with only 20-minute breaks for meals. The 17th Middlesex then entrained at Pont-de-Briques Station and, after a further train journey of some 9 hours duration, the battalion marched to its billets in the small agricultural village of Les Ciseaux, a few miles south-west of Hazebrouck. For the first time on active service, the men could clearly discern the sound of the guns, the front lines being only about 16 miles away. The billets, consisting of farmhouses, barns and outbuildings, were scattered throughout the village. First impressions were not good, as 2/Lt Cosmo Clark recalled:

On looking ruefully at what was to be my home for at least the next few days, this is what I saw. A long, very low old house standing by itself with just a few barns and outhouses tacked on. No lights anywhere, about twelve doors all of which might be front doors and a good rich niff of 'cochons'. However, I waded through a sort of front garden and farmyard combined, and as I was very tired and didn't want to waste time, gave a hearty bang on one of the doors. Immediately about fifty dogs started barking, grunts came from the outhouses, and jabbering from a female inside the house. Soon a door opened and a French madame holding a candle, and in somewhat scanty attire, demanded if I was 'l'officer d'etre loge ici?' I gave her a most emphatic 'oui' and she bade me enter in a very motherly way. I was agreeably surprised how well I got on with the lingo and soon we were the best of friends.[3]

During their stay at Les Ciseaux there was plenty of time for letter writing. For the young officers with a middle-class background, whose duty it was to censor their men's letters home, the experience was frequently a bewildering one:

I censored about sixty men's letters tonight. It was a queer job. Some were very funny and some rather pathetic. They all start with 'I hope this finds you as it leaves me in the pink'. One man said that he couldn't get any sleep because of the 'terrible roaring of the guns'. As a matter of fact we can only just hear the faintest rumble. They all ask for fags and socks – they want both, poor beggars, their money all goes on little extra comforts – not beer.[4]

After a few days at Les Ciseaux, the 17th Middlesex marched to the small manufacturing town of Isbergues, where one of the largest munitions factories in France was situated. Some of the battalion's officers went on a tour of the factory: 'It was most interesting, the whole place was about twice as big as Harrods – simply palatial. Everything was most up-to-date. There was hardly any skilled labour, a little boy or old man standing beside a huge machine which did all the work. They were turning out shells in thousands. I think one might even say millions.'[5]

On 25 November a hastily arranged football match took place against some men from the Royal Engineers billeted nearby. The 17th Middlesex were handicapped by a lack of kit, playing in their uniform and army boots, but the team of Royal Engineers must still have played well to earn a 2–2 draw. The following day the 17th Middlesex proceeded to Guarbecque, where the battalion remained for the rest of November. Several of the men were sent on a bombing course, which took place near a canal. L/Cpl Joe Bailey could not resist dropping a grenade into the water 'to see what it would do'. After the explosion, several dead fish floated up to the surface.

On 1 December a 17th Middlesex team played a match against a battalion of the Northamptonshire Regiment, winning 7–0. The next day the battalion marched to Béthune, an important supply town for the British, where it encountered a Scottish unit returning from the front line. Its soldiers were caked in mud, but were surprisingly cheerful. Some good-natured banter ensued, one Scotsman gesturing towards the German lines: 'They are leading over there at half time 1–0, go and have a shot at equalising it.'[6]

During their stay in Béthune, the 17th Middlesex was billeted in the College des Jeunes Filles, a large building of solid construction, which had been used for medical tuition prior to the war.[7] Second-Lieutenant Archie Brown, 2/Lt Samuel Dunton, 2/Lt Fred Stansfeld and 2/Lt Lionel Bradstreet reported to the Brigade Machine Gun Officer for a course of instruction. The men were kept busy with various fatigues and training, but there was still time for some local sightseeing around the town, the impressive Belfry situated in the main square proving a particular attraction. Chelsea reserve goalkeeper Pte William Krug took the opportunity to send a postcard to Stamford Bridge, stating that he was fine.

On 8 December the 17th Middlesex were transferred from the 33rd Division to the 2nd Division, commanded by Maj Gen William Walker VC.[8] Brig Gen Robert Twigg, the officer commanding 100th Brigade, sent a message to Col Henry Fenwick in which he expressed his regret at losing the battalion and thanking all ranks for their good and wholehearted work while under his command. Similar exchanges of battalions were taking place between several regular and New Army divisions in France around this time, the rationale being that the inexperienced New Army divisions would be 'stiffened' by the incorporation of regular battalions.

The catalyst for the re-organisation of BEF had been the Battle of Loos in September 1915, which had raised doubts about the military effectiveness of the New Army divisions arriving in France, notwithstanding the fact that two Scottish New Army divisions, the 9th and the 15th, had performed with great credit in the battle's opening stages. As a result of the reorganisation, the original pals-type composition of the 33rd Division disappeared at a stroke. The 17th Middlesex and five other battalions of the 33rd Division were transferred to the 2nd Division, and three public schools battalions of the Royal Fusiliers were disbanded, the majority of their men being persuaded to apply for commissions.[9] Prior to the reorganisation the 2nd Division had consisted almost entirely of battalions from the pre-war regular army. It had embarked at Southampton for France on 12 August 1914 and had been heavily engaged in the fighting to date.

The 17th Middlesex were now part of 6th Brigade, which had been commanded since May 1915 by Brig Gen Arthur Daly, an experienced career soldier.[10] The son of a general, Daly had been commissioned into the West Yorkshire Regiment in 1890 and had been badly wounded in the Boer War. On 9 December the 17th Middlesex marched to Annequin, where their billets were situated only a couple of miles from the front line. The following evening the 17th Middlesex's war started in earnest. The weather was wet and cold. Officers and NCOs from 'A' and 'B' Companies were sent into the line between La Bassée and Loos for 'instructional purposes'. Accompanied by guides, small groups of the 17th Middlesex made their way to the front line through a matrix of muddy communication trenches.

On their arrival in the front line, 2/Lt Fred Stansfeld and NCOs from the Machine Gun Section were attached to their counterparts in the 1/1st Hertfordshires. Maj John Pretyman–Newman and 'A' Company were also attached to the 1/1st Hertfordshires, while Capt Frank Buckley and 'B' Company were attached to the 1st

Royal Berkshires of the 99th Brigade. The Reading players in 'B' Company were given a warm welcome by the officers and men of the 1st Royal Berkshires, who plied them with food and drink. L/Cpl Joe Bailey was grateful for the hospitality: 'We had plenty of rum to keep the wet out: it poured with rain the whole time. The mud and water was up to our waists: we did look some nice boys . . . I don't think I have met a more sociable and better lot of fellows than the Berks, they are top hole.'[11]

After 24 hours' experience of trench warfare, 'A' and 'B' Companies were relieved in the front line by officers, platoon sergeants and section commanders from 'C' and 'D' Companies; the former company being attached to the 1/1st Hertfordshires, and the latter being attached to the 1st King's Royal Rifle Corps. During the evening of 11 December Donald Stewart, serving under the alias Pte James MacDonald, became the battalion's first fatality on active service. While on sentry duty, he was caught by a burst of enemy machine-gun fire, having entered the trenches for the first time just 7 hours previously. According to his service record, the farm servant from Leslie, near Fife, was 21 years old at the time of his death, but it is quite possible that he was an under-age enlistment, having used an alias to help conceal his true age from the authorities. The only other casualty of the battalion's first spell in the trenches was Pte William Perry, who was wounded in the head by a spent rifle bullet on 14 December.

Over the next few weeks the officers and men of the 17th Middlesex adapted to the routine of life in the trenches. Half an hour before dawn would come the 'Stand To', when the men stood on the trench firestep with their bayonets fixed in anticipation of a German attack. Half an hour after dawn, came the 'Stand Down'. The rum ration might be issued. The men would then clean their rifles before eating breakfast, which would invariably be washed down with strong, sweet-tasting tea. All manner of officer inspections might follow: gas helmets, rifles, ammunition, iron rations and socks. Throughout the day the men would be kept occupied with a seemingly endless selection of tasks, such as sentry duty, repairing trenches, digging latrines, or bringing up duckboards, grenades and other trench stores from the rear. If enemy artillery and snipers were active, wounded men might need to be carried back to the regimental aid post, usually situated in a reserve trench, where the regimental medical officer (RMO) would perform his duties.

Mealtimes provided some welcome relief from the routine. Lunch was taken around midday. Dinner would take place in the early evening. Half an hour before dusk, the men would again 'Stand To' for an hour. Once darkness fell, the trenches would become a hive of activity. Wiring parties would go out into No Man's Land to repair gaps in the wire entanglements, and patrols would be sent out to report on enemy activity and the state of their defences. This was also usually the time that ration carriers would bring up supplies to the front line, such as water, bread and tins of food.

While various half-companies of the 17th Middlesex were rotated in and out of the front line trenches, the remainder of the battalion spent its time digging, wiring and filling sandbags. Several officers reported to the Divisional School of Instruction at Fouquereuil to attend a ten-day course on the use of grenades. On 22 December the 17th Middlesex completed their first tour of duty and marched back to billets in Beuvry, a dilapidated village about 2 miles behind the front line. On Christmas Eve a concert was organised for the men:

The band played selections. There were two very scratchy films (a Charlie Chaplin and a cowboy one), funny men recitations and cornet and violin solos – also songs and carols. Everything was excellent bar the air which was as thick as a gas attack, due to the Christmas smokes!! It seemed very funny to think that we were only two miles away from the Germans – all this time our guns were booming away and straffing the old Bosche - no truce this year! Fortunately the Germans didn't shell our village as is their custom.[12]

The evening's entertainment was organised by Maj Maclaine of Lochbuie, the 17th Middlesex War Diary recording that he 'contributed greatly to the success of the evening'. It is quite possible that he performed one of the 'funny man recitations' in person. His usual act consisted of three songs, each sung while wearing an appropriate costume:

84

The first was a Scottish song, sung in his kilt and wearing an embroidered satin waistcoat worn by Bonnie Prince Charlie. The second song in the ducks and serge uniform of a ship's officer, and the third in a purple cutaway, with silk hat, gold-tipped cane, and white-topped boots. The third song, reportedly his best, was about a 'London Johnny', who called himself 'Monte of Monte Carlo'.[13]

On Christmas Day all training was suspended and a Divine Service was held during the morning. Sgt Ted Hanney and L/Cpl Joe Bailey went to visit their friends in the 1st Royal Berkshires for Christmas lunch. The 17th Middlesex War Diary noted laconically that 'as far as possible the usual festivities were indulged in'. At least the battalion was out of the front line. Other soldiers, such as Sgt Ernest Parfitt of the Queen's Regiment, were spending a miserable Christmas in the trenches. Within a few months, Sgt Parfitt, a salesman of leather goods in North London, would be commissioned and posted to the 17th Middlesex. On Christmas Day he wrote of the men's efforts to keep up their spirits in a letter to his fiancée Alice:

We are all having imaginary drinks & of course offering everyone that passes [the dugout] a port & lemon or something stronger & also cigars. The boys keep asking me to open another bottle or to pass the nuts, oranges or sweets, and believe me, we are quite enjoying the fun.[14]

After Christmas lunch, a 17th Middlesex side played a game of football against a team comprised of men from the Royal Engineers. The match ended in a resounding 19–1 victory for the 17th Middlesex.[i] That evening the officers dined together for the first time since leaving England. Second-Lieutenant Cosmo Clark described the event to his parents:

[i] The 17th Middlesex team: Pte Jimmy Hugall (Clapton Orient), Pte Edward Jennings (Amateur), Pte Joseph Raw (Clapton Orient), Pte John Nuttall (Millwall), L/Cpl Ben Butler (Queen's Park Rangers), Pte William Jonas (Clapton Orient), Pte Hugh Roberts (Luton Town), Sgt Bob Dalrymple (Clapton Orient), Pte Joe McLauchlan (Watford), Pte Edward Foord (Chelsea) and Pte Thomas Codd (Leicester Fosse).

We had a huge feed that night – turkey and plum pudding and all the usual etceteras – including hundreds of crackers which came from goodness knows where. Unfortunately, the Colonel made me sit next to him so I had to be on my best behaviour. However, he went immediately after dinner . . . Afterwards we had a gramophone and dancing, singing and games. The contents of the crackers made good get-ups. We all drank the King's health which was a solemn proceeding. It was rather strange but just as we all said 'the king', Big Lizzie (a huge gun of ours) shot a present over to the Bosche with a big bang. I hope that the shell found a good billet.[15]

On Boxing Day the battalion undertook a route march in the morning and everyone was given free time in the afternoon. The younger officers took the opportunity to go ice-skating at a local rink, while the battalion band played an assortment of popular tunes. On 27 December the 17th Middlesex marched back to Busnes for a period of rest. Over the next few days many men took the opportunity to reflect on their first experience of the trenches. Ptes Edward Foord and William Krug were fairly upbeat in their correspondence with Chelsea, the following note appearing in the programme ahead of the club's 1–1 draw with Fulham:

Teddy Foord and Krug have written to say they are fit and well after a spell in the trenches. Foord has put in a good many shots, some of which he hopes have caused the opponents to be one or two down and Krug (goalkeeper) does not seem at all disappointed at the fact that he has let everyone go past without stopping a single shot.[16]

The former Brighton & Hove Albion goalkeeper, Pte Bob Whiting, was rather more circumspect in a letter to Albert Underwood, the club secretary:

We are having a rest after our first dose of the trenches, and I can tell you we have well earned it . . . I can honestly tell you it is all work and very little play. You feel a bit fatigued in the trenches after you have been there for 24 hours building up parapets, which the fellows across the way knock down with their whizzbangs. What delightful toys they are to be sure. But for every one they send our fellows, the good old RFA [Royal Field Artillery], give them back about twenty, so I suppose they are pretty busy making their rabbit holes look a bit shipshape afterwards and by goodness, they must be busy sometimes, as our artillery does give them a doing every now and then.[17]

One feature of life at the front was the prevalence of rumours. In such an environment it is hardly surprising that rumours of every description were rife, ranging from colourful accounts of enemy atrocities to the reported death of an individual soldier. Such stories might subsequently feature in a soldier's letters to friends and family, or be circulated in England by wounded men returning from the front. On 29 December one such story appeared in the *Sporting Chronicle*, which informed its readers that the Footballers' Battalion had been in action for the first time. Tim Coleman of Nottingham Forest, Bob Dalrymple of Clapton Orient, and George McDonald of Norwich City were reported as killed:

Perhaps the best known of these footballers was Tim Coleman, a wonderfully clever and versatile footballer who represented England against Ireland in 1907. Although of a roving disposition, he was wonderfully popular wherever he went, for he was a born humorist and was the life and soul of every club he was travelling with. He was an inside forward and could play right or left, but his favourite position was inside right. He was tricky with his feet but did not overdo it, and was a rattling good shot.

His first important club was Kettering but from there he joined Northampton Town in its first season and then went south to Woolwich Arsenal. Everton next attracted him to the north, later he did excellent work at Roker Park before the more genial climate of the south once more appealed to him and he joined Fulham. From there he went to Nottingham Forest, where he was playing when he heard his country's call. Poor Tim, many will miss his cheery face and ever-ready joke.

Dalrymple was a Scot who came south from Hearts and was also an inside forward. He was older than Coleman and was going rather bald, but he was an excellent fellow and a good footballer. He played for Portsmouth and did good service for several seasons for Fulham before going to Orient.

McDonald was a young forward who played with Norwich City.[18]

George McDonald of Norwich City had obviously been confused with the unfortunate James MacDonald, the first soldier of the 17th Middlesex to be killed on active service. George McDonald was actually in hospital, having recently undergone an operation to remove his cartilage, which had been causing him persistent problems since his enlistment. It is unclear why Coleman and Dalrymple were reported to have been killed. The reports of their deaths certainly made no sense to the men's families and clubs. Tim Coleman's wife had only just received a letter from her husband, dated Boxing Day, in which he had stated that the battalion was 'resting' out of the front line. She felt sufficiently alarmed to visit the War Office, where officials were unable to either confirm or deny the report. The Orient chairman, Capt Henry Wells-Holland, who had not proceeded overseas with the battalion, was equally bemused by these reports.[19] Richard McFadden and Jimmy Hugall had made no mention of their team-mate's death in recent letters. In his last communication to Capt Wells-Holland, McFadden had stated merely that 'we have been a fortnight in the trenches and now are back at base for a little time', while Jimmy Hugall had even alluded to the conspicuous bravery of Sgt Bob Dalrymple in rescuing a wounded man under fire.

In France the reports caused some amusement. On reading the report of his death, the 'rather bald' Sgt Bob Dalrymple cracked jokes about his second time on earth. CSM Tommy Gibson, the Nottingham Forest captain, handed Pte Tim Coleman an anxious telegram from the club while on parade. Coleman replied immediately: 'I am pleased to say, gentlemen, there is absolutely no truth in the report at all.'[20] The genial Coleman was renowned for his sense of humour. On returning from one spell in the trenches, he told his former Everton teammate, Pte Jack Borthwick: 'This is the worst team I ever signed for and I am not going to sign for them again'. Percy Barnfather of Croydon Common recalled an occasion when:

He was on fatigue duty when a shell came rather too close, and the officer in charge asked who would get him the nose of the shell. Coleman was missed, but presently returned bringing a nose cap. The officer was pleased and gave him five francs. Tim looked at it and said: 'What, five francs for a nose! How much will you give me if I fetch the gun that fired it!'[21]

Several players wrote home to set the record straight. Phil Kelso of Fulham received a letter from Pte Ernest Coquet stating that everyone was quite well contrary to newspaper reports. Pte John Nuttall wrote to Bert Lipsham, the Millwall manager:

> I expect you have read that Dalrymple, Coleman & MacDonald have been killed but the statements are false, as they are all in the pink and MacDonald has been sent back to England. Things are very quiet here just now. I trust it will not be long before I will be able to look you up again and in the meantime I wish you a Prosperous New Year and ask you to remember me to all the players and others connected to the club and tell Elijah (dressing room attendant) I could do with one of his Sunday morning baths just now.[22]

After only a few weeks in France, the men were already infested with the ubiquitous lice. These much detested parasites were one of greatest miseries of the trenches, causing intense discomfort and sometimes blood poisoning. Usually of a greyish hue and some 3–4mm in length, the body louse would reside in the seams of men's clothing, feeding daily on the blood of its host. In the squalid environment of the trenches, the men did what they could to rid themselves of these parasites. Popular counter-measures included the application of commercially available powders, such as Harrison's Pomade, which were widely believed by soldiers to be wholly ineffectual, or the running of a candle flame along the seams of one's clothing. However, the lice, commonly called 'chats' by the soldiers, were virtually impossible to eradicate in such conditions, particularly given that the female louse was capable of laying around five eggs a day.

At Busnes the men had the opportunity to delouse themselves in the divisional baths. While their clothes were being disinfected, small groups of men took turns to soap themselves in large vats of lukewarm water before receiving a change of underclothes. The relief was short-lived. Several eggs would often remain unaffected by the disinfecting process. Within a few hours of putting their uniform back on, many men would be scratching again, their body heat having caused the remaining eggs to hatch.

The 17th Middlesex and the other units of 2nd Division were now 'resting' around Busnes. The term 'rest' was somewhat misleading. Over the next few days the battalion trained daily in the art of open warfare, practising skirmishing and attack formations. Nonetheless, time was made available for recreational pursuits. The authorities had not been slow in recognising the important role of sporting activity in maintaining the morale of the burgeoning armies in France, as well as its positive effect on men's physical fitness. Football was invariably the most popular, although soldiers would enjoy a diverse range of activities, including wheelbarrow races, swimming and boxing. During this period of rest several men of the 17th Middlesex competed unsuccessfully in a Brigade Boxing Tournament, failing to win a single prize at any weight. Not that anyone was particularly troubled by this fact. Of far greater interest was the forthcoming Divisional Football Tournament. After all, the 17th Middlesex had a reputation to uphold.

1. TNA: WO 95 /1361.
2. Clark, C., *The Tin Trunk*, p. 24.
3. *Ibid.*, p. 25.
4. *Ibid.*, p. 26.
5. *Ibid.*, p. 29.
6. *Ibid.*, p. 30.
7. This building was recently demolished to make way for a car park.
8. Maj Gen W.G. Walker (4th Gurkha Rifles, Indian Army, attached to Bikanir Camel Corps), then a captain, won his VC in Somaliland on 22 April 1903. Following the action at Daratoleh, he remained with a wounded officer, keeping the enemy at bay, while another officer went in search of help.
9. The other five battalions were the 13th Essex, 17th Royal Fusiliers, 22nd Royal Fusiliers, 23rd Royal Fusiliers and the 24th Royal Fusiliers. Several men who were commissioned from the ranks of the disbanded Public Schools battalions would later be posted to the 17th Middlesex.
10. Following its reorganisation in December 1915, the 6th Brigade consisted of the 1st King's Liverpool, 2nd South Staffords, 1/1st Hertfordshires, 17th Middlesex and 13th Essex. The 1/1st Hertfordshires were transferred to GHQ in February 1916.
11. BNL: *Berkshire Chronicle*, 7 January 1916.
12. Clark, C., *The Tin Trunk*, p. 34.
13. Although it is highly unlikely that Maclaine of Lochbuie would have taken such a treasured heirloom as Bonnie Prince Charlie's waistcoat to France, a makeshift costume would undoubtedly have been improvised for the occasion.
14. PC: Letter to Alice Simpson, 25 December 1915.
15. Clark, C., *The Tin Trunk*, p. 25.
16. BNL: *The Chelsea FC Chronicle: Official Programme*, 22 January 1916.
17. BNL: *Argus*, 14 January 1916.
18. BNL: *Sporting Chronicle*, 29 December 1915.

19. After a spell with the 27th Middlesex, Wells-Holland served with the No 5. Works Company of the Royal Sussex Regiment. He was later discovered to have been 'drawing more money than was required for Company purposes and had been using it for private purposes'. Admitting 'considerable errors', Wells-Holland applied to resign his commission on 27 November 1916, narrowly avoiding a court martial. The GOC, Aldershot Command, considered him 'unfit to be trusted as an officer'. His friend, Capt Foxcroft-Jones, was similarly disgraced. Having commandeered a local grocer's car for his own private use, while the battalion was stationed at Holmbury St Mary, he was subsequently cashiered by sentence of court martial on 21 March 1916. A few months later, he was discovered to be serving as a staff sergeant in the ASC Forage Department under the name of Evans Foxcroft Wyndham.

20. BNL: *Grimsby News*, 8 February 1916.

21. BNL: *Berkshire Chronicle*, 2 December 1916. Tim Coleman is the subject of a recent biography. See Myerson, G., *Fighting for Football: From Woolwich Arsenal to the Western Front*.

22. BNL: *Athletic News*, 10 January 1916.

CHAPTER 5

THE DIVISIONAL CUP

*It is a very monotonous life out here when one is
supposed to be resting and most of the boys prefer
the excitement of the trenches.*
L/Sgt Walter Tull F/55 (Northampton Town)

Awarded a bye in the first round of the Divisional Football
Tournament, the 17th Middlesex were drawn against the
winners of the match between the 1/1st Hertfordshires and the 13th
Essex. Understandably, both sides were keen to pit their skills against
a team of famous footballers and the match was a hard-fought
contest, in which the 13th Essex ultimately triumphed 4–3.

The 17th Middlesex's first match took place on 7 January at the
ground of the 13th Essex, or rather the field, which had been
hastily commandeered for the purposes of playing football. The
weather was dreadful. In a letter to H.N. Hickson, the Grimsby
Town secretary, Pte Sid Wheelhouse wrote that there were strong
gusts of wind and that it was raining hard. Faced with the prospect
of a 4-mile walk to the playing field, many men decided not to
make the trip. Nonetheless, a steady succession of men trudged
through muddy country lanes to watch the match. In the event
there were 500 or so spectators huddled around the pitch when
the game commenced.

The weather made no difference to the outcome of the game,
which ended in a 9–0 victory for the 17th Middlesex.[i] L/Cpl Joe
Bailey scored four goals, L/Cpl Jack Cock and Pte Hugh Roberts
scored two apiece, and even Capt Frank Buckley, hardly a prolific
goalscorer, got his name on the score sheet. The final score would

---

[i] The 17th Middlesex team: Pte Tommy Lonsdale (Southend Utd), goalkeeper; Pte Sid
Wheelhouse (Grimsby Town) and L/Cpl Fred Bullock (Huddersfield Town), backs; Pte
George Scott (Clapton Orient), Capt Frank Buckley (Bradford City) and L/Cpl Billy Baker
(Plymouth Argyle), halfbacks; Pte Hugh Roberts (Luton Town), Capt Vivian Woodward
(Chelsea), L/Cpl Jack Cock (Huddersfield Town), L/Cpl Joe Bailey (Reading) and Sgt Percy
Barnfather (Croydon Common), forwards.

have been far more emphatic, had it not been for the heroics of the 13th Essex goalkeeper. Most observers agreed that his performance had single-handedly prevented the 17th Middlesex scoring in the region of 30 goals. Players and spectators alike roundly applauded him when the final whistle blew. Afterwards, everyone was entertained to tea and a concert given by the 13th Essex.

No one was under any illusions that the result of the Divisional Football Tournament would be anything other than a foregone conclusion. CSM Tommy Gibson, of Nottingham Forest, predicted that 'the lads will walk the tourney'. Another well-known player wrote home: 'We have undoubtedly enough players in the Battalion to produce a dozen teams capable of beating any regimental eleven out here.'[1] Nonetheless, there was stiff competition for places in the 17th Middlesex football team. The next day Pte Bob Whiting, in a letter thanking Albert Underwood for a parcel of chocolate and cigarettes, mentioned that the battalion had played its first competitive game in France: 'I am sorry to say that none of the Brighton players were in the team, though I think Billy Booth was picked to play, but was on transport duty.'[2]

On 10 January an unchanged team played in the 6th Brigade Final against the 2nd South Staffords, who had beaten the 1st King's Liverpool 3–1 three days earlier. The morning was spent practising rifle drill and undergoing instruction in the art of throwing grenades and the proper fixing of gas masks. In the afternoon the band of the 17th Middlesex accompanied virtually the whole battalion to the ground, where the players and supporters of the 2nd South Staffords had also gathered. The match was once again a one-sided affair and the 17th Middlesex ran out 6–0 winners, L/Cpl Jack Cock bagging four goals and L/Cpl Joe Bailey scoring a brace. The fact that there were fewer goals this time could be attributed to the condition of the pitch, rather than any improvement in the quality of the opposition. Pte Sid Wheelhouse recalled that:

The ground we played on was awful. It was over the boot tops in mud and the ball would not bounce. It put me in mind of the Huddersfield ground when we played them two seasons ago, when the ball would not bounce and we had to hook it out of the mud before we could kick it.

I nearly forgot to tell you that we had a penalty and they shouted Tommy Lonsdale [the Southend Utd goalkeeper] up to take it, as he'd had nothing to do in both the matches, for he only got a kick when Fred Bullock or myself passed it back to him to let him know he was in the game. Well, Tommy took the kick and put it out of the goalkeeper's reach all right – right over the bar! And before he got back into the goal the whistle blew for time.[3]

For their opponents, the 2nd South Staffords, the result was hardly surprising. Their regimental history would comment that 'the Middlesex team was almost entirely composed of International and First League players'.[4] After the match, Col Henry Fenwick arranged a dinner for both teams.

A few days later a mischievous report of unknown origin appeared in England that the 2nd South Staffords football team had actually beaten the famous Footballers' Battalion. Capt Edward Bell, who had assumed the responsibilities of battalion adjutant shortly before the battalion had proceeded overseas, quickly wrote home to set the record straight. Capt Bell was the son of a major in the Royal Fusiliers. A useful right-winger in his day, Bell had made a handful of appearances in the Southern League for Southampton and had also played for Portsmouth reserves.

The recent football matches had provided a welcome distraction from the war, but the period of rest was coming to an end. In a letter to R. Turner, the Nottingham Forest trainer, CSM Tommy Gibson wrote resignedly that he expected to '. . . be moving off again shortly to our little mud trench in the West to have another go at Old Fritz'.[5] On 15 January the 17th Middlesex played a 'Best of Brigade Team', winning 3–1. Two days later the 17th Middlesex were ordered to proceed to Gorre. For some men the news came as a relief. Although they had been safe from German shells and snipers, several individuals had found the routine of drill, inspections and route marches tedious in the extreme. L/Sgt Walter Tull wrote home:

For the last three weeks my Battalion has been resting some miles distant from the firing line but we are now going up to the trenches for a month or so. Afterwards we shall begin to think about coming home on leave. It is a very monotonous life out here when one is supposed to be resting and most of the boys prefer the excitement of the trenches.[6]

Not everyone was preparing to move back into the front line. Even though the battalion had only been on active service a few weeks, the health of some men had already broken down. A couple of weeks earlier Maj Pretyman-Newman had returned to England, having 'found that life in a dugout increased his pain and stiffness and on sudden alarms he found that he could not get out of his dugout without help'.[7] Back in England, he lost no time in entering the ongoing conscription debate in his capacity as a Member of Parliament, convinced that young men were best equipped to withstand the rigours of trench life: '. . . it is not the young who suffer but the middle-aged men of thirty-five or forty years, who undoubtedly do get rheumatism in the trenches. Young men, I find, go through their duties splendidly . . . To my mind, the class of men you want in Flanders are young fellows of 18 years of age.'[8]

The problem was that 18-year-olds were not supposed to be serving in the trenches. Maj Pretyman-Newman had clearly, like many officers, chosen to turn a blind eye to the 'one or two' under-age soldiers in his own Company:

I had a letter from the mother of a lad in my company who stated that he was only sixteen years old, that he was too young to serve in the trenches, and that he should be sent home. I sent for the lad, a very well-grown young fellow, though he is certainly not nineteen, and I told him: 'Your mother says you must go home. Here is your birth certificate showing that you joined under sixteen'. The lad said that he did not want to go home and that he wanted to serve . . .[9]

On the evening of 20 January the 17th Middlesex moved into the front line trenches at Givenchy, where the respective front lines were in places only 20–30yd apart. It was in this sector that 2/Lt Cosmo Clark had his first encounter with the enemy:

The men told me that the Bosche were trying to fraternise with us. I went down and went up one of our saps which went quite close to brother Bosche and poked my nose round a traverse and there was a German standing exposed to the waist and waving to me! I was jolly careful not to look for long because they expose themselves sometimes for you to look over whilst they have another man training a rifle on you. Soon he signalled me to get down by waving his hands towards the ground and then pointing a little higher up the line. At the same time he shouted in a German accent 'Get Down' – I took his hint and sure enough some bombs came over from where he had pointed. He was a Saxon, about 23 years old and quite good looking – clean shaven. He had a trench cap on, the round soft cap which you've seen in the papers, and a grey uniform. He laughed at me when he was signalling. We shouted back for him to try and entice him to come over and give himself up but he hadn't quite enough confidence in us. Prisoners are always made welcome by us!

The colonel was very amused when he got to know about it. He came up to the trenches the morning after and said 'Hulloa Nobby' (my nickname), 'I hear you've been holding a conversation with a German.'[10]

The men spent their time working on the trenches, pausing to watch the ever-increasing number of dogfights occurring in the skies. The war in the air was a source of fascination to soldiers living in the rat-infested squalor of the trenches. Cpl Joe Bailey wrote to Harry Matthews, the secretary of Reading FC:

It is a lovely day. I am writing this at the side of my dug out, sitting on a bag of coke. Two German aeroplanes have just been over my head observing. It was a fine sight to see our aeroplanes firing at them with machine guns in their planes, but no such luck as to see one come down.[11]

On the night of 2 February the 17th Middlesex were relieved by the 1/1st Hertfordshires and marched back to billets in Gorre. The Battalion War Diary recorded that: 'During our tour to the front line and supports our casualties were: Wounded Capt VJ Woodward, LT EBD Brunton and Major Maclaine of Lochbuie. Other Ranks: Killed 4, Wounded since died 6, Wounded: 33.'[12] Virtually all these casualties were sustained as a result of rifle grenades, of which the Germans appeared to have an abundant supply.

Above left: *Frederick Wall, secretary of the Football Association, 'a tireless and efficient worker during the formative years of the Association'. His younger son Herbert was an officer in the 17th Middlesex before transferring to the Royal Flying Corps.* (Football Association)

Above right: *Lord Kinnaird, president of the FA, who played in nine FA Cup Finals and finished on the winning side on five occasions. Two of his sons were killed on the Western Front.* (Football Association)

Below left: *William Joynson-Hicks MP, the man responsible for the raising of the 17th Middlesex.* (Authors' collection)

Below right: *Fred 'Spider' Parker. The Clapton Orient captain was the first footballer to step on to the recruiting platform at Fulham Town Hall in December 1914.* (Colorsport)

Above: *Frank Buckley of Bradford City and England, pictured early in his career as a Brighton & Hove Albion player. Buckley was one of the few professional footballers in the 17th Middlesex with previous military experience.* (Brighton & Hove Albion Collectors' and Historians' Society)

Below: *Encouraged by their club chairman, Henry Wells-Holland, the players and supporters of Clapton Orient made a significant contribution to the ranks of the 17th Middlesex. Three Orient players – William Jonas, George Scott and Richard McFadden – would lose their lives while serving with the battalion.* (Stephen Jenkins)

Above: *Archie Needham of Brighton & Hove Albion. Former clubs included Sheffield United, Crystal Palace and Wolves. Needham played a large part in ensuring that virtually the entire Albion team enlisted in the 17th Middlesex.* (Brighton & Hove Albion Collectors' and Historians' Society)

CLAPTON ORIENT FOOTBALL CLUB, 1913-14.

Above: *The response of Brighton & Hove Albion team was remarkable. No less than 13 players in this photograph would enlist in the 17th Middlesex. Three of them – Jasper Batey, Charles Dexter and Bob Whiting – would lose their lives.* (**Brighton & Hove Albion Collectors' and Historians' Society**)

Below left: *Recruiting poster for the 17th Middlesex. Extract from* Frankfurter Zeitung: *'The young Britons prefer to exercise their long limbs on the football ground, rather than to expose them to any sort of risk in the service of their country.'* (**IWM PST 12126**)

Below right: *Percy Barnfather of Croydon Common whose former clubs included Barnsley, New Brompton, and Norwich City.* (**Alan Futter**)

Above left: *Hugh Roberts of Luton Town. His previous clubs included Leeds City and Scunthorpe.* **(Roger Wash)**

Above right: *Alexander Stewart of Watford was an accomplished left-back and captain of the club. He relinquished the captaincy soon after joining the 17th Middlesex at the public meeting in Fulham Town Hall.* **(Trefor Jones)**

Below: *The recruiting desk in West Africa House, Kingsway. The original caption reads: 'Prominent players attend at the headquarters of their battalion to receive their Army pay. By the table on the right are Frederick Wall, secretary of the Football Association, Colonel Grantham and Captain Elphinstone'.* **(Authors' collection)**

MEN OF MILLWALL

Hundreds of Football enthusiasts are joining the Army daily.

Don't be left behind.

Let the Enemy hear the "LION'S ROAR."

Join and be in at

THE FINAL

and give them a

KICK OFF THE EARTH

Apply:
West Africa House, opposite National Theatre, Kingsway.

Above left: *Nottingham Forest players, from left: Tommy Gibson, Joe Mercer and Harold Iremonger, outside West Africa House in January 1915.* (Gary James)

Above right: *A recruitment poster aimed at Millwall supporters.* (Dave Sullivan)

Below: *The 17th Middlesex march through the streets of Central London en route to White City in January 1915.* (Authors' collection)

Above: *Vivian Woodward of Chelsea, Tottenham Hotspur and England. One of the greatest forwards of the age, Woodward remained England's leading goalscorer until 1958.* (Colorsport)

Right: *Walter Tull was an early enlistment in the 17th Middlesex. He was killed in 1918 while serving with the 23rd Middlesex.* (Phil Vasili)

Below: *The 17th Middlesex getting ready for the 'forthcoming match against the Huns' at White City.* (Authors' collection)

PROMINENT FOOTBALLERS.

E. BELL,
SOUTHAMPTON.

Above: *Charles Bunyan, the former goalkeeper, who once conceded 26 goals in an FA Cup match against Preston North End in 1887. Bunyan had to lie about his age to enlist in the 17th Middlesex.* **(Stuart Basson)**

Left: *Cigarette card featuring Edward Bell, who played briefly for Southampton and Portsmouth. Bell was battalion adjutant when the unit proceeded overseas in November 1915.* **(Duncan Holley)**

Below: *The 17th Middlesex attending church parade at White City in early 1915.* **(Jane Jones)**

Above: *Officers of the 17th Middlesex in Spring 1915. Front row, from left: Maj Pretyman-Newman, Col Grantham, Capt Elphinstone. Second row: Lt D. Evans, Capt Foxcroft-Jones, Lt Scotland, Lt Bell. Third row: Lt & Quartermaster Morris, Lt Oxenbould, Capt Wells-Holland, Lt Tickler, Lt Parsons. Fourth row: Lt Hoad, Lt Wilkinson, Lt Woodward, Lt Wall, Lt Palmer, Lt King, Lt B. Evans.* (Courtesy of the Council of the National Army Museum, London)

Below: *Joe Webster of West Ham United. Before joining the Hammers in April 1914, Webster had made 131 appearances for Watford in the Southern League.* (Trefor Jones)

Below: *Fred Bartholomew of Reading signed as an amateur on Good Friday 1904 and later turned professional. He would serve the club in various roles until 1957.* (David Downs)

Among the dead were Pte Frank Howell, a grocer's assistant from Lewisham, and Pte Robert Harding, a porter from Chelsea. Harding was a 'boy soldier'. At the time of his death he was only 17 years old. Another casualty was Pte Frederick Holland, a stockbroker's clerk, who was badly wounded in the stomach. With scant regard for his own safety, L/Cpl Joe Bailey carried him across open ground in order to speed up his evacuation from the front line. The Reading player's efforts were in vain. Pte Frederick Holland died later that evening. A few days later, Frederick Holland's wife – whose maiden name, 'Eckert', suggests that she was of German descent – received the news that she had become a widow.

Capt Vivian Woodward was among the wounded. The 'idol of football London' had been hit in his right thigh by grenade splinters. Initial reports suggested that the Chelsea star's wounds were 'so severe that his days of athletic activity are at an end'.[13] A few days later the newspapers were able to report that his wounds were not as serious as previously believed. Nonetheless, his condition was such that he needed to be sent back to England for further treatment. Maj Maclaine of Lochbuie, who had been badly wounded in the foot, was also evacuated from France. Recently promoted to rank of major, Frank Buckley assumed the role of second-in-command.

During the period of rest at Gorre the men were kept occupied with gas helmet inspections and various schedules of training, with particular emphasis on 'bomb throwing'. Officers of the 1st King's Liverpool gave lectures to small groups of 17th Middlesex on aspects of trench warfare. Working parties were engaged in sandbagging parapets and revetting breastworks with wire frames and hurdles on a daily basis around Gorre Wood.

On 11 February the 17th Middlesex moved to Festubert, south of Aubers Ridge. In this 'pestilential part of the line' conditions were so bad that the front line consisted solely of 16 isolated breastworks,situated in an expanse of mud and water between 150 and 300yd from the German lines. The garrisons of these breastworks, anything between 7 and 13 men, could only be relieved under the cover of darkness, as any relief had to be undertaken across open ground. Some 600yd to the rear lay the old front line prior to the costly British attack at Festubert in May

1915. The village of Festubert had been almost totally destroyed in the fighting. All that remained standing was the crucifix in the ruins of the church.

The next few days were quiet. Intermittent shelling wounded three other ranks, and Sgt Stanley Banham was wounded by a spent rifle bullet. The body of an unknown officer from a Canadian Scottish Regiment was discovered in front of No. 15 Island and given a decent burial. His body had been lying there for several months. On 13 February there was some excitement when two young German deserters from Infantry Regiment 57 crossed No Man's Land, shouting '*Kameraden*', and surrendered to men of 'B' Company: 'The Bosche were hulking chaps, officers' servants, and because they had been maltreated, had deserted, fetching with them a good supply of their officers' cigars, cigarettes and wine in sandbags!'[14]

On 14 February the 17th Middlesex were relieved by the 1st Royal Irish Rifles, and marched five miles to new billets in Essars, north-east of Béthune. The next few days were spent in and out of the line, and the battalion furnished several working parties to assist the Royal Engineers. On 20 February Capt Alan Burgoyne, Unionist MP for Kensington North, was struck off battalion strength as being medically unfit for service. A noted expert on submarines and a man of diverse business interests, Burgoyne had travelled extensively prior to the war, and had once been arrested and imprisoned in Russia on a charge of spying. That same day Lt Fred Nunn and 2/Lt Laurence 'Ivan' Horniman joined the battalion from the 16th Lancers and the 12th Middlesex respectively. Lt Frederick Nunn had been a pre-war ranker, while 2/Lt Ivan Horniman, educated at Rugby and Exeter College, Oxford, had been studying to become a barrister at the outbreak of war.

On 21 February the Germans launched a massive attack on the French positions around Verdun. Under mounting pressure, Gen Joffre, the French commander, asked Gen Sir Douglas Haig, who had replaced Sir John French as the Commander-in-Chief of the BEF after the Battle of Loos, to take over a section of the French line. Haig acceded to Joffre's request, and arrangements were duly made for the BEF to relieve two corps of the French Tenth Army along a 20-mile section of front between Ransart and Loos. The 2nd Division was one of the first British divisions instructed to take over a portion of the French line, relieving the French 18th Division in the Angres-Calonne sector, a few miles north-west of Vimy Ridge.

On 26 February the 17th Middlesex took over trenches from French troops near Calonne. The men chatted and joked with the outgoing French soldiers, and lost little time in 'anglicising' the sector. Trenches were given appropriate names, such as Footballers' Avenue and Middlesex Walk. Unlike many of the French positions taken over by the British around this time, which were found to be poorly-constructed and maintained, the trenches in this sector were found to be comfortable and of solid construction.

The weather was bitterly cold. In such inclement conditions the rum ration was one of the few comforts for men in the line. Usually issued after the 'Stand Down' in the morning, half-gill measures of thick rum would be poured out from one-gallon earthenware jars, marked with the initials: SRD (Supply Reserve Depot). Soldiers would frequently ascribe their own meaning to these initials, such as 'Soon Runs Dry' or 'Seldom Reaches Destination'. Another comfort was the daily deluge of letters and parcels, delivered by the remarkably efficient Army Postal Service. These usually reached soldiers within a few days of being posted back home, and played an important role in maintaining morale at the front.

At home, friends and family made every effort to keep up the men's spirits. Maj Buckley's wife, Madge, was reckoned to have 'probably made more puddings and sent out more parcels to soldiers in the trenches than any lady in the country'.[15] Mrs Buckley was also doing her bit on the home front, entertaining wounded soldiers from local hospitals at Birmingham City home games. At the FA offices in Russell Square, Frederick Wall was overseeing the administration of the Footballers' Battalion Comforts Fund, successfully resisting the best efforts of the Office of Works to commandeer the premises:

Two surveyors from the department of the Office of Works inspected 'No. 42.' Then three officers came and went over the building. They praised the Council Chamber and the Committee Rooms. They said that the premises were just what they were needing for war purposes. 'Yes,' said one of the officers, 'but where's the bath?'

Of course, every place was a store-room filled with thousands of pairs of socks, tons of cigarettes and many other necessities and comforts. I was Honorary Secretary, and I got in touch with Lord Derby and made representations to him that there were other houses equally as good in Russell Square without disturbing our work for the troops.

The officers were persistent . . . I received a telegram that some men had taken possession and had started to pull up the drains. I got into communication with the Office of Works, and during the morning, while the men were getting on with their job, an official came and told me that he had ordered them to stop, and that we should not have any further trouble. We were left in peace because we were doing so much good work.[16]

As a result of Wall's 'good work', approximately £40 was being expended weekly on the provision of extra socks, Vaseline, cigarettes, toffee, peppermint lozenges and candles for the battalion. Parcels of leather for boot repairs and leather laces were also sent out to France on a regular basis. Much of the money came from collections at football matches, but the clubs themselves did their bit. On the Saturday between the end of the Principal and the start of the Supplementary Tournaments in January 1916, a programme of matches was played by London Combination clubs, the entire gate receipts (£731 2s 11d) being donated to the Fund. This money was subsequently topped up with a £100 donation from Col Fenwick. The results of the matches were:

Arsenal	2–0	Fulham
Millwall	3–1	Reading
Luton Town	3–1	Watford
Chelsea	1–2	Brentford
Tottenham Hotspur	0–1	Clapton Orient
Croydon Common	0–2	Crystal Palace
West Ham Utd	0–0	Queen's Park Rangers

On 27 February the 17th Middlesex were paid a surprise visit by their founder, William Joynson-Hicks MP, who brought with him a letter from King George V, conveying his good wishes to the battalion. After dropping by IV Corps HQ, where he engaged in a

frank discussion with Gen Sir Henry Wilson about the shortage of aircraft, shells and munitions, Joynson-Hicks arrived at 6th Brigade HQ, only to discover that the 17th Middlesex were in the front line. Undaunted, Joynson-Hicks set off for the trenches in a car driven by Maj Gen John Heath, recalling that: 'General Heath drove a little further in our car and left it behind a house in the outskirts of the village. We crossed an open field where small German shells were bursting fifty to seventy yards from us. The General's only anxiety was lest they should "get that d------ motor car". He seemed to set much greater store on that than by our own lives.'[17] Joynson-Hicks' biographer recorded what happened next:

> Soon they stepped into trenches, and into the mud; and eventually, after what seemed to be miles of walking, they reached a coal cellar on the outskirts of Calonne, where they found Colonel Fenwick, the Footballers' Commanding Officer, and two others, lunching on the inevitable bully-beef stew, and tea from tin mugs. Joynson-Hicks was remarkably impressed by the spectacle of the Colonel, whose bedroom here was an inner cellar without any light or ventilation, and who was practically a millionaire, living this life for his country's sake, when he was long past the age when men were expected to serve in the trenches.[18]

Accustomed to the sight of their founder immaculately dressed in a top hat and frock, the rank and file found the spectacle of a muddy Joynson-Hicks in the trenches highly amusing. Clearly dissatisfied with the view of No Man's Land afforded by a trench periscope, Joynson-Hicks put his head over the parapet. At that moment a German shell landed nearby. Fortunately for everyone present the shell was a dud. The next one, which landed a little further away, was not. In the subsequent explosion, parts of a nearby brick wall were tossed high into the air. Maj Gen Heath and Col Fenwick immediately 'began to contemplate what might happen to them, if he were killed, and they put an early end to this part of his tour'.[19] The next day after a visit to Béthune, Joynson-Hicks went to watch heavy artillery in action near Loos. Interestingly, the visit of their founder in February 1916 was not mentioned in the 17th Middlesex War Diary. Joynson-Hicks would pay one further visit to the Western Front in June 1917 to watch the Royal Flying Corps at work.[20] It is not known whether he paid a second visit to the battalion.

Over the next few weeks the 17th Middlesex were rotated in and out of the front line. Snow seemed to fall on an almost daily basis. There were no fatalities, but a few men were wounded. Once again it was German rifle grenades causing the trouble, one of which nearly accounted for L/Cpl Joe Bailey, the Reading forward:

> We had two footballers wounded . . . Summers, of Grimsby; and Gray, of Dundee; they are in my section. I must say it was lucky I saw the rifle grenade coming or it might have wounded more. I was only four yards away from them, and a piece cut my lips and nose, and I did not notice it till one of the boys said to me 'Your face is all covered with blood'. I thought it was the blood from Gray, as I took him in my dug out to dress him. It was a nasty wound in the back, hope it will not touch his lung.[21]

On 18 March the 17th Middlesex moved back to Bruay for a period of rest. After 20 days in the trenches, the 12-mile march to Bruay was a gruelling one. Time spent in the trenches, even in a relatively quiet sector, sapped a man's energy and fitness. By the time the battalion reached its billets, all ranks were thoroughly worn out. Nonetheless, Brig Gen Arthur Daly was impressed and saw fit to congratulate the battalion on its excellent march discipline.

That same day it was reported that two 17th Middlesex men, who had remained behind at the regimental depot in England, Pte Wilfred Nixon of Fulham and Pte Oscar Linkson, the former Manchester Utd player, had absented themselves without leave for 7 hours to play for Queen's Park Rangers against Tottenham in a 0–0 draw at White Hart Lane. They had been arrested at the final whistle and remanded for an escort at Enfield Petty Sessions. The players had argued that they had applied for leave and although promised it had been cancelled at the last moment. At the time of their arrest Nixon and Linkson were found to have return rail tickets in their possession, which had helped counter any suspicion that they might have been intending to desert. Both players received a severe ticking-off from the authorities, and the FA wrote to Queen's Park Rangers to demand an explanation. Within a few months, both men would be sent out to serve with the battalion on the Western Front.

On 21 March the 6th Brigade was inspected by Gen Sir Henry Wilson, the officer commanding IV Corps. That same day the first officers and men of the 17th Middlesex went home on leave. Earlier in the war, the leave system had been at best haphazard. By this stage of the war a fairer system was beginning to emerge. Rotas were drawn up and lists kept for future reference. The men would often be informed of their leave at the last minute and lost little time in making their way home. The son of Sgt James McCormick, the Plymouth Argyle player, remembered his father standing in front of the kitchen fireplace with the dried mud of the trenches still on his tunic.

Col Fenwick was one of the first men to return to England. 'Though naturally reticent about the movements of the Battalion', he was reported as having 'nothing but praise for the men under his command'.[22] In his absence, the imposing figure of Maj Frank Buckley assumed command of the battalion. Buckley had a remarkable affinity with the men, as Col Fenwick recalled: 'If I was walking down the lines with Major Buckley – no matter where we were – the men would salute in the ordinary way, but they took no further notice of me. Their eyes were for Buckley. They whispered "That's Buckley – the footballer".'[23] Lt Herbert Wall, the younger son of the FA Secretary, was another officer who enjoyed a period of leave at this time. Within a few months he would transfer to the Royal Flying Corps.[24]

One of the first other ranks to be selected for leave was Sgt Richard McFadden. During his few days in England, he found time to play for Clapton Orient in a 1–1 draw against QPR at Homerton, much to the delight of the home supporters. He was clearly affected by his time in the trenches. Observers noted that he was 'not altogether in happy touch with the ball but he did well, and as the game wore on, he improved greatly'.[25] Pte Allen Foster spent his leave back in Reading, where he told a representative of the *Berkshire Chronicle* that the men 'were all well provided for and they were as well fed as they were in England'.[26]

Not everyone returned to England. Lt Bertie Wade spent his

first leave in the Latin Quarter of Paris, where he had been studying art at the outbreak of war. A friend recalled that Wade 'was beloved by the long-haired untidy-looking denizens of that fascinating spot, all of whom knew the spruce-looking little Englishman in their midst'.[27] Lt Bertie Wade was touched by their reaction, writing to a friend: 'They all remembered me and all seemed pleased to see me again, that it fairly brought the tears to my eyes; but then I always was a sentimental ass.'[28]

On 30 March the 17th Middlesex played the 1st King's Royal Rifle Corps, the winners of the 99th Brigade competition, in the semi-final of the Divisional Tournament. The line-up was virtually identical to the team that had played against the 13th Essex in January. Pte Frank Martin of Grimsby Town played instead of Maj Buckley, and Capt Woodward was replaced by Pte William Jonas of Clapton Orient. By all accounts, Woodward was now making a good recovery from his wounds and had recently been spotted in the Directors' Box at Stamford Bridge.

The 17th Middlesex won 6–0. L/Cpl Jack Cock of Huddersfield Town scored a hat-trick. The other scorers were L/Cpl Joe Bailey, Pte Hugh Roberts and Pte Frank Martin. That afternoon Maj Frank Buckley wrote about the match to a friend, pointing out that the battalion's sporting prowess was not just limited to the football pitch: 'We are in a Divisional Cup competition, and won the semi-final today against the KRR's 6–0. We also played the Kings at Rugger the other day and won by 69 points to nil, so you can see we still keep having a game.'[29]

In between the sporting activities, the military training continued.[ii] On 1 April some men attended a training session on *Flammenwerfer* at Ruitz. Flamethrowers had first been employed by the Germans against the British at Hooge in July 1915. Operated by two men, one man would carry the tank, which looked rather like a 'potato-spraying device'; the other would be responsible for

---

[ii] A friendly match took place around this time against the 8th Railway Company, RE. The team was: Pte Percy Summers (Grimsby Town) goalkeeper; Sgt Tommy Gibson (Nottingham Forest) and L/Cpl Fred Bullock (Huddersfield Town), backs; Sgt Joe Smith (Chesterfield Town), Sgt Ted Hanney (Manchester City) and L/Cpl Billy Baker (Plymouth Argyle), halfbacks; Pte Jackie Sheldon (Liverpool), L/Cpl Joe Bailey (Reading), Pte George Pyke (Newcastle Utd), Pte Tommy Barber (Aston Villa) and L/Cpl Fred Goodwin (Exeter City) forwards.

aiming the hose, which could spout a stream of liquid fire 30–50yd in the direction of the chosen target. Unsurprisingly, flamethrowers were a much-feared weapon, notwithstanding the fact that if the tank itself were hit a predictably explosive result would ensue. The 100 or so men who attended the demonstration of this terrifying weapon were reported to have found it 'very interesting'.[30]

Over the days that followed, the 17th Middlesex were preoccupied with the usual route marches and rifle inspections. Each evening large parties of men were sent up to improve sections of the line around Souchez at the northern end of Vimy Ridge, the scene of heavy fighting between the French and Germans in 1915. The work proved particularly gruesome, on account of the large number of rotting German and French corpses unearthed during the excavations.

The final of the Divisional Football Tournament was fast approaching. The Liverpool player Pte Jackie Sheldon was still smarting over the permanent ban on his 'taking part in football or football management'. Other 'guilty' players, who had been involved in the infamous Good Friday match had already experienced problems in relation to playing Army football. On Christmas Day 1915 the Manchester Utd players Sandy Turnbull and Arthur Whalley had been due to represent the 23rd Middlesex in a match against Birmingham City, but they had not been allowed to play. Even though the FA had issued its final verdict on the Good Friday match over three months previously, Pte Jackie Sheldon wrote to the editor of *Athletic News* asking him to publish a declaration of innocence. The editor of the newspaper duly obliged, taking particular note of the fact that its author was 'somewhere in France':

Would you kindly grant me space in your valuable paper to explain my position re suspension? Perhaps it is unfair for me to ask this favour after my case has been dealt with so long ago by the FA. But you will understand how difficult it is for me to explain while doing my bit somewhere in France. I am now taking the first opportunity I have had, and wish to let the numerous followers of football know how I stand. I emphatically state to you, as our best and fairest critic, that I am absolutely blameless in this scandal, and am still open as I have always been to give to any Red Cross Fund or any other charitable institute the sum of £20 if the FA or anyone else, can bring forward any bookmaker or any other person with whom I have had a bet. Assuming I return safely from this country, I intend taking action against my suspension, and in the meantime you would do me a great favour if you would kindly insert me this letter in your next week's issue.[31]

On 11 April the 17th Middlesex played the 34th Brigade RFA in the final of the Divisional Cup at Hersin.[iii] It was not much of a match, the 17th Middlesex running out 11–0 winners. Maj Gen William Walker was unable to attend the game, so it fell upon Brig Gen Arthur Daly to present the winning team with the Cup. As part of the celebrations, the Cup was filled with an appropriate celebratory beverage by the acting CO, Maj Frank Buckley, and the adjutant, Capt Edward Bell. Over the course of the competition the 17th Middlesex team had scored 44 goals without reply. In time a commemorative medal would be struck for each member of the team. The medals were made of silver and were described as being of 'handsome design'. In addition to the name of the player, each medal bore the following inscription: 'B.E.F. France, Association Football Cup'. By the time these medals were ready for distribution, four members of the winning team would no longer be alive to receive them.[32]

[iii]The 17th Middlesex team: Pte Tommy Lonsdale (Southend Utd) goalkeeper; Pte Sid Wheelhouse (Grimsby Town) and L/Cpl Fred Bullock (Huddersfield Town), backs; Pte George Scott (Clapton Orient), Pte David Kenney (Grimsby Town) and L/Cpl Billy Baker (Plymouth Argyle), halfbacks; Pte Hugh Roberts (Luton Town), Pte William Jonas (Clapton Orient), L/Cpl Jack Cock (Huddersfield Town), L/Cpl Joe Bailey (Reading) and Sgt Percy Barnfather (Croydon Common), forwards.

1. BNL: *Athletic News*, 31 January 1916.
2. BNL: *Argus*, 14 January 1916.
3. BNL: *Grimsby News*, 15 January 1916.
4. Jones, J., *A History of the South Staffordshire Regiment 1705–1923*, p. 318.
5. BNL: *Grimsby News*, 11 February 1916.
6. Vasili, P., *Colouring Over the White Line*, p. 52.
7. After a short period of attachment to the 10th East Surreys, Maj Pretyman-Newman would spend the rest of the war at the Central Recruiting Depot in Whitehall.
8. *Hansard* HC, vol. 78, cols 92, 17 January 1916.
9. *Hansard* HC, vol. 78, cols 91–92, 17 January 1916.
10. Clark, C. *The Tin Trunk*, p. 45.
11. BNL: *Berkshire Chronicle*, 4 February 1916.
12. CWGC records the deaths of only eight soldiers during this period.

13. BNL: *Athletic News*, 31 January 1916.

14. Clark, C., *The Tin Trunk*, p. 45.

15. BNL: *Athletic News*, 27 March 1916.

16. Wall, F., *50 Years of Football 1884–1934*, pp. 14–15.

17. Taylor, H., *Jix: Viscount Brentford*, p. 138.

18. *Ibid*.

19. *Ibid*.

20. Throughout the war Joynson-Hicks concerned himself primarily with matters relating to the design and production of aircraft and air defence, harrying the government at every opportunity. In 1916 he published a pamphlet, *The Command of the Air*, which he described as 'the last despairing effort I can make by the pressure of public opinion to force the Government to take in hand the formation of a real national, or indeed, imperial air service'.

21. BNL: *Berkshire Chronicle*, 7 April 1916. David Gray recovered from his wounds. In October 1916, he was able to play for a Footballers' Battalion team against Portsmouth, scoring two goals in a 3–2 victory at Fratton Park.

22. BNL: *Athletic News*, 1 April 1916.

23. BNL: *Sporting Chronicle*, 20 September 1916.

24. Lt Herbert Wall would survive the war, winning a Military Cross and Bar.

25. BNL: *Athletic News*, 10 April 1916.

26. BNL: *Berkshire Chronicle*, 7 April 1917.

27. Sewell, E., *The Rugby Football Internationals' Roll of Honour*, p. 219.

28. *Ibid*.

29. BNL: *Football Post*, 8 April 1916. The 1st King's Liverpool War Diary recorded the score as 42–0.

30. TNA: WO 95/1361.

31. BNL: *Athletic News*, 10 April 1916. In July 1917 Sheldon would admit in the witness box that he had played a key role in fixing the match during a libel action brought by Enoch 'Knocker' West against both the FA and E. Hulton & Co Ltd (publishers of the *Daily Dispatch* and the *Sporting Chronicle*). West was one of the Manchester Utd players given a lifetime ban as a result of the Good Friday game.

32. The match ball, which was signed by a total of 42 players, was sent home to be auctioned for charity. The auction took place in December 1916. The ball was described by *Athletic News* as 'a football worth possessing... the historic ball bearing the signatures of many good lads... some alas will take the field no more'.

CHAPTER 6

FOOTBALL CRATER

Not bad for a start, eh?
Sgt Percy Barnfather F/43 (Croydon Common)

On 12 April 1916 the 17th Middlesex moved by train to Bruay, marching to Calonne the next day. There the battalion entrained for Aire, before undertaking a 13-mile march to billets in Radinghem. The march was a trying one, as the men had a north-west gale blowing clouds of dust in their faces the whole way. Over the next few days the 17th Middlesex underwent company training and participated in brigade training exercises round Bomy, a pretty village surrounded by woods within a picturesque valley.

The 17th Middlesex went back into the front line near Calonne on 19 April. A draft of 2 officers and 50 other ranks arrived to make good the battalion's losses to date, bringing the fighting strength up to 32 officers and 856 other ranks. The next few days were uncomfortable, largely on account of the wet weather. The rain was relentless. Trench walls collapsed and several trenches were knee-deep in water. Each night working parties were busy repairing the front and reserve lines. On St George's Day the rain subsided and the Germans began to shell the British lines with artillery and trench mortars. There were no fatalities, but ten men were wounded.

On 26 April the 17th Middlesex were relieved by the 13th Essex and took over comfortable billets in support. The men were housed in cellars, many of which contained beds and furniture. Two days later 6th Brigade HQ organised an Easter Sports Day for local children aged 4–11 years, living within 2,500yd of the front line. The children were presented with chocolate and sweets on arrival, before participating in a variety of events, including a 'threading the needle' competition, a sack race and an Easter egg trail. After tea the children were treated to a conjuror show and presented with an orange and bun to take home. It was a pleasant day, particularly for those men with sons and daughters on the other side of the Channel, but the reminders of war were never far away. A gramophone had played a selection of popular tunes throughout the afternoon, but it had done little to mask the incessant rumble of the guns, which grew in volume as the day wore on.

On 29 April the Germans discharged a mixture of chlorine and phosgene from cylinders to the left of the 17th Middlesex. Clouds of gas rolled over the British trenches to where the 17th Middlesex were in support, bleaching vegetation in their path. Anti-gas measures had progressed considerably since soldiers had been advised to hold a urine-sodden handkerchief over their mouth and nose. From early 1916 onwards the PH (phenate-hexamine) gas helmet had begun to be issued to British soldiers, replacing the earlier P (phenate) gas helmet, which had failed to give the wearer adequate protection against phosgene.[1] As soon as the gas alarm was sounded, 17th Middlesex hastily donned their PH helmets until the gas had sufficiently dissipated an hour or so later. No casualties were sustained.[2]

On the evening of 30 April the 17th Middlesex moved back into the front line. Over the next few days six men were wounded, including Cpl Alf Gregson of Grimsby Town and Cpl Ben Butler of Queen's Park Rangers. Ten days later, Cpl Butler died of his wounds. Rev Samuel Green, a chaplain at Casualty Clearing Station No. 22, recorded his impressions of the rugged centre-half:

A great, big chap lies in this bed – a guard bulges up the blankets over his leg.

'Well, Corporal, how are you now?' – 'Bad. This leg is done in. No more football for me. I'm a 'pro' and play for —.'

I look at the papers and see his thigh is shattered – always dangerous, these wounds. However the danger is not immediate, and I shall have many more half-hours at this bedside. He fights for dear life for ten days, and then goes out. He has played the game. I doubt not he has won. A fine fellow – may he rest in peace.[3]

Cpl Ben Butler was the first professional footballer in the ranks of the 17th Middlesex to give his life for his country. Before signing for

Reading, Butler had been an engine cleaner for South-Eastern Railway Company. During the 1909/10 season, in which Reading were relegated from the Southern League First Division, Butler had made 17 appearances for the club. The following season, when Reading won the Second Division Championship, the centre-half had played 'the game of his career' in a vital 2–0 victory over Croydon Common, before moving to Queen's Park Rangers. Butler left a widow and two young children at the family home in West Hampstead.

On 4 May the 17th Middlesex were relieved by the 13th Essex and moved back to billets in Bully-Grenay. Four days later the battalion was back in the front line. Even though the 17th Middlesex had been on active service for only a few months, and had yet to see any serious fighting, several men were already beginning to suffer psychological damage from the effects of war. Pte Allen Foster would later write to his wife that the whole business was 'very trying to the nerves, and lots of fellows get what they call shell shock. What with the continual bursting of shells etc, and the thundering of the guns, they seem to go all to pieces. So I am afraid you wont last long out here, but there is no need to worry, as I am A1.'[4]

One soldier who had recently begun to display symptoms of shell shock was L/Sgt Walter Tull of Northampton Town. His condition did not improve and Tull was sent home on 9 May, diagnosed as suffering from 'acute mania'.[5] Other men suffering such conditions were often not so fortunate, being labelled as malingerers or worse and classified as fit for duty. The authorities had been slow to recognise that the stresses of war could have an adverse impact on a soldier's mind, although there was growing alarm at the increasing numbers of men claiming to be suffering from shell shock. War neurosis, or battle fatigue, manifested itself in a multitude of ways. Some men went berserk, others became withdrawn. Some men would even develop a wide range of physical conditions, such as sensory loss, or the paralysis of one or more limbs.

During this spell in the front line, the 17th Middlesex positions were strafed by German artillery and trench mortars on several occasions. Several men were wounded. On 11 May L/Cpl Horace Wass, one of the Grimsby men recruited by Lt Arthur Tickler and a good friend of Pte Sid Wheelhouse, was struck and killed instantly by a shell fragment. The following day the battalion moved back into support.

On 15 May the 17th Middlesex returned to the front line, near Calonne. The enemy's trenches were about 300yd away and the Germans could often be heard singing or shouting. The next couple of days were quiet, although German aeroplanes did drop some bombs on nearby trenches, as well as green flares over British gun emplacements in order to highlight their positions to the German gunners. The British front line ran in front of the village and the support and communication trenches wound their way through its houses and gardens. Various salad vegetables and rhubarb were found growing nearby. Servants decorated their officers' dugouts with 'iris, big red anemones, pansies and all manner of flowers'.[6] On 18 May having suffered only four men wounded, the 17th Middlesex were relieved by the 8th Royal Berkshires and marched back to billets in Fosse 10. For the next couple of days the battalion provided working parties. All seemed quiet. There was no hint of the trouble that was brewing nearby on Vimy Ridge.

As soon as the British had taken over Vimy Ridge a few months earlier, they had lost little time in making use of the extensive mining system inherited from the French. The tunnelling companies of the Royal Engineers, the first of which had been formed in February 1915, were largely comprised of miners in civilian life, or 'clay-kickers' previously employed in the construction of sewerage systems, or projects such as London's underground railway. Tunnels would be painstakingly driven under No Man's Land towards the enemy lines. At the end of these tunnels a chamber would be excavated, packed with explosives and detonated. The tunnelling companies were also responsible for counter-mining measures, which involved listening for evidence of German mining activity and destroying their mine galleries before they could be fired under British positions.

Before the British arrival on Vimy Ridge, the German miners had been in the ascendancy. Within a couple of months everything had changed. It was now the turn of Allied mining activity to have a detrimental effect on German morale. One of the German units serving at the northern end of Vimy Ridge was Infantry Regiment 163, of the 17th Reserve Division. Its regimental historian recorded that:

These continual mine explosions in the end got on the nerves of the men. The posts in the front trenches and garrisons of the dug-outs were always in danger of being buried alive. Even in the quietest night there was the dreadful feeling that in the next moment one might die a horrible and cruel death. One stood in the front line defenceless and powerless against these fearful mine explosions. Against all other fighting methods there was some protection – against this kind of warfare, valour was of no avail, not even the greatest foresight. Running back, retirement were useless: like lightning from the clear heavens, like the sudden occurrence of some catastrophe of nature, these mine explosions took place.[7]

The success of British mining operations on Vimy Ridge prompted the Germans to take action. Gen Freiherr von Freytag-Loringhoven, the temporary commander of the IX Reserve Corps of 6th Army, decided to launch a limited operation against the British line in the Berthonval sector. His plan was to capture the British mine shafts, thereby neutralising the threat from mining operations for the foreseeable future.

On the evening of 21 May, after a 4-hour bombardment during which an estimated 70,000 shells fell on a frontage of only 1,800yd, the Germans attacked between Momber Crater and Broadmarsh Crater in the Berthonval Sector. The brunt of the assault fell on the 140th Brigade of the 47th Division. Whole sections of the British line had been obliterated by the bombardment and the dazed survivors were swiftly taken prisoner. Such was the fury of the German assault that Gen Sir Edmund Allenby, the commander of Third Army, initially thought that the city of Arras might be the German objective. The 2nd Division was in reserve around Bruay, over 10 miles away. Urgent orders were received to move up to the front. The 17th Middlesex hastily vacated their billets and were taken up in lorries to support the 25th and 47th Divisions.

The British were pushed back to the Reserve Line, known as the

Talus des Zouaves, which ran along the road cutting at the bottom of the Zouave Valley. Plans were immediately drawn up for a makeshift counterattack to recover the lost ground, which was duly launched on the evening of the 23rd. The 17th Middlesex were fortunate not to be involved. British artillery preparation was woefully inadequate, owing principally to a lack of heavy ammunition, and a deserter had reportedly given full details of the impending counterattack to the Germans. The attack failed at a cost of several hundred casualties.

On 26 May the 17th Middlesex marched back to reserve billets at Villers-au-Bois. Having achieved their primary objective, the possession of the entrances to the British mining system, the Germans decided not to occupy the former British support line, as this would leave their troops more exposed to shellfire. Over the next few days soldiers from the 6th and 99th Brigades, pushed out saps 300yd from Talus des Zouaves back up the western slopes of Vimy Ridge, where a new front line was painstakingly excavated.

On 30 May the 17th Middlesex relieved the 13th Essex in the front line, near the village of Souchez at the northern end of Vimy Ridge. Between Souchez and Givenchy-en-Gohelle the British mine shafts were still intact, as the Germans had not attacked here on 21 May. The sector had already seen considerable mining activity, and the narrow strip of land between the respective front lines was pockmarked with an array of craters. Beneath the trenches held by the 17th Middlesex, the 176th Tunnelling Company were in the final stages of preparing another three mines for detonation in the vicinity of an existing group of craters, known as the Northern Group of Craters, Carency Section.[8] Most prominent in this group were three large craters – Broadbridge, Mildren and New Cut – which ran on a north-to-south line through No Man's Land, with only a few yards between craters.[9]

The detonation of the three mines was to be preceded by an intense bombardment by corps and divisional artillery on the German front and support lines between 4.05 p.m. and 8.30 p.m. on the evening of 1 June. The three mines were to be detonated as soon as the bombardment finished. A few hundred yards to the south of the 17th Middlesex, the 1st King's Liverpool would launch an immediate raid on the German front line. Forty-three minutes later, provided that any retaliatory German barrage had died down, it would be the turn of the 17th Middlesex to move forward, the artillery having lifted onto the enemy support and second-line trenches, some 300yd east of the anticipated craters.

The plan was that a raiding party would pass between Broadbridge Crater and Mildren Crater. Covering parties with two Lewis guns were to seize and hold the far lips of the new craters, while consolidating parties would incorporate the near lips within the British front line. Col Fenwick was given some discretion as to exactly when he should order his men forward, but his orders made it clear what was expected: 'If the hostile barrage does not permit of the attack being launched at 0.43 hours, the parties will be held in abeyance till the barrage slackens when the advance will be vigorously pushed <u>at once</u>'.[10]

At 4.05 p.m. the British guns began to pound the German lines, in accordance with the artillery fire plan. For 2/Lt Cosmo Clark and 18 men of the 17th Middlesex, sheltering in an isolated section of the front line, the British bombardment was a nerve-shattering experience:

I knew that if our gunners bombarded the German lines the German guns would be sure to retaliate on us, so I got all my men sitting at the bottom of the trench and had two sentries only, looking through periscopes. At two o'clock in the afternoon our guns started registering and at four o'clock they started an intense bombardment. Never have I experienced such a time. There was a long continuous scream and groan of our shells whistling over our heads and a continuous roar made everybody literally tremble with anticipation and excitement. The Germans retaliated but they gave us not an eighth of what we gave them.[11]

At 8.30 p.m. there were three immense explosions as the mines went up.[12] Col Fenwick noted that 'very little vibration of earth took place when the mines were blown'.[13] That was not the case for 2/Lt Cosmo Clark and his men in their section of trench:

At eight thirty our mines went up and I had a splendid view of them. They don't make much noise but they make the ground rock

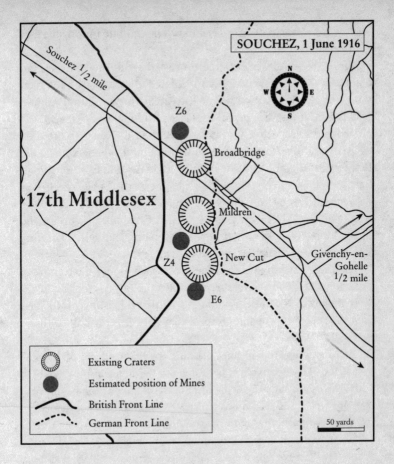

SOUCHEZ, 1 June 1916

Souchez 1/2 mile

Z6

Broadbridge

17th Middlesex

Mildren

New Cut

Z4

Givenchy-en-
Gohelle
1/2 mile

E6

Existing Craters

Estimated position of Mines

British Front Line

German Front Line

50 yards

backwards and forwards for a good half minute. All you can see of the explosion is an immense tongue of flame about twice the size of our house. Great chunks of earth flew into the air like so much paper, as did some Bosche spread-eagled against the sky. Then the Bosche started with his artillery. The shells simply came over and burst in thousands – great flashes everywhere which burned one's skin and yet the bits of metal which flew around missed one.[14]

The German bombardment caused considerable damage to the British front line and communication trenches. Several German shells also fell on British troops in their exposed support positions in Zouave Valley, a branch of the Souchez Valley running southwards, causing many casualties among units not involved in the operation.

The 17th Middlesex suffered no casualties during the German bombardment. Col Fenwick had ordered the men to remain in their dugouts in anticipation of such retaliatory shelling. Around 9.40 p.m. German fire began to slacken and Col Fenwick gave the order for the respective parties to leave their dugouts. The raiding party of ten men, consisting mainly of 'expert bombers', was the first to venture into No Man's Land. Originally 2/Lt Ivan Horniman had been the officer selected to lead the party, but when it was discovered that he was due to go on leave the next day, his place was taken by 2/Lt Edgar Lee. There was little enthusiasm for the forthcoming operation within the battalion. The general feeling was that heavy casualties were inevitable.

The three covering parties of ten men each, under the command of Lt John Engleburtt, were next to leave the British trenches. They were followed by the consolidating parties consisting of 40 men from 'A' and 'B' Companies respectively. Col Fenwick recalled that:

> The expectation was on that reaching the line it would be found that the great damage had been done to the German front line by the explosion, and also by the five hours' continuous bombardment of our artillery. In fact, it was anticipated that the German front line would be practically non-existent. However, the reverse was the case. Our front line and communication trenches suffered very severely from both the explosion and the German artillery, and the Germans were quite ready to meet the troops on their arrival with machine-gun fire.[15]

The German defenders had indeed remained alert. Heavy machine-gun fire opened up on the raiding party as soon as it began to pick its way between Broadbridge Crater and Mildren Crater. Second-Lieutenant Edgar Lee was hit in the head straightaway and died without regaining consciousness. Realising that entering the German front line was not a viable option, Sgt Herbert Bear withdrew the remainder of the raiding party to assist Lt Engleburtt's covering parties.

The weight of enemy fire ensured that none of the covering

parties were unable to progress to the far lips of the craters, although initial reports received by Col Henry Fenwick suggested otherwise, so they positioned themselves on the sides of the craters. The two Lewis guns proved particularly effective in keeping the Germans at bay. A series of bomb fights ensued. At one stage the Germans came close enough to disrupt the consolidation work going on behind them, but Sgt Charles Cook led a party of bombers forward to force the Germans back. Casualties began to mount. One of the stretcher-bearers, the Reading player Pte Angus Seed, dragged several wounded men back to the British line, including the Arsenal assistant trainer Pte Thomas Ratcliff, who had been buried by an explosion. Col Fenwick sent an order to Lt Engleburtt, who had been wounded in the hand and arm, that he should withdraw his two Lewis Guns to the near lips of the crater.

While the covering parties, ably assisted by Sgt Bear and the intended raiding party, continued to keep the Germans at bay, the consolidating parties worked hard to construct a tenable line of defence. In his subsequent report, Col Fenwick reported that the results of the consolidation process were mixed:

First, the left, led by 'B' Company under Captain Salter. Here a crater of considerable size was found on the left of Broadbridge. Explosions had only damaged our line in two places. The crater itself was of a favourable nature to consolidate. Much work was done here, and by daylight on the 2nd it was pretty safe. Second, as regards the crater on the right. This was a matter of such magnitude and difficulty, which difficulty was enhanced by the fact that two platoon leaders, 2nd Lieuts. L.A. Bradstreet and J.B. Skerry, were killed within five minutes of entering trenches by machine gun-fire. It took some time to send up two officers to replace them [one of these officers was 2/Lt Ivan Horniman], and consequently work proceeded much slower. Also, Captain Rollason, who commanded this part of the line, did not have the advantage of expert advice, the Engineer Officer who accompanied the consolidating parties confining his attention strictly to the crater on the left. Of two sappers who accompanied this party one was instantly killed by shell-fire before reaching the trench. Captain Rollason found himself without any technical advice and assistance, and had to do the best he could, which consisted in clearing and digging a trench and sap to the crater to gain as much cover as possible. The front trench here was completely obliterated, and a dangerous position thus created.[16]

By daybreak, this minor operation had cost the 17th Middlesex the lives of three officers and five other ranks. One officer and 38 other ranks had been wounded. To the south, the 1st King's Liverpool had incurred heavier casualties in the execution of their raid, losing around 60 men killed, wounded and missing. One of the 1st King's Liverpool parties had managed to occupy a section of the German line under severe fire, but had been forced to withdraw three quarters of an hour later. Although the operation had clearly not fulfilled all its objectives, the commander of the 2nd Division, Maj Gen William Walker, was clearly impressed with the performance of the 17th Middlesex. In his report to IV Corps HQ, he wrote: 'This is the first occasion on which the 17th Middlesex have been engaged in serious fighting, but I consider they carried out the operation with steadiness and gallantry under very trying circumstances'.[17]

The fears of heavy casualties had not been realised, but the loss of officers had been disproportionately high. Second-Lieutenant Edgar Lee, only 21 years old at the time of his death, was the only son of a local magistrate in Willesden. Lee had enlisted as a private in the Motor Section of the Army Service Corps on the outbreak of war. During the winter of 1914/15, he had acted as a Motorist Observer to the General Staff before being invalided home suffering from jaundice. He was subsequently commissioned and had been posted to the 17th Middlesex in May 1915. An accomplished linguist, able to speak French, German, Russian and Romanian, 2/Lt Lee had been called upon to act as an interpreter by Brig Gen Arthur Daly on several occasions.

Second-Lieutenant Lionel Bradstreet was a bank clerk in civilian life. He was one of the officers who had joined the 17th Middlesex at Holmbury from the Inns of Court OTC. Originally from York, 2/Lt James Skerry was another bank clerk, residing in Crouch End on the outbreak of war. On 1 September 1914 Skerry had enlisted in the 1/28th Londons before being commissioned in the 17th Middlesex in January 1915. The bodies of all three officers were subsequently recovered and lie today in Cabaret-Rouge British Cemetery, Souchez, alongside the other ranks of the 17th Middlesex killed on 1 June.

Among the other ranks killed were Pte Reginald Pearless, a resident of Thornton Heath, and Cpl Herbert Derisley, nephew of a Crystal Palace FC director and an honorary steward of the club. Killed by shellfire, Cpl Derisley, had only rejoined the battalion on 28 May after spending a period of leave at his home in Upper Norwood. His death must have been particularly devastating for his parents, as Herbert's younger brother Frank had been killed the previous November.

Cpl Billy Baker of Plymouth Argyle and Pte Thomas Codd of Leicester Fosse were among the wounded. Several wounded men, including Pte George Blades, a keen amateur footballer from Walthamstow, and Pte Matthew Watson, a baker from Fulham, later succumbed to their wounds.

The next couple of days were spent consolidating the new front line. The crater of considerable size, north of Broadbridge, was christened Football Crater. Two loopholes were constructed in its near lip, and a dense tangle of wire thrown inside. The Germans attempted to establish a position on the far side, but were bombed out. The position was a good one, overlooking the German lines in the vicinity of the Pimple. On 3 June L/Cpl Joe Bailey spent a few hours sniping from one of these loopholes, accounting for two or three Germans, including an officer. L/Cpl Bailey was later joined by Sgt Norman Wood of Stockport County, who had brought up some protective sniper plates. The two men fitted these plates in the loopholes and took turns sniping throughout the afternoon. That evening Col Fenwick came up to inspect the positions for himself. At 11 p.m. the 17th Middlesex were relieved by the 13th Essex and moved back into support.

Over the next few days the relatives of the dead began to receive the customary letters of condolence from the front line. The father of 2/Lt Edgar Lee, the first officer of the 17th Middlesex to be killed in the war, received several such letters from the battalion's officers and the men under his son's command. One spoke of Edgar dying a 'glorious death at the head of his men'. Others, like that written by his company commander, Capt William Wilkinson, were perhaps more sensitive to the grief of a father who had lost his only son:

. . . Always merry and bright, often chaffed but never ruffled, he was a favourite with all ranks, and his brother officers and N.C.O.s and the men of his company will never cease to regret his loss and miss his cheery presence. I cannot hope to express my sympathy with you in your bereavement, but poor little Edgar died doing his duty like the fine officer and gentleman he was.[18]

For the remainder of June the 17th Middlesex were rotated in and out of the front line around Souchez, undergoing the novel experience of being shelled with lachrymatory shells, which 'made things very disagreeable'. On 5 June, the same day on which Lord Kitchener drowned when HMS *Hampshire* struck a mine in the North Sea, Pte John 'Ginger' Williams, the stocky Millwall forward, was killed.[19] Before becoming a professional footballer, Williams had worked at the Mountain Colliery in his native Flintshire and was often to be seen riding around the streets of Buckley on what was described by bemused locals as a 'bamboo bike', as part of his fitness regime.

Williams had played for Bury, Accrington, and Birmingham City before moving to Crystal Palace in 1909. At Palace he had enjoyed considerable success, once scoring five goals in a match against Southend and being capped for Wales. Moving to Millwall in 1913, this 'plucky, fearless and clever' player had scored 12 goals in 59 appearances for the Lions. Within a few months, a fund would be set up to provide support for his widow Sarah and their son, Kenneth, who was less than a year old at the time of his father's death. His last two clubs, Crystal Palace and Millwall, would also play a fund-raising match in 1917 before 5,000 spectators at the Den.[20] Pte John Williams has no known grave and is commemorated on the Arras Memorial to the Missing.[21]

Over the next couple of weeks around 20 men were wounded. Among their number were two professional footballers, Pte Joe McLauchlan of Watford and Pte Angus Seed of Reading, both of whom sustained serious shrapnel wounds to their legs.[22] On 17 June the recently promoted Cpl Joe Bailey visited the RMO, having cut his hand badly on some barbed wire. It failed to heal and he was evacuated to a hospital out of the line. Within a couple of weeks he would arrive back at Dover on a hospital ship. The Reading player's active service with the 17th Middlesex was over. On recovery from his injury, Cpl Bailey would be commissioned, returning to the Western Front to serve with the 2nd Suffolks in October 1917.

As the war had progressed, increasing numbers of men were being commissioned from the ranks to replace officer casualties. L/Sgt Jimmy Hugall of Clapton Orient would also leave the 17th Middlesex in this way, being commissioned as a second lieutenant in the Durham Light Infantry in the summer of 1916.[23] On 19 June the newly commissioned 2/Lt Ernest Parfitt joined the 17th Middlesex in France. On reporting for duty with the 17th Middlesex he discovered straightaway that Capt Edward Bell, the adjutant, was 'the man other than the CO'. As a keen amateur footballer himself, he was especially delighted to discover that 'McFadden of the Orient' was his platoon sergeant. Over the next few days 2/Lt Parfitt was made to feel welcome by his brother officers, a 'jolly set of fellows' whose messing was fairly cheap, being only 4-5 francs a day. By the end of June he would write to his wife that: 'I rather like my new regiment & my brother officers are a most mixed lot. Some are varsity men, other solicitors, others like myself & the most peculiar thing of all is – that at one time or another they were in the ranks, several in the Public Schools battalions of the Fusiliers'.[24]

On 24 June, the day on which the British guns started their bombardment of the German lines and support areas north of the River Somme, the 17th Middlesex received notification of honours awarded 'for acts of bravery and good work' on 1 June. Capt Thomas Rollason, Capt William Salter and Lt John Engleburtt were awarded the Military Cross.[25] It was generally agreed that Lt Engleburtt was the hero of the hour. Wounded three times, he had refused to leave his post, waiting until the consolidation work had been completed before walking back to the dressing station 'as cool as a cucumber'. Distinguished Conduct Medals were bestowed upon Sgt Herbert Bear and Sgt Charles Cook.[26] Sgt Frederick Jackson, Cpl Billy Baker, Pte Angus Seed, Pte Edward Davey and

Pte George Crowther were each awarded the recently instituted Military Medal.[27] The Hurst FC centre-forward, George Crowther, had worked in a shipbuilder's yard before becoming a professional footballer and had seen service with Manchester Utd, Halifax Town and Huddersfield Town.

Amid scenes of great enthusiasm, Brig Gen Arthur Daly presented the awards at a full muster roll of the battalion.[28] It was a proud day for the 17th Middlesex. Sgt Percy Barnfather wrote to a friend: 'I don't know if you heard that we had been in a "little affair" a week or two back. We were complimented on the good work we did, and two [three] of our officers have got the Military Cross, two Sergts the DCM, and about five men Military Medals. Not bad for a start, eh?[29]

News that the 17th Middlesex had been in action soon reached England. In the eyes of the game's sternest critics, football was at last beginning to pull its weight, although some chose to qualify their praise. As Lord Hawke, a leading figure in the world of cricket, remarked:

Even the professional footballers, though they came in a bit late, have shown true English grit and pluck, and won renown by their fine achievements on the fields of battle, whilst the splendid exponents of Cricket, Rowing, Rugby and Golf who have died fighting so gallantly, have raised the name and fame and the tone of sport for all time. I am against men still playing football as a spectacle for thousands when their mates are dying on the bloody fields of France and other lands.[30]

On 30 June the 17th Middlesex were holding support trenches near Cabaret Rouge. The Battalion War Diary recorded: 'Occasional shelling from enemy. Otherwise quiet.' Further south on the Somme it was anything but quiet. British and French guns had been pounding the German lines for the past week in preparation for the long-awaited 'Big Push' on the Somme.

During the first two weeks of the Somme offensive the 17th Middlesex were rotated in and out of the front line at the northern end of Vimy Ridge. Although this sector had quietened down in recent weeks, the front remained an active one with intermittent shelling and the occasional trench raid. Sgt Percy Barnfather wrote home:

Things are very lively all along this front, and have been for a few weeks now, and I think poor old Fritz must be wondering what has come over us all . . . It is very exciting, and also very interesting, especially when you know you are giving more than you are receiving. As soon as our artillery starts at night after the first few shells, you see the red and green lights go up from Fritz, and then there is some fun. That is a signal for their guns to start.

The night before last we were watching the effect of our guns; then they sent their lights up, and the first two shells they sent over burst right over our heads. We were standing just outside our dugout, and there was such a rush to get inside that everyone got jammed in the doorway, and nobody got inside. You talk about a laugh, it was a scream. One chap was lying on his back, and about four or five on top of him. No one was hurt, luckily, I am glad to say.[31]

On 4 July Pte Frank Taylor of Northampton Town was killed. Taylor was also a useful cricketer, playing for Finedon Cricket Club during the summer months. Fellow Northampton Town player, Pte George Whitworth, wrote home that at the time of his team-mate's death the air 'was like red-hot iron and the sky was lit up by bursting shells'.[32] Also among the casualties during this spell in the trenches was Pte Alexander Stewart. The former Watford captain, who had been one of the first professionals to enlist in the 17th Middlesex, was badly wounded in the back and legs.[33]

Out of the line time was still found to play football. Faced with a lack of competitive fixtures, the 17th Middlesex had decided to set up their own miniature football league consisting of five teams, one from each of the four companies, and a team made up of officers and NCOs.[34] A request was sent to the Footballers' Battalion Comfort Fund for equipment. Within a matter of days Frederick Wall sent out 'two dozen footballs, 60 pairs of blue knickers, a dozen shirts in each of five colours, 60 pairs of stockings and 60 pairs of boots'.[35] Arrangements were immediately put in place for a continuous supply of kit to be sent out to France, but before long a letter from the Front was received at the FA offices in Russell Square. It instructed Wall to 'suspend all orders as we are likely to be in the thick of it again before many days are over'.[36]

131

For some time, the men of the 17th Middlesex had suspected that that their turn on the Somme was about to come. Letters home contained references about 'going to a famous place', or to going 'down South where all the fighting has been'. Morale was good, as 2/Lt Cosmo Clark recalled in a letter to his parents:

Everybody is in the best of spirits and I expect to the average onlooker it would seem we are off for a holiday instead of to a somewhat lively sector. The men are all keen on having a real good go at the Bosche. I heard a sergeant saying 'If only I can 'ave an 'and to 'and fight with one – to be able to say "Look 'ere chummy, it's either you or me – if I'm the better man you go under and if you're the better man I go under and good luck to us both" – WALLOP. The last remark was accentuated by fetching his fist very smartly against his other hand.[37]

The men's ardour was dampened somewhat by the journey southwards. Having left the billets in Houdain at 2 a.m. on 20 July, the 17th Middlesex marched 8 miles to the country town of Bruay, where the battalion boarded a train to Longeau, on the outskirts of Amiens. After a 6-hour journey they marched a further 15 miles to billets at Ville-sous-Corbie, arriving just after midnight. In a letter to his wife requesting two sets of clean underclothes, 2/Lt Ernest Parfitt asked her to send out some mouth organs: 'Also I want 4 mouth organs, the name of which is 'Up to Date' & in case you cannot get this particular brand, please get 4 of any one name, but must be vampers, Key G. Vamper means a mouth organ that one can vamp on. They are those with only one set of teeth.'[38]

On 23 July the 17th Middlesex arrived at the woodland camp in the Bois des Tailles, south of Méaulte. Water was a precious commodity in the chalk uplands of the Somme. One of the Reading men wrote home that: 'We are now under canvas just behind the lines, and water is very scarce. You would laugh to see the lads washing in cups of water. You ought to hear the guns. You would marvel how men could live through it all, but when they come out they are all smiles, and you would not think they had just come away from the jaws of death.[39]

1. Phosgene had first been used against British troops in December 1915.

2. As the war progressed, both sides would employ a wide range of toxic agents, including lachrymators (causing eye-watering), sternutators (causing sneezing) and vesicants (causing blisters). The infamous 'mustard gas', a particularly unpleasant vesicant, would make its appearance on the battlefield at Ypres in 1917.

3. McLaren, S. (ed.), 'Somewhere in Flanders'. A Norfolk Padre in the Great War: The War Letters of The Revd Samuel Frederick Leighton Green MC, Army Chaplain 1916–1919, p. 55.

4. BNL: Berkshire Chronicle, 18 August 1916.

5. Tull would not return to the 17th Middlesex. After recovering from shell shock, he was posted overseas to the 23rd Middlesex on 20 September 1916. Two months later, having impressed his superior officers, Tull was recommended for a commission, his application form being signed by Lt Col Alan Haig-Brown, who had played football as an amateur for Brighton & Hove Albion, Tottenham Hotspur and Clapton Orient. Returning to the 23rd Middlesex as a second lieutenant in the summer of 1917, Tull became one of the first black combat officers in the British army. Given the extreme prejudice faced by non-whites at that time, this achievement was truly a remarkable one.

6. Clark, C., The Tin Trunk, p. 57.

7. Edmonds, Sir J., Official History of the War, Military Operations: France and Belgium 1916, vol. 1, p. 225.

8. The three mine shafts used were: Z6 (14,150 lbs of ammonal and 1,200 lbs of guncotton), Z4 (20,000 lbs of ammonal) and E6 (13,000 lbs of ammonal and 1,200 lbs of guncotton).

9. New Cut had been blown by the Germans on 26 April 1916. The huge Broadbridge Crater, situated 100yd or so to the north of New Cut, had resulted from the British firing a camouflet three days later, which had in turn set off the original German charge. By way of retaliation, the Germans had then blown Mildren Crater between Broadbridge and New Cut.

10. TNA: WO 95/1354.

11. Clark, C., The Tin Trunk, p. 61.

12. Ammonal consisted of 65% ammonium nitrate, 15% TNT, 17% coarse aluminium and 3% charcoal.

13. TNA: WO 95 /1361.

14. Clark, C., The Tin Trunk, pp. 61–3.

15. TNA: WO 95 /1361.

16. Ibid.

17. Report by Maj Gen W.G. Walker in Wyrall, E., The History of the Second Division 1914–1918, p. 257.

18. De Ruvigny, Marquis, The Roll of Honour: A Biographical Record of Members of His Majesty's Naval and Military Forces who Fell in the Great War, vol. 2, part III, p. 172.

19. John William Williams was also known as James William Williams at various stages of his football career, but his name is registered as John William Williams on his birth certificate.

20. Crystal Palace won this match 4–1.

21. Shortly before proceeding to France on active service with the battalion, John Williams had guested for Clapton Orient in an away match against Crystal Palace in a London Combination match. Crystal Palace supporters were incensed by their former favourite playing for the opposition, and subsequently lodged a complaint that William had not received the necessary permission from his last club, Millwall, to play for the Os. Clapton Orient won the match 2–1, but were later fined a guinea.

22. Joe McLauchlan was evacuated back to England, where he was treated at Southampton Hospital. On the occasion of his marriage six months later, he was still recovering from his wounds at the Convalescent Camp, Shoreham.

23. While serving with the Durham Light Infantry, Jimmy Hugall was wounded in the legs and shoulder during the attack on Le Sars on 7 October 1916. Returning to the front in April 1917, Hugall was wounded in the face within a month and was then diagnosed as suffering from shell shock ('trembling, restless, irritable, exhaustion, headache'). Returning to England, he underwent treatment at Craiglockart War Hospital where Wilfred Owen and Siegfried Sassoon were also patients. Despite considerable pain in his shoulder, the Orient goalkeeper was able to resume his playing career, missing only seven matches of the 1919/20 season. His benefit match in 1920 against Spurs drew a crowd of over 10,000. In 1922 Hugall moved to Hamilton Academicals, later joining Durham City. He died in 1927 at the age of 38.

24. PC: Letter to Alice Parfitt, 27 June 1916.

25. *London Gazette*, Issue 29684, 25 July 1916.

26. *Ibid.*

27. *London Gazette*, Issue 29701, 8 August 1916.

28. Cpl Billy Baker and Pte Angus Seed were not awarded their medals at this muster roll, as both men were in hospital. Seed had been evacuated to England, where he was being treated at King George's Hospital in London.

29. BNL: *Croydon Advertiser*, 15 July 1916.

30. BNL: *Athletic News*, 3 July 1916.

31. BNL: *Croydon Advertiser*, 15 July 1916.

32. BNL: *Athletic News*, 10 July 1916.

33. On 27 July 1916 Chaplain Davis wrote from a hospital in France: 'I am pleased to be able to tell you that Stewart is getting on nicely and is ready to be sent down to the base by the next train. He is in excellent spirits and we shall be quite sorry to lose him from the ward. Always cheery and interesting to talk to.' Stewart was subsequently discharged from the Army, as a result of his wounds.

34. One team which played in an inter-company game around this time was: Pte Peter Roney (Bristol Rovers), goalkeeper; Pte Alf West (Notts County) and Pte Jack Doran (Coventry City), backs; Pte Frank Martin (Grimsby Town), Sgt Joe Mercer (Nottingham Forest) and Pte John Lamb (Sheffield Wednesday), halfbacks; Pte Tommy Barber (Aston Villa), Pte Tim Coleman (Nottingham Forest), L/Cpl Jack Cock (Huddersfield Town), Pte David Kenney (Grimsby Town) and Pte William Ripley (Stoke City), forwards.

35. BNL: *Athletic News*, 24 July 1916.

36. *Ibid.*

37. Clark, C., *The Tin Trunk*, p. 65.

38. PC: Letter to Alice Parfitt, 21 July 1916.

39. BNL: *Berkshire Chronicle*, 11 August 1916.

CHAPTER 7

THE DEVIL'S WOOD

By gum, I saw some sights there! I shall never forget them.
Sgt Ted Hanney F/1613 (Manchester City)

Then, as now, the partly-canalised River Somme meandered in a westerly direction, between Peronne and the city of Amiens with its magnificent Gothic cathedral, on its way to the English Channel, through a largely agricultural landscape dotted throughout with villages and woodland. Before the British arrival the previous summer, the Somme had been a largely quiet sector, which had enabled the Germans to construct a formidable First Position, supported by a Second Position some 2,000-4,000yd to the rear. Each position consisted of a succession of well-constructed lines of trenches, linked by communication trenches and protected by thick belts of barbed wire. Situated between the First and Second Positions there were several intermediate defences, strongly fortified woods and villages, all of which were likely to prove serious obstacles to any Allied advance. Around 3,000yd behind the Second Position, a Third Position was already in the early stages of construction by the spring of 1916.

It was Gen Joseph Joffre, the French Commander-in-Chief, who first suggested a Franco-British offensive on the Somme. On 30 December 1915 Joffre had written to Haig that 'I think that it will be a considerable advantage to attack the enemy on a front, where for long months the reciprocal activity of the troops opposed to each other has been less than elsewhere. The ground is, besides, in many places favourable to the development of a powerful offensive.'[1] The French commander neglected to give any details of exactly why the ground was favourable for such an offensive.

The Somme was selected primarily because it was the junction of the British and French armies on the Western Front. In view of the fact that the German defences on the Somme formed a pronounced bulge in the Allied lines, there was little chance that even a successful offensive could ever seriously threaten enemy lines of communication. Haig would rather have launched an attack in Flanders with the strategic objective of clearing the Channel coast but, charged by Kitchener to co-operate closely with the French, he acceded to Joffre's request.

In February 1916 Allied plans were thrown into disarray by the German offensive at Verdun. Increasing numbers of French troops were drawn into the fighting and it soon became clear that it would be the British playing the major role on the Somme. The final plan was that Fourth Army, under Gen Henry Rawlinson, and elements of Third Army, under Gen Edmund Allenby, would attack the German positions along a front of 16 miles between Gommecourt and Montauban after a lengthy preliminary bombardment. To the south, the French Sixth Army would attack in support on a front of 8 miles astride the banks of the River Somme. In the event of a breakthrough, Gen Hubert Gough's Reserve Army was waiting to push through the gap in the direction of Bapaume. The Fourth Army would then wheel northwards and roll up the German lines in the direction of Arras.

On 24 June the preliminary bombardment began. Over the next week British artillery fired over 1,500 000 shells into the German defences. The incessant deluge of shells raining down on enemy positions did much to inspire the watching British troops with confidence, but the impression of wholesale destruction was somewhat illusory, given the fact that many German soldiers were sheltering in deep dugouts, some of which were 30ft underground, immune to all but a direct hit from the heaviest shells. Furthermore, the density of artillery employed, one field gun to every 21yd of front and a heavy gun to every 57yd, was less that it had been in the first major attack of the war by the BEF at Neuve Chapelle in March 1915. The effectiveness of the bombardment was further undermined by the relative inexperience of many British gunners in the art of wire-cutting, and the fact that the direction of artillery fire and the assessment of its effect on the German defences were severely hampered by periods of bad weather.

Whatever the deficiencies of the preliminary bombardment, the German troops had still undergone a hellish ordeal at the hands of the British guns. Heavy casualties had been suffered and supplies of food and water severely disrupted. Numerous trenches and dugouts had been destroyed, but a significant number had survived intact and in several sectors the wire remained uncut.

Morale in the British trenches was high. Before the offensive, a company commander in the 8th East Surreys, Capt Wilfred 'Billie' Nevill, had bought two footballs for his men to dribble across No Man's Land. One football bore the words 'NO REFEREE'; the other was inscribed:

> The Great European Cup-Tie Final
> East Surreys v Bavarians
> Kick Off at Zero[2]

At 7.30 a.m. on 1 July the British artillery lifted and the first waves of British infantry clambered out of their trenches. Near Montauban, a private of the 8th Royal Sussex witnessed the launch of the 8th East Surreys' attack: 'As the gun-fire died away I saw an infantryman climb onto the parapet into No Man's Land, beckoning others to follow. As he did so he kicked off a football; a good kick, the ball rose and travelled well towards the German line. That seemed to be the signal to advance.'[3]

As soon as the alarm sounded, German soldiers raced up the steps of their dugouts to man their fire trenches and machine-gun posts. Artillery batteries, which had remained silent during the bombardment in order to avoid detection from the insufficient number of British guns engaged in counter-battery work, erupted into life and brought down a protective curtain of fire across No Man's Land.

Faced with massed ranks of infantry advancing across No Man's Land, German machine-guns were soon operating with deadly effect. Capt 'Billie' Nevill and many of his men were cut down. Up and down the front, with a few exceptions, similar scenes were replaying. By the end of the day the British had sustained 57,470 casualties, of whom 19,240 had been killed. Among the dead was Lt Evelyn Lintott, the first professional footballer to receive a commission. Only a few months before his death, when the battalion had been stationed in Egypt, Lintott had written home

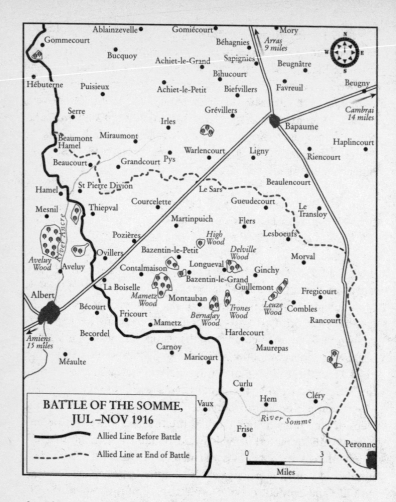

BATTLE OF THE SOMME, JUL –NOV 1916

———— Allied Line Before Battle

- - - - - Allied Line at End of Battle

that 'he was ashamed to put 'On Active Service' on the envelope as he had so little to do'. Lintott was killed at Serre while serving with the 15th West Yorkshires, better known as the 'Leeds Pals'.[4]

Between the villages of Serre in the north and Fricourt in the south, the attack had been bloodily repulsed. South of Fricourt, the British had enjoyed a considerable degree of success. The Fourth Army had advanced a mile into the German defences along a 3½ mile front. XV Corps had captured Mametz. XIII Corps, attacking alongside the French and supported by their artillery, had taken all its first day objectives, including the village of Montauban. To the right of XIII Corps, the French XX Corps, which had employed a concentration of heavy guns nearly four times greater than that of the British, had taken all its first day objectives.

Rawlinson proposed a renewal of the offensive in the north and centre where the attack had failed, but Haig was keen to exploit the first day's success in the southern sector of the battlefield so that the British could advance alongside the French Sixth Army. Accordingly, Rawlinson was urged to concentrate his efforts around Mametz Wood–Contalmaison, as a precursor to an attack on the German Second Position along the Longueval–Bazentin–le-Petit Ridge. Responsibility for operations north of the Albert-Bapaume Road was subsequently transferred to Gen Gough and the Reserve Army.

Over the next ten days the Fourth Army made a concerted effort to cover the flanks of the forthcoming assault on the German Second Position.[5] On 3 July Bernafay Wood was occupied at the cost of only six British casualties. On 7 July the bitter struggle for the possession of Mametz Wood started. The following day Trônes Wood was attacked for the first time. On 10 July 2/Lt Donald 'Donny' Bell, a professional footballer with Bradford Park Avenue, who was serving with the 9th Yorkshires, was killed near the village of Contalmaison. Bell was posthumously awarded the Victoria Cross for an act of bravery a few days before his death.

By 12 July the Fourth Army was finally in a position to launch an attack against the German Second Position, having sustained a further 25,000 casualties since the opening day of the offensive. Rawlinson had formulated an innovative plan for an attack on the German defences between Longueval and Bazentin-le-Petit, involving the assembly of the attacking battalions under the cover of darkness in No Man's Land, and a massive intensification of a three-day preliminary bombardment, 5 minutes before Zero Hour. At 3.25 a.m. on 14 July the assaulting troops advanced behind a 'creeping barrage', which moved forward in short lifts as the attack progressed, remaining about 50–100yd ahead of the infantry. The attack was remarkably successful, overrunning the front and support systems of the German Second Position on a front of 6,000yd. The villages of Bazentin-le-Petit and Bazentin-le-Grand were captured, but High Wood and the newly constructed

Switch Line remained in enemy hands and German troops still clung to the northern ruins of Longueval, a small village that lay to the immediate west of Delville Wood.

By now the chances of an Allied breakthrough in July had virtually disappeared. Within ten days of the opening of the Somme offensive, no less than 15 fresh German divisions had either already arrived on the Somme, or were in the process of doing so. Rawlinson turned his attention to the untaken objectives of 14 July. One of these objectives was Delville Wood, an area of woodland covering some 156 acres. 'The Devil's Wood, as it soon became known, consisted 'of a thick tangle of trees, chiefly oak and birch, with dense hazel thickets intersected by grassy rides'.[6] The South African Brigade, which was serving with the 9th Division, received orders to take it 'at all costs'.

On 15 July the South Africans attacked Delville Wood from its south-western corner. By early afternoon, they had captured virtually the entire wood, with the exception of its north-western corner. Three days of intense shelling and desperate fighting followed. On 18 July, after heavy preliminary shelling, the Germans made a concerted effort to recapture the wood. After a heroic defence in heavy rain, the dwindling number of South African troops was slowly pushed back. The Germans retook most of the wood and forced their way back into the northern half of Longueval.[7] Over the next few days the British made several attempts to capture Delville Wood and Longueval, but a series of under-resourced and poorly planned attacks failed to make much progress in the face of determined German resistance.

On 23 July, while Gough's Reserve Army were beginning a bitter struggle for the possession of the village of Pozières astride the Albert-Bapaume Road, Rawlinson's Fourth Army launched another large-scale dawn attack on the German defences between the Switch Line, west of High Wood and the village of Guillemont, south-east of Delville Wood. As part of this operation the 3rd Division attacked Delville Wood. Inadequate artillery support and haphazard planning severely undermined any prospect of success. Due to the late arrival of the final orders, the attacking battalions of the 3rd Division were not fully briefed until less than two hours before the attack was due to commence. Their officers were wholly unfamiliar with the ground, and matters were not helped by the fact that there was only one map of the operational area available.

Rawlinson immediately issued new orders for the capture of Delville Wood and the northern section of Longueval. A massive concentration of guns would be employed and a sufficient number of fresh troops would be made available. The 5th Division would attack Longueval and the western edge of Delville Wood. The 2nd Division, which had only just arrived from the First Army on Vimy Ridge to join XIII Corps of Fourth Army, was given the objective of capturing the greater part of the wood, attacking northwards from its southern edge. This part of the operation was to be carried out by the 99th Brigade.

On 25 July the 17th Middlesex left their woodland camp at Bois des Tailles, and moved up to the reserve line, through the ruined villages of Fricourt and Mametz.[i] On the way up to the front, the 17th Middlesex passed several batches of German prisoners being escorted back to the rear. It was clear from the demeanour of these men that they had endured hell on earth. Even though these individuals were enemy soldiers, the sight of such broken men aroused feelings of compassion. Second-Lieutenant Parfitt wrote home:

My word! Our guns are giving the Boche something. All day yesterday & all night long our guns were going as fast as they could be worked . . . One Boche prisoner was telling that they could not hope to last much longer, owing to the enormous number of casualties & also they are worn out. Poor devils . . . it makes one feel sorry for them. What they must have endured nobody knows except those concerned.[8]

[i]On 24 July, a match took place between 'B' Company and a team of NCOs. 'B' Company won 1–0. The respective teams were: 'B' COY: Pte Peter Roney (Bristol Rovers), goalkeeper; Pte Alf West (Notts County) and Pte Oscar Linkson (formerly of Manchester Utd), backs; Pte George Scott (Clapton Orient), Pte Joe Mercer (Nottingham Forest) and Pte Frank Martin (Grimsby Town), halfbacks; Pte David Kenney (Grimsby Town), Pte Jack Doran (Coventry City), Pte George Whitworth (Northampton Town), Pte David Chalmers (Grimsby Town) and Pte Tommy Barber (Aston Villa), forwards. NCOs: L/Cpl Humphreys (Sutton Town), goalkeeper; Cpl Lyndon Sandoe (Cardiff City) and L/Cpl Fred Bullock (Huddersfield Town), backs; Sgt Maurice Woodward (Southend Utd), Sgt James McCormick (Plymouth Argyle) and Sgt Joe Smith (Chesterfield Town), half-backs; Sgt George Welsh (Amateur), Sgt Ted Hanney (Manchester City), L/Cpl Jack Cock (Huddersfield Town), Sgt Norman Wood (Stockport County) and L/Cpl George Ford (Arsenal), forwards.

The 17th Middlesex, with a fighting strength of 38 officers and 872 men, occupied former German trenches astride the Montauban-Carnoy Road, relieving the 10th Royal Welch Fusiliers. The trenches were in a terrible state, having been badly battered by the British guns prior to capture:

The majority of the deep dug-outs had been blown in by our heavy shells. Bits of German equipment and bits of Germans were all over the place, the latter making a nuisance of themselves, even after death, by the stench. We found many clips of German cartridges with the bullets reversed, ample evidence to show that they are still as brutal as ever. Higher up, nearer to our present front line, there are literally hundreds of dead lying – German, Britishers and horses.[9]

It was now the turn of the German artillery to torment the occupants of these positions. One heavy shell landed in one section of trench occupied by the 17th Middlesex. Ptes William Freeman, Henry Oldroyd, Alfred Smith and William Welch were killed outright. Another four men were wounded. Later that evening the 1st King's Royal Rifle Corps and 23rd Royal Fusiliers of 99th Brigade moved into their assembly positions in readiness for the forthcoming assault on Delville Wood

At 6.10 a.m. on 27 July a massive barrage, provided by 369 guns, was unleashed on Delville Wood and Longueval, which resulted in the area being torn apart by some 125,000 shells. An hour later the 99th Brigade attacked Delville Wood from trenches just north of South Street. At the same time the 15th Brigade attempted to clear the northern part of Longueval. The principal German defenders of the Delville Wood were the Lieb Grenadier Regiment 8. This regiment belonged to the 5th Infantry Division from Brandenburg and had recently seen heavy fighting at Verdun. It was a highly regarded division, being described by Haig in his diary as 'the crack corps of Germany'.[10]

As the 1st King's Royal Rifle Corps and the 23rd Royal Fusiliers advanced into the smoking wood, it was immediately apparent that the British guns had done their work. The officer commanding 99th Brigade, Brig Gen Richard Kellett reported:

Our artillery was most effective. Hundreds of freshly killed Boches were met in the line of advance, and at least three Boche machine guns were destroyed, thus saving hundreds of our lives . . . Their shooting inspired our men with complete confidence, and though we apparently suffered a good many casualties from short shells (principally Heavies), the shooting of our guns was admirable and provided a curtain of fire close behind which our men moved with little loss, encountering men (Boche) out of whom the fight had been knocked by our shell-fire.[11]

Those German soldiers who were able to resist were shot down or bayoneted by the advancing waves of the 1st King's Royal Rifle Corps and the 23rd Royal Fusiliers. Behind these battalions came four companies of the 1st Royal Berkshires, which had been tasked with 'mopping-up' and consolidation duties, detachments of the 1st (East Anglian) Field Company, Royal Engineers, and the trench mortar and machine-gun sections. By 9 a.m. the attacking troops had reached their final objective, a line about 150yd inside the northern perimeter of the wood. As soon as the Germans realised that their troops had been evicted from the wood, heavy shellfire systematically began to sweep the wood and its southern approaches. The fact that Delville Wood formed such an advanced salient in the German lines meant that the shells were coming from three directions.

While countless shells exploded around them, the officers and men of 99th Brigade worked hard to consolidate their new positions before the inevitable counterattacks began. The consolidation process was rendered considerably more difficult by the matted tangle of tree roots that lay just beneath the surface, but a makeshift line of defence was gradually established 150yd inside the northern, north-eastern and eastern perimeters of the wood. To the west of Delville Wood the attack of the 15th Brigade had made initial progress, but was being held up in the ruins of Longueval around the crossroads in Duke Street.

By 9.30 a.m. large numbers of German troops were reported to be massing north and east of the wood. Half an hour later a heavy bombing attack was launched on the eastern fringe of Delville Wood against two companies of the 1st King's Royal Rifle Corps.

Further counterattacks developed from the north and north-east. Throughout the morning several bomb fights took place and there was much sniping from shell holes and the thickets of undergrowth. With casualties mounting, the 99th Brigade called for assistance.[12]

Col Henry Fenwick received the orders to move up to Delville Wood, shortly after 11'o'clock. The 17th Middlesex passed through Montauban, Bernafay Wood and Trônes Wood. Each man was carrying three grenades and two Very lights. Due to the continued scarcity of drinking water, several men were ordered to take up petrol tins of water. By 2.15 p.m. the 17th Middlesex had reached the Battalion HQ of the 17th Royal Fusiliers, situated in Longueval Alley. Behind the 17th Middlesex came the 2nd South Staffords and two companies of the 22nd Royal Fusiliers bearing tools and boxes of grenades and ammunition.

Progress was painfully slow on account of a heavy German artillery barrage designed to prevent reinforcements reaching Delville Wood. Prior to the Somme offensive, the German guns had carefully registered the probable routes of an advancing enemy in the event of the First Position being breached. Shells of all calibres fell on Delville Wood and its southern approaches. One shell landed on 2/Lt William Hendry's platoon with tragic consequences, as Pte George Whitworth, of Northampton Town, recalled: 'We were going up through the wood [either Delville Wood or Trônes Wood] when a shell came over and buried all my platoon, killing fourteen: but I got out of it and went on with shells dropping all around us.'[13] By 5.15 p.m., the first two companies of the 17th Middlesex had reached the Wood's southern perimeter. Fifteen minutes later a British aeroplane on a reconnaissance flight reported that Delville Wood appeared to have been totally destroyed by the British and German bombardments.

From 9:20 p.m. onwards, three companies of the 17th Middlesex undertook the relief of the three right companies of the 1st King's Royal Rifle Corps, who moved back to hold the line between Rotten Row and South Street. At 10.30 p.m. two platoons of the 17th Middlesex reinforced the left company of the 1st King's Royal Rifle Corps. There were now three and a half companies of the 17th Middlesex in Delville Wood, working hard to consolidate their positions. Along with one company of the 1st King's Royal Rifle Corps, the 17th Middlesex held a line facing north-east from Regent Street to a point just south of Princes Street. On their left, the 2nd South Staffords had relieved the 23rd Royal Fusiliers on the northern and western edges of the Wood. A major of the 23rd Royal Fusiliers described the conditions that evening: 'the scene . . . was awful, the wood being ablaze in many places. I read messages and wrote out the relief orders by the light of a blazing tree, which had fallen across the shell-hole then being occupied by Battalion headquarters.'[14]

The incoming soldiers of the 17th Middlesex and 2nd South Staffords were shocked by the scenes of utter devastation. After nearly two weeks of constant fighting, Delville Wood was now little more than a cratered tangle of blackened tree stumps, splintered branches and rusty barbed wire, interwoven with the debris of battle:

The horrors of that ghastly place were now everywhere evident. The fearful havoc created by our barrage of the early morning, when no less than 369 guns of all calibres had poured a continuous storm of shells upon the unfortunate enemy, had piled destruction upon destruction. Branches of trees had been flung about in all directions; the thick undergrowth of the wood was pitted with shell-holes into which the enemy had crept for shelter – the whole place was in a state of indescribable confusion – to the attackers it was almost like creeping through a jungle, not knowing where the enemy was lurking or at what minute he might be encountered. The dead were everywhere – equipment littered the ground; and above all, in the momentary pauses between shell-burst and another, the moans or agonised cries of the wounded, calling for water or assistance, lent a final touch to an altogether ghastly scene.[15]

By 11.30 p.m. on 27 July the 17th Middlesex had suffered in the region of 50 casualties. Two officers, 2/Lt John Guest and 2/Lt William Hendry, and 14 other ranks had been killed. Second-Lieutenant Guest had died of wounds in the regimental aid post of the 1st Royal Berkshires. He had been hit approaching an apparently unoccupied trench, which was found to be full of Germans. A bank clerk in civilian life, 2/Lt Guest had enlisted in the 16th Middlesex before being commissioned from the ranks. Before becoming an officer in the 17th Middlesex, 2/Lt William Hendry, a stockbroker's clerk, had been a pre-war territorial, proceeding to France with the 1/14th Londons in September 1914.[16]

Among the 14 other ranks killed was one of the battalion's first recruits, the bustling Clapton Orient forward Pte William Jonas, who had scored 23 goals in 74 appearances for the club. Originally a miner at Cambois Colliery, Jonas had started his career with local sides, Havannah Rovers, Washington Utd and Jarrow Croft FC, scoring two goals for the latter club in the Gateshead Charity Cup Final. Clapton Orient had signed him in 1912 on the recommendation of Company Serjeant Major Richard McFadden, a friend from childhood.

CSM McFadden was utterly devastated by his friend's death: 'Both Willie and I were trapped in a trench . . . Willie turned to me and said, "Goodbye Mac. Best of luck, special love to my sweetheart Mary Jane and best regards to the lads at Orient." Before I could reply to him he was up and over. No sooner had he jumped up out of the trench, my best friend of nearly twenty years was killed before my eyes.'[17] When the Orient goalkeeper Jimmy Hugall heard the news of his team-mate's death, he wrote to the club that 'I was also very grieved to hear of poor Billy Jonas' death. He was just the same old Billy out here as he was in the football field, and was liked by everybody. I think he had the heart of a lion and was the life and soul of the Footballers' Battalion. He was one of my best pals, and no one could have wished for a better chum.'[18]

William Jonas was also a popular figure with the Orient supporters, particularly with the ladies. At one stage he was reported as being the recipient of over 50 letters a week from female admirers. Although no doubt flattering, such attention could hardly have been welcome given that he had married his sweetheart Mary Jane some four years earlier. A 1914–15 club programme had taken pains to conclude an article about William Jonas with the following words: 'For the interest of the young ladies of Clapton Park, we have to state that Jonas is married to a very charming young lady.'[19]

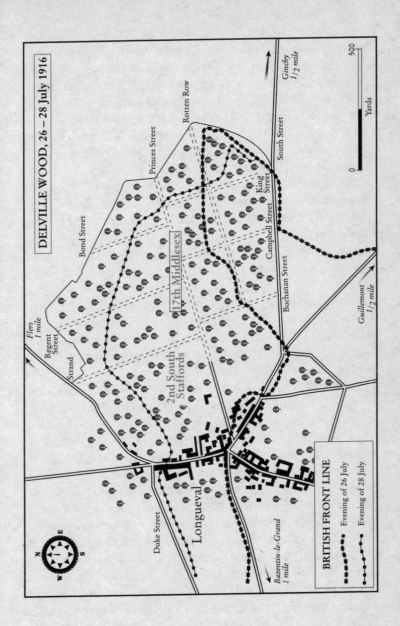

DELVILLE WOOD, 26 – 28 July 1916

Flers
1 mile

Regent
Street

Strand

Duke Street

Longueval

Bazentin-le-Grand
1 mile

2nd South
Staffords

17th Middlesex

Bond Street

Princes Street

Rotten Row

King
Street

Campbell Street

Buchanan Street

South Street

Gincby
1/2 mile

Guillemont
1/2 mile

500

0

Yards

BRITISH FRONT LINE
Evening of 26 July
Evening of 28 July

Early on the morning of 28 July all other British units apart from the 17th Middlesex and the 2nd South Staffords were withdrawn from Delville Wood in order to minimise casualties from shellfire. The exhausted men of the 1st King's Royal Rifle Corps went back to Montauban Alley. Their line, which consisted of little more than fragments of former German trenches and shell holes, was taken over by the 17th Middlesex. The 2nd South Staffords and the 17th Middlesex were now the sole defenders of the wood.[20] Shortly after 9 a.m. 6th Brigade HQ received a report from Col Fenwick that German troops were assembling east of the wood. British artillery was quickly brought to bear, but no attack materialised.

Throughout the day German artillery continued to pound Delville Wood, the accurate fire of a battery, situated near Ginchy, causing particular problems. The shallow trenches and bombing posts offered scant protection from the incessant artillery fire. Many men were buried in the ensuing explosions. Lt Arthur Elliott, who was commanding 'C' Company, was buried for 15 minutes before being dug out in a state of concussion. In the words of a fellow officer: 'He was absolutely a mad lunatic when he came back.'[21] Second-Lieutenant Roy Beaumont was unconscious by the time his men had managed to extricate him from the loose earth. He would not regain consciousness for another 6 hours.[22]

Other men were wounded by shrapnel and fragments of shell casing. Col Henry Fenwick was hit. Maj Frank Buckley was badly wounded in the shoulder and the lung. The second-in-command was clearly in a bad way. Pte George Pyke, of Newcastle Utd, recalled that it did not look like Maj Buckley would make it to the casualty clearing station. The former Portsmouth and Southampton player, Capt Edward Bell, assumed command of the battalion and ensured that the men held their positions in the face of severe pressure. Capt Bell would later be awarded a Military Cross for his 'conspicuous gallantry during operations' at Delville Wood.[23]

The strain of the constant bombardment was almost too much to bear, as the men huddled together in their trenches and shell holes. One soldier wrote resignedly that 'their big guns are awful, but still we stand them and wait for our turn to stop one'.[24] Several soldiers 'stopped one' that afternoon. From a Liverpool hospital a few months later, Pte Jack Borthwick, the Millwall player, would write to his manager, the former England outside-left, Bert Lipsham:

We were being very heavily shelled, dead and wounded all over the place, Germans as well as our own . . . our Captain came and gave orders for four men to take a wounded Captain [probably Acting Capt John Engleburtt] to the dressing station, and I was one to be chosen. There wasn't a whole stretcher in the place, and all the stretcher bearers were knocked out except one.

We were kept busy all the time bandaging the wounded, and if they were not able to walk to the dressing station, they had to be left until someone could take them out. We got two stout branches of a tree, put two waterproof sheets across them, placed the Captain on it, and then started off. The trenches were very badly knocked about and full of troops so we had to go over the top and what a journey.

We had to go three-quarters of a mile to the dressing station, and God knows how we got there with shells flying all around us, scrambling up and down shell holes and over broken tree trunks. I expected that we should all go up in the air any minute. However, we arrived all safe and I was thankful as I was well beat.

We had an hour's rest before starting off back again. Everything was going well until I stopped my packet. I never heard the shell coming but felt it as my neck was very near set in. The piece must have been rather large and I was afraid I should be under the turf with a little wooden cross on top. I managed to get back to our trench and the stretcher-bearer dressed the wound. I lay down in the side of the trench for nearly half an hour until the shelling quietened down.

Our Captain wanted to send four men to carry me out, but I didn't fancy it, so I told him I would rather walk across if he sent a man with me to see I didn't collapse. Jack Nuttall [his Millwall team mate] came with me and you ought to have seen us dashing across the wood. Donaldson couldn't have run faster [Jack Donaldson, legendary Australian sprinter of the early 20th century]. I remember getting to the dressing station but I must have lost consciousness as I don't remember seeing our Doctor [Lt Richard Felton] on the trip down the line. I was operated on next day, but I remember nothing about it. I was placed on the danger list and the missus had word to come, but I took a turn for the better. What a ward I was in, not one able to get up. We had six deaths in 24 hours and one fellow off his head.[25]

Earlier in the day several companies of Lieb Grenadier Regiment 8 and Grenadier Regiment 12 had been sent forward to reinforce the German line. The subsequent interrogation of a German prisoner revealed that a major counterattack was planned for the evening. At 9 p.m. the German bombardment suddenly intensified on the positions of the 17th Middlesex and the 2nd South Staffords. Entire sections of British trenches were obliterated. Half an hour later the Germans launched a series of attacks against the 2nd South Staffords and 17th Middlesex, consisting primarily of bombing parties supported by snipers.

The 17th Middlesex were ready for them. Pte George Whitworth recalled that: '. . . the Germans attacked us, and what a reception they got. They didn't get twenty yards before they turned and ran away'.[26] Pte Allen Foster wrote to his wife: 'We made old Fritz hop about a bit. They were running about like lost sheep, but we were popping away at him like blazes. I don't think he expected us to be quite so near him, but we were, of course. We had to pay for getting so near but as luck would have it I managed to get back without a scratch.'[27]

The confused nature of the fighting in the descending darkness meant that men had little idea of what was occurring barely a few yards away. In places small parties of Germans managed to slip between the 17th Middlesex posts. Having taken over command of 'D' Company after Capt John Engleburtt had been shot in the head and seriously wounded, Capt Ivan Horniman recalled that: 'The enemy obtained a momentary footing on the left of my Coy front (D) but were dislodged after hand-to-hand fighting: the field of fire was very poor owing to trees and branches felled by artillery fire. The enemy made numerous counterattacks'.[28]

Sgt Ted Hanney was hit in the face and neck by shrapnel later that evening, but he decided to remain with the battalion rather than leave the trenches: 'I was hit on the night of the 28th of July about 10.30pm, but did not leave the trenches until the next morning about 8.30. The Germans counterattacked that night three times, and as I felt quite all right I stopped and gave them a few extra rounds of ammunition . . . By gum, I saw some sights there! I shall never forget them.'[29]

By midnight the 17th Middlesex had lost 38 men killed and in excess of 150 wounded. Sgt Percy Barnfather reckoned that the majority of these casualties were caused by shellfire. One of the footballers killed was Sgt Norman Wood, the Stockport County inside-left. Born in Streatham, the 26-year-old Norman Wood, with his 'brushed dark hair and deft touches of the ball with the side of the foot', had been associated with a number of football clubs, including Tottenham Hotspur, Crystal Palace, Plymouth Argyle, Croydon Common, Chelsea, and Stalybridge Celtic: 'His type of play was unselfish, for with a crafty left foot he made openings and opportunities for colleagues. Unquestionably he was a fine initiator, but did not make the mark that he should have done.'[30]

Norman Wood had taken some time to settle down at Stockport County. On 4 October 1913, in only his sixth game for the club, he had scored an own goal, conceded a penalty and missed a penalty at the other end. Wood had gone on to make 37 appearances for Stockport County that season, scoring 10 goals. During the 1914/15 season, he had scored 2 goals in 21 appearances for the club. Also among the dead was Cpl Thomas Heller from Birkenhead. He had been the goalkeeper of the Preston Marathon rink hockey team, which had won the World Championship at Putney. Another soldier killed was Pte Henry Woolger, a barber from Fulham, who was shot dead by a sniper.[31]

On 29 July the 17th Middlesex witnessed another day of 'terrific artillery fire', but no infantry attacks materialised.[32] It would appear that the battalion escaped the worst of the shelling, as the casualties appear to have been remarkably light. Only four soldiers of the 17th Middlesex died on this date, and only two of these men, Sgt Charles Elliott and Pte James Flanagan, are listed as killed in action. The other two, Pte Cecil Selley, who had previously worked for the famous piano manufacturer, Messrs J. Broadwood & Sons in Conduit Street, London, and 19-year-old Pte Charles Wilson, are listed as dying of wounds, quite possibly sustained in the fighting of the previous day.[33]

That same day the 5th Division launched another attack on the northern part of Longueval, the 12th Gloucesters and the 1st East

Surreys finally clearing the village and the strongpoints in the orchards north of Longueval. At 9 p.m. the 13th Essex relieved the 17th Middlesex and the exhausted men stumbled back to the support line in Montauban Alley. The 17th Middlesex War Diary recorded that: 'All ranks behaved with great gallantry. The devotion to duty was magnificent. The Division has been thanked by GHQ for capturing the wood.'[34]

Since entering Delville Wood on the evening of 27 July, the 17th Middlesex had lost one officer killed, 2/Lt John Guest, and a further eight wounded: Col Henry Fenwick, Maj Frank Buckley, Capt Edward Bell, Lt Arthur Elliott (shell shock), Lt George Robertson, Lt Roy Beaumont (shell shock), 2/Lt John Engleburtt and Lt Richard Felton, the RMO. The Battalion War Diary recorded the casualties of the other ranks as 35 killed and 192 wounded.[35] The 2nd South Staffords had incurred a similar number of casualties in holding their section of the line.

Such was the intensity of the fighting in and around Delville Wood during the summer of 1916 that only 13 men of the 17th Middlesex, who died during this period, have known graves. Twelve of these graves can be found in Delville Wood Cemetery, which was created after the Armistice. Designed by Sir Herbert Baker, the cemetery contains 5,523 graves, including those of 19-year-old Pte Abraham Marks, the eldest son of Mark and Rachel Marks of Somers Town, London, and L/Cpl Thomas Collett, a coal porter from Gillingham, with three young children. Others no doubt lie in the same cemetery as unidentified burials beneath headstones bearing inscriptions such as 'An Unknown Soldier of the Middlesex Regiment' or as 'A Soldier of the Great War, Known unto God'. The remainder still lie beneath the trees of Delville Wood.

In the preliminary pages of the battalion history of the 23rd Royal Fusiliers, there appears a poem by 'Touchstone' of the *Daily Mail*, which was composed in honour of that battalion's exploits on 27 July. The 23rd Royal Fusiliers lost a great many men in the process of capturing Delville Wood, including the famous boxer Pte Jeremiah 'Jerry' Delaney. Given that the 23rd Royal Fusiliers was a battalion comprised of fellow sportsmen, one might say that this poem is equally appropriate to the memory of those officers and men of the 17th Middlesex, who lost their lives in the vicinity of the 'Devil's Wood' during the summer of 1916:

SPORTSMEN of every kind,
God! we have paid the score
Who left green English fields behind
For the sweat and stink of war!
New to the soldier's trade,
Into the scrum we came,
But we didn't care much what game we played
So long as we played the game.

We learned in a hell-fire school
Ere many a month was gone,
But we knew beforehand the golden rule,
"Stick it, and carry on!"
And we were a cheery crew,
Wherever you find the rest,
Who did what an Englishman can do,
And did it as well as the best.

Aye, and the game was good,
A game for a man to play,
Though there's many that lie in Delville Wood
Waiting the Judgment Day.
But living and dead are made
One till the final call,
When we meet once more on the Last Parade,
Soldiers and Sportsmen all![36]

1. Edmonds, J., *Official History of the War, Military Operations: France and Belgium 1916*, vol. 1, p. 27.
2. Although the 8th East Surrey War Diary states that 'B' Company 'took four footballs out with them which they were seen to dribble forward into the smoke of our intense bombardment on the Hun front line', no more than two footballs were, in fact, used. See further: TNA WO 95/2050 and Harris, R., *Billie: The Nevill Letters 1914-1916*, pp. 195-197.
3. Middlebrook, M., *The First Day on the Somme*, p. 124.
4. There had been much speculation that Lintott, a former chairman of the Players' Union, was to be transferred to the 17th Middlesex in January 1915, but the move never materialised. A schoolmaster by profession, Lintott had played for Plymouth Argyle, Queen's Park Rangers, Bradford City and Leeds City during the course of his career, gaining seven full and five amateur England caps.
5. Bell had been an assistant master at Starbeck Council School near Harrogate, where he

had supplemented his income by playing professional football for Bradford Park Avenue. He had made his Football League debut against Wolverhampton Wanderers at Molineux on 13 April 1913, having previously played amateur football with Crystal Palace, Newcastle Utd and Bishop Auckland.

6. These rides were named after streets in London and Edinburgh.

7. The South Africans had gone into Delville Wood with a fighting strength of 121 officers and 3,032 men. When the brigade was relieved a few days later, there were only 29 officers and 751 other ranks left.

8. PC: Letter to Alice Parfitt, 24 July 1916.

9. Clark, C., *The Tin Trunk*, p. 68.

10. Haig, D. (eds Sheffield, G. and Bourne, J.), *Douglas Haig: War Diaries and Letters 1914–1918*, p. 210.

11. Report by Brig Gen R.O. Kellett (99th Infantry Brigade) in Wyrall, E., *The History of the Second Division*, p. 280.

12. Total casualties of the 99th Brigade on 27 July 1916 were 45 officers and 1,119 other ranks.

13. BNL: *Sporting Chronicle*, 9 August 1916.

14. Ward, F. *The 23rd (S) Battalion Royal Fusiliers (First Sportsman's): A Record of Its Services in the Great War 1914–1919*, p. 88.

15. Wyrall, E. *The 17th (S) Battalion Royal Fusiliers 1914–1919* , pp. 37–8.

16. On 31 October 1914 at Messines the 1/14th Londons (London Scottish) had become the first territorial infantry battalion to see action against the Germans

17. BNL: *Oriental Notes*, 18 November 1916.

18. *Ibid.*, 2 September 1916.

19. *Ibid.*, 5 September 1914.

20. The 17th Middlesex War Diary is of little assistance in piecing together the events of 28 July. The entry for this date states only that: 'At 12 p.m. the enemy counter-attacked but we beat them off with great loss to him & held our line & consolidated'. Interestingly, there is no reference to such an attack in any other source. During periods of action it was not unusual for a unit war diary to be written up several days later and it may be that the diarist inadvertently confused 'p.m.' with 'a.m.'. Even if the Germans did attack the 17th Middlesex at noon on 28 July, it is quite clear that the War Diary omitted to mention much of what happened that day.

21. Clark, C., *The Tin Trunk*, p. 68.

22. Both men were severely traumatised by their experiences in Delville Wood. On 31 August 1917 a medical board concluded that Lt Arthur Elliott was 'pale looking, below weight, breaks down into tears readily under any slight occasion'. On 14 July 1919, a medical board found that 2/Lt Roy Beaumont still suffered: 'Insomnia. Sleep disturbed by nightmares . . . Frequently very depressed and irritable. Lack of energy and easily fatigued. Frontal headaches after concentrating for long. Nervous in traffic . . .'

23. 'For conspicuous gallantry during operations. Finding himself in command of the battalion he repelled a counter-attack with great determination. On another occasion he rescued several men from a blown-in dugout.' *London Gazette*, Issue 29793, 20 October 1916.

24. BNL: *Sporting Chronicle*, 9 August 1916.

25. BNL: *Athletic News*, 16 October 1916.

26. BNL: *Sporting Chronicle*, 9 August 1916.

27. BNL: *Berkshire Chronicle*, 18 August 1916.

28. PC: Annotation made by Capt L.I. Horniman in the margin of his copy of Wyrall, E., *The History of the Second Division 1914–1919*.

29. BNL: *Berkshire Chronicle*, 18 August 1916.

30. BNL: *Athletic News*, 4 September 1916.

31. Pte Henry Woolger F/482 had enlisted on 30 January 1915.

32. TNA: WO 95/1361.

33. Pte Cecil Selley F/1590 had enlisted on 30 May 1915.

34. TNA: WO 95/1361.

35. The 2nd Division War Diary records that the casualties of the other ranks were 46 killed, 216 wounded and 18 missing between the dates of 27 July and 2 August 1916. Further investigation reveals that the deaths of 67 officers and men occurred during this period.

36. Ward, F., *The 23rd (S) Battalion Royal Fusiliers*, p. 3.

CHAPTER 8

GUILLEMONT

This is worse than a whole season of cup ties
Pte Jack Borthwick F/14 (Millwall)

On 30 July, 'after a very trying time in Delville Wood', the 17th Middlesex moved back to Montauban Alley in support.[1] It was a difficult time for the survivors, many of whom had witnessed first hand the death and mutilation of comrades. Several men relived their recent experiences and wondered how they had managed to come through the fighting unscathed. Recommended for a Military Cross on account of his bravery in Delville Wood, 2/Lt Ernest Parfitt wrote to his wife:

We went into action on Friday morning & succeeded in taking a wood which is nic-named [sic] Devil's Wood & I can assure you the name is very appropriate. We held the wood until yesterday (Monday) morning, when we were relieved & if you read last Saturday's papers you will agree with me that I am certainly being guarded by a higher power. I felt it myself. I had no fear & was out in the wood on many occasions when my orderlies had turned back. Don't think that I <u>tried</u> to run risks because I didn't but just carried out my duties, as you would expect of your husband.[2]

On 1 August the 17th Middlesex were heavily shelled. Four men were killed and another fourteen were wounded. The next day the 17th Middlesex were relieved by the 1st King's Royal Rifle Corps and marched back to Breslau Trench, north-east of Carnoy, for a brief period of recuperation. Forty-seven reinforcements had been advised, but they had yet to appear. Recognising that his battalions were utterly worn out, Brig Gen Arthur Daly, the officer commanding 6th Brigade, sought to bring this fact to the attention of 2nd Division HQ. He set out his views in a report, pointing out that the brigade had lost 32 officers and 905 other ranks killed, wounded and missing during recent operations:

I hope that no misinterpretation will be placed on this report. I merely wish to bring existing facts to notice. The fighting spirit of the Brigade is entirely undiminished, but numbers are greatly reduced and, of course, the heat and general conditions cause a good deal of physical exhaustion. All ranks are determined that any attack they are called on to undertake shall be a success if such is humanly possible. I merely wish . . . to point out that an attack undertaken now is, with all the will in the world, a different proposition to what it would have been a week ago with Battalions all intact. The physical strain of the last 6 days holding Delville Wood has been very great, and there is no use in blinking one's eyes to the fact.[3]

His words fell on deaf ears. The 6th Brigade would be in action again within a few days. Haig had instructed Rawlinson to capture Guillemont, Falfemont Farm and Ginchy as soon as possible, in order to assist the French advance on the right of Fourth Army.

Previous attempts to take Guillemont on 23 July and 30 July had ended in failure. Situated about a mile south-east of Longueval, the fortified village had originally formed part of the German Second Position. Approximately halfway along the road connecting the two villages lay the ruins of Waterlot Farm, a sugar refinery before the war. On the eastern side of the road, about halfway between Waterlot Farm and Guillemont, was a house, which the Germans had converted into a formidable defensive position, known as Machine Gun House to the British soldiers. German defences were also strong in the vicinity of the railway station and the quarry to the north-west, and west of Guillemont. To the south-west of the village, the ground was open and its approaches were heavily wired and entrenched. Guillemont itself was honeycombed with deep dugouts and a warren of subterranean tunnels. On 2 August XIII Corps HQ issued orders for another attack. The capture of the village was to be undertaken by the 2nd Division and the 55th Division. Originally scheduled for the 4th, Zero Hour was eventually set for 4.20 a.m. on 8 August.

The infantry attack was to be preceded by a 17-hour bombardment to carry out wire-cutting and to destroy the German defences. In many respects the artillery fire plan was little different from those employed during the earlier attacks on Guillemont. Fifteen minutes before the start of the infantry assault, XIII Corps artillery would lift from the German front line to a line running through the centre of Guillemont. A further two artillery lifts, over the next 20 minutes, would move the barrage through to the eastern perimeter of the village. A standing barrage would then be placed on the slopes between Ginchy and Guillemont, and in front of Leuze Wood, some 1,300yd east of Guillemont. Divisional artillery would lift from the German front line at Zero Hour, moving through the village in a series of five lifts at 10-minute intervals to its eastern edge. In order to minimise enfilade fire, artillery barrages would be maintained on both flanks of the attack.

Three battalions of the 55th Division – the 1/8th King's Liverpool, 1/4th King's Own Yorkshire Light Infantry and 1/5th King's Liverpool – would attack Guillemont from the west and south-west. The 2nd Division was given the task of dealing with the German defences between Waterlot Farm and the northern edge of the village. Its attack was to be carried out by two battalions of 6th Brigade. The 1st King's Liverpool would capture the railway station, Brompton Road, High Holborn and Machine Gun House, while the 17th Middlesex were to take the northern half of ZZ trench, and the section of trench running south-west from ZZ Trench to Machine Gun House.

The 2nd South Staffords were to be held in support, occupying trenches in Trônes Wood and Bernafay Wood. 'A' Company of the 2nd South Staffords was placed at the disposal of the 1st King's Liverpool and 'B' Company at that of the 17th Middlesex. The 13th Essex would be held in brigade reserve in Mine Alley. Nos 2 and 3 Sections of the 5th Field Company, Royal Engineers, were to be attached to the 17th Middlesex and the 1st King's Liverpool respectively. One company of the divisional pioneers, the 10th Duke of Cornwall's Light Infantry, would be allotted to each attacking battalion to assist with the consolidation of the German positions once they had been captured.

During the evening of 5 August the 17th Middlesex relieved the

13th Essex in the trenches around Waterlot Farm, now little more than a mound of bricks, a few hundred yards south-east of Delville Wood. Following the wounding of Maj Frank Buckley, Maj William 'Harry' Carter had been posted as the new second-in-command of the 17th Middlesex. Given that Col Fenwick had remained with the out-of-battle cadre, Maj Carter was now in temporary command of the battalion. The son of a gas tube maker from Wolverhampton, Carter had enlisted as a private in the 2nd South Staffords in 1899 and had seen action during the Boer War. Still only a signal sergeant at the outbreak of war, he had been commissioned in the field in January 1915. An outstanding leader of men, Carter was an officer who led from the front, his fearlessness in action having already resulted in the award of a Military Cross.

On 6 August the 17th Middlesex were subjected to heavy shelling throughout a fine hot day. Seven other ranks were killed, including Pte Franz Hemberger from Marylebone, and Pte Eli Wardley, a resident of Tunstall in Suffolk. At 9 a.m. on 7 August the heavy artillery of XIII Corps opened up on Guillemont and the German positions east of Waterlot Farm. Forty 18-pounders and twelve 4.5in howitzers of the divisional artillery were also in action throughout the day, firing three rounds and two rounds per minute respectively. Incorporated within the bombardment were several so-called 'Chinese attacks', whereby there would be a momentary lull in the barrage in an attempt to fool the Germans that the attack was about to commence. At that time, the village of Guillemont and its defences to the north were defended by Infantry Regiment 124 and Grenadier Regiment 123 respectively. Both units formed part of the 27th Infantry Division, which had taken over the defence of the vital Ginchy-Guillemont-Maurepas sector a week earlier, having recently arrived from the Ypres Salient. The 27th Infantry Division was a formidable opponent, and was rated as one of the best German divisions by the Allies.

In accordance with the fire plan, the British bombardment ceased at nine o'clock that evening. Patrols were immediately sent out to ascertain the state of the German defences. These patrols reported back that the line was held in strength, and that the trenches appeared to be practically undamaged by the bombardment. At midnight the British resumed their pounding of the German positions. Another patrol, consisting of L/Cpl James Connolly, Pte Tommy Barber and Pte David Kenney, went out to inspect the German defences at the northern end of ZZ Trench. An hour later they returned to report that 'the ground between trenches was cut up with plenty of shell holes. They have a little wire out but of no danger to troops going across . . . No sign of Germans moving about in trench'.[4]

The 17th Middlesex spent an uncomfortable night in the trenches around Waterlot Farm waiting for Zero Hour. The morning of 8 August was very misty and the atmosphere was thick with smoke and dust. An easterly wind swept the dust thrown up by the British bombardment across No Man's Land into the faces of the attacking troops. These conditions would negate many of the visual signalling measures, such as mirrors, lamps and ground flares, which had been employed to ensure that communications would not break down. British aircraft, which were detailed to monitor the progress of the attack, would later report that they were unable to distinguish much of what followed.

At 4 a.m. Capt William Salter, CSM Arthur Cater and the four platoons of 'B' Company left their jumping-off trenches near Waterlot Farm and fanned out across No Man's Land in anticipation of the barrage lift at 4.20 a.m. Nos. 5 and 6 platoons were to attack the left section of ZZ Trench, while Nos. 7 and 8 platoons were to attack the right section. They were supported on the flanks by bombing parties from 'A' and 'C' Companies. The men formed up behind a low ridge in the middle of No Man's Land. Capt Salter was carrying a rifle and bayonet, rather than a revolver, in order to make himself less conspicuous to German marksmen looking to pick off British officers. Positioning himself in the centre between Nos. 6 and 7 platoons, Capt Salter took out his pocket watch and waited for the barrage to lift. The second line of the assaulting party took their places in the trenches. In accordance with orders issued before the attack, one man per section carried wire cutters and a pair of hedging gloves. Each man taking part in the assault had also been instructed to carry a water bottle of cold tea without sugar and milk. In addition to their iron ration, each man was ordered to carry two extra biscuits and, if possible, two slabs of chocolate.

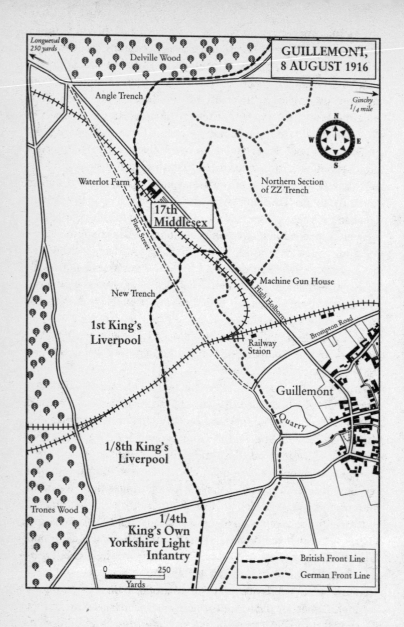

GUILLEMONT,
8 AUGUST 1916

Longueval
250 yards

Delville Wood

Angle Trench

Ginchy
1/4 mile

N
W E
S

Waterlot Farm

Northern Section
of ZZ Trench

17th
Middlesex

Fleet Street

Machine Gun House

New Trench

High Holborn

1st King's
Liverpool

Brompton Road

Railway
Staion

Guillemont

1/8th King's
Liverpool

Quarry

Trones Wood

1/4th
King's Own
Yorkshire Light
Infantry

0   250
Yards

British Front Line
German Front Line

On this occasion, there was to be no period of intense artillery fire just before the barrage lift to warn the Germans that an attack was imminent. As the British guns lifted to the first barrage line, ten Stokes mortars opened rapid fire on ZZ Trench and the strongpoints in front of Machine Gun House. Simultaneously, Capt Salter and 'B' Company prepared to surmount the low ridge into a maelstrom of fire. The fact that the attack on Guillemont was an isolated operation meant that German artillery could bring every gun in the sector to bear. Within seconds, a mass of shells came crashing down, turning No Man's Land into what 2/Lt Cosmo Clark recalled as 'a perfect blaze of heavy shellfire'.[5] The deadly German barrage accounted for several men during the initial moments of the attack. Pte Ronald Jeffery recalled that:

I was about the third man from the right of No. 8 platoon. I was looking towards Capt Salter for the signal to advance. As we got up, a whizz-bang caught him and CSM Cater, who was with him. I saw them both fall . . . I was hit in the head by shrapnel four or five minutes afterwards, and at the dressing station I was told that both Capt Salter and CSM Cater had been killed.[6]

In the region of 300 officers and men of the 17th Middlesex dashed through the smoke towards ZZ Trench. Second-Lieutenant Clark was caught in the back of the thigh by a piece of shell: 'I'd got about halfway across when I got winged and I managed to keep on with the men for a little while before it gave out.'[7] Pte George Cave witnessed the death of 2/Lt Edward Cocks: 'He was leading his men in the charge when a shell caught him, and blew him up. It was a clean hit'.[8]

Four minutes after the barrage lifted, a green Very light lit up the sky, having apparently been fired from the German lines in the direction of Waterlot Farm. This was the pre-arranged signal that the 17th Middlesex were in ZZ Trench. It was immediately followed by several similar lights spiralling into the sky. Maj Carter decided to wait for confirmation by runner before issuing further orders. In the absence of further news, he sent another platoon to reinforce the assaulting party via the German sap leading to the northern end of ZZ Trench.

Large sections of the wire remained uncut. As small groups of 17th Middlesex searched for gaps they came under accurate machine-gun fire, which cut several men down. Sgt George Brown saw 2/Lt William Henderson 'leading the company forward under heavy machine-gun fire. He waved the men to go on and was hit on the edge of the German trench and fell forward into it'.[9] Some men found gaps in the wire and jumped down into ZZ Trench, but their numbers were too few to capture and hold the position. Their task was made more difficult by the fact that only one Lewis Gun had made it across No Man's Land.

At 5 a.m. a runner reported that the assaulting party had been bombed out of ZZ Trench by the junction of the sap leading to Machine Gun House. Maj Carter immediately dispatched 6 bombers and 13 bayonet men from 'A' Company to push up this sap to reinforce the men in ZZ Trench, but the party came under fire as it neared Machine Gun House. A Lewis gun team was sent up in support, but by 6.10 a.m. it was being held up by enemy bombers. A few minutes later the party came under heavy machine-gun fire and withdrew.

At 7.15 a.m. Maj Carter received the unwelcome news that all 17th Middlesex who had managed to enter ZZ Trench had been killed, wounded or captured. He immediately sent a patrol up the German sap leading to the northern end of ZZ Trench in order to verify this information. His worst fears were soon confirmed. ZZ Trench was held in strength by the Germans. This information was duly relayed back to 6th Brigade HQ. At 9.45 a.m. Brig Gen Daly telephoned 2nd Division HQ with the news that all 17th Middlesex in ZZ Trench had been killed or captured. This was not quite true. One man, L/Cpl Thomas Pearson, of Clapton Orient, had managed to get back to the British lines. His report to Maj Carter made it abundantly clear that the attack of the 1st King's Liverpool to the south was not proceeding to plan either.

At 10.30 a.m. a message was received from 6th Brigade HQ that the 17th Middlesex should endeavour to link up with the 1st King's Liverpool to the south. Such were the conditions around Guillemont that it had taken 1 hour 40 minutes for this message to reach the front line from Bernafay Wood. Earlier that morning a bombing party under 2/Lt Fred Nunn had made its way down the German front line trench to a point north-west of Guillemont railway station, seeking to link up with the 1st King's Liverpool. Orders were issued for 2/Lt Nunn to push on further. The party almost reached the railway line, but there was still no sign of the Liverpool men.

Further south, the 1st King's Liverpool had met with disaster. At 5.20 a.m. a carrier pigeon had appeared at 6th Brigade HQ with a message from Lt Col Charles Goff, the young commanding officer of the 1st King's Liverpool: 'First – ['First' was the codeword signifying capture of the German front line trench] we have taken front line and station and I think High Holborn. Everything is rather mixed. Machine-guns are firing at us from Guillemont and from our left. I am at present in German front line and am going forward to clear up situation.'[10]

The problems faced by 'B', 'C' and 'D' Companies of the 1st King's Liverpool had been compounded by the fact that touch had been lost with the 1/8th King's Liverpool on the right. The Germans had managed to push reinforcements through the gap, enabling the front line to be reoccupied. When 'A' Company of the 1st King's Liverpool, which had been tasked with mopping-up duties, advanced across No Man's Land, it was met with a shower of grenades and rifle fire. The survivors of the other three companies of the 1st King's Liverpool had been left stranded around the station and the northern part of the village, where they had been swiftly surrounded by German reinforcements.

To the south of 6th Brigade, the attack of the 55th Division had also failed. The 1/8th King's Liverpool had doggedly fought their way into Guillemont either side of the quarry, but there they had been left similarly isolated once the Germans had reoccupied their front line. At the south-western corner of Guillemont, the advance of the 1/4th King's Own Yorkshire Light Infantry had been checked by uncut wire. Near Maltz Horn Farm, the 1/5th King's Liverpool had made some progress along Cochrane Alley, but their attack had stalled in the face of fierce German resistance.

At 3 p.m. orders were received at 6th Brigade HQ to mount another attack after dark in order to attain the objectives of the morning. The 17th Middlesex were called upon to organise an attack on Machine Gun House, with the intention of isolating it from the German defences, but the operation was postponed. The rest of the afternoon passed quietly. As darkness fell, search parties went out into No Man's Land to collect the wounded. Everywhere had been badly knocked about by the German artillery and the front line and communication trenches were littered with dead and wounded. The 17th Middlesex War Diary recorded the losses of the day's fighting as follows: 'Capt Salter, 2/Lt Cocks, and 2/Lt Henderson are missing. 2/Lt Clark and 2/Lt Banks are wounded. 29 killed, 9 died of wounds, 115 wounded and 45 missing were our casualties'.[11] The brunt of the losses had been borne by 'B' Company, which had emerged from the fighting only ten men strong, under the command of L/Cpl Thomas Pearson.

The three missing officers were subsequently confirmed killed. Recently awarded a Military Cross for his actions at Football Crater, Capt William Salter had been commissioned from the ranks of the 2/5th Londons in August 1915. Salter had a link with football in that his brother, Alfred, had once played in a friendly for Norwich City and had also represented Norfolk County. Second-Lieutenant Edward Cocks was a resident of Bath, where he had worked as draper's assistant. Described as 'very Scotch' by a fellow officer, 2/Lt William Henderson was formerly a valuation assistant with the Inland Revenue. He had only joined the battalion three months earlier, having seen earlier service with the 7th Cameron Highlanders.

Among the 51 other ranks of the 17th Middlesex who lost their lives on 8 August were several footballers. The legs of former Aston Villa inside-forward Pte William Gerrish had been shattered when a shell exploded nearby. He 'lay quietly smoking a cigarette, until picked up by the stretcher bearers'.[12] He died soon after. Maj Frank Buckley would later describe him as' a splendid soldier, most willing and brave'. After joining Bristol Rovers in 1905, Willie Gerrish had made 49 Southern League appearances for the club, scoring 11 goals. Four years later he had moved to Aston Villa, scoring 18 goals in 59 matches, and winning a Football League Championship medal. In 1912 he had signed for Preston North End, but had soon fallen out with the club's directors. Within a matter of months, Gerrish had moved to Chesterfield Town, breaking a leg on his debut for the club. In a letter describing his friend's death, Pte Peter Roney of Bristol Rovers alluded to an unusual incident, which had occurred the previous year. Accounts of this episode subsequently featured in several newspapers:

Definite news was received in Bristol last week of the death in action of Willie Gerrish, the well known forward of Bristol Rovers, Aston Villa and Preston North End. Gerrish was one of the first to enlist into the Footballers' Battalion. An interesting war happening concerning Gerrish has now seen light for the first time. In Feb 1915, he was in hospital for a slight operation when he heard that a patient was sinking from the loss of blood. Gerrish offered to have some of his own pumped into the patient who was ever after grateful for the extension of his own life by about a year.[13]

The former Manchester Utd right-back, Pte Oscar Linkson, who had incurred the wrath of the authorities when absenting himself to play for Queen's Park Rangers earlier in the year, was also among the dead. Initially reported as missing, no trace of him was ever found. Linkson had played for Barnet Alston FC, the works team of a local dental manufacturing company, and Pirates FC before signing for Manchester Utd in 1908. After making 55 appearances for the club, Linkson had moved to Shelbourne FC in August 1913. His mother would never accept that her son was dead, choosing instead to believe that he had run away to escape what she believed to be an unhappy marriage. Pte Linkson left behind a widow and two young children at the family home in Barnet.

Another casualty was the Reading player Pte Allen Foster. He had been caught in the arm, leg and abdomen by a burst of machine-gun fire. Although quickly evacuated from the front line, Foster subsequently died of his wounds. Originally from Rawmarsh, near Rotherham, the stocky forward had played for local side Parkgate Athletic, while working at a colliery in the fitter's room. At the age of 18 Foster was signed by Rotherham Town, moving to Bristol City in 1909. His career had stalled in the West Country and Foster had managed only 13 appearances for the first team. Nonetheless, his performances for the reserves in the Great Western Suburban League were sufficiently impressive to persuade Harry Matthews, the Reading club secretary, to part with the sum of £75 to secure his services in August 1911.

At Elm Park, Allen Foster's career had flourished. His excellent vision and his ability to link 'his wings together by discreet distribution' won many admirers.[14] Despite being predominantly left-footed, Foster became the recognised pivot of the Reading attack. Over the next four seasons he appeared in 146 Southern League matches and scored 68 goals for the club. One goal in particular, against the mighty Aston Villa in an FA Cup tie, had made him a legend among the Reading supporters. On learning of the centre-forward's death, Harry Matthews said: 'He was liked by all, and he has done a very great deal for our club . . . Of all the players, I devoutly hoped that he might be spared to come back and be with us all again. I am hoping when the better days come that the club can do something in appreciation of his good deeds.'[15]

Also among the dead was professional cricketer L/Cpl James Connolly, who had gone out on a patrol with Pte Tommy Barber and Pte David Kenney the previous evening. Six weeks after his death his parents in Oxford would receive official notification that their late son had been awarded the Military Medal. Also among the dead were Pte George May, a docker from Dartford, and Pte George Hendriks, of Dutch descent, who had been born on the Monte Rosa Rubber Plantation in Malaya.

Two sets of brothers serving in the 17th Middlesex had also suffered at Guillemont. The three Potter brothers had enlisted together at Deptford on 6 February 1915. Now the eldest of the three, L/Cpl William Potter, a widower with three children, was dead, and his brothers, Ernest and Walter, had been wounded. Pte Sidney Jerram had lost his elder brother Herbert. Few of the 17th Middlesex men who died on 8 August have a marked grave. The greatest concentration of 17th Middlesex graves is to be found in Delville Wood Cemetery. Eleven men, including L/Cpl James Connolly, are buried here. As in the fighting at Delville Wood, the vast majority of 17th Middlesex who fell at Guillemont have no known grave and are commemorated on the Thiepval Memorial.

Not all the missing of 8 August were dead. Several 17th Middlesex had been captured in ZZ Trench. Generalleutnant Otto von Moser, the commander of the 27th Infantry Division, recorded his impressions of some British prisoners in his diary entry for 8 August. The majority of these men would have been from the 1st King's Liverpool and 1/8th King's Liverpool, but there were probably a few 17th Middlesex among them.

At 6.00 a.m. a report arrives. 'Large scale British attack for the past hour!' Into the car and race towards Sailly! There I receive some happy news: Regiments 123 and 124 have beaten off the attack, which was directed mainly towards Guillemont. There, in the grey dawn, numerous dense waves of attackers were bloodily repulsed after bitter hand to hand fighting. Already the great courtyard of the farmhouse adjoining Divisional Headquarters is full of prisoners, including several officers. The British soldiery are a real mish mash: some of them have the faces of low criminals, obviously the scum of the population. Others both young and old, look to be far more agreeable types.[16]

One soldier, who fell into enemy hands on 8 August was the Plymouth Argyle player Sgt James McCormick of 'C' Company. He was lucky to be alive, having been badly wounded in the head by a piece of shrapnel: 'Half of my forehead was blown away and my nose was split in two parts'.[17] Temporaily blinded by a flap of skin hanging over his eyes and the blood streaming down his face, Sgt McCormick had been determined to get back to the British lines. Hearing the groans of a soldier with shattered legs lying nearby, he attempted to carry the man on his back, following the wounded man's directions. Unfortunately, the pair lost their bearings and ended up in a German trench where they were taken prisoner. Such was Sgt McCormick's fury at being captured that the Plymouth Argyle player flung the wounded man to the ground. Another footballer captured by the Germans was the Clapton Orient player Pte George Scott, who had been badly wounded. Within a few days Pte Scott would succumb to his injuries.[18]

Born in West Stanley, George Scott had started his football career in the Sunderland District Amateur Leagues, where he played for Braeside FC and Sunderland West End FC. Signed by Clapton Orient as a general utility player in 1908, Scott had soon proved himself to be a very capable centre-half, also featuring as an inside-left and outside-left for the club. Over the next seven seasons, Scott made 205 league appearances and scored 33 league goals for the Os. On learning of his death, one newspaper said of him that he 'would tackle a steam engine if he saw a goal in prospect. With such a disposition it is small wonder that he has fallen in the great fight'.[19] As Scott was reported missing, his family and friends would face an agonising wait for news. A couple of months would elapse before C.W.H. Deane, the club secretary, received official confirmation of his death: 'Big hearted and daring – as Scott always was, we can imagine the impetuosity with which he confronted the enemy. To those who knew him personally he was one of the best, and the thousands who have witnessed his football career will undoubtedly express feelings of sorrow at his untimely end.'[20]

During the evening of 8 August the preparations were made for another attack on Machine Gun House, involving 'C' and 'D' Companies of the 2nd South Staffords, which had been placed at the disposal of Maj Carter earlier in the day. At 2.30 a.m. the following morning a bombing party under Capt Walter Fluke of the 2nd South Staffords assembled at a sap-head about halfway between Waterlot Farm and Machine Gun House. Capt Fluke reported that:

I left our trenches with a party consisting of 19 Brigade bombers and 50 Bayonet men and carriers. We went forward in single file under heavy machine gun and artillery fire. The ground was very uneven and full of shell holes, and great difficulty was found in trying to keep the party closed up: this was all the more difficult since the men were dead tired and had been shelled heavily all day. On arriving at the trench I found that I had only three men with me, the others having lost a great deal of distance: we jumped into the trench and at first met with no resistance, the sentries appearing to be asleep leaning against the parapet. These numbering about a dozen we shot: they seemed quite dazed.

The trench was in the form of a horseshoe and we continued down one arm for some distance until a large party of the enemy came up bombing heavily. We had exhausted our small supply of bombs, but opened fire into their midst and retired slowly back to

Above: *A group of the 17th Middlesex with the battalion mascot.* (Courtesy of the Council of the National Army Museum, London)

Below: *Tim Coleman of Nottingham Forest and England. A consistent goalscorer throughout his career, Coleman 'was wonderfully popular wherever he went, for he was a born humorist and was the life and soul of every club he was travelling with'. His former clubs included Woolwich Arsenal, Everton, Sunderland and Fulham.* (Colorsport)

Below: *Fred Goodwin of Exeter City.* (Colorsport)

Above left: *Joe Orme of Millwall. One of several goalkeepers in the 17th Middlesex, Orme was sent off for fighting with fellow recruit William Jonas of Clapton Orient during an FA Cup tie in January 1915.* **(Dave Sullivan)**

Above right: *William Spittle of Arsenal. The inside-forward made his Football League debut against Manchester City in November 1912.* **(Colorsport)**

Below: *A group of the 17th Middlesex at Holmbury.* **(Rupert Casey)**

Above: *Jack Cock was playing for Huddersfield Town at the outbreak of the First World War. Described by one newspaper as 'a magnificent specimen of healthy manhood', Chelsea paid a transfer fee of £2,650 to secure his services after the war.* **(Dave Sullivan)**

Above right: *Cardiff City players, Fred Keenor and Lyndon Sandoe, lived on the same street in Cardiff. Sandoe was awarded the Distinguished Conduct Medal & Bar and the Military Medal during the course of his war service.* **(Bern Stacey)**

Below: *Officers and men of the 17th Middlesex: Front row, from left: Pte Pat Gallacher (formerly of Tottenham Hotspur), Capt Edward Bell (formerly of Portsmouth and Southampton), Lt Vivian Woodward (Chelsea), Capt Frank Buckley (Bradford City), Pte Sid Wheelhouse (Grimsby Town), Pte Tommy Barber (Aston Villa), L/Cpl Fred Bullock (Huddersfield Town). Back row: Sgt Percy Barnfather (Croydon Common), Pte William Jones (Brighton & Hove Albion), Pte William Booth (Brighton & Hove Albion), Pte George Beech (Brighton & Hove Albion), Pte Tommy Lonsdale (Southend United), Sgt Joe Smith (Chesterfield), Sgt Yeoval, Pte Frank Martin (Grimsby Town), Pte Jack Sheldon (Liverpool).* **(Colorsport)**

Above left: *Reg 'Skilly' Williams, the legendary Watford goalkeeper. During the 1914/15 season the performances of Williams in the Watford goal helped the team to the Southern League Championship.* (Trefor Jones)

Above right: *Jackie Sheldon of Liverpool. The skilful outside-right was a key protagonist in the 'fixed' Good Friday match at Old Trafford in 1915.* (Colorsport)

Below: *William Joynson-Hicks (second row, far left) with a 17th Middlesex football team in 1915. Also in photograph, front row: Fred Parker, Richard McFadden (2nd from left). Middle row: Frank Buckley (2nd from left), Col Grantham (3rd from left). Back row: Edward Bell, James McCormick (2nd from left), Allen Foster (5th from left), Joe Mercer (7th from left).* (Courtesy of the Council of the National Army Museum, London)

Above: *The 17th Middlesex camp at Holmbury.* (**Julia Rhys**)

Below: *Pte Fred Holland is standing second from right in the back row. His friend, Pte Cyril Gooding, standing in the middle of the back row, was wounded at Delville Wood in July 1916, then captured on the Redan Ridge on 13 November 1916.* (**Rupert Casey**)

Above: *Field kitchen at Holmbury.* (Julia Rhys)

Below: *Field oven at Holmbury.* (Julia Rhys)

Above left: *James McCormick as a Sheffield United player. At the outbreak of war McCormick was playing for Plymouth Argyle.* **(Patrick McCormick)**

Above right: *Pte William Reed of Brighton & Hove Albion, in uniform.* **(Bill Reed)**

Below: *A group of the 17th Middlesex at Holmbury. James McCormick is nearest the camera with his legs crossed and a pipe in his mouth.* **(Patrick McCormick)**

Above: *The barber's tent at Holmbury.* (Julia Rhys)

Below: *The 17th Middlesex on a route march near Clipstone Camp.* (Julia Rhys)

the bend where we found another strong party coming up the other arm of the trench and gradually closing in on us. We continued firing at them and they bombed us very heavily and we were forced to retire back to our trenches.[21]

On the return of this party to the British trenches, Maj Harry Carter ordered Capt Fluke to reorganise and prepare for a second attack. An artillery barrage was requested on Machine Gun House and ZZ Trench, which was now reported to be full of Germans. Maj Carter also ordered 2 machine-guns, 2 Lewis guns and 60 rifles of the 17th Middlesex to open rapid fire on the German lines. As the barrage came crashing down, their concentrated fire cut down several enemy soldiers seeking to escape the deluge of shells.

While preparations were made for a fresh attempt on Machine Gun House, another attack was being mounted on Guillemont. At 4.20 a.m. the 13th Essex attacked Guillemont from west of the station, using the same jumping-off trenches that had been used the previous day by the 1st King's Liverpool, while three battalions of the 55th Division attacked to the south-west of the village. At 4.30 a.m. a bombing party of the 17th Middlesex, supported by Lewis guns, launched a diversionary raid on ZZ Trench in order to divert the enemy's attention from the area around Machine Gun House. Once Maj Carter thought that the attention of the enemy had been sufficiently diverted, he ordered Capt Fluke to try again, but the attempt was unsuccessful. At 5.45 a.m. Maj Carter decided to cancel a third attempt to secure Machine Gun House, as it was now being shelled by British heavy artillery and German shells were also falling short in the vicinity. To the south, the attack on Guillemont had once again broken down, in the face of unsuppressed machine-guns and uncut wire.

Later that morning Maj George Dawes of the 2nd South Staffords visited 17th Middlesex HQ to obtain from Maj Carter the full details of Captain Fluke's attempts to 'cut out' Machine Gun House. Maj Carter was nowhere to be seen:

I was told that he was 'over the top'. To get to him I had to cross our block, on the other side of which I found a small party digging out the trench, which was little more than a series of shell holes. Some yards further on I came upon a Sergeant and a man with satchel of bombs; in the next shell hole was Major Carter, making observations on the positions of the enemy posts, and arranging points round the shell hole for the guidance of the sentries of the bombing posts, which he, on his return, organised and pushed forward to the point reconnoitred. He signalled to me not to join him, and I waited with the bomber until he came back

This was not his first reconnaissance this morning, he had on a previous occasion encountered and shot a German [In Maj Carter's words: 'One of the enemy was creeping along the railway in a south westerly direction. This man I shot, but it was impossible to get at his body in daylight'] and been forced to return by the appearance of several others in an adjacent trench.[22]

Maj Carter would later be awarded the Distinguished Service Order for his leadership at Guillemont in August 1916: 'For conspicuous gallantry during operations. He commanded the battalion after his CO was wounded and displayed great skill and personal courage. He went about everywhere encouraging his men and making personal reconnaissances during three days of heavy fighting. He set a fine example to his command.'[23]

For the rest of the day the 17th Middlesex worked hard to repair the damaged trenches, while sentries reported on what was happening around Guillemont. At about 4 p.m. Maj Carter was informed that a group of British soldiers was beginning to surrender in the vicinity of the railway station:

I at once gave orders for as many Machine guns, Lewis guns and rifles to open rapid fire on the right and left . . . The 'Rally' was sounded on several whistles and the party surrendering turned around and acknowledged it. Immediately after the signal I personally saw the whole of the party put up their hands. They then commenced to move off . . . The next time they were seen they were 900 yards in the German system of trenches. As the escort passed an open space they were shot down by an officer of the 17th Middlesex. At this time 5 of the party made a rush . . . [back to the British lines]. The Germans opened fire with rifles and two of these were seen to fall. The remaining three went on and dropped into shell-holes . . . Shortly afterwards one man was seen to get into the British Trench. In my opinion 40% of the surrendering party could have got back had they rushed, but they seemed to have no leader.[24]

Maj Carter's appraisal of the situation was somewhat harsh. This party of men was probably from the 1st King's Liverpool and the 1/8th King's Liverpool. They had held out in the vicinity of the railway station since the previous morning, resisting numerous German attempts to evict them. By now they were out of grenades and ammunition and water was running low. It must also have obvious to these brave officers and men that there was no chance of relief, given the failure of the attack on Guillemont earlier that morning.

During the evening of 9 August the 17th Middlesex were relieved by the 1st Royal Fusiliers and marched to Breslau Trench before moving back to a camp in Happy Valley, a few miles behind the front line the next day. Lightly wounded at Delville Wood, Col Fenwick had remained with the 'left out of battle' cadre and the transport to await his battalion's return. He ensured that the survivors were given a rousing reception. Second-Lieutenant Parfitt recalled what was undoubtedly an emotional experience for all concerned: 'It was like coming back to civilisation to meet the other officers that had been left behind with the transport as reserves & to get something decent to eat & a clean change & a good sleep. My word! I felt awfully proud & not a little choked at the welcome we received by these officers & the men of the transport.'[25]

As soon as they were out of the line, many officers and men took the opportunity to write home. Second-Lieutenant Parfitt wrote to Alice, acknowledging safe receipt of the mouth organs that he had requested before entering Delville Wood:

We had some very hard fighting lately & unfortunately we have lost almost the whole of the regiment. We have made two attacks since coming out of the wood again. I must ask you to offer up a special prayer with me in thanking God for bringing me through & also instilling me with a sense of safety & that no amount of shelling ever upsets me.[26]

Many officers and men were at the limits of their endurance. Sgt Percy Barnfather recalled that he had hardly eaten for three or four days, and that all available drinking water had been contaminated by petrol. The Croydon Common player was recognised by some Royal Engineers from Croydon, who took him out for dinner. While his men were resting, Brig Gen Arthur Daly had other matters on his mind. A conscientious and professional officer, he was appalled by recent events. The haphazard and under-resourced attack of 9 August had particularly infuriated him: 'I consider that the attack of the 9th instant was most ill-advised and, except for a miracle, had no chance of success, whilst it was bound to cost the lives of many valuable officers, NCOs and men.'[27]

Like many other 'pals' battalions of Kitchener's armies, the 17th Middlesex had been well and truly 'blooded' on the Somme. The fighting at Delville Wood and Guillemont had cost the battalion dearly. The 2nd Division War Diary recorded that between the dates of 24 July and 11 August, 15 officers and 498 other ranks of the 17th Middlesex had become casualties. Over the next few weeks the families of these officers and men would receive notification from the War Office that their loved ones had been killed, wounded, or posted missing. Others received the news from unofficial sources. Mrs Foster, of 14 Kent Road, Reading, first received news of her husband's death in a letter from a nursing sister in France. Her husband had only been able to give the nurses his address before lapsing into unconsciousness. He had died barely an hour after his admission. In his last letter to his wife, Pte Allen Foster had written:

I often wonder how long it will be before we are back to the old times again. Sometimes, I think that it will not last long, and yet there does not seem to be any sign of it finishing yet; but of course, we can't tell, and we can only hope and trust that it will not be too long before it is over.[28]

Over the next few weeks newspapers carried numerous reports of footballers in the 17th Middlesex who had been wounded in the recent fighting around Delville Wood and Guillemont. Among their number were the young Cardiff City player, Pte Fred Keenor, who had been wounded in the knee, and the Brighton & Hove Albion outside-left, L/Cpl Alfred Tyler, who had had been badly wounded in the leg and shoulder.[29] Not all the wounds were physical. CSM Tommy Gibson was suffering from shell shock. The former captain of Nottingham Forest had been 'partially buried by a shell explosion, and when extricated appeared to be in a serious condition'.

The lightly wounded men, such as the Clapton Orient players Pte Joseph Raw and Sgt Bob Dalrymple, whose wounds were 'not good enough for a Blighty', were treated in France before returning to the battalion. The more seriously wounded soldiers, like Cpl Nolan Evans of Clapton Orient, 'invariably good-tempered and exceptionally witty', who had nearly lost his leg as a result of wounds sustained at Delville Wood, remained in France until it was considered safe to evacuate them.[30]

On arrival back in Blighty, the wounded officers and men of the 17th Middlesex were transported to hospitals up and down the country: Maj Frank Buckley became a patient of the Birmingham University Military Hospital; L/Cpl Fred Bullock, of Huddersfield Town, was treated at the 2nd Southern Hospital in Bristol; the Croydon Common player Pte Cyril Smith recovered from the effects of gas poisoning in a Liverpool hospital; Sgt Ted Hanney was a patient at the 5th General Hospital in Portsmouth; and the Aston Villa player Pte Tommy Barber underwent treatment for serious gunshot wounds in his leg at hospital in Aberdeen.

While recovering from their wounds, several footballers had to come to terms with the fact that that their playing careers were over, which must have been particularly difficult for those with wives and families to support. From Belmont Military Hospital in Liverpool Pte Jack Borthwick of Millwall outlined the extent of his injuries in a letter to Bert Lipsham:

> I am glad to say that my wound is going on all right, but I am afraid I am finished with football. I feel rather sorry as I am sure the army training had done me a lot of good. I was looking forward to coming home and making good. However, I must be thankful I am alive. My head has been trepanned, as the skull was knocked in. The cut extends from nearly the top of my head down to my eyebrow. It was a near thing of my losing my right eye. I left on 19 August [hospital

in Rouen] and had the good fortune to get to Liverpool. This is worse than a whole season of cup ties.[31]

The fighting around Guillemont, Waterlot Farm and Delville Wood would continue for the rest of the month. From a hospital near Étaples, 2/Lt Cosmo Clark wrote to his parents:

I think that these three places are the most terribly awful spots in the whole world. The sight one sees are like the most dreadful nightmares and life up there is a nightmare. Nothing but death. Nothing but death and horrors everywhere. At night when you're being shelled and you can hear the wounded fellows crying out where you can't get to them and when you do, you can't get them to the Aid Post because of the hellish fire. The stench is awful due to this boiling hot weather we've been having. Dead men, friend and foe, lie about in heaps often with their wild grinning faces turned to you, others sleeping peacefully. Perhaps I shouldn't have told you all this, but I expect now you understand why we all think that the life of an infantryman a hard one and why he thirsts to get away from it.[32]

Guillemont would survive another costly British attack on 18 August, before finally falling on 3 September. Only with the capture of Guillemont, was the British tenure of Delville Wood and Waterlot Farm rendered secure.

1. TNA: WO 95/1361.
2. PC: Letter to Alice Parfitt, 31 July 1916.
3. TNA: WO 95/1357.
4. TNA: WO 95/1357.
5. Clark, C., *The Tin Trunk*, p. 70.
6. TNA: WO 339/28928. Capt William Salter's date of death is recorded by the CWGC as 9 August 1916, but it is clear from the correspondence in his record of service that he was, in fact, killed the previous day.
7. Clark, C., *The Tin Trunk*, p. 70.
8. TNA: WO 339/61290.
9. TNA: WO 339/62497.
10. Wyrall, E. *The History of the King's Regiment (Liverpool) 1914–1919*, p. 305.
11. The 6th Brigade War Diary noted the casualties of the 17th Middlesex on 8 August as: officers, 2 wounded, and 3 missing; other ranks, 19 killed, 143 wounded, and 43 missing.
12. *Villa News and Record*, August 30–September 1 1919, p. 13.
13. BNL: *Athletic News*, 11 September 1916.
14. BNL: *Sporting Chronicle*, 16 August 1916.
15. BNL: *Berkshire Chronicle*, 8 August 1916.
16. Sheldon, J., *The German Army on the Somme 1914–1916*, p. 246.
17. PC: Papers relating to Sgt James McCormick.

18. The grave of Pte George Scott can be found today in St Souplet British Cemetery. Situated nearby is the grave of 2/Lt Will Lawrence, the younger brother of Lawrence of Arabia. An observer in the Royal Flying Corps, 2/Lt Lawrence was shot down on 23 October 1915.

19. BNL: *Athletic News*, 20 November 1916.

20. BNL: *Oriental Notes*, 18 November 1916.

21. TNA: WO 95/1362.

22. TNA: WO 95/1357.

23. *London Gazette*, Issue 29793, 20 October 1916.

24. TNA: WO 95/1361.

25. PC: Letter to Alice Parfitt, 15 August 1916.

26. PC: Letter to Alice Parfitt, 10 August 1916.

27. TNA: WO 95/1354.

28. BNL: *Berkshire Chronicle*, 18 August 1916.

29. On 16 October 1916 Fred Keenor had recovered sufficiently to play for Brentford, along with Alf Gregson, in a 3–0 defeat to Millwall.

30. BNL: *Oriental Notes*, 21 November 1914. Nolan Evans was named after his uncle, Capt Nolan Crawshaw, who had been reputedly one of the finest horsemen in the British army.

31. Borthwick was discharged on 12 April 1917 as being ' no longer physically fit for war service'.

32. Clark, C., The Tin Trunk, p. 72.

CHAPTER 9

AN AUTUMN
ON THE SOMME

*There are only myself and two others left of the battalion team
that won the Divisional Cup out here*
Pte Tommy Lonsdale F/906 (Southend Utd)

The 17th Middlesex were brought back up to strength over the
next few days. By 15 August a total of 716 reinforcements had
arrived. These men were from several battalions of the Middlesex
Regiment, including its sister battalions, the 23rd and 27th
Middlesex.[1] The majority of the newcomers were first-timers on
the Western Front, but there were a few experienced soldiers like
Sgt William Glenie, who had recovered from wounds sustained in
earlier fighting. Having been passed fit again for active service,
these men were posted to any battalion of their regiment in need of
reinforcements. Sgt Glenie had joined the Middlesex Regiment in
1904, serving in both the 1st and 2nd Battalions before transferring
to the Army Reserve in 1911 on completion of seven years' service.
After spending some time in Australia, where he had joined the
Legion of Frontiersmen,[2] Glenie had rejoined the 1st Middlesex on
the outbreak of war and had been badly gassed at Loos.

On 17 August, having been transferred to the Reserve Army, the
2nd Division began the relief of the Guards Division in the vicinity
of Hébuterne, a village some 9 miles north of Albert. The next day
the 17th Middlesex marched 18 miles from Vacquerie to Bois de
Warnicourt, where the men were billeted in an assortment of huts
and tents. On 22 August the 17th Middlesex relieved the 13th
Essex in the front line, east of La Signy Farm. The enemy was
quiet, but two men were killed over the next four days.[3] One of
the dead, Pte Frank Mason from Stockwell, was barely 17 years
old at the time of his death, having originally enlisted in the 16th
Middlesex on 12 July 1915. Two men were accidentally wounded

when Pte Biggs forgot to remove his bolt when cleaning his rifle. It is likely that CSM Richard McFadden, of Clapton Orient, was one of 18 men wounded during this spell in the front line:

> Your humble got two pieces in the head (Shrapnel) and one in the chin. I was sent out of the line suffering from shell shock, but did not know I was wounded in the head until I got to the dressing station. I only knew I was wounded in the chin, but am all right now and back at work . . . I was sleeping with my "batman" and the shell came through my dugout and killed him. It must have knocked me out, for when I came to I had my arm round him, and I was wounded as I have told you. So I must have been very lucky.[4]

Towards the end of August the weather deteriorated. Much time was spent revetting and repairing the trenches after prolonged spells of heavy rain. The 2nd Division was instructed to prepare for the resumption of offensive operations. Divisional artillery began to register targets in the German lines and started the task of cutting the wire. Working parties struggled up to the front line in cloying mud, bearing supplies of ammunition, duckboards and gas cylinders. On 30 August the 17th Middlesex relieved the 1st King's Liverpool in the front line at Serre for another four-day tour. The weather was still bad and the trenches were by now in an appalling state.

Even though the Allied attacks on the Somme had achieved their primary objective in that they had forced the Germans to halt their attacks at Verdun back in July, Haig was determined not to allow the German army a moment's respite. He ordered Rawlinson to draw up plans for a large attack involving the use of tanks for the first time in the history of warfare. On 15 September the Fourth Army attacked on a frontage of nearly 6 miles, supported by thirty-two tanks. Results were mixed. High Wood was finally cleared and the villages of Martinpuich, Courcelette and Flers were taken, but the attack failed to drive the intended wedge into the German defences between Morval and Gueudecourt. During the Battle of Flers–Courcelette, the Fourth Army sustained nearly 30,000 casualties, including the Prime Minister's son Raymond Asquith, who died near Guillemont. This battle was also the baptism of fire for the 23rd Middlesex, which had arrived on the Western Front in May 1916. In heavy fighting around Flers Wood the battalion lost nearly half its strength, including Lt Col William Ash, its commanding officer.

For the first half of September the 17th Middlesex had been rotated in and out of the front line around Serre. Out of the line, the men were engaged in training. Back in England, Maj Frank Buckley was doing his best to ensure that the exploits of the 17th Middlesex did not pass unnoticed. His arm and shoulder were healing well, but some shrapnel remained lodged in his lung. Doctors had advised him that he would have to 'go slow' for a few years. On 16 September Maj Buckley and his wife Madge attended Birmingham City's match against Sheffield Wednesday. A journalist recorded that:

> Major Buckley spoke with such sincerity of the part the Football Battalion had played in France that he was clearly proud of his regiment. The behaviour of the men of all ranks had been extremely good, and the valour and soldierly qualities proved. Those who doubted them at first were firm believers in the merit of the professional footballer. He admitted that he himself had been astounded. Men from Plymouth Argyle, Clapton Orient, Nottingham Forest and other clubs had particularly distinguished themselves. When volunteers were required for perilous undertakings the footballers were eager to join in, and in the mass they acquitted themselves as well as any men in the line. It was an honour to have been associated with them.[5]

On 17 September, the day on which Captain Thomas Rollason left the battalion with a bad case of trench fever, the 17th Middlesex were back in the front line, near Serre. The day had been spent repairing trenches in heavy rain. At 9.10 p.m. the Germans opened a violent *Minenwerfer* bombardment. Over the next 30 minutes an estimated 750 mortar shells fell between Grey Sap and Warloy Sap. Col Fenwick reported that at one stage 11 shells were counted in the air at the same time. An SOS signal was immediately sent to the divisional artillery requesting retaliatory fire, but the response was limited to around 80 shells, the artillery being under strict orders to stockpile shells for offensive operations. The 17th Middlesex had to sit it out as best they could. The front line 'was obliterated and a month's work rendered useless'.[6] Second-Lieutenant John Stagg and four other ranks were killed, including Cpl Samuel Smith from Burnley, an early enlistment in the battalion. Second-Lieutenant Robert Templeman, 2/Lt Gordon Fowler and 25 other ranks were wounded.

Born in 1878, 2/Lt John Stagg had been educated at Haileybury, and had become a successful journalist and novelist, writing several novels under the pseudonym 'John Barnett'. A keen sportsman, Stagg had excelled at golf and represented Kent at rugby. In October 1914 he had enlisted in the 16th Middlesex, before being recommended for a commission. His commanding officer had noted in his report that Stagg was 'a particularly good NCO, absolutely fearless under heavy fire. Specially recommended although somewhat over the age for candidates'.[7] This fearlessness under fire had already led to the award of a Distinguished Conduct Medal, when Stagg had carried a wounded man to safety under very heavy rifle fire.[8]

On 18 September it rained for most of the day. Men were detailed to work through the night in an effort to repair the damage sustained during the previous day's bombardment. At dusk, several working parties were still engaged on this task, when several *Minenwerfer* shells started to fall nearby. One working party took cover in the rear entrance to the Grey Sap, a mineshaft being prepared for detonation under the German lines. The timing was unfortunate. The Germans had detected British mining activity, and were preparing to detonate a charge of their own. Col Henry Fenwick recalled that:

A few minutes after the men took shelter, the enemy blew up a mine in the Grey Sap, and some of the mine gas was expelled through the rear entrance to the Sap; the men in the entrance . . . were overcome by the fumes and when eventually discovered and dragged out only one could be restored to life . . . The Tunnelling Officer, Captain Wood of the 252nd Tunnelling Company, who finally discovered the unfortunate men, being armed with a Box Respirator, was able to fetch them out; he displayed the greatest gallantry and was ably assisted by three of his own Engineers.[9]

Six men were already lifeless by the time their bodies were dragged out of Grey Sap. Contrary to Col Fenwick's report, two men were pulled out alive: L/Cpl Ernest Bowerman, a printer from Tottenham, and L/Cpl Sid Wheelhouse, the Grimsby Town captain. Both men subsequently died. At first, L/Cpl Sid Wheelhouse did not seem to have been badly hurt, managing to walk unaided down to the advanced dressing station, but the next day he was dead. His friend and team-mate Pte Frank Martin wrote to Mr Hickson, the Grimsby Town secretary: 'Sid Wheelhouse got gassed up the line on Sunday night (17th) and I am sorry to tell you he died in hospital on Monday. I was going to see his grave today, but I could not get away, but I am going to see it one day this week. I can tell you we all feel cut up about it.'[10]

A few days later, Pte Frank Martin was able to pay a visit to the grave. He was accompanied by Pte Tommy Lonsdale, who wrote home of the devastation wrought by the recent fighting on the battalion football team, and his sense of despair at the loss of a close friend:

Frankie and I walked over to the British cemetery today to see where he was buried . . . Almost opposite Sid's grave rests Captain Basil Hallam of 'Gilbert the Filbert' song fame. Sid has a cross up with his name and date of death, and we shall see that he has a wreath as soon as possible. We all feel his loss very much as he was a universal favourite with us all. There are only myself and two others left of the battalion team that won the Divisional Cup out here . . . .

I am not much in the mood for letter writing at present. I am a bit too much shaken up as yet to think and write as I should like. I don't seem able to realise yet that Sid has gone. We were, as you know, from the same town before we came away to pro football and had practically always been together.[11]

The death of L/Cpl Sid Wheelhouse caused much sorrow back in Grimsby, where a newspaper columnist commented that he was 'one of the most popular players who ever donned the Town's colours – perhaps the most popular with the supporters during the past few years'.[12] A skilful right-back, Wheelhouse was described as 'a fine man, clean living, high minded, chivalrous and a model professional'.[13] He had first played football as a boy for Bishop Auckland, helping them to win the Darlington and District League and Cup, before moving to Shildon Athletic at the age of 16. During the 1907/8 season he was signed by Grimsby Town and immediately placed in the first team. His qualities, both as a man and as a footballer, had made such a favourable impression on the club's directors that before long he was appointed club captain. Wheelhouse had gone on to make a total of 235 appearances for the club. At the time of his death, he was 28 years old and married with four children, the youngest of whom was only three months old.[14]

On 19 September divisional artillery and trench mortars carried out a heavy bombardment of the German front line in retaliation for recent enemy mortar activity. The following evening the 17th Middlesex were relieved in the front line by the 17th Sherwood Foresters of 39th Division. The battalion marched back to billets in Bus-les-Artois. For the rest of September the 17th Middlesex were engaged in musketry training and bomb throwing practice. Much work was also done with the Lewis gun teams. On one occasion the 17th Middlesex practised ground communication with aircraft in preparation for future offensive operations.

Following the attack at Flers on 15 September, Rawlinson's Fourth Army had continued with its attempts to batter a path through the German defences. The fortress villages of Morval and Lesboeufs were captured on the 25th. Gueudecourt had fallen the next day, and the Germans were forced to evacuate Combles. North of the Albert-Bapaume Road, Gough's Reserve Army were making a concerted effort to wrest the Thiepval Ridge from the Germans. The village of Thiepval, a first day objective of the Somme offensive, was finally captured on 27 September. Optimistic intelligence reports at GHQ suggested that German morale was ebbing away. Such a view was shared by Sgt Fred Parker, the Clapton Orient captain, who wrote to the club that: 'The saying with the Tommies is "Do you think we are winning, chum?" and the answer is "YES".'[15]

Even though winter was drawing near, Haig was determined to

land a decisive blow, believing that German reserves were almost expended. While it was true that the Germans had been badly mauled by the recent fighting, fresh troops and artillery were already beginning to replace the under-strength divisions holding the line between Le Transloy and the River Ancre. The key question was whether the British could move quickly enough to exploit this situation. On 29 September, 'the first wet day for some time', Haig instructed the commanders of the Third, Reserve and Fourth Armies to make preparations for a major attack by all British forces south of Gommecourt. A combination of the weather and stiffening German resistance would ensure that this ambitious plan would never come to fruition.

On 1 October Maj Harry Carter left the battalion to take over command of the 13th Essex. Until his replacement arrived, Capt Vivian Woodward, who had returned to the battalion on 18 August, temporarily assumed the role of second-in-command.[16] The 17th Middlesex spent the next few days unloading stores at Beaussart Station and providing working parties to carry up supplies, predominantly mortar shells, to the front line. Fifty men, under the command of 2/Lt Charles Koop, were sent to assist the 252nd Tunnelling Company, Royal Engineers. On 6 October Maj James Walsh reported for duty as the new second-in-command of the 17th Middlesex. Only commissioned in January 1916, Maj Walsh was a pre-war ranker who had served on the Western Front since the earliest days of the war. During the afternoon Col Henry Fenwick attended a meeting at 6th Brigade HQ at Bertrancourt to discuss the imminent Reserve Army attack astride the River Ancre, a small tributary of the Somme flowing across the northern part of the battlefield. The role of 2nd Division would be to secure the Redan Ridge, an area of high ground between Serre and Beaumont Hamel.

On 7 October the 17th Middlesex marched to Puchevillers, a village situated on the main road between Amiens and Thiévres, and a major railhead for the British. The billets were situated in an apple orchard and the huts were in a poor condition. Along with the rest of the 2nd Division, the 17th Middlesex underwent training for forthcoming operations. A small-scale model of the German positions on the Redan Ridge was constructed from aerial photographs and patrol reports, the enemy trenches being represented by lines of white tape and the advancing British barrage marked out by flags. Although tanks did not participate in the various exercises, there were plenty of rumours that they would be employed in the forthcoming attack.

Initially known as 'landships', these ungainly machines had been labelled tanks (as in 'water tanks') in order to conceal their development from the Germans. Rhomboidal in shape, the more heavily-armed 'male' Mk I tank weighed 28 tons and was armed with two 6-pounder naval guns and four machine-guns. With a crew of eight, a tank had a top speed of 3.7 miles per hour, which was significantly reduced over cratered ground. The 'female' Mk I tank differed in that its armament consisted solely of machine-guns. Following their deployment at Flers in September, press reports had made much of this new weapon's fighting capabilities, omitting to mention that they were vulnerable to enemy shellfire and prone to mechanical breakdown. The majority of British soldiers still had to see tanks in action, but many believed the stories that the tank was the weapon to win the war. Second-Lieutenant Ernest Parfitt outlined the apparent fighting abilities of this new weapon to his wife:

It is also rumoured that there will be another big advance in which the 'tanks' will be a big feature & will probably bring about the termination [of the war]. What wonderful things these tanks must be!! I read in a paper some days ago that they simply go over the Boche, smash everything that comes in their way such as trees, houses, barbed wire etc. & they cannot be hurt unless a large shell pitches directly on it, which would be rather hard to hit as the [tank] keeps on the move the whole of the time . . . These tanks are supposed to be wonderfull [sic] things & everyone is bursting with excitement to see what they can do'.[17]

Pte William Krug, the Chelsea reserve goalkeeper, was even more emphatic in his appraisal of the tank's capabilities. While attending Chelsea's 0–0 draw with Millwall during a period of leave, he reportedly told a club official that: 'I'm tickled to death with the antics of our tanks over there. They waddle about like ducks and spit death like a thousand vipers in a tin case. Fritz fears them as much as the devil fears holy water.'[18]

On 16 October the proposed attack of the 2nd Division on the Redan Ridge was rehearsed in full for the third time at Raincheval, with proceedings being watched by Gen Gough, the commander of the Reserve Army. Afterwards Maj Gen William Walker presented awards to officers and men of the 2nd Division for acts of bravery on the battlefield. Five NCOs of the 17th Middlesex received Military Medals from their divisional commander: CSM Lyndon Sandoe, Sgt Jack Gammon, Sgt Albert Drury, Cpl Frank Anderson and CSM Richard McFadden. The Clapton Orient inside-left had impressed everyone with his bravery. A newspaper commented of CSM McFadden that 'it has been said of him that when in action scarcely a day passed without this fine soldier-player going out into the shell-swept open to rescue a fallen chum'.[19] It was not the first occasion that the selfless bravery of CSM McFadden had been given official recognition:

McFadden has shown bravery as a civilian, and it is recalled that one Sunday a year or two ago he was walking along the banks of the River Lea when he saw two boys in danger of drowning. He at once jumped into the water and rescued both of them. Sometime later, while walking in Clapton Park, he heard screams from a house on fire. A mother was frantically crying that her child was in the building. McFadden, without hesitation, rescued the child, which must have been burnt to death but for the footballer's timely rescue. For these deeds McFadden was publicly presented with a gold medal.[20]

On 18 October the 17th Middlesex vacated their billets in Puchevillers and marched to Acheux Wood. Four days later the 17th Middlesex undertook the relief of the 1st Royal Berkshires in the front line, near Serre. It was a slow march on account of the congested tracks and the waterlogged state of the trenches. Accurate German artillery fire wreaked havoc. Two footballers were among the casualties. Sgt Billy Baker, the Plymouth Argyle left-half, was one of four men killed. Described as a 'pocket Hercules', Sgt Baker had languished in the Plymouth reserves for four seasons before breaking into the first team in 1909. A loyal servant of Plymouth Argyle, he had made a total of 193 appearances for the club in the Southern League.

CSM Richard McFadden was one of 19 other ranks wounded. His wounds were so severe that he died the following day. McFadden was one of the battalion's earliest recruits, having followed the example of his Clapton Orient club captain Fred Parker at Fulham Town Hall on 15 December 1914. Born in Cambuslang, Scotland, his family had subsequently moved to Blyth where he had befriended William Jonas. At the age of 12, McFadden had started work as a tub-boy at Ashington Colliery, playing for local youth sides Ashington Black Watch and Hirst St John. Before moving to Wallsend Park Villa for 'less than a £5 note', McFadden had played for several local sides, including Newburn (5s per week plus expenses) and Blyth Spartans (12s 6d per match). In May 1911 McFadden had joined Clapton Orient, for whom the slight inside-left would score 66 goals in 144 matches. A skilful player and a great passer of the ball, he had once been selected to play in a Southern XI team against England, scoring the only goal of the game. His platoon officer, Lt Ernest Parfitt, described the circumstances of his death in a letter to Alice:

He and I have been together in all the scraps that the Regt. has been engaged in, except Delville Wood when I was in charge of the signallers. I was also mainly responsible for getting him the Military Medal. And curiously enough I was with him when he got hit . . . I led the Coy in, with McFadden beside me. When we arrived in the trenches we met with a rather warm reception. He (Mac) and I were hustling the fellows into our particular part of the line when there was a huge gap in the ranks. I started to swear at the other fellows for hanging behind, and promptly went up to chase them down. I had hardly got 10 yds away from Mac, when one shell burst in the trench and caught Mac. I got him away with the help of some stretcher-bearers, and they told me there was every hope for him. Three days, later the RAMC sent word that he had gone under . . . Don't think I'm callous, but that's always the way, one gets so used to this and that. As regards writing [to] his wife, that has been done, and I can assure you, that if there's any possible way out of . . . writing [to] mothers and wives we take it. It's no pleasant task.[21]

His club captain, Sgt Fred Parker, was on leave in England and only found out about his friend's death on his return:

> The first thing I heard on getting back was that poor old Mac had died of wounds. It is a terrible blow to all the boys who are left. I could not believe it at first, but it is too true . . . Mac feared nothing. All the boys are going to visit his grave as soon as they get a chance . . . We have had a splendid cross made for him with a football at the top of it, but that will not bring him back. No one will miss him like I do out here. We were always together.[22]

CSM Richard McFadden was the third Clapton Orient player in the 17th Middlesex to lose his life. Within a few months the directors of the club would commemorate the sacrifice of their players by unveiling a polished oak shield at the club, bearing the names of CSM Richard McFadden, Pte William Jonas and Pte George Scott.[23]

On 26 October the 17th Middlesex were back in reserve in Mailly-Maillet after a relatively quiet couple of days in the front line. A large flight of German aeroplanes attacked the gun batteries engaged in wire cutting. British aircraft intervened, and the troops watched the ensuing dogfights from the trenches. Three British and two German aircraft were shot down. One of the enemy aircraft was brought down at the junction of Legend Trench and Sackville Street, near Serre. Second-Lieutenant John Howard noted laconically that the 'Pilot was badly wounded and the Observer was mixed up with the machinery. The enemy shelled this plane for a long time, but a few pieces of the Observer were recovered together with his map.'[24] Four days later the 17th Middlesex, with a fighting strength of 37 officers and 1,011 other ranks, marched back to Bertrancourt and took over huts in North Camp. The camp was in a shocking state; the recent heavy rainfall had turned it into a muddy quagmire.

The treacherous state of the ground was having serious repercussions for the British across large swathes of the Somme battlefield. Throughout October the repeated efforts of Fourth Army to force its way through to Le Transloy had increasingly foundered in the deep mud. North of the Albert–Bapaume Road the Reserve (soon to be renamed Fifth) Army had become similarly bogged down:

> By the middle of the October conditions on and behind the battle-front were so bad as to make mere existence a severe trial of body and spirit . . . The ground was so deep in mud that to move one 18-pdr. ten or twelve horses were often needed, and to supplement the supplies brought by light-railway and pack-horse, ammunition had to be dragged up on sledges improvised of sheets of corrugated iron. The infantry, sometimes wet to the skin and almost exhausted before Zero Hour, were often condemned to struggle painfully forward through the mud under heavy fire against objectives vaguely defined and difficult of recognition.[25]

Haig had been forced to abandon his scheme for a large-scale attack involving three armies, but had decided that Gough's Fifth Army should still proceed with its planned offensive astride the Ancre, supported by elements of the Fourth Army on its left. The Ancre attack had been scheduled originally for 23 October, but bad weather had once again intervened. On 27 October the provisional date for the Fifth Army offensive was rescheduled for 1 November.

Twenty-two millimetres of rain fell over the next three days. The date of the attack was put back to the 5th. Haig was becoming increasingly concerned about the viability of the attack given the state of the ground and the fact that more and more men were falling sick. On 3 November Gough was given permission to postpone the offensive indefinitely 'with the proviso that arrangements are made to bring on the attack without delay as soon as the weather shows some signs of improvement'.[26] Two days later Haig visited Fifth Army HQ to suggest an alternative operation astride the Ancre with limited objectives, namely the reduction of the German salient between Serre and the Albert–Bapaume Road. The attack was rescheduled for the 9th. That same day Captain Parfitt wrote to Alice: '. . . awful rain every day and night – but shush, it's a blessing in disguise!!! Can't explain but perhaps you can guess.'[27]

Twelve millimetres of rain fell the following day. The attack was postponed yet again, but the foul weather did not prevent a football match taking place in which the 17th Middlesex beat the 2nd South Staffords 5–0. Back in England, an extract of a 'characteristic letter' to Nottingham Forest from Pte Tim Coleman was published in *Athletic News*: 'Joe Mercer is just getting into form again, you know what that means. Look out for another Big Push.'[28] This made perfect sense to the newspaper's readers. Over 6ft tall and weighing some 13st, Joe Mercer, although a skilful player, had a reputation for his ability to 'mix it up'. When playing for a local team in Ellesmere Port, he had been watched by an Everton scout who reported back to Goodison Park that 'He's a good player all right, but he'd get us thrown out of the League'.[29]

On 7 November the 17th Middlesex relieved the 22nd Royal Fusiliers opposite the German positions on Redan Ridge. At Serre, and all along the Redan Ridge, the German front line was in the same position that it had been on the opening day of the Somme offensive. Following the disaster that had befallen the 31st and 4th Divisions in this sector on 1 July, the British had not renewed their assault here, attempting instead to exploit their success south of the Albert–Bapaume Road. For the last four months the Germans had continued to strengthen their already formidable defences and had multiplied the number of guns in this sector. The recent increase in activity behind the British lines had not passed unnoticed. Sensing that an attack was imminent, German artillery routinely destroyed whole sections of the British trench system.

During this spell in the front line the 17th Middlesex cleared 'jumping off' trenches, stockpiled grenades and dragged ladders and other equipment up through the mud. Even though the weather was at last beginning to improve, conditions in the front line remained appalling. The average depth of water in the trenches was reported to be above the knee. In places Capt Horniman recalled that the water reached 'the buttons of the breast tunic pockets' and that 'Floating trench boards made progress by wading very difficult'.[30] On 9 November the 17th Middlesex were relieved by the 1st King's Liverpool and returned to Bertrancourt where the battalion was notified that Zero Hour had been provisionally fixed for 5.45 a.m. on 13 November.

At 5 a.m. on 11 November, once the normal night firing

programme had finished, the British heavy guns began the preliminary bombardment of the German lines, building up to a crescendo at 6 a.m., when the field batteries joined in. The object of the British fire plan was to leave the German defenders unsure of the exact timing of the attack. After 15 minutes of intense shelling the British guns fell silent. Fearing an attack, German artillery immediately put down a heavy barrage on No Man's Land and the British front line. Once it became apparent that no attack was in progress, the German guns ceased fire. An hour later the British gunners resumed their usual daily firing programme, but foggy weather hindered the registration of targets.

On 12 November the British artillery, repeating the tactic of the previous day, were again successful in drawing German fire, which died down when no infantry attack materialised. The day was a clearer one, and the British guns were able to carry out their registration on the German defences more effectively. The results were encouraging. Maj Victor Walrond of the Royal Field Artillery wrote in his diary:

We did careful registration on to points on the Violet, Green, and Yellow Lines, which the 'show' has been cut down to, the Blue and Brown lines having been abandoned. Then later it came to registering the front line, which was no easy matter, especially as all the telephone wires were broken. Meanwhile a heavy bombardment was going on, and Serre was practically in flames, 12-inch, 15-inch, 9.2-inch, and 8-inch shells falling in torrents on to it. All the rear communications, O.P.'s [observation posts] etc, were being shelled to blazes by the big stuff, and in retaliation the Boche put up two quite good barrages on to the White City and the Redan Ridge.[31]

When making the final decision about whether the attack should proceed, Gough was in a difficult position. While expressing concern at the state of ground, Haig had continually stressed the advantages of a successful attack to the Fifth Army commander. Earlier that afternoon, Haig had paid a visit to Fifth Army HQ to discuss the final arrangements. The forthcoming conference of Allied commanders, which was due to take place at Chantilly on 15 November, was very much on Haig's mind:

I told him [Gough] that success at this time was much wanted – firstly, on account of the situation in Roumania, we must prevent the Enemy from withdrawing any divisions from France to that theatre. Next the feeling in Russia is not favourable either to the French or to ourselves. We are thought to be accomplishing little . . . Lastly on account of the Chantilly conference which meets on Wednesday. The British position will doubtless be much stronger (as memories are short!) if I could appear there on the top of the capture of Beaumont Hamel for instance, and 3000 German prisoners. It would show too that we had no intention of ceasing to press the Enemy on the Somme.[32]

There was no change to the timing of the attack as a result of this meeting. Haig left Fifth Army HQ sufficiently reassured that the attack had reasonable prospects of success. At nightfall, Zero Hour was confirmed for 5.45 a.m. the following day. The *History of the Second Division* records that this was 'news which gave the troops the greatest satisfaction'.[33] Such a sentiment was later dismissed by Capt Ivan Horniman, the officer commanding 'D' Company of the 17th Middlesex, as: 'Pure staff flap-doodle! No infantry soldier liked going over the top.'[34]

The attacking troops began to assemble in their positions during the evening. For the last few days patrols had reported that No Man's Land was in a treacherous state. The ground had been churned up by months of shelling and weeks of rain. The gaping shell holes and numerous mine craters filled with water made the ground impassable for the tanks, which had moved up from Beaussart Station on the evening of 11 November. Much to the disappointment of all ranks, the tanks were ordered to withdraw.

At 9.30 p.m. Gough conferred with his corps commanders to determine how the offensive would progress, if success were achieved the following morning. No firm decision was taken, but it was understood that a further advance towards Pys and Irles would be undertaken. By this time several of the attacking battalions had already begun their march up to the front line through thick fog, which was rapidly descending across the battlefield. On arrival at their assembly positions, the men prepared for an uncomfortable night exposed to the elements, waiting for Zero Hour. One of these battalions, shivering in the dense fog a few hundred yards south-east of Serre, was the 17th Middlesex.

1. These men came from the 1st, 2nd, 4th, 6th, 1/7th, 1/8th, 10th, 11th, 12th, 13th, 14th, 15th, 16th, 20th 21st, 23rd, 24th, 27th, and 28th Battalions of the Middlesex Regiment.
2. An organisation set up by the adventurer and author Roger Pocock in 1904.
3. The 17th Middlesex War Diary states that four men were killed, but this figure is not supported by CWGC records.
4. BNL: *Oriental Notes*, 2 September 1916.
5. BNL: *Sporting Chronicle*, 20 September 1916.
6. TNA: WO 95/1361.
7. TNA: WO 339/60533.
8. *London Gazette*, Issue 29631, 20 June 1916.
9. TNA: WO95/1355.
10. BNL: *Grimsby News*, 29 September 1916.
11. *Ibid.*
12. *Ibid.*
13. BNL: *Athletic News*, 2 October 1916.
14. On 8 October 1916 a memorial service would be held for Sid Wheelhouse at St Aidan's Church, New Cleethorpes.
15. BNL: *Oriental Notes*, 21 October 1916.
16. Within a couple of months, Woodward would leave the 17th Middlesex to become an army physical training instructor.
17. PC: Letter to Alice Parfitt, 10 October 1916.
18. BNL: *Chelsea FC Chronicle, 28 October 1916.*
19. BNL: *Athletic News*, 18 September 1916.
20. *Ibid.*
21. PC: Letter to Alice Parfitt, 5 November 1916.
22. BNL: *Oriental Notes*, 18 November 1916.
23. It was placed on the wall of the boardroom at Millfields Road, and was first displayed on the occasion of Clapton Orient's 3–4 defeat to West Ham on 24 February 1917.
24. NAM: Papers relating to Capt J.G. Howard (1999-03-95-2).
25. Miles, W. *Official History 1916*, vol. II, pp. 457–8.
26. *Ibid.*, p. 462.
27. PC: Letter to Alice Parfitt, 5 November 1916.
28. BNL: *Athletic News*, 6 November 1916.
29. James, G., *Football With a Smile: The Authorised Biography of Joe Mercer*, p.11.
30. PC: Annotation made by Capt L.I. Horniman in the margin of his copy of Wyrall, E., *History of the Second Division 1914–1919*.
31. Wyrall, E., *The History of the Second Division*, p. 308.
32. Haig, D., *Douglas Haig: War Diaries and Letters 1914–1918*, p. 254.
33. Wyrall, E. *The History of the Second Division*, p. 308.
34. PC: Annotation made by Capt L.I. Horniman in the margin of his copy of Wyrall, E., *The Second Division 1914–1919*.

CHAPTER 10

THE REDAN RIDGE

All ranks were extremely cheerful
and success seemed inevitable.
17th Middlesex War Diary, 13 November 1916

On the morning of 13 November 1916 the British were attacking the German lines on a 9,000yd front from north-east of Thiepval to a mile north-west of Serre. South of the Ancre, the 19th and 39th Divisions of II Corps were to push towards St Pierre Divion and Grandcourt, securing the remains of the German front line system and clearing the south bank of the river. The main attack was to be launched north of the Ancre, between Beaucourt and Serre, by the Royal Naval, 51st, 2nd and 3rd Divisions of V Corps, with the 31st Division of XIII Corps providing a defensive flank north-west of Serre.[1] With the 3rd Division on the left and the 51st Division on the right, attacking Serre and Beaumont Hamel respectively, the 2nd Division's objective was to capture the Redan Ridge. Two brigades were to carry out this task. The 5th Brigade would form up on the right and the 6th Brigade on the left. The 99th Brigade would be held in divisional reserve.

Of the two attacking brigades, the 6th Brigade had the more difficult task. The ground on its frontage of attack was in a deplorable condition. Another problem was that the battalions of 6th Brigade were confronted by the Quadrilateral, a strongly fortified German redoubt, which was described by one soldier as being about the size of Piccadilly Circus. An officer of the 1st King's Liverpool would later write of the Quadrilateral, lying in a hollow between Serre and Beaumont Hamel, that 'its defences were wonderfully complete; dugouts 400 to 500 yards long, too deep for a shell to batter in, and all trench mortars and machine guns working on lifts. The German is a very continuous and thorough worker and has concentrated on this point ever since trench warfare began.'[2]

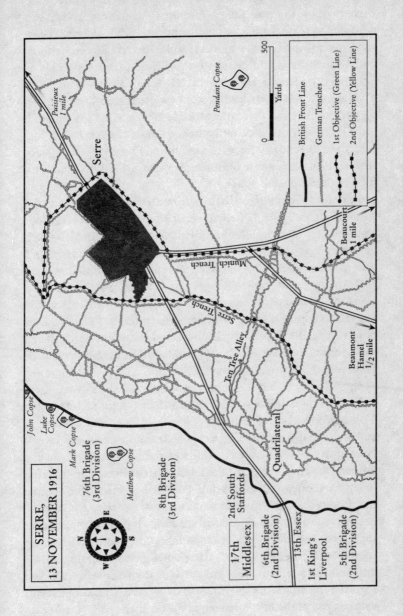

SERRE, 13 NOVEMBER 1916

N
W — E
S

Puisieux 1 mile

Serre

Pendant Copse

Beaucourt 1 mile

Munich Trench

Serre Trench

Beaumont Hamel 1/2 mile

Ten Tree Alley

John Copse
Luke Copse
Mark Copse
76th Brigade (3rd Division)
Matthew Copse
8th Brigade (3rd Division)

Quadrilateral

17th Middlesex

6th Brigade (2nd Division)
2nd South Staffords

13th Essex

1st King's Liverpool

5th Brigade (2nd Division)

British Front Line
German Trenches
1st Objective (Green Line)
2nd Objective (Yellow Line)

0   500
Yards

201

On the 6th Brigade front, the 13th Essex were on the right, supported by the 1st King's Liverpool, while the 2nd South Staffords were on the left, supported by the 17th Middlesex. There were two planned phases to the assault. The 2nd South Staffords and 13th Essex would penetrate the German defences as far as Serre Trench (The Green Line). The 1st King's Liverpool and 17th Middlesex would then 'leap-frog' these battalions and push on towards the second objective, Munich Trench (The Yellow Line). Sited on the reverse slope of the Redan Ridge, Munich Trench was well short of Pendant Copse, the small wood behind the hamlet of Serre, which was to have been the objective of the 17th Middlesex in the original plan of attack.

In order to minimise casualties from German artillery crossing No Man's Land, each battalion was instructed to advance in four waves 100yd apart, in columns of half-companies in single rank, a gap of at least three paces between each man. In addition to his rations, each soldier was to carry 150 rounds of ammunition, two Mills bombs and two sandbags. Around 20 men from each company were ordered to carry picks and shovels to consolidate the enemy trenches once they had been captured. To facilitate air observation, the troops of the 2nd Division wore a patch of red material on their haversacks. Such identification aids would be rendered wholly useless by the fog.

Opposite the 2nd Division, the German lines were held principally by Battalions I and III of Infantry Regiment 23 of the 12th Division. This division was made up of men from the mining and industrial districts of Upper Silesia, and there were several Poles in its ranks. Severely mauled in the opening stages of the Somme offensive, the 12th Division had been withdrawn from the line for a short period of refitting. Further fighting on the Somme had followed around Pozières in mid-July before the 12th Division had moved to a quiet sector south of Arras. It had only taken over the defence of this sector in late October. The enemy lines to the south of Serre were held by III Battalion of Infantry Regiment 169. This unit belonged to the 52nd Division from Baden, which had repulsed the attack in this sector on 1 July. The 52nd Division was rated as one of the best divisions in the German army.

The 17th Middlesex had marched up to the front line from

Mailly-Maillet at 11.15 p.m. and had taken up their positions shortly after midnight. Owing to the wretched condition of the trenches, the men formed up on open ground, their movements screened from enemy observation by the dense fog. Hot coffee and cocoa were issued. At 4 a.m. several messages bearing the code word 'Smith' began to be received at 2nd Division HQ. This was the pre-arranged signal that all troops were now in position. Throughout the night German artillery fire had been sporadic, and the 17th Middlesex had not sustained any casualties. The 17th Middlesex War Diary recorded that 'All ranks were extremely cheerful and success seemed inevitable'.[3]

At 5 a.m. the siege batteries opened their customary fire on the German positions, so that the enemy would not expect the day to be any different to those that had preceded it. The response of the German artillery was slight. At 5.45 a.m. the siege batteries were joined by the 18-pounders and 4.5in howitzers, which put down a heavy barrage on the German front line trenches. From their positions some 500yd behind the British front line, the 17th Middlesex waited for the order to advance. Even though dawn had broken during the bombardment, the thick fog, which still hung over the battlefield, limited visibility to 30yd. In such a scenario, officers of the attacking battalions had been instructed to advance using compasses. A Brigadier-General would afterwards point out that 'marching by compass bearing as a peace manoeuvre is a very different thing to doing so under fire'.[4] This comment subsequently appeared in the divisional history, prompting Capt Ivan Horniman to scrawl in the margin of his copy: 'especially in a "tin hat" made of steel and with both legs sunk in the mud'.[5]

Col Fenwick ordered the 17th Middlesex forward. 'B' and 'A' Companies went first on the left and right respectively. A few minutes later, they were followed by 'D' and 'C' Companies. In an act of remarkable sangfroid, 'B' and 'D' Companies of the 17th Middlesex advanced to meet the enemy playing mouth organs. At the time many of the battalion's officers were far from impressed. Second-Lieutenant Barnfather would recall that the 'officers were angry because they could not stop the men singing and playing mouth organs'.[6] After the attack the same officers would cite this incident of going 'over the top' playing mouth organs as proof of their men's indomitable spirit.

The troops disappeared into the mist. Even at the start, Capt Horniman recalled that his men experienced 'great difficulty in keeping direction, owing to trenches running at various angles across the line of advance'.[7] Prior to the attack, 'bridges' had laid across the network of water-logged trenches behind the British lines, but they were not always visible in the fog. Second-Lieutenant Charles Koop recalled that:

> I was in command of the rear left platoon of 'C' Coy, which was in support of 'A' Coy, with 'D' Coy on the left in support of 'B' Coy. The attack started, the battalion advancing in artillery formation, and for some time I was able to keep touch with the rear right platoon of the company on my left. After a time, however, this became impossible owing to the fact that the fog was so dense and also that everybody as far as possible was heading for the bridges and consequently got very mixed up.[8]

At 5.51 a.m. the artillery began to lift forward at the rate of 100yd every 5 minutes. In order to adhere to the artillery timetable, the 2nd South Staffords would need to have captured the Serre Trench (Green Line) within 56 minutes of Zero Hour. At that time artillery would stop moving forward and provide a standing barrage 150yd beyond the Green Line, so that the trenches could be consolidated without interference from enemy counterattacks. At 7.41 a.m. the artillery would resume its forward lifts and the 17th Middlesex would advance to Munich Trench (Yellow Line). By 8.31 a.m. the 17th Middlesex were to have reached the Yellow Line and the artillery would thereafter provide another standing barrage while the consolidation of Munich Trench was undertaken.

By 6.15 a.m. the first waves of 2nd South Staffords had taken the German front line. A few casualties had been sustained, largely as a result of the left-hand company advancing too closely on the heels of the British barrage. It was then that things started to go wrong. When the 2nd South Staffords reached the immediate support line, the wire was found to be practically uncut. Only a few men found a way through the entanglements. One officer of the 2nd South Staffords began to bomb his way up Ten Tree Alley before he was wounded and obliged to return. Matters were further complicated by the fact that elements of 8th Brigade, which was attacking Serre to the left, had become completely disorientated in the fog, and had proceeded on a southerly course virtually parallel to German front line. Officers and men of these battalions soon found themselves cutting across the supporting waves of the 2nd South Staffords, and complete pandemonium ensued. Lt Col George Dawes of the 2nd South Staffords would later report that a 'senior officer of one of these units was running about in a highly excited state waving a revolver and threatened to shoot at least three of my officers on the grounds that they were going the wrong way, when they were doing the best to rally parties in front of the German wire'.[9]

Things were no better by the time 'B' and 'D' Companies, on the left of the 17th Middlesex advance, began to cross No Man's Land, as 2/Lt Stanley Read recalled:

I was threatened with a revolver by a 2nd Lieut. of the Royal Scots who remarked that I was crossing his front. He mistook me for a Private as I was wearing a Private's tunic, with a star upon the shoulder. He afterwards noticed that I was an officer . . . I reasoned with him, and explained the exact position where we were and he quite realised that he was wrong. He apologised, but made no attempt to get into his correct position. We eventually arrived near the north face of the Quadrilateral where I found mixed men of the Shropshires, E. Yorks and Royal Scots.

As the officers of the mixed-up battalions tried to disentangle their men, the creeping barrage went on ahead and German soldiers emerged from the safety of their dugouts. Machine-gun fire from Serre and the Quadrilateral began to cause many casualties among the small groups of British soldiers struggling through the morass of No Man's Land. Another problem was enemy artillery, which was by now putting down a heavy barrage. Sgt Henry Bush was approaching the German front line with 2/Lt Leslie Christmas, a 20-year-old bank clerk from Muswell Hill, and Sgt Henry Croker: 'when a shell burst near and they turned off a little to the left. Almost immediately I saw a shell burst right on them. I was thirty yards away and I could see nothing of them when the smoke cleared away'.[10]

Even if the mix-up of units had not occurred, it is likely that the battalions of 6th Brigade would have struggled to keep up with the barrage. Along their frontage, much of the ground had the consistency of porridge and several men were reported to have sunk up to their waists. Capt Horniman commented laconically that he 'found it quite impossible to advance at the rate of 100 yds in 5 minutes in the thick treacly mud'.[10] The men's predicament was neatly summarised by the *Official History*:

> In front of it [the Quadrilateral], and farther north, the German wire was mostly still intact and, because of the fog, the stormers, often foundering in deep mud, could not see their way either to the gaps or to the firmer ground. The barrage lifted forward and was lost, whilst the German machine guns, as they were designed to, took most of the brigade frontage in enfilade . . . Parties of all four battalions forced their way into the German front trench, but were held there by deadly bursts of machine-gun fire at close range; others remained in shell-holes outside the enemy parapet.[12]

Despite this storm of machine-gun bullets, several men from 'A' and 'C' Companies of the 17th Middlesex did manage to progress beyond the German front line. Second-Lieutenant Athole Murray was commanding No. 3 Platoon, 'A' Company:

> We reached the first German trench, first system, and found no one at all there not even the moppers up of the Battalion [2nd South Staffords] in front. At this period, the barrage was becoming heavier and several of my men were knocked out; however it was not until attempting to jump the second trench that I was hit [in the left leg and arm], and therefore failing to clear it I fell in . . . Here I found myself enveloped in a sea of mud from which I was unable to extricate myself. Those of my men who were left carried on under Lieut. Marchant. I sank up to my thighs, and found after considerable trouble that the more I struggled the worse I got . . . I was there for about half an hour without seeing anyone, not even the supporting waves.[13]

Lt Ernest Marchant pushed on towards the Green Line with No. 4 Platoon of 'A' Company and the remnants of 2/Lt Murray's platoon. It was not long before he suddenly found himself alone with his servant:

We continued on but almost immediately my servant was killed. I soon came to another German trench, hoping to find it occupied by the Essex. It was empty. I made my way along it, bombing 2 dugouts on the way. I could see no signs of the first 4 waves of the attack or of any Germans. After proceeding some way, I found 2 men of the Middlesex, who were wounded.

I decided to bomb along the trench to the right in the hope of getting in touch with the King's. In the act of taking the wounded men's bombs I was hit in the head & arm by, as I was told by one of the men afterwards, a hand grenade, which rendered me temporarily unconscious.[14]

Only a few months previously, 2/Lt Charles Flint had been a corporal. Due to a shortage of officers in the 17th Middlesex after the attack on Guillemont, Col Fenwick had been authorised to grant commissions in the field to two suitable NCOs. Although L/Cpl Flint was barely 20 years old, the former clerk from Chiswick had clearly impressed Col Fenwick and he had been selected for promotion along with Sgt Percy Barnfather of Croydon Common.[15] On 13 November 2/Lt Flint repaid Col Fenwick's faith, leading a platoon from 'C' Company into the heart of the German defences:

We reached the enemy's fourth line without suffering any great loss. After passing the fourth line *Lewis* and rapid fire was opened on us and we were unable to get nearer than fifty yards, owing to enormous number of killed and wounded. I was hit at the same moment in two places and fell into a shell hole where I was picked up by the enemy several hours later in a semi-conscious condition.[16]

The fact that the fog in the valley was now beginning to be dispersed by the wind did little to assist the attackers, as Unteroffizier Otto Lais, a machine gunner of Infantry Regiment 169, recalled:

This enabled us to fire very precisely at individual craters. Emerging from the Heidenkopf [Quadrilateral] and from the battalion trenches, our infantry moved forward against them. They were surrounded and captured to a man. On all sides our hand grenade troops closed in on the British. As the visibility improved, the machine guns from the Heidenkopf joined in with us. The British were caught in a witch's cauldron. Unholy confusion prevailed amongst them. They wanted to break through but, caught in cross fire from three machine guns, they did not get ten metres. Taking cover in the crater field they cowered in the shell holes and, in their section groups, were wiped out or captured.[17]

Back in the British trenches, Col Henry Fenwick waited impatiently for news. He had already despatched 2/Lt Percy Barnfather to select a suitable site for Battalion HQ in the German front line, but the Croydon Common player had yet to return. By 7.20 a.m. nothing had been heard of the attack's progress. For the last hour or so, a steady stream of wounded had appeared at the advanced dressing station, but their reports were contradictory. Capt Horniman, who had been wounded in the thigh by shrapnel, then appeared at the parapet of the British front line. He reported that several units were mixed up in No Man's Land and that German machine-guns 'were causing a lot of trouble'.[18]

Around 7.30 a.m. 2/Lt Barnfather returned to report that 'the Staffs had not got on', and that Lt Col Dawes had sent him back to tell Col Fenwick that there had been a 'slight check'.[19] By this time the 17th Middlesex and the 1st King's Liverpool of 6th Brigade, and the 17th Royal Fusiliers and the 2nd Oxford and Bucks Light Infantry of 5th Brigade were supposed to be preparing to advance towards the second objective, the Yellow Line, on the heels of the creeping barrage. Only the attacking battalions of 5th Brigade were in a position to continue the advance, assisted by a few men from the 13th Essex and 1st King's Liverpool on the extreme right of 6th Brigade's attack.

At 7.50 a.m. Cpl Frank Anderson, one of the 17th Middlesex signallers, returned with a message from 2/Lt Robert MacIntyre, who had gone over the top that morning despite suffering from rheumatism and acute sciatica. The message stated that 'B' company was held up by wire opposite the German trenches, and that the fog was causing great difficulty. By this stage the British soldiers still in No Man's Land had used their two grenades, and many of their rifles were clogged up with mud, useless for anything except bayonet fighting. The remnants of 'B' Company were manning a bank along the Serre Road, barely 100yd in front of the British line. Enemy machine-guns were still 'doing a great deal of damage'.[20] On hearing that Capt James Kessack of 'A' Company had been killed, 2/Lt MacIntyre conferred with 2/Lt Stanley Read, and both officers decided to withdraw. The composition of 2/Lt Stanley Read's small party, which subsequently arrived back at the British lines, was indicative of the chaos prevalent in No Man's Land. There were two men each from the 2nd Royal Scots, 17th Middlesex and 2nd South Staffords; three from the 7th King's Shropshire Light Infantry and a soldier from the 8th East Yorks. Around the same time Sgt George Boyce and CSM Albert Drury, of 'C' and 'D' Companies respectively, reported that their advance had been held up by wire, and that the survivors were also pulling back. Other stragglers would arrive back at the British front line throughout the day.

In his subsequent report, Col Henry Fenwick saw the fog as the principal reason for the failure of the attack. Interestingly, he made no reference to the state of the ground:

I attribute failure chiefly to the fog and to a lesser degree to the uncut wire. The fog undoubtedly caused Brigade on our left to come across us. This was a mistake easily made in a fog as the boundary line at FLAG [Flag Avenue] and BORD [Board Street] is very difficult. After crossing FLAG unless a sharp turn to the left is taken a body of men would find themselves marching South.

In my humble judgment the formation for drawing up, the best under normal conditions, is wrong in a fog, where I consider that troops should be drawn up much closer together and much nearer the front, also blob formation in a fog is most difficult as small parties of men in any form of fog are well known to have a great tendency to wander.

I can't help attribute thinking that there were far more gaps than were seen and reported, but again fog prevented them from being seen. In fair light they could be spotted from a distance. Whenever men could be seen in front getting through others behind could follow but the fog stopped all that.[21]

Shortly after 9 a.m. Brig Gen Arthur Daly, concerned by the possibility of a German attack on the thinly-held British line, ordered that all survivors be grouped together in two composite battalions; the right hand battalion consisting of some 250 men from the 1st King's Liverpool and the 13th Essex, and the left battalion consisting of around 300 men from the 17th Middlesex and 2nd South Staffords. Unaware of the extent of the disaster that had befallen 6th Brigade, Maj Gen William Walker, the officer commanding 2nd Division, was keen to mount a fresh attack, but Brig Gen Daly sent word that the 6th Brigade was 'unfit for a fresh effort'.[22] At 2.15 p.m. orders were received to hold the front line by forming strong machine-gun posts in case of enemy counterattack. For the remainder of the day German artillery shelled the British lines remorselessly. Only as darkness fell were the stretcher cases able to be evacuated from the front line.

The results of the fighting on 13 November could best be described as a partial success for the British. Once again the shell-blackened ruins of Serre had proved elusive, as they had done on 1 July. North-west of the village, the 92nd Brigade of 31st Division had been forced to withdraw from its lodgement in the German lines once the attack of 3rd Division had broken down. South-west of Serre, the attack of the 6th Brigade on the Redan Ridge had been a costly failure, notwithstanding the fact that the 13th Essex and the 1st King's Liverpool had played an important role in protecting the left flank of the successful 5th Brigade attack, which had resulted in the capture of a section of Beaumont Trench and more than 150 prisoners. Further south the attack had been more successful. The 51st Division had taken Beaumont Hamel, and the Royal Naval Division was close to securing Beaucourt. South of the Ancre, the 19th and 39th Divisions had gained all their objectives to a depth of 1,600yd.

In terms of loss of life, the attack of the 17th Middlesex on the Redan Ridge had proved far more costly than the actions at Delville Wood and Guillemont. The 17th Middlesex War Diary recorded the losses of the day's fighting, as 3 officers killed, 2 wounded and 8 missing; 15 other ranks killed, 145 wounded and 133 missing. In time it would emerge that Captain James Kessack, 2/Lt Edward Brunton, 2/Lt Gordon Wade, 2/Lt Leslie Christmas, 2/Lt William Austen and 2/Lt Sidney Rothe were dead. A post office clerk before the war, Lt Patrick Fall, described by Captain Parfitt as 'a grand little chap and a typical Irishman', died of his wounds that evening at the advance operating station in Authie. Capt Ivan Horniman and 2/Lt Fred Stansfeld had been wounded. It would later transpire that four of the missing officers, Lt Ernest Marchant, 2/Lt Athole Murray, 2/Lt Charles Koop and 2/Lt Charles Flint, had been taken prisoner.

Prior to the attack at Guillemont, 2/Lt Gordon Wade, the son of an actor, had written out an informal will. Following his death in action on 13 November, his wife Maggie would receive this document, along with his identity disc and 'lucky bean' talisman. One can only imagine how Maggie, at their home in Sudbury, Middlesex, must have felt when reading her late husband's words for the first time:

I am writing this as I feel that I may shortly be going into action, which may be of very serious consequence to me, although I pray to God that for my darling wife Maggie's sake I shall be spared; however I don't suppose this war has been so horrible as at this point which this Battalion has to face . . .

Lastly, I would proclaim before the whole world how much I have loved her and what a noble character is hers. Surely everyone must admire her and I charge one and all to be as kind and patient with her as possible and help to relieve her suffering, which must be terrible knowing how well we have loved one another. May God bless and protect my darling faithful little girl always until we meet again in heaven.[23]

Ninety-three other ranks of the 17th Middlesex had lost their lives, including the Arsenal reserve player L/Cpl Robert Houston, who had enlisted in the 17th Middlesex within days of its formation, and L/Sgt Archie Strike, Football League linesman and employee of the company registration agent Richard Jordan & Son in Chancery Lane. Also among the dead was the Chesterfield Town left-half, CSM Joe Smith. Although wounded, CSM Smith was reported to have 'again dashed into battle, only to be shot down'. A former miner, Smith had played football and cricket for Hickleton Main Colliery before joining Birmingham City in 1911. At St Andrew's, Smith had struggled to establish himself in the first team, making only eight appearances for the Blues. After a couple of seasons languishing in the reserves, Smith had moved to Chesterfield during the 1913/14 season, making a total of 30 appearances for the club in the Midland League. At the time of his death Smith was earmarked for a commission 'in recognition of his good work in France'.[24] Within only a few weeks of his death, CSM Joe Smith would receive a mention in despatches.

Among the many wounded was a former storekeeper, Pte John Paterson, who had previously spent time in West Africa working as a trader.[25] Pte Paterson had only rejoined the 17th Middlesex a few weeks earlier, having been wounded at Delville Wood.[26] It was the end of his service with the 17th Middlesex. On recovery from his wounds he would successfully apply for a commission and be posted to the 1st Essex in 1917. One footballer wounded was Sgt George Ford, the Arsenal full-back, who had joined the club as an amateur in 1912. Four months later, when Sgt Ford attended Arsenal's 2-1 victory over Portsmouth, it was still considered unlikely that he would ever regain complete use of his left arm.

Given the difference between the number of confirmed deaths and those reported missing, it is clear that in the region of 50 officers and men of the 17th Middlesex fell into German hands on 13 November. One of them was 2/Lt Athole Murray, who had been unable to extricate himself from the mud:

The first I knew of the German counter attack was the arrival of some stick bombs to which I replied with my two Mills bombs which were all I had available. The German infantry then arrived and finding I was in a helpless condition carried on the attack and finally about an hour later, by which time I was up to my waist in mud, brought means of getting me out and did so.[27]

The majority of men taken prisoner were from 'A' and 'C'

Companies. Having penetrated the German defences in the vicinity of the Quadrilateral, small groups of 17th Middlesex had surrendered once they had been surrounded. The Germans had also picked up the wounded men who were unable to make their way back to the British lines. Second-Lieutenant Charles Koop was lying dazed in front of a German trench, a bullet having shattered his left arm:

> I do not know how long I lay there and the next thing I remember was seeing some Germans in front of me with some of our men, whom they had apparently captured. They saw me lying there and ordered two of our men to help me into their trench, where my wound was dressed by a German stretcher bearer. I was then taken down a dugout close by and laid on a bed and looked after by a German soldier.[28]

Like their British counterparts, German soldiers were not averse to picking up 'souvenirs' when the opportunity presented itself. One of those who fell victim to a souvenir hunter was Lt Ernest Marchant, who had been knocked unconscious by the explosion of a grenade: 'When I regained my senses I found myself on my back in the trench with Germans around me, one of whom was cutting my revolver lanyard.'[29]

Other soldiers captured that day included the Croydon Common goalkeeper Pte Tom Newton, Pte Sidney Jerram and Pte Richard Humphries, a builder from Stoke Newington. Pte Frederick Hodges, a worker in a textile mill, who had been badly wounded by a hand grenade in 'both legs and privates', would not be found for a couple of days, subsisting on his iron rations and rainwater. His daughter recounted what her father told her in later life:

> Help finally arrived in the form of a young German – he waved aside the offer of a watch, indeed the wounded man offered all he had for a little food. The young man gave Fred a little block of something (my memory tells me that it was coffee but that seems a strange thing to give in those circumstances). He then went away to return with two stretcher bearers. They carried the wounded man on their heads through heavy shelling (my father told me that if he had been in

213

their shoes, he would have been very tempted to throw down the stretcher and run).[30]

The morning of 14 November was misty. Enemy artillery was active, and CSM Albert Drury, a waiter in civilian life, was killed. Where sections of the German line had been captured, dugouts were immediately appropriated for use by British troops, notwithstanding the fact that their entrances were vulnerable to enemy shellfire. British soldiers were astonished by what they found. One such dugout, situated to the right of the Quadrilateral, was 'about thirty steps deep and a clear 500 yards in length under the front-line parapet. Accommodation is provided for about 400 men, dormitories, mess rooms, bath places and separate rooms for the officers and NCOs. Officers' quarters are most luxurious – papered – with greater quantities of wine, cigars, beer and soda water.[31]

The next morning the 17th Middlesex were relieved by the 4th Royal Fusiliers and moved back to support trenches around Ellis Square. During the afternoon the survivors marched back to Mailly-Maillet. The following day the remnants of the battalion were taken by lorries to billets in Louvencourt, where stock could be taken of the losses.

Most of the battalion's dead would not be recovered until the German withdrawal to the Hindenburg Line in the spring of 1917. Only then could the burial parties begin their gruesome work. Over the preceding months, the remains of many men had either disappeared in the mud, or had been blown to pieces by shellfire. Those bodies that remained could often not be identified. For such reasons, 46 17th Middlesex, who were killed in the fighting of 13 November, have no known grave and are commemorated on the Thiepval Memorial to the Missing.

The majority of the 17th Middlesex dead with a known grave lie today only a few yards from where they fell. The graves of 14 men, including 2/Lt Leslie Christmas, CSM Joseph Smith and L/Sgt Archie Strike, can be found in Serre Road Cemetery No. 1, which contains the last resting places of nearly 2,500 officers and men. Of this figure only 698 are identifiable burials. Another 27 17th Middlesex, including early recruit Pte Leslie Oliver and Pte Albert

Bourne, a farmhand from Kent, are buried in Serre Road Cemetery No. 2 close to the site of the infamous Quadrilateral. Not long before the attack on the Redan Ridge, Pte Bourne had written home to his sister Emily, asking to be remembered to 'all the girls' and one in particular: 'Tell Rose Bryant I should like to be picking up potatoes long with her. Tell her there's not many girls out here where I am . . .' Today there are over 7,000 First World War graves in this cemetery, mostly dating from 1916. Of this number, nearly 5,000 are unidentified burials. It is likely that several of the 'missing' 17th Middlesex, who were killed in the fighting of 13 November, are buried in these cemeteries as unknown soldiers. The remainder still lie in unmarked graves beneath the surrounding fields.

On 18 November the Battle of the Somme petered out as the final British attacks on the Ancre stalled in the face of driving sleet and heavy machine-gun fire. Back in England that afternoon, a match took place between Reading and a 'Footballers' Battalion' team, comprising of soldiers from the 27th Middlesex.[i] The game had been organised by the Reading directors to raise money for Allen Foster's widow and young son. Sgt Ted Hanney was one of the linesmen, and Cpl Joe Bailey turned out for Reading. Heavy snow fell throughout the match, but more than 1,000 spectators braved the elements to watch a convincing 5–2 victory for the 27th Middlesex. Cpl Arthur Wileman, of Luton Town, scored a hat-trick, while his club team-mate, L/Cpl Arthur Roe, and Sgt David Gray of St Mirren, scored a goal apiece.

On 27 November the 17th Middlesex arrived at Agenvillers, north-east of Abbeville, for a period of rest and training. By the end of the month 316 men had arrived to make good the battalion's losses, bringing the fighting strength of the 17th Middlesex up to 26 officers and 936 other ranks. Over the next few weeks the deficit in officers would also be remedied; 13 officers would report for duty, including 2/Lt Allastair McReady-Diarmid and 2/Lt Norman Dick. Several football matches took

---

[i] The 27th Middlesex team: L/Cpl Fred Durston (QPR) goalkeeper; Pte David Girdwood (Chelsea) and Cpl Amos (Brentford), backs; Pte Bailey (Sutton Junction), Pte Henry Pennifer (QPR) and Pte Green (QPR), halfbacks; Sgt David Gray (St Mirren), Cpl Arthur Wileman (Luton Town), L/Cpl Arthur Roe (Luton Town), Pte Arthur Mounteney (Hinckley Athletic) and Cpl Muncer, forwards. Several of these players had seen active service with the 17th Middlesex.

place during this spell out of the line. Having earlier beaten the 1st King's Liverpool 12–0, the 17th Middlesex played the 2nd South Staffords in the final of the 6th Brigade Competition on 14 December, winning 2–0. Three days later, another inter-battalion competition started and in the first match the 17th Middlesex put ten goals past the 1st King's without reply. On 18 December the 17th Middlesex once again met the 2nd South Staffords in the 6th Brigade Final, beating them 6–1. The next day the battalion team won the tug-of-war event at a Brigade Sports Day.

On Christmas Day the 17th Middlesex attended divine services held in the Divisional theatre, with the 'rest of the day given up to celebrations'.[32] On 27 December Maj Gen Cecil Pereira took over command of the 2nd Division from Maj Gen Walker, who had recently returned home. Born in 1869, Maj Gen Pereira was educated at the Oratory School and was commissioned into the Coldstream Guards in 1890. After service in Niger and Uganda, Pereira had seen plenty of action in the Boer War. At the outbreak of war he was in command of the 2nd Coldstreams. In May 1915, Pereira had been promoted to the command of 85th Brigade and had been wounded later that month near Vermelles. Wounded again at Loos in September 1915, Pereira had assumed command of the 1st Guards Brigade the following June.

That same afternoon, the final of the Divisional Football Competition took place against the 34th Brigade RFA.[ii] After a hard-fought game, the 17th Middlesex edged it 2–1. Sgt Bob Dalrymple, of Clapton Orient, was reported to have played an especially good game. Pte Alonzo 'Olly' Poulton, who had made his League debut for West Bromwich Albion against Newcastle in September 1914, scored both goals. Earlier in the month the burly forward had won the battalion heavyweight-boxing championship. The following day Col Fenwick arranged a celebratory tea for the team in the Recreation Hut. On 30 December the 17th Middlesex beat an Army Service Corps team in Abbeville 5–1, the battalion team and band being transported in

[ii]The 17th Middlesex team: Pte Tommy Lonsdale (Southend Utd) goalkeeper; L/Cpl John Woodhouse (Brighton & Hove Albion) and Sgt Fred Bartholomew (Reading), backs; Pte John Nuttall (Millwall), Pte David Kenney (Grimsby Town) and Pte John Gregory (Queen's Park Rangers), halfbacks; Pte Edward Foord (Chelsea), Pte Alonzo Poulton (West Bromwich Albion), Pte George Pyke (Newcastle Utd), Sgt Bob Dalrymple (Clapton Orient) and 2/Lt Percy Barnfather (Croydon Common), forwards.

ambulances to and from the match. On New Year's Day 1917 the 17th Middlesex had use of the baths at Gapennes and clean linen was issued to the men. News was received that Lt Ernest Marchant and 2/Lt Athole Murray were prisoners of war.

The prolonged spell of rest and training was much needed to restore morale after the hardships of the previous few months. Although other battalions had suffered higher casualties over the course of the campaign, the Somme had been a truly dreadful experience for the 17th Middlesex. Since its arrival in July, the battalion had sustained casualties in the region of 800 officers and men killed, wounded or taken prisoner. Two hundred and sixty-nine officers and men had lost their lives. Of this number, 144 individuals have no known grave. Their names can be found on Panels 12D and 13B of the Thiepval Memorial to the Missing, which commemorates the officers and men of the United Kingdom and South African forces who died in the Somme sector before 20 March 1918. This imposing monument, visible from several sectors of the battlefield today, bears the names of more than 72,000 officers and men who have no known grave. Over 90 per cent of these officers and men lost their lives between the dates of 1 July and 18 November 1916.

The attritional nature of the Somme fighting had taken a terrible toll on the British army. Although the offensive had achieved its primary objective in July, namely relieving the pressure on Verdun, the Allies had kept battering away at the German defences in order 'to wear down' the enemy. There had also been several occasions, most notably during the latter half of September, when Haig had entertained the prospect of a breakthrough, but such hopes had ultimately proved illusory. By the time the snows of early winter had brought the fighting to an end, the Allies had clawed back a 20-mile strip of devastated land some 6 miles deep from the Germans at a cost of over 600,000 casualties, more than two-thirds of them British.

The German army had also suffered greatly. One German staff officer would later declare that 'the Somme was the muddy grave of the German field army and of the faith in the infallibility of the German leadership'.[33] The true extent of German losses on the Somme has been much debated over the years, due to their policy of excluding the lightly wounded from casualty returns. Estimates range from 437,000 to 680,000. Even if the lower figure is taken as the correct one, the total number of casualties sustained by both sides had exceeded one million, and it was clear that the fighting would continue well into 1917. While the various options for the next 'campaigning season' were discussed behind the lines, the soldiers in the trenches devoted their energies to surviving the winter, and the customary pattern of trench warfare resumed. Local inhabitants, who had remained close to the front, would later maintain that the winter of 1916/17 was the worst for 50 years.

1. After hard fighting at Gallipoli in 1915, the Royal Naval Division had arrived in France in May 1916.
2. Letter written by Lt Ninian Bannatyne, in Wyrall, E., *The King's Regiment*, p. 353.
3. TNA: WO 95/1361.
4. Wyrall, E., *The History of the Second Division* p. 311.
5. PC: Annotation made by Capt L.I. Horniman in the margin of his copy of Wyrall, E., *The History of the Second Division 1914–1919*.
6. BNL: *Croydon Advertiser*, 2 December 1916.
7. PC: Annotation made by Capt L.I. Horniman in the margin of his copy of Wyrall, E., *The History of the Second Division 1914–1919*.
8. TNA: WO 339/ 55296.
9.TNA: WO 95/1355.
10. TNA: WO 339/3731. On 27 January 1917 the widow of 2/Lt Christmas would give birth to a son, Roy Leslie.
11. PC: Annotation made by Capt L.I. Horniman in the margin of his copy of Wyrall, E., *The History of the Second Division 1914–1919*.
12. Miles, W., *Official History of the War, 1916*, vol. II, p. 495.
13. TNA: WO 339/5466.
14. TNA: 339/55296.
15. On 2 December 1916 a dinner in 2/Lt Barnfather's honour was held at the Greyhound Hotel in Croydon to celebrate the fact the Robins player had received a commission. Local dignitaries presented him with a silver cigarette case, an amber mouthpiece and a silver-mounted briar pipe.
16. TNA: WO 339/28019.
17. Sheldon, J., *The German Army on the Somme 1914–1916*, p. 383.
18. TNA: WO 95/1361.
19. *Ibid*.
20. *Ibid*.
21. *Ibid*.
22. Miles, W., *Official History of the War, 1916*, vol. II, p. 496.
23. TNA: WO 339/64940.
24. BNL: *Football Post*, 2 December 1916.
25. Paterson's medical notes show that he was wounded in the head on 13 November 1916. However, his military history sheet describes his injury as 'Gunshot wound left hand'.
26. Details of Paterson's wound received at Delville Wood are similarly contradictory. His military history sheet states he was evacuated with shell shock. His medical notes record a gunshot wound to his neck.
27. TNA: WO 339/5466.
28. TNA: WO 339/55296.
29. *Ibid*. Lt Ernest Marchant made several attempts to escape from captivity. He succeeded at the third attempt, arriving back in England on 14 December 1918.
30. LC: POW 048.
31. Letter written by Lt Ninian Bannatyne, in Wyrall, E., *The King's Regiment*, pp. 352–3.
32. TNA: WO 95/1361.
33. Terraine J., *Douglas Haig: The Educated Soldier*, p. 232.

CHAPTER 11

THE GERMAN WITHDRAWALS AND THE BATTLES OF ARRAS

It has been freezing very keenly out here,
and my fingers are nearly frozen
Pte Peter Roney F/306 (Bristol Rovers)

On 15 November 1916, two days after the 17th Middlesex attack on the Redan Ridge, Haig and Joffre met with military representatives of Belgium, Italy, Japan, Romania, Russia and Serbia at Chantilly to decide upon Allied strategy for 1917. Their outlook was generally optimistic, despite the losses on the Somme and at Verdun. While the year of 1916 had not exactly gone to plan, it was felt that the tide of the war was at last beginning to turn. The massive Russian offensive, launched in June, had met with much success against the Austro-Hungarian army, forcing Germany to transfer troops from the Western Front to shore up its ally in the East. After a series of reverses against the Austro-Hungarian army earlier in the year, the Italians had mounted moderately successful counterattacks on the Isonzo. Although German submarines were exacting a heavy toll on Allied shipping, the British naval blockade was causing significant shortages of raw materials and foodstuffs in Germany.

The Allied representatives were determined to ensure that the Germans did not seize the initiative again, as they had done earlier in the year with the Verdun offensive. Accordingly, it was decided that a series of synchronised offensives should be launched 'from the first fortnight of February 1917 with all the means at their disposal'.[1] In the intervening period, ongoing operations were to 'be continued to the fullest extent permitted by climatic conditions'.[2] Whereas the military representatives of the Allied powers were still confident of success, the lengthy casualty lists had given rise to mounting disquiet in England and France over the conduct of the war. Shortly after the Chantilly conference Prime Minister Herbert Asquith resigned. He was replaced by David Lloyd George, former Secretary of State for War. The mercurial Welshman had scant regard for Haig's abilities as a military commander.

In France, too, there was a change of direction. Gen Joffre was replaced by the relatively unknown Gen Robert Nivelle, who had masterminded a series of successful local counterattacks at Verdun in the autumn of 1916. Joffre's intention for 1917 had been to destroy the enemy capacity for resistance by broadening the Somme front in early February, with the French attacking between the Oise and Somme, and the British between the Somme and the Scarpe. The designs of his successor were far more ambitious. Nivelle proposed a Franco-British attempt 'to destroy the main body of the enemy's Armies on the Western Front' by unleashing a massive French offensive on the Aisne.[3] The operation would be preceded by subsidiary Franco-British attacks elsewhere on the Western Front to pin down German reserves before the main blow fell. The British role in this plan would be to launch a subsidiary attack around Arras.

Over the winter months the German High Command had also re-evaluated its strategy for 1917. It decided to introduce a policy of unrestricted submarine warfare, whereby all ships, regardless of their country of origin, would be sunk without warning if they entered defined zones around Britain, France and Italy, and in the Eastern Mediterranean. Although such a decision would undoubtedly bring the United States into the war, Ludendorff was prepared to gamble on Britain being forced to sue for peace before American troops could arrive on the Western Front in significant numbers.[4]

Alert to the likelihood of renewed Allied offensives on the Western Front, the German High Command decided upon a defensive strategy for 1917. Plans were duly made to evacuate the large salient between Arras and Soissons, and to undertake a strategic retirement to the Siegfried Stellung, a well-prepared defensive position which had been constructed towards the end of

1916. Known as the Hindenburg Line to the British, its formidable defences ran from the northern bank of the Aisne to the southern bank of the Scarpe. The withdrawal would have the effect of shortening their lines on the Western Front by about 25 miles, thereby releasing some 14 divisions for duty elsewhere. The retirement was scheduled to be completed by the middle of March.

The first few days of the New Year saw the 17th Middlesex training and practising various schemes of attack at Agenvillers. Plenty of time was made available for recreational activities. On 3 January the 17th Middlesex officers played a football match against their counterparts in the 1st King's Liverpool at football and won 6–1. The game was watched by Maj Frank Buckley, who had decided to pay his former battalion a visit in France. On 6 January the Battalion War Diary recorded awards to officers and men in the New Year's honours list: 'Col H.T. Fenwick CMG. Mentioned in despatches Col H.T. Fenwick, Major Buckley, L/Sgt G. Pargeter, Sgt J.D. Blair (since killed in action) and CSM J. Smith (since killed in action)'.[5] A surprised Capt Ernest Parfitt wrote home:

Our Major told me he was very sorry that my Military Cross had not come through in the New Year's Honours. Of course I said I had given up all idea of it a month after the wood [Delville]. He then informed me that it wasn't for the wood, but this last stunt . . . I'm really glad I didn't get it because nothing is worse in my opinion than getting an MC for doing absolutely nothing!!![6]

On 9 January 1917 the 17th Middlesex undertook a 16-mile march to dilapidated billets at Autheux, the 2nd Division having received orders to proceed back to the Somme. For the next week or so the battalion were in support at Aveluy, providing working parties for the front line. The weather was bitterly cold and there was heavy snow. On 20 January the 17th Middlesex relieved the 17th Royal Fusiliers in the front line, about 2,000yd north of Courcelette. The following day Brig Gen Richard Walsh DSO assumed command of 6th Brigade, Brig Gen Arthur Daly having been invalided home on account of ill-health. The son of a former surgeon-major-general, Brig Gen Walsh was another career soldier, having been commissioned into the Royal Scots Fusiliers in 1894. Like most of his contemporaries, he had seen plenty of action in the Boer War.

The conditions around Courcelette were dreadful. The section of front line taken over by the 17th Middlesex consisted of 18 disconnected posts. Such was the barrenness of the ground that it proved impossible to locate a post to the left of the battalion, estimated to be about 300yd away. Early in the morning of 22 January soldiers of the 6th Northants, who were holding the post, sent up two Very lights so that a compass bearing might be taken. Second-Lieutenant Edward King, an electrical engineer in civilian life, and two men crawled out into No Man's Land. An hour later, there was still no sign of the post in the featureless landscape. Second-Lieutenant King decided to turn back:

I then commenced my return journey on a reversed compass bearing being about two degrees to the right hoping to strike the Northamptonshire post on my way. I had proceeded for about two hours when I was challenged in English 'Halt! Who are you?' at about ten yards. I replied 'Friend, Middlesex. Are you Northants?' On a reply of 'Yes,' I said 'I am coming in,' and proceeded to cross a few strands of wire in front of the post.

It was extremely dark and I did not see that I had approached an enemy post until I was within about two yards of a sentry standing on the top. There were several men immediately behind him. The sentry presented his bayonet at my chest saying 'Hands up,' I therefore surrendered.[7]

Over the next few days relief and ration parties frequently got lost on their way up to the front line. In order to reach the posts, the men had to follow makeshift brushwood tracks that could only be used at night. Their difficulties were compounded by the fact that Ironside Avenue, a communication trench that ran 800yd forward from the West Miraumont Road up to the front line, was frequently impassable on account of the mud. On 24 January the 17th Middlesex were relieved by the 2nd South Staffords. The battalion went back into support, being billeted at Wolfe Huts, Ovillers.

The 17th Middlesex spent the next three weeks in reserve and support, working predominantly to deepen trenches and improve communications to the front line. Parties of men also worked in sawmills, supervised by officers of the Royal Engineers. The cold chilled the men to the bone. Capt Ernest Parfitt wrote to a friend: 'We are having a real freezing time out here. We have had a frost every morning for the last three weeks, and we've got all our work cut out to fight frostbite. We are awfully proud because we've only had four cases up to now.'[8] Colonel Fenwick did what he could to alleviate his men's suffering. His provision of coke for the men's braziers in the trenches was particularly appreciated. Sgt Fred Parker, to date the only Clapton Orient player in the 17th Middlesex not to have been killed or wounded, wrote to Billy Holmes, the club secretary: 'Talk about cold, you ought to be here – it's terrible. Thank goodness I have been extra busy of late, but it is almost a matter of impossibility to keep oneself warm. We have a fine CO, he buys us coke, and I can assure you it is appreciated.'[9]

Many men were at the limit of their endurance, but they were more fortunate than Pte Richard Humphries, who had been captured at Serre on 13 November. Only three days after his capture, he had been put to work behind the German lines along with 150 other British prisoners:

We lived on 8 oz of bread and dirty water. We started work at 6 a.m. and did not leave off until 7.30 at night. We had to make trenches, dug-outs, wire entanglements, and the Germans kicked and hit us about with their rifles. If we went sick we had our bread stopped.

We had to sleep on the ground in a little French house the roof of which had been blown off, so that rain and snow used to come through. We had no blankets to put over us, and had to sleep in our clothes, which were all alive [infested with lice]. We had to find tins to get our turnip water in, which the Germans called soup, and which was given to us once a day; we could not eat it. The bread was made of sawdust and potato peelings and bones of some kind.

When our boots got worn they gave us wooden clogs to wear, made of tree trunks, which cut our feet to bits. Our sanitary arrangements were very bad; we only had a wash once a week, and had beards about 4 inches long on our faces. They knocked me about and beat me from head to foot because I could not work, and spat in my face. Some of us had to work with no boots on our feet.

We did not receive any parcels or letters all the time I was there, which was from 16th November 1916 till 15th February 1917. Some of the men died from the cold, ill-treatment and hunger.[10]

Despite the severity of the weather, the Fifth Army had already resumed offensive operations on the Ancre. On 17 February an effort was made to secure the high ground overlooking Miraumont. The operation was undertaken by the 2nd and 18th Divisions, with the Royal Naval Division attacking on the north bank of the Ancre. Three companies of the 17th Middlesex were attached to the 99th Brigade, which was attacking Hill 130, south-east of Miraumont.

At 5.45 a.m. the 99th Brigade attacked behind a creeping barrage. The attacking troops were greatly hindered by the state of the ground. A rapid thaw had resulted in pools of glutinous mud, which made any movement difficult. The gains fell far short of what had been anticipated, but the 99th Brigade managed to capture and hold their first objective, Grandcourt Trench, in the face of determined German counterattacks. By the evening the Royal Naval Division had gained all its objectives on a front of about half a mile, and the 18th Division had reached the south-western outskirts of Petit Miraumont. Throughout the day 'A' Company of the 17th Middlesex had carried up munitions and supplies to the new front line. Five men were killed, most probably as a result of artillery fire. Among their number was 22-year-old Pte Walter Tookey, a warehouseman from Leicester. His mother, Mary Jane, would lose her other son, John, in 1918.

On 20 February 'B', 'C' and 'D' Companies of the 17th Middlesex relieved the 13th Essex in the front line near Miraumont, while 'A' Company remained in support in the old front line. After the heavy rain the series of shell holes that constituted the new front line were full of water. The relief was not completed until the morning, owing to the difficulties of identifying the exact position of the front line and the bog-like condition of the tracks. Several men sank deep into the mud and had to be either dug out or hauled out with ropes. Over the next couple of days enemy artillery and trench mortars were active.

Six other ranks were killed, including L/Cpl Edward Monk, a pre-war regular from Gravesend.

On 24 February the 17th Middlesex were relieved by the 17th Royal Fusiliers after a trying few days. Capt Ernest Parfitt described the preceding days in the trenches, as 'the worst time I've ever experienced . . . standing up to one's knees in thick mud'.[11] The battalion moved back to the town of Albert for a period of training. Albert was the largest town within the British sector of the Somme battlefield. It was famous for its statue of the Virgin and Infant Christ, which leaned precariously from the top of the Basilique Notre Dame de Brebiéres in the centre of the town, having been dislodged by shellfire earlier in the war. When the 17th Middlesex reached Albert, everyone was still caked in mud. Capt Parfitt tried to describe the scene to Alice: 'Try to imagine one of the mud-carts, one sees in the streets of London, then picture a man that has fallen in it just coming out . . . There you have the picture of the whole [battalion] coming out of the line. My word! We haven't had such a mud bath since we were children'.[12]

The ground captured during the previous week had given the British excellent observation over the German artillery positions in the upper Ancre Valley. To minimise casualties, the Germans abandoned Pys and Miraumont. At II Corps HQ, plans were immediately formulated for a series of minor operations to secure the remaining high ground between Bapaume and Achiet-le-Petit. As part of this scheme, the 2nd Division and the 18th Division were tasked with capturing Grevillers Trench and Irles, the only positions still held by the Germans in advance of the Le Transloy-Loupart Line.

On 3 March the 17th Middlesex moved back into support at Ovillers. Another week of providing working parties followed. The weather was atrocious. Capt Parfitt wrote home:

We are still having bitter weather: March winds and snow, and to add to these discomforts, the barrenness of the ground for miles about here. It's not too rosy. Everything about this part of the line is absolutely blasted: no whole trees for miles, only the stumps and of course no houses. Places where villages once stood are also unrecognisable. Not a very cheery outlook.[13]

On 10 March the 99th Brigade attacked and captured Grevillers Trench and Lady's Leg Ravine, supported by a highly effective artillery barrage, and covering fire from the 2nd Australian Division on its right. On the left, the 18th Division made a similarly well-executed assault on the village of Irles. By the following morning, preparations were already underway to capture Loupart Trench, a few hundred yards in front of Grevillers Trench. That evening the 17th Middlesex marched to Courcelette and battalion working parties assisted with the construction of communication and 'jumping off' trenches. All units were ordered to complete arrangements for the attack on Loupart Trench by 14 March. In the event, the attack was destined not to take place.

About 1.30 a.m. on 13 March Australian patrols reported that the Germans appeared to have vacated the Loupart Line. The 1st King's Liverpool immediately occupied Loupart Trench and Loupart Wood. The 13th Essex moved forward on their left. The advancing troops had to remain on their guard, numerous booby traps having been left to trap the unwary soldier looking for a souvenir:

> The dug-outs vacated by the enemy in the Loupart line have been found to contain many traps. As our troops were on their guard against these no harm was caused by them. The following were found: artificial flowers, bits of evergreen, pieces of shell or a bayonet on the floor or walls. A wire was attached to these, running to an explosive charge near the entrance. If an object is picked up the charge is ignited and the entrance blown in. Pieces of wood lightly fastened to the wall, as though intended for us as a hand rail when going down the steps. Wires with an electric spark attached to an explosive charge were attached to these rails.[14]

That evening the 17th Middlesex moved up in support to Grevillers Trench and Gallwitz Switch. Behind them working parties of infantry, sappers and pioneers laid tracks and rebuilt shattered roads so that the guns could be hauled forward. Ahead of the advancing British troops lay the Bihucourt Line, which was reported to be held in strength by the enemy, with sentries posted at 25yd intervals. The trenches were protected by 4ft-high wire entanglements, some 25ft in depth. Preparations for an attack on the Bihucourt Line were soon underway. On 16 March the 17th Middlesex relieved the 2nd South Staffords in front of Loupart Wood. That night a succession of mysterious red lights were seen burning all along the German line,

At 6 a.m. the following day Col Fenwick received word from 6th Brigade HQ that the Germans were retiring. The 17th Middlesex were 'ordered to push forward and keep touch with the enemy'. The battalion duly advanced and occupied the Bihucourt Line west of Biefvillers. A 17th Middlesex patrol ventured a mile beyond the front line and found no sign of the enemy. Another patrol moved into Sapignies. Finding the blazing ruins unoccupied, the patrol proceeded to the far side of the village, although this news would not reach 6th Brigade HQ until the following morning.

The night passed without incident. Sapignies burned fiercely and several green and white lights were seen behind the German lines. During the morning of 18 March an advance guard consisting of the 1st King's Liverpool, a company of the 2nd South Staffords, one section of the 483rd (East Anglian) Field Company, one section of the 6th Brigade Machine-Gun Company, and two troops of the Queen's Own Yorkshire Dragoons passed through the 17th Middlesex and entered Sapignies. By nightfall cavalry patrols, supported by the 1st King's Liverpool, had pushed forward to occupy the high ground north-east of Mory.

The German withdrawal had been codenamed 'Alberich', after the malevolent dwarf in Wagner's Ring cycle. The codename was particularly appropriate. Everything that lay between their former front line and the Hindenburg Line had been laid to waste by the retreating German army. Under a systematic programme of destruction, anything that could conceivably be of use to the advancing troops was destroyed:

There was not much to be seen of the enemy . . . He worked out his retreat with usual German thoroughness. Every tree had been sawn down to a foot of the ground, fruit trees and all telephone wires taken down and crops burnt.

In the villages he had started systematically at one end and destroyed every single thing that could ever be of any considerable use to anyone. Craters from thirty to fifty yards across had been blown up at intervals along the main roads and at every crossroad. Every house had been blown up or set fire to; every well poisoned.

In one of his engineering yards he had gone to the trouble breaking the handles of every pick and shovel, firing the bags of nails, wetting the bags of lime and cement.[15]

The retreat to the Hindenburg Line would necessitate a few changes to Haig's plans for the forthcoming offensive. The Fifth Army was to have attacked in a north-easterly direction, in conjunction with a Third Army attack around Arras. Much of the area, which had previously been designated for capture by the Fifth Army, had now been abandoned. The revised role of Gough's Fifth Army would be to press the retreating Germans and to take up positions opposite the Hindenburg Line. Preparations would then be made to attack these formidable defences between Quéant and Bullecourt.

On 19 March the 17th Middlesex marched back to camp at Courcelette. After a day's rest a working party of 400 men was detailed to recover salvable war material in the vicinity of Miraumont. This task involved collecting up weapons, equipment and unexpended ammunition lying about the battlefield. On completion of this work, the battalion marched back to their billets in Ovillers Huts. The following day the 17th Middlesex marched to good billets in Warloy, where the battalion remained for the next three days. On 26 March, the 2nd Division having been transferred to XIII Corps of First Army, the 17th Middlesex began a long march northwards. Four days later the battalion arrived at billets in Boyaval, near St Pol, for a period of rest and training.

On 3 April the 53-year-old Col Fenwick relinquished command of the 17th Middlesex. It was sad day for everyone. His avuncular manner would be much missed by officers and men alike. Second-Lieutenant Percy Barnfather said of Col Fenwick that 'His motto was "My men". If the food was short the men had what there was, and the officers went without.'[16] Only recently Col Fenwick had sent a cheque for £200 to the Footballers' Battalion Comforts Fund to buy canvas 'rest' shoes for his men, when out of the line. Needless to say, his retirement did not pass unnoticed by the sporting press:

Colonel Fenwick went to France with the battalion in November 1915, and has been through all their severe fighting and many hardships. He was loved by the many fine and famous players under him. He has been the father of the battalion, and has looked after the welfare of his men in a manner which they will never forget. As a man of wealth he has been able to do a great deal for them.[17]

The new commanding officer was the 36-year-old Lt Col George Kelly. Educated at Wellington College, Kelly was commissioned into the King's Royal Rifle Corps in 1899. During the Boer War he had been wounded at the Battle of the Tugela Heights, recovering in time to take part in the advance through Natal. In 1904 Kelly had been present at the defeat of the 'Mad Mullah' at Jidballi, Somaliland, spending the next few years with the West Africa Frontier Force. As a staff captain of 6th Brigade in 1914, Kelly had seen plenty of action. He had returned to England after being wounded at the Battle of Loos in September 1915. On recovering from his wounds, Kelly was appointed to a post at the Reserve Training Centre at Cannock Chase, returning to the Western Front towards the end of 1916. Col Fenwick was a hard act to follow. While Lt Col Kelly was regarded as 'an extremely able officer', he was unsurprisingly less popular than his predecessor, being described by one of the 17th Middlesex officers, as 'rather a snorter'.

The first few days of April were spent training in preparation for the Arras offensive. The divisional schools were busy instructing soldiers in the most effective use of grenades and Lewis guns. Plenty of entertainment was organised for the men between these training courses. During the day there were the usual football matches and recreational activities, while the divisional troupe performed an assortment of shows in the evening. On 7 April the 17th Middlesex, with a fighting strength of 41 officers and 904 other ranks, vacated their billets in Boyaval and marched to Camblain Châtelain. By the following evening the three infantry brigades of the 2nd Division were under orders to be prepared to move at 4 hours' notice once the infantry attack started. The preliminary bombardment had been underway for the last four days.

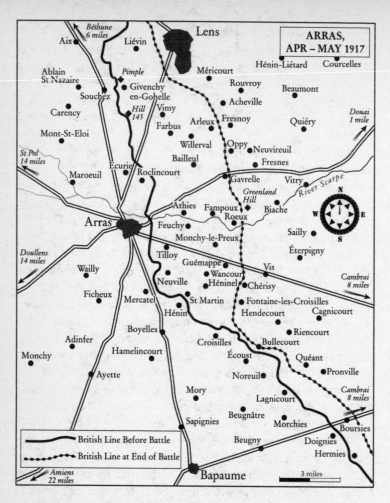

ARRAS,
APR – MAY 1917

Béthune
6 miles
Aix
Liévin
Lens
Hénin-Liétard   Courcelles
Ablain
St Nazaire
Pimple
Méricourt
Rouvroy
Beaumont
Givenchy
en-Gohelle
Souchez
Acheville
Douai
1 mile
Carency
Hill
145
Vimy
Arleux
Fresnoy
Quiéry
Mont-St-Eloi
Farbus
St Pol
14 miles
Willerval
Oppy
Neuvireuil
Bailleul
Fresnes
Ecurie
Roclincourt
Maroeuil
Gavrelle
Vitry
River Scarpe
Greenland
Hill
Athies
Fampoux
Biache
Arras
Roeux
Feuchy
Monchy-le-Preux
Sailly
Doullens
14 miles
Tilloy
Éterpigny
Wailly
Guémappe
Vis
Neuville
Wancourt
Héninel
Cherisy
Cambrai
8 miles
Ficheux
Mercatel
St Martin
Fontaine-les-Croisilles
Cagnicourt
Hénin
Hendecourt
Boyelles
Riencourt
Adinfer
Croisilles
Bullecourt
Monchy
Hamelincourt
Écoust
Quéant
Pronville
Ayette
Noreuil
Cambrai
8 miles
Mory
Lagnicourt
Sapignies
Beugnâtre
Morchies
Boursies
Beugny
Doignies
Hermies

—— British Line Before Battle
•••• British Line at End of Battle

Amiens
22 miles
Bapaume
3 miles

On 9 April the British launched their Arras offensive in a snowstorm, 14 divisions attacking on a frontage of nearly 15 miles. Attacking astride the River Scarpe, the objective of Allenby's Third Army was to break through four lines of German defences and to open up the way for an advance on Cambrai, the axis of the advance being the Arras-Cambrai Road. North of Arras, the First Army had been allocated the unenviable task of capturing the seemingly impregnable Vimy Ridge. By the standards of the First World War, the results of the first day's fighting were a resounding success. This was largely due to improvements in artillery techniques, and the density of heavy guns employed, which was nearly three times that of 1 July 1916. North of the River Scarpe, XVII Corps of the Third Army penetrated German defences to a depth of some 3½ miles, the furthest advance in a day by either side since the onset of trench warfare in the autumn of 1914. South of the river, the gains of VII and VI Corps, although less spectacular, were significant nonetheless. North of Arras, the Canadian Corps of the First Army captured virtually all of Vimy Ridge.

On 10 April the 17th Middlesex left Camblain Châtelain in a heavy snowstorm and proceeded south, the 2nd Division having received orders to relieve the 51st Division in the trenches north of the Scarpe. That same day the Canadians captured Hill 145 on Vimy Ridge and VI Corps pushed forward towards Monchy-le-Preux and Guémappe. The hilltop village of Monchy-le-Preux fell the next day. South of the Arras–Cambrai Road, the Fifth Army launched a poorly planned attack on the Hindenburg Line at Bullecourt with inadequate artillery support.

During the early hours of 12 April the 5th and 99th Brigades of 2nd Division completed the relief of the 154th Brigade in the front line. The 6th Brigade went into reserve, the 17th Middlesex taking over trenches south of Écurie. Working parties from all four battalions of 6th Brigade repaired roads and laid a duckboard track from Roclincourt to the forward areas. To the south of the 2nd Division, the Third Army took the villages of Héninel and Wancourt, capturing 2,000yd of the Hindenburg Line. To the north, the First Army seized The Pimple and Bois-en-Hache, thereby completing the capture of the Vimy and Lorette Ridges.

These successful operations disrupted German plans to recover Vimy Ridge by way of a counterattack from the direction of Givenchy-en-Gohelle, as their lines were now overlooked by the First Army positions. Under the cover of darkness, the Germans undertook a 2–3 mile retirement to their original third line of defences in the sector, the Oppy–Méricourt Line, which ran between Gavrelle and Méricourt before looping around the western outskirts of Lens. The following morning, once it became clear that the Germans were vacating their forward positions, the British and Canadians pushed forward. By the evening of 14 April the 2nd Division had advanced to within 500yd of the Oppy–

Méricourt Line. Patrols sent out to examine the German defences reported back that the wire was 'very thick and formidable'.[18]

After the initial success of the Arras fighting, the British advance had slowed considerably. Fresh German reserves were arriving on the Arras front in increasing numbers. Having undergone several days of hard fighting, the First and Third Armies were close to exhaustion and there were insufficient troops available to renew the attack on a wide front. The poor condition of the roads also meant that the guns were struggling to get forward to provide the infantry with effective artillery support. On 15 April Haig ordered a temporary suspension of offensive operations in order to prepare for the next series of attacks. Thus, the First Battle of the Scarpe on the Third Army front, and the Battle of Vimy Ridge on the First Army front, had come to an end. Over the last six days the British line had advanced 4 miles eastwards. More importantly, the British had performed their role in pinning down significant numbers of enemy reserves ahead of Nivelle's great offensive on the Aisne.

On 16 April the French delivered their main thrust on the Aisne. Although over 10,000 prisoners and several villages were taken by nightfall, the promised breakthrough failed to materialise and the French had lost over 40,000 men. That same day in St Pol, Haig outlined his future plans for the next phase of the British offensive at a conference attended by the army commanders of the First, Third and Fifth Armies. The First Army would assault the Oppy–Méricourt Line and capture Gavrelle, while the Third Army would launch further attacks astride the River Scarpe. To the south, the Fifth Army would capture Riencourt and Hendecourt.

On 20 April the 17th Middlesex were in support trenches opposite Oppy Wood, between Arleux and Gavrelle. Under the supervision of Capt Percival Edwards, formerly a tea planter in Ceylon, working parties dug assembly trenches for the planned attack on Oppy. Morale was good. Captain Ernest Parfitt had just returned from a spell of leave in North London, which had been spent making plans with Alice for the arrival of their first child:

We are at present in some trenches situated on top of a big ridge and my word, you can see for miles!!! You can see our shells falling in amongst their villages and on their trenches . . . I feel quite confident we could capture the line he is holding, if they sent for us for it now. And if we took that line from him, he would have to fall back another 2 or 3 miles, as there are no more trenches between.[19]

The following day Gen Henry Horne, the commander of the First Army, acting on reports that the wire in front of the Oppy–Méricourt Line had been insufficiently cut, requested a postponment of the attack on Oppy. Haig acceded to this request. The First Army's objectives were limited to the capture of Gavrelle. Thus, the Second Battle of the Scarpe would be predominantly a Third Army operation with the First Army playing only a subsidiary role

On 23 April the British attacked on a 9 mile-front between Fontaine-les-Croisilles and Gavrelle. About 10.45 a.m. a heavy German barrage was directed against the British positions all along the front. Reports were received of German infantry massing to recapture Gavrelle, which had fallen to the Royal Naval Division on the immediate right of the 2nd Division. Having moved up towards the front line the previous evening, the 17th Middlesex were ordered to form a defensive line along an embankment of the Lens-Arras railway, west of Bailleul. In the event, the wave of German counterattacks was directed solely at Gavrelle.

Battalion HQ of the 17th Middlesex provided an excellent vantage point from which to observe the progress of these counterattacks, all of which were broken up by British artillery at considerable loss to the Germans. Pte Wilf Nixon, the Fulham goalkeeper, saw a deluge of British shells come crashing down on a party of around 200 German soldiers moving towards Gavrelle. He recalled that the survivors ran back 'like bloody hell'.[20] At 9.30 p.m. a 17th Middlesex working party was sent out to dig a defensive trench in front of the railway embankment. Second-Lieutenant Basil Last and three other ranks were killed. Estranged from his wife for several years, 2/Lt Last had enlisted as a private in the London Regiment before being commissioned in the Middlesex Regiment. He had only been with the battalion since the beginning of the month.

On 24 April the Germans mounted further counterattacks to

recapture Gavrelle, which were once again repulsed. The Second Battle of the Scarpe had seen the British line advance 1 or 2 miles. Despite fierce German counterattacks all along the front, the British had managed to retain possession of Gavrelle and Guémappe, and the high ground above Fontaine-les-Croisilles and Chérisy. Progress had also been made east of Monchy-le-Preux and on Greenland Hill. That evening the 17th Middlesex moved back to Tent Camp at Roclincourt.

By this time, it was clear that the French offensive had failed to achieve the results predicted by Nivelle. Despite repeated French assurances that the Aisne offensive would continue, Haig had his doubts. There was already talk of replacing Nivelle with Gen Henri-Philippe Pétain, the doughty defender of Verdun. Haig decided to continue attacking around Arras, hoping that it would encourage the French to sustain their offensive. Accordingly, he proceeded to make plans for a major attack in early May, involving the First, Third and Fifth Armies. A preliminary series of operations was scheduled for 28 April. Attacks would be launched along an 8-mile front running southwards from Arleux to Monchy-le-Preux, in order to secure a better starting position for future operations. The 1st Canadian, 2nd and Royal Naval Divisions of the First Army were to seize the Oppy–Méricourt Line, north of Gavrelle, and to capture the villages of Arleux and Oppy, while the Third Army was tasked with securing Roeux and Greenland Hill. The 2nd Division's role in this operation was to capture the village of Oppy. On 26 April, while the 17th Middlesex were making final preparations for the forthcoming attack, Captain Ernest Parfitt wrote to Alice, by now only a few months from her due date:

Tomorrow evening I shall probably be going to a place where I shall not be able to write for several days, so remember NOT to worry . . . I will write at every opportunity as you know, but little girl please don't worry, think of what it means to us if you get upset . . . Give my love to Mum and all at home. Look after yourself and our little kiddie. I remain your ever loving Hubby.[21]

1. Miles, W., *Official History of the War, 1916*, vol. II, p. 532.
2. *Ibid.*
3. Falls, C., *Official History of the War, Military Operations: France & Belgium 1917*, vol. 1, p. 37.

4. Unrestricted submarine warfare was introduced on 1 February 1917. The United States formally declared war on Germany on 6 April.

5. TNA: WO 95/1361.

6. PC: Letter to Alice Parfitt, 8 January 1917.

7. TNA: WO 339/72157.

8. PC: Letter to Mrs Haynes, 29 January 1917.

9. BNL: *Oriental Notes*, 24 February 1917.

10. TNA: WO 161/100.

11. PC: Letter to Alice Parfitt, 2 March 1917.

12. *Ibid.*

13. *Ibid.*, 9 March 1917.

14. Divisional Intelligence Diary, in Wyrall, E., *The History of the Second Division*, p. 391.

15. Letter written by officer of the 1st King's Liverpool, in Wyrall, E., *The King's Regiment*, p. 380.

16. BNL: *Croydon Advertiser*, 2 December 1916.

17. BNL: *Sporting Chronicle*, 23 April 1917.

18. Wyrall, E., *The History of the Second Division*, p. 412.

19. PC: Letter to Alice Parfitt, 20 April 1917.

20. LC: POW 047.

21. PC: Letter to Alice Parfitt, 26 April 1917.

CHAPTER 12

OPPY WOOD

*I do hope that it will soon be over. I want to
get back to my home and little wife*
Capt Ernest Parfitt

In the days preceding the attack on Arleux and Oppy, divisional
and corps artillery pounded the German defences. Effective
artillery support proved problematic because the field guns were
either positioned on the reverse slope of Vimy Ridge, in which case
they were firing at extreme range or, if they were emplaced on its
forward slopes, they were exposed to German counter-battery fire.
Nonetheless, the work of wire-cutting continued unabated and
'reports showed that the wire had been sufficiently destroyed to
enable the infantry to assault without difficulty'.[1]

The attack was scheduled to take place at 4.25 a.m. on the 28th.
It was to be delivered by the 6th and 5th Brigades on a frontage of
2,200yd, with the 99th Brigade being held in reserve. At the same
time, the 1st Canadian Division would assault Arleux to the north,
and the Royal Naval Division would capture the high ground
north-east of Gavrelle to the south. The nature of the task facing
2nd Division was outlined in the *Official History*:

> It had first to break through the strongly-wired Oppy line. Then it
> would be faced by Oppy Wood, with its tangle of fallen trees, lying to
> its right centre. Behind the wood was the village, the two stretching a
> thousand yards from east to west. And a village with a wood on its
> near side to break up the formation of an attack had proved on many
> occasions one of the most difficult of all obstacles.[2]

Another problem was the 2nd Division was significantly under-
strength in that several battalions were still awaiting
reinforcements. The number of troops available for the assault on
Oppy was further eroded by the instruction that each battalion

should leave 108 soldiers out of the line in order to assist with its rebuilding in the event of heavy casualties. This meant that only 3,518 officers and men of the 5th and 6th Brigades would be available for the attack, less than the established strength of a single infantry brigade.

On the left of 2nd Division's attack, the 5th Brigade was to capture the enemy positions between Arleux and Oppy Wood. From right to left, its attack would be carried out by the 2nd Highland Light Infantry and the 2nd Oxford and Bucks Light Infantry with the 17th Royal Fusiliers in close support. The 24th Royal Fusiliers would be held in brigade reserve. On the right, the 6th Brigade was to seize Oppy Wood, Oppy and the trench systems to the immediate south of the village. The 13th Essex would advance on the right, the 17th Middlesex on the left. The 2nd South Staffords would be in close support, providing carrying parties, 'moppers up' and consolidating parties for the two strongpoints, which were to be established north-east and east of the village.[3] The 1st King's Liverpool were to remain in close support in the railway cutting west of Bailleul, and were to provide four carrying parties to haul supplies of ammunition, grenades and mortar shells up to the front line.

The 17th Middlesex had three objectives for the attack on Oppy. The first objective (Blue Line) followed the road, which ran between the wood and village. The second objective (Green Line) traced the eastern outskirts of the village. The third objective (Brown Line) crossed the Oppy-Neuvireuil Road, a few hundred yards east of the village, near the cemetery. In order to attain all three objectives the 17th Middlesex would have to advance a total of some 1,200yd.

The plan was that the 17th Middlesex would advance in three waves behind a creeping barrage. The barrage would be supplied by 18-pounder field guns, with one half of the guns moving 200yd ahead of the other firing high explosive shells, the remaining half firing shrapnel shells. The 4.5in howitzers, heavy artillery and machine-gun barrages would move ahead of the 18-pounder barrage. On reaching the Blue Line, the first wave would consolidate their gains, while the artillery placed a protective barrage in front for half an hour or so. During this pause the second wave was to form up in the rear, ready to advance through Oppy towards the second objective as soon as the artillery began to move forward again. Similar arrangements were to be carried out by the second and third waves in respect of the Green and the Brown Lines.

Two Stokes mortars of 6th Trench Mortar Battery were to follow the third wave along the southern edge of Oppy Wood on their way to occupy 'Strong Point C', near the Oppy–Neuvireuil Road. Three Vickers machine-guns would also move up behind the third wave to protect the flanks of the attack. A further two Vickers guns were to assist the 17th Middlesex with the task of clearing Oppy, before moving up to garrison 'Strong Point D', north-east of the village. Fierce opposition was to be expected, as 'Instructions' issued by 2nd Divisional HQ made clear:

All indications and information lead to the assumption that the enemy troops have received orders to oppose strenuously our advance on the north bank of the river Scarpe, which, if successful, will not only bring us up to the Siegfried Line before it is completed, but also threaten his hold on the valuable mining area of Lens. Violent counter-attacks are, therefore, to be expected, and will probably develop very shortly after our capture of Oppy and Arleux.[4]

On the morning of 28 April 1917 Oppy was defended by Infantry Regiment 75. This regiment was part of the 17th Division. It recruited principally from the Hanseatic towns and the Duchies of Mecklenburg, although there were several Danes and Poles within its ranks. It was rated as one of the most formidable divisions in the German army. Only a few months earlier the 17th Division had been an opponent of 2nd Division on the Ancre in the vicinity of Miraumont and Grandcourt before being withdrawn from the line in March. After a period of rest near Douai, it had been one of the German divisions rushed to the Arras sector, a few days after the opening of the British offensive.

The 17th Middlesex moved up to the front line on the evening of 27 April. Their assembly positions had been taped out by No. 4 Section of the 483rd Field Company behind the front line trench. In absolute silence the men formed up in three waves along a

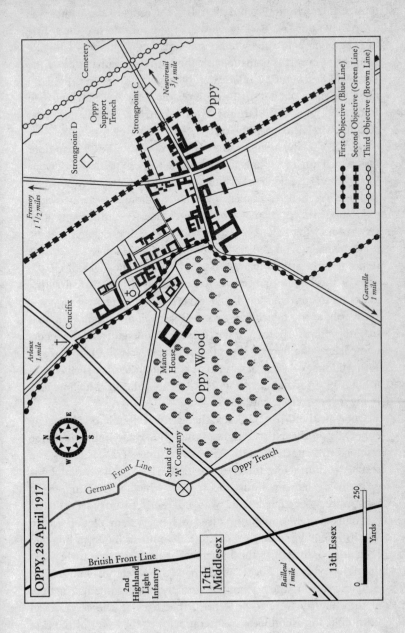

OPPY, 28 April 1917

First Objective (Blue Line)
Second Objective (Green Line)
Third Objective (Brown Line)

Cemetery

Strongpoint D

Oppy Support Trench

Strongpoint C

Newireuil 3/4 mile

Oppy

Fresnoy 1 1/2 miles

Crucifix

Arleux 1 mile

Gavrelle 1 mile

Manor House

Oppy Wood

Stand of 'A' Company

German Front Line

Oppy Trench

British Front Line

2nd Highland Light Infantry

17th Middlesex

13th Essex

Baillenl 1 mile

0   250
Yards

N
E
W
S

239

four-company front. From right to left, the order of companies was 'D', 'C', 'B', and 'A'. Each wave was organised into two lines: first line, bombers and riflemen; second line, Lewis gunners and rifle bombers. Contact was made with the battalions either side of the 17th Middlesex, the 13th Essex on the right and the 2nd Highland Light Infantry of the 5th Brigade on the left. The attached men from the 2nd South Staffords assumed their respective positions behind each wave, with the carrying parties at the rear.

At 4.25 a.m. the barrage came crashing down on the German front line, which ran a few yards in front of the western perimeter of Oppy Wood. The 17th Middlesex clambered out of their assembly trenches. Red and green flares immediately shot up from the German lines requesting artillery support. Two minutes later the British guns lifted forward and the battalion started its advance, immediately coming under machine-gun fire. It had been previously impressed on the troops that the artillery barrage was to be 'the guiding factor as to the pace of the infantry advance'.[5] A warning had been issued to the attacking troops that they should 'expect to find machine-guns a few yards behind the trench line assaulted, as well as in front of it, and that they must go straight for these machine-gun emplacements immediately the barrage lifts off the trench'.[6] As the first wave of 17th Middlesex dashed across No Man's Land, German shells began to drop in great numbers 150–200yd behind the British front line, trying to 'seal' off the battlefield.

Opposite the 17th Middlesex, the wire was 'found to be perfectly cut'. Only on the extreme right of the 6th Brigade front were large sections still intact, the 13th Essex suffering several casualties as a result. Within a few minutes the first waves of both battalions were in the enemy front line trench, which was found to be practically unoccupied. This was not entirely unexpected. The Germans had recently introduced a new system of defence in depth, whereby the number of machine-guns in the front line had been increased, while the trenches themselves were to be only lightly garrisoned. Such tactics had the effect of minimising casualties during the preliminary artillery bombardment. The bulk of the infantry were to be kept further back in the second and third lines for use in local counterattacks, in the event of the first line of defence being breached.

Above: *Kenneth Maclaine of Lochbuie was second-in-command of the 17th Middlesex when the battalion proceeded overseas in November 1915.*

(Lorne Maclaine)

Above: *Joe McLauchlan of Watford.*

(Trefor Jones)

Below: *Lt Maurice Oxenbould on the ranges at Perham Down.* (Julia Rhys)

Above and below: *Men from 'C' Company of the 17th Middlesex on field exercise near Perham Down.* (Julia Rhys)

Above: *Gravestone of Donald Stewart who was serving under the alias of James MacDonald. He was the first soldier of the 17th Middlesex to be killed in action.* **(Authors' collection)**

Below left: *A group of the 17th Middlesex at Givenchy, trying to keep warm, sketched by Cosmo Clark.* **(Julia Rhys)**

Below right: *Albert 'Ben' Butler pictured in his days as a Reading player. The Queen's Park Rangers centre-half was the first professional footballer in the 17th Middlesex to be killed.* **(RGBW Wardrobe & Museum Trust)**

Above: *L/Cpl Herbert Derisley, nephew of a Crystal Palace director, who was killed on Vimy Ridge on 1 June 1916.* (Jane Jones)

Above right: *2/Lt Edgar Lee, the first officer of the 17th Middlesex to be killed in the war.* (Jane Jones)

Below: *A mine crater on Vimy Ridge in 1919.* (IWM Q37095)

Above: *A 17th Middlesex patrol venturing into No Man's Land, sketched by Cosmo Clark.* (Julia Rhys)

Below left: *A German trench at Souchez.* (Julia Rhys)

Below right: *John 'Ginger' Williams of Millwall and Wales. Williams was killed on Vimy Ridge in June 1916 and has no known grave.* (Vicky Moore)

Above: *The ruins of Longueval during the summer of 1916. Delville Wood is in the background.*
(Julia Rhys)

Below left: *Ted Hanney of Manchester City. A fine centre-half, Hanney played for Great Britain in the 1912 Stockholm Olympic Games. He was wounded at Delville Wood on 28 July 1916.*
(Colorsport)

Below right: *Norman Wood of Stockport County was known for his 'brushed dark hair and deft touches of the ball with the side of the foot'. Wood lost his life in Delville Wood on 28 July 1916.*
(Alan Futter)

Above left: *Jack Borthwick of Millwall was fortunate to survive a serious head wound at Delville Wood on 28 July 1916.* **(Dave Sullivan)**

Above right: *Despite being wounded in the knee on the Somme during the summer of 1916, Fred Keenor (seated behind the FA Cup) later became one of the greatest players in the history of Welsh football. In 1927 he famously captained the Cardiff City side which defeated Arsenal in the FA Cup Final.* **(Colorsport)**

Below: *The shattered remnants of Delville Wood, August 1916.* **(Julia Rhys)**

Above: *Guillemont Railway Station, September 1916.* **(Julia Rhys)**

Below left: *William Gerrish pictured in his days as an Aston Villa player. Gerrish's legs were shattered by a shell at Guillemont on 8 August 1916. He 'lay quietly smoking a cigarette, until picked up by the stretcher bearers', but died soon after.* **(Colorsport)**

Below right: *Wounded at Guillemont on 8 August 1916, Cosmo Clark was a young art student at the outbreak of war.* **(Julia Rhys)**

Both the 17th Middlesex and the 13th Essex took a few prisoners. During the early stages of the fighting, about 80 prisoners, mostly from I Battalion of Infantry Regiment 75, would arrive back at the British lines. Three minutes later, the creeping barrage resumed its forward movement at a rate of 100yd every four minutes. Keeping up with the barrage, the first wave moved on into Oppy Wood and past the ruined white manor house in the north-eastern corner of the wood. Snipers and machine-guns concealed in the trees and undergrowth were not the only danger. In order to clear the wood effectively, the shrapnel shells fired by the British guns needed to burst high above the trees. The attacking troops had been warned that 'though the shells may be bursting over the heads or even a little behind them, they must watch the strike of the bullets on the ground and get as close to this as possible'.[7] The 17th Middlesex War Diary, which contains a fairly detailed summary of the day's events, recorded the initial moments of the attack:

The battalion pressed forward behind the creeping barrage and the 1st Objective was reached with only a few casualties. Shortly after the advance commenced the Officer Commanding A Coy on the left noticed that the battalion on our left [2nd Highland Light Infantry] had either lost touch or had been unable to make progress. He therefore placed a Lewis gun section and some bombers in the enemy front line trench with instructions to block the trench and prevent any movement by the enemy against the left flank. The right flank during the advance to the first objective appears to have kept well in touch with the 13th Essex.[8]

As the second wave of the 17th Middlesex prepared to assault the village, the British guns laid down a standing barrage 50–100yd in front of them, while the 'moppers-up' cleared Oppy Wood. Under the supervision of Capt Ernest Parfitt, the first wave of 17th Middlesex, which had been charged with the consolidation of the first objective, went about their work. An immediate problem was that there were several houses in the gap between the positions being consolidated by the 17th Middlesex and the protective standing barrage. The officer commanding 2nd Division, Maj Gen Cecil Pereira, would later write:

If I had to attack Oppy Village again I should prefer not to make a pause at the Western edge of the village or inside the village itself, as this entails a depth of 200 yards in front of the leading wave being untouched by barrage during the period of the halt. I should prefer to halt either half-way in the wood or else carry on through the village dropping strong lines of mopping up and consolidation parties en route.[9]

Taking full advantage of the gap in the barrage, the defenders of Oppy were free to maintain their fire from loopholes cut in the walls. There were even reports of enemy machine-guns being seen mounted on roofs. Under a hail of fire, brave men did what they could to silence the machine-guns. Lt John Sebright remembered one particular act of heroism:

> Shortly after reaching our first objective a large number of enemy snipers and machine guns, hidden in various houses and barns, started firing and caused a considerable annoyance. One enemy machine gun on my Company front (C Coy) was particularly severe on my men and Corpl. W. White asked for permission to try to silence it. He returned in about half an hour having effectually silenced the gun and disposed of its crew single-handed. Apart from this very plucky action he was always infusing cheerfulness and a spirit of action into the men and was happiest when in greatest danger.[10]

At 5.35 a.m. the creeping barrage started moving forward again towards the Green Line. The second wave of 17th Middlesex started its advance through the village under heavy fire. It was not long before the gap between the second wave and the barrage began to widen. There were particular problems on the right of the 17th Middlesex attack, where the Germans were not only holding their ground, but beginning to launch counterattacks supported by a withering machine-gun fire. Cpl Arthur Dettmer of No. 14 Platoon, 'D' Coy, was hit shortly before his platoon officer, 2/Lt Alfred Henderson, a pre-war territorial, was shot in the head:

> I was wounded first and, while he was looking at me, he was killed by a machine gun bullet. We were absolutely overcome by Germans

and it was a trying time for us to save our lives. I was very sorry to see what had happened as he was one of the best officers one could wish for. Although he was only with us a short time he proved to be one of the best.[11]

By now, the advance of 'D' Company had ground to a halt. Lt Sebright recalled: 'I received an urgent message from the Company Commander on my right [D Company] for help, as he was being counterattacked. He kept my men for an hour, by which time our Artillery had finished its support to our furthest advance.'[12] The 17th Middlesex War Diary recorded that:

Very heavy fighting now ensued on the Right, but on the left . . . Crucifix Lane [a German trench running north-south, north-east of Oppy] . . . was reached. The fighting had now become so serious that both the 2nd and 3rd waves were fully involved in the struggle for the 2nd Objective while the 1st Objective was still being consolidated. Up to this juncture reports from wounded men and reports by runner had been received confirming the capture of the 1st Objective and of the struggle for the 2nd Objective, but owing to the hostile shelling all reports were somewhat late in making in reaching Battn. HQ and the situation on the left did not seem clear, as although A Coy. were known to have gained ground, a report came in from the H.L.I. [Highland Light Infantry] on our left to the effect that they were hung up by fire in the Sunken Road in the neighbourhood of the Crucifix. A senior officer [Capt Percival Edwards] was now sent from Battn HQ to clear up the situation on the left and to locate a suitable forward position for Battn HQ to move to.[13]

Almost as soon as the 17th Middlesex had reached the first objective, stubborn German resistance had started to delay the advance. At 6.29 a.m. when the British artillery started to lay down a protective barrage in front of the Brown Line, the third objective, there was no sign of the 17th Middlesex. Seriously behind schedule, and now bereft of effective artillery support, the second and third waves of the 17th Middlesex were still fighting their way towards the second objective.

Around 7 a.m. British aircraft circled above Oppy monitoring the progress of the attack. It was a mild bright day. The 17th Middlesex lit flares and flashed mirrors to signal the extent of their advance. Fifteen minutes later a message and map were dropped near 6th Brigade HQ showing that flares had been lit on the line of the first objective along the line of the road running south-east to north-west through Oppy. No flares were reported to have been seen either to the north-west, or to the south of the village. Of even greater concern were the large numbers of German reinforcements, which could be clearly discerned crossing the ridge to the east of Oppy, moving up towards the fighting.

In Oppy, the struggle for the second objective raged unabated. Without effective artillery support and sufficient weight of numbers to drive the Germans out of the village, the plight of the 17th Middlesex was growing more desperate by the minute. Second-Lieutenant Norman Dick was in the thick of it. Only the previous week, the Aldenham School maths master, who had played rugby for Saracens, had 'turned down' a staff appointment in order to remain with the battalion. Second-Lieutenant Sebright recalled what happened next:

There was considerable amount of confusion now owing to great loss of officers and men. 2/Lt Dick came up to me and asked whether we could not 'DO SOMETHING'. From reports of a patrol the enemy were massing at the other end of the village. We collected all the men we could, charged through the village and succeeded in taking about 12 prisoners and breaking up the counter-attack.

I passed the word along for a further rush to a low brick wall some forty yards ahead. I waited a few minutes and ran followed by only two or three men who were killed or wounded on the way. I immediately tried to get back but a hail of machine gun bullets around my head prompted me to lie low for a few minutes. Soon I heard a tremendous clatter of machine guns and looked up to see Lt Dick, with rifle and bayonet in hand, rushing towards me. In spite of great danger he continued his course until he fell on his face about ten yards from me and never moved again.

This gallant officer, who refused to remain with the Brigade staff the week before, because he 'wished to fight', ran the gauntlet in face of what he knew was almost certain death to assist a brother officer.

He had seen what had happened to us, but this did not deter him from attempting as brave a deed as I have ever witnessed. A few moments after many bombs were sent over and I was almost buried and lost consciousness until I was being carried away by four Huns.[14]

By now, the situation on the left flank was also beginning to deteriorate. Strong parties of the enemy had been able to maintain their positions in the vicinity of the Crucifix, north-east of the wood, causing the 17th Middlesex to lose touch with the 2nd Highland Light Infantry. Slipping through the resulting gap between the two battalions, an estimated two companies of German troops entered the north-eastern corner of Oppy Wood from their positions around the Crucifix. One party proceeded west through the wood past the white manor house back towards Oppy Trench; the other moved south and attacked Capt Parfitt and the first wave of the 17th Middlesex from the rear.

On the right flank of the 17th Middlesex, the 13th Essex were also in difficulties, having reached a point south-east of Oppy Wood. Once the 1st Royal Marine Light Infantry of the Royal Naval Division, who were attacking to the south, had been virtually annihilated in the face of heavy machine-gun fire and uncut wire, the Germans had been able to focus their attention on the right flank of the 13th Essex and had started bombing up Oppy Trench from the south. Back at Battalion HQ it must have been increasingly apparent to Lt Col Kelly that the 17th Middlesex were now in serious trouble:

It was now nearly 8 o'clock and a few minutes later a report came in from the O.C. A Coy, the left Coy, to say that the enemy was working round both his flanks. The only available reserve inside the Battn, viz: the Moppers Up of the 1st Objective (who had reported the completion of this task) had already been sent forward to strengthen the right in the hope that the 2nd Objective might still be reached. Capt. Edwards the officer, who had been sent out to clear up the situation found that the enemy had pressed down in strength from the North both down the German Front Line Trench [Oppy Trench] and by the Crucifix Road on the flank of our two left Coys ['A' and 'B' Companies] and had driven them back through the wood to the enemy Front Line Trench.

Here these two Coys were making a stand, but had by now maintained very heavy losses. The enemy also appears to have counter attacked against the front & right flank as well and had succeeded in re-entering the wood and getting in between the troops consolidating on the 1st Objective and those who had been driven back to the Oppy Trench. The enemy had also worked up the Oppy Trench from the south and were bombing up from that direction also. All communication with the remnants of the troops in the 1st Objective was now cut off and runners who attempted to get through to the troops still holding the OPPY Trench were either killed or wounded. Lt Col Martin, 13th Essex Regt commanding, sent forward a Company of 1st Royal Berks to endeavour to relieve the situation, but they could not get beyond the OB line [British front line][15]

The 17th Middlesex in and around Oppy were now completely cut off. The Germans would later claim to have sidestepped to the flanks of the front attacked, allowing the 17th Middlesex to enter the wood, before moving back in their rear, 'as if a door into a great reception room had been opened and then closed again as soon as sufficient guests had entered'.[16] The 17th Middlesex War Diary recorded that 'the troops on the 1st Objective (Blue Line) were not heard of again until a wounded officer succeeded in making his way back during the night. His evidence made it clear that these troops had fought till they were practically exterminated by the superior pressure of the enemy; the few survivors probably surrendered'.[17]

In Oppy Trench the remnants of 'A' and 'B' Companies of the 17th Middlesex continued to hold out against the odds until the supply of grenades was exhausted. Refusing to surrender, around ten survivors dashed across No Man's Land back towards the British front line. Only one officer and three other ranks made it. To the south of Oppy Wood small parties of the 13th Essex also tried to hold their section of Oppy Trench, but their predicament proved similarly hopeless. British reports maintain that small isolated parties held out in Oppy Trench until dusk, before withdrawing to the British front line. This version of events differs from that provided by the regimental history of Infantry Regiment 75, which maintains that Oppy Wood and village had been completely retaken by 11.15 a.m. This view would appear to be supported by the 2nd South Staffords War Diary, which records that the enemy had managed to reoccupy their front line opposite the 17th Middlesex by 10.45 a.m.

The stunned survivors of the 17th Middlesex remained for the rest of the day in the British front line. That evening the 6th Brigade was relieved by the 99th Brigade, who were to launch another unsuccessful assault on Oppy the next morning, and the 17th Middlesex moved back to Roclincourt. The day had been a complete disaster. The Battalion War Diary recorded that:

Had the flanks remained secure it is believed that the 1st objective could have been held against counter attack and possibly the 2nd objective would have been gained in its entirety, although in view of the strength of the enemy in the village, this may be doubtful.

As it was, the sudden onrush of the enemy from both flanks, which enabled them to re-occupy the wood, combined with their vigorous counter-attacks, was disastrous; and in the confused nature of the fighting it was impossible to know where to ask for fresh artillery barrages to be placed.[18]

While skilful German defence had undoubtedly played an important part in the failure of the attack, Maj Gen Cecil Pereira correctly identified the principal cause of failure in his subsequent report. Too few men had been allocated to the initial assault, and there had been insufficient reserves available:

It is evident that, even with our heavy and accurate artillery barrage which was well followed up, there must be sufficient men per yard to give weight to the impetus of the waves, to provide sufficient moppers up to deal with dug-outs, shell holes, strong points without delay, and to afford a suitable reserve to meet contingencies and counter-attacks. On the 28th April, a sufficient number of men per yard was not available, and I attribute the failure of the attack very largely to this fact: the exposure of the right flank undoubtedly contributed to this failure.[19]

The only success of the day's fighting, later known as the Battle of Arleux, had occurred north of Oppy, where the 1st Canadian

Division had taken Arleux. All the 2nd Division had to show for its efforts was a small section of ground on the northern side of Oppy Wood, which had been taken by 5th Brigade. The 2nd Oxford and Bucks Light Infantry were secure in their positions along the Green Line, following the successful assault of the Canadians on their left and the limited advance of the 2nd Highland Light Infantry on their right. Although the latter battalion had reached the Oppy–Arleux Road, the Scotsmen had been forced to pull back once the 17th Middlesex had been ejected from Oppy Wood.

Of the two brigades of 2nd Division that led the attack around Oppy on 28 April, the 6th Brigade had fared the worst. Its casualties amounted to 38 officers and 1,066 other ranks. These figures included 11 officers and 451 other ranks of the 17th Middlesex. The Battalion War Diary recorded the casualties as: 2 officers and 11 other ranks killed, 3 officers and 106 other ranks wounded, and 6 officers and 334 other ranks missing. Of the officers and men who had gone over the top that morning, only 1 officer and 41 men had returned unscathed. When one compares these casualty figures with the number of dead recorded by the Commonwealth War Graves Commission (CWGC), it is clear that around 250 officers and men must have fallen into enemy hands on 28 April. Many of them, like Capt Ernest Parfitt and three footballers, Pte Charles Abbs of Norwich City, Pte Wilf Nixon of Fulham and Sgt Joe Mercer of Nottingham Forest, had been wounded prior to capture.[20]

Despite the large number of prisoners, the 17th Middlesex had nonetheless incurred what would prove to be the battalion's heaviest loss of life in a single day's fighting during the entire war. Six officers and 133 other ranks of the 17th Middlesex were dead. Another 20 or so soldiers would later die of their wounds. The six officers killed on 28 April 1917 were 2/Lt Frank Bonathan, 2/Lt Norman Dick, 2/Lt Alfred Henderson, Capt Stanley Read, 2/Lt Albert Secrett and 2/Lt Cyril White. Another officer, 2/Lt John Abercrombie, a former bank clerk at the British Linen Bank in Threadneedle Street, died of his wounds the following day at the 1st Canadian Casualty Clearing Station. Two of these officers, 2/Lt Frank Bonathan and Capt Stanley Read, were holders of the Military Cross.

Second-Lieutenant Frank Bonathan had only been with the battalion a few weeks. Only 5ft tall, with tattooed forearms, he was, in many respects, an unlikely officer. Born in 1893, Bonathan had grown up in a children's home in Milton, where the superintendent had described him as 'an industrious, willing, and obedient boy'.[21] Enlisting in the Middlesex Regiment shortly after his 14th birthday, Bonathan had struggled with the discipline of army life and had fallen foul of the authorities on several occasions. Wounded in August 1915, he was sent back to England, being posted to the 23rd Middlesex on recovery from his wounds. Promoted to the rank of company sergeant major, Bonathan had distinguished himself by winning a Military Cross in the autumn of 1916 and had subsequently been commissioned.[22] Capt Stanley Read, from Ealing, had joined the battalion from the 1/13th Londons following the unsuccessful attack on Guillemont in August 1916. The son of Frederick and Rosa Read of West Ealing, London, Capt Read was only 21 years old when he was killed. His Military Cross would be gazetted a few weeks after his death.[23]

Another officer of the 17th Middlesex killed on 28 April 1917 was the former Scottish rugby international Lt Bertie Wade, who had been attached to the 6th Brigade Trench Mortar Battery since December 1916. He was hit in the eyes and chest: 'His lads, who loved him . . . carried his body to the front line German Trench which they were taking, determined to have him with them to the end'.[24] An officer wrote to Wade's father that 'he died a very gallant little gentleman'.[25] Fellow Old Alleynian, 2/Lt Stanley Cross, serving in the London Regiment, later wrote of his reaction to the news of his friend's death:

We were sitting outside our dug-out, my Company Commander and I; the mail from home had just come in, and both of us were deep in the contents of letters and newspapers. 'Haven't I often heard you speak of a great pal of yours named Wade, well-known Rugger man, wasn't he?' I looked up at the sound of Captain T___'s voice, and seeing that he was reading *The Times*, an icy fear stole into my heart as I replied, 'Yes, what's up?' 'Sorry, old man, he has gone under; here's a notice about him'. The bright spring afternoon seemed to grow darker at his words, and I went off to a quiet spot I knew of, just to have a good think about the best pal I ever had.[26]

Among the 133 other ranks of the 17th Middlesex killed at Oppy was Pte Bob Whiting, the former Brighton & Hove Albion goalkeeper, who had been killed by shellfire while tending to the wounded. Whiting left a widow, Nellie, and three young boys, the youngest of whom was barely 3 months old. The previous year Whiting had fallen foul of the military authorities when he had overstayed a period of home leave, possibly on account of some family crisis. He was brought back to France and held briefly in the military prison at Étaples before being returned to the 17th Middlesex on 26 November 1916. On 28 February 1917, at a Field General Courts Martial, he was found guilty of being absent from duty without leave between 3 June 1916 and 13 October 1916.[27] His sentence of 9 months imprisonment and hard labour was subsequently suspended and he had remained with the battalion.

Renowned for the phenomenal distance of his goal kicks, 'Pom-Pom' Whiting was reputed to have once cleared the opposing team's crossbar with a kick from his own goal-area. He had started out as a shipbuilder before playing professionally for West Ham Utd reserves. After a two-year spell at Tunbridge Wells Rangers, Whiting was signed by Chelsea in April 1906, following an impressive performance during an FA Cup match against Norwich City. During his time at Stamford Bridge, Whiting made 52 League appearances, helping Chelsea secure promotion to the First Division in his first season. In 1908 he moved to Brighton & Hove Albion, where he soon became a firm favourite of the club's supporters. In December 1914, when Whiting unexpectedly announced his intention to retire from the game, the Albion directors agreed to cancel his contract and voted him a sum of money in lieu of a promised benefit match.

At the family home in Tunbridge Wells, Nellie Whiting received the news of her husband's death from the chaplain, Rev Donald Murray. Unfortunately for Nellie Whiting, there was a deeply unpleasant postscript to the tragedy of her husband's death. Within a few weeks a malicious and wholly unfounded rumour reached Brighton that Pte Bob Whiting had, in fact, been shot as a deserter. When this shocking news reached the ears of his widow, Nellie immediately sought to disprove this 'foul calumny' by passing on letters from the chaplain, her husband's company commander and the battalion adjutant, 2/Lt John Howard, for publication in local newspapers. The subsequent publication of these letters put a welcome end to the speculation. Bob Whiting's tally of 320 appearances in the Albion goal would not be surpassed until 1972.

By far the majority of the other ranks killed at Oppy were men who had arrived as reinforcements in the wake of the attacks on Guillemont and the Redan Ridge. These men were predominantly from London and Home Counties. Only 18 of the men killed at Oppy were original enlistments in the battalion. Among their number were Cpl Philip Furneaux from Hackney, who had enlisted in the Footballers' Battalion at the age of 16, Pte John Abear, who left a widow and young son back home in Wantage, and Pte Henry Spurgeon, a 37 year-old dyer from Shepherd's Bush. At a Field General Courts Martial on 24 August 1916 Pte Spurgeon had been convicted of attempted desertion and had been given a sentence of three years penal servitude, later commuted to two years' imprisonment and hard labour. After nearly four months in a military prison at Rouen, the sentence was suspended and Pte Spurgeon had been returned to the 17th Middlesex. At Oppy Wood he gave his life for his country.

Of all the officers and other ranks of the 17th Middlesex who were killed on 28 April, only three – Pte George Chambers and two early enlistments, Pte John Abear and Drummer William Sharpe – have a known grave. The remainder are commemorated on Bay 7 of the Arras Memorial to the Missing, which commemorates almost 35,000 servicemen from the United Kingdom, South Africa and New Zealand who lost their lives in the Arras sector between the spring of 1916 and 7 August 1918.

On 3 May 1917 Oppy Wood was attacked again as part of a series of operations by the First, Third and Fifth Armies along a 14-mile front. Haig had already taken the decision to limit the scope of the Arras offensive with a view to shifting the focus of British operations north to Flanders, but he wanted to keep the

Germans occupied ahead of a renewed French effort on the Aisne. Despite the fact that it had been severely mauled, the 2nd Division was ordered to attack Fresnoy Trench, north of Oppy.[28] The three brigades of the 2nd Division were so depleted that Maj Gen Pereira decided to form a single composite brigade to carry out the attack. The only battalion not to feature in this composite brigade was the 17th Middlesex. By the time that the survivors of 28 April had rejoined the transport and battle cadre, the total strength of the battalion was 12 officers and 180 men.

The fighting of 3 May, known as the Third Battle of the Scarpe, was a disaster for the British, the Third and Fifth Armies making little progress at a heavy cost in men. Among the dead was L/Sgt Sandy Turnbull, who had transferred from the 23rd Middlesex to the 8th East Surreys towards the end of 1916. On 19 February 1910, Turnbull had scored the first ever goal at Old Trafford, as well as the winning goal in the FA Cup Final against Bristol City the previous year. Reported wounded and missing during the attack on the village of Chérisy, 10 miles east of Arras, Sandy Turnbull was never seen again and is commemorated on the Arras Memorial.

North of the Scarpe, the First Army attacked Fresnoy and Oppy. The capture of Fresnoy by the 1st Canadian Division, whose right flank was partially secured by the Composite Brigade of 2nd Division, was described in the *Official History* '. . . as the relieving feature of a day which many who witnessed it consider the blackest day of the war'.[29] Attacked by the 92nd Brigade of 31st Division, Oppy once again proved an insurmountable obstacle. An impressive memorial commemorating the men of Hull, who died that day was erected in the village after the war. It is situated on the eastern edge of the wood, close to the spot where Capt Parfitt and his men were overwhelmed. At the time of writing there is a small football pitch nearby, an inadvertent memorial perhaps to the officers and men of the 17th Middlesex who fell in the vicinity of Oppy on 28 April 1917.

The Arras offensive petered after the disastrous attack of 3 May. By the time, the fighting had come to an end, the Third Army had captured Roeux and its notorious Chemical Works, but the Germans had retaken Fresnoy. During the bitter fighting of April and May 1917 the First, Third and Fifth Armies had sustained casualties of 158,660 officers and men.[30] Once again, accurate German casualty figures are unavailable, but there is little doubt that their losses were significantly less, particularly in view of the recent changes to their defensive doctrine.

A few weeks after the 17th Middlesex attack at Oppy Wood, Alice Parfitt gave birth to a baby girl. Joyce Parfitt never did meet her father. Badly wounded in the right leg, Capt Parfitt had lost a lot of blood by the time he received medical treatment. On 7 May, the same day that Haig briefed his army commanders that the Arras offensive would be scaled down ahead of impending operations in Flanders, Capt Parfitt wrote a short note to Alice from a hospital in Bavaria, telling her that he had been wounded, and that he had been taken prisoner. He gave no indication of the seriousness of his condition. A week or so later he lapsed into a delirious state and died on 28 May 1917.

Capt Parfitt was buried in Kempten Protestant Cemetery with full military honours, the British officers and men in the hospital providing a 'beautiful floral wreath' for the occasion. A Canadian officer, Lt Harold Bridge, who had been treated in the same ward as Capt Parfitt, sent word to Alice, via the German authorities, that her late husband had received 'every attention and kindness possible'.[31] After the war he told her the truth. The manner of the treatment and the lack of food were to blame: 'If I met that Prussian Doctor Hauptmann Grunewald, I would have him shot.'[32] After the war, the body of Capt Parfitt was moved to Niederzwehren Cemetery, a few miles south of Kassel, where his grave can be found today.

1. TNA: WO 95/1296.
2. Falls, C., *Official History of the War, 1917*, vol. 1, p. 419.
3. On 28 April 1917 4 officers and 120 men of 'D' Company were attached to the 17th Middlesex for mopping-up and consolidation duties. One officer and 68 other ranks of 'C' Company formed carrying parties for the 17th Middlesex.
4. Quoted in Wyrall, E., *The History of the Second Division*, p. 419.
5. TNA: WO 95/1356.
6. *Ibid.*
7. *Ibid.*
8. TNA: WO 95/1361.
9. TNA: WO 95/1296.
10. TNA: WO 339/34919. Unfortunately, it has not proved possible to identify Cpl W. White conclusively. Pte F. White MM (F/ 608) is the most likely candidate. He was killed on 28 April 1917 and was an acting corporal at the time of his death.
11. TNA: WO 339/37013.

12. TNA: WO 339/34919.

13. TNA: WO 95/1361.

14. TNA: WO 339/34919.

15. TNA: WO 95/1361.

16. Falls, C. *Official History of the War, 1917*, vol. 1, p. 420.

17. TNA: WO 95/1361.

18. *Ibid.*

19. TNA: WO 95/1296.

20. The history of the German Infantry Regiment 75 records that 7 officers and 228 other ranks of the 'South-Strasford-Shire Regiment' [sic] were captured unwounded on 28 April 1917. These figures excluded prisoners who were sent straight back to the prisoners' cage, or evacuated wounded. The casualties of Infantry Regiment 75 were: 5 officers and 62 other ranks killed; 7 officers and 190 other ranks wounded; and 114 other ranks missing.

21. TNA: WO 339/86173.

22. *London Gazette*, Issue 29837, 24 November 1916.

23. *Ibid.*, Issue 30111, 1 June 1917.

24. DCA: Letter from John Luvian Wade to 'Slacker' Christison, 25 May 1917.

25. BNL: *Sportsman*, 10 May 1917.

26. Sewell, E., *The Rugby Football Internationals' Roll of Honour*, p. 218.

27. Being absent without leave was a lesser offence than desertion. The key distinction between the offences was the *intention* of the soldier: 'The offence of desertion - that is to say, of deserting or attempting to desert His Majesty's service - implies an intention on the part of the offender either not to return to His Majesty's service at all, or to escape some important service . . .' War Office, *Manual of Military Law*, para. 13, p.18. Paragraph 14 goes on to deal with the crucial question of ascertaining 'intention': 'It is obvious that the evidence of intention to quit the service altogether may be so strong as to be irresistible, as for instance, if a soldier is found in plain clothes on board a steamer starting for America, or is found crossing a river to the enemy; while, on the other hand, the evidence is frequently such as to leave it extremely doubtful what the real intention of the man was. Mere length of absence is, by itself, inconclusive as a test, for a soldier who has been entrapped into a bad company through drink, or other causes, may be absent some time without any thought of becoming a deserter; but in the case above put, of a soldier found on board a steamer starting for America, there could be no doubt of the intention, though he might only have been absent for a few hours.' *Ibid.* p. 18. Even so, the fact that Whiting, having been absent for 133 days, faced a charge of being absent without leave, rather than one of desertion, suggests that there might have been extenuating circumstances in his case.

28 Between 15 and 30 April 1917 the 2nd Division sustained the following casualties: officers: 39 killed, 72 wounded and 28 missing; other ranks: 349 killed, 1,054 wounded and 1,089 missing. Most of these casualties were sustained in the attacks of 28 and 29 April.

29. Falls, C., *Official History of the War, 1917*, vol. 1, p. 450.

30. The daily casualty rate of the British army during the Arras offensive exceeded those of Passchendaele and the Somme.

31. Letter to Alice Parfitt, 3 June 1917.

32. *Ibid.*, 2 November 1920.

CHAPTER 13

HOLDING THE LINE

Brooks our company kitten is busy catching fleas. There is a
German aeroplane overhead, which our anti-aircraft guns are
shelling – apart from that I don't think there is much news
Capt Cosmo Clark

On 1 May the 17th Middlesex left the camp at Écurie and
marched to Maroeuil. Four days later the battalion moved to
Roclincourt where it spent the next few days working on the
Bailleul light railway before moving back into the rest area around
Diéval. There was plenty of time to reflect on recent events. Recently
promoted to the rank of captain, Percy Barnfather wrote to a friend
in Croydon:

> I am very glad to say my good fortune is still sticking to me, and I
> hope it may continue to do so. You want a lot of luck out here to keep
> free from injury. I had a charmed life in the last attack. We have been
> having glorious weather, but today it is raining very hard, I'm afraid
> it will spoil our game tonight. We have a big match on. We are still
> unbeaten, and likely to remain so, although we lost a good many of
> the old boys in this last attack . . . They are all heroes, every one of
> them, and we realise it more and more every day. I saw plenty of men
> knocked out in the last affair, but I never heard one word of
> complaint, they were simply glorious.[1]

After a period of reorganisation and training, the 2nd Division
was sent back into the line around Oppy towards the end of May.
Still under-strength, the 17th Middlesex were kept in divisional
reserve. On 3 June the 17th Middlesex, organised into two double
companies, went back into front line near Fresnoy, relieving the
17th Royal Fusiliers. The following evening a 17th Middlesex patrol
ran into trouble in No Man's Land. Second-Lieutenant Herbert
Sanders, a bank clerk from Surrey, was wounded in the head and

taken prisoner. On 5 June the Germans raided the 17th Middlesex trenches, but were easily repulsed, leaving two dead behind. These men were identified, as belonging to Bavarian Infantry Regiment 10 of the 6th Bavarian Division. The next day 2/Lt Stephen Kempster, a commercial traveller in civilian life, went out to visit listening posts in No Man's Land. He lost his way on his return and was tragically killed by a Canadian grenade while attempting to crawl through the wire. Second-Lieutenant Kempster left a widow and two young daughters at his home in Switzerland.

While the 17th Middlesex were experiencing one of their quietest periods of the war, British preparations for offensive operations were continuing around Ypres. On 7 June, as a precursor to the main thrust in Flanders, Gen Herbert Plumer's Second Army executed a well-planned assault on the Messines-Wytschaete Ridge, which dominated Ypres from the south. The key feature was the detonation of 19 mines containing nearly 1,000,000lb of high explosive, which virtually destroyed the German forward positions and entombed many of their occupants.[2] The success of the Messines operation owed much to Plumer's chief of staff, the meticulous Maj Gen Charles 'Tim' Harington. Several years earlier Harington had been Frank Buckley's company commander in the King's Liverpool Regiment, and had once written a letter to the young soldier congratulating him on his prowess on the football field.

On 19 June the 17th Middlesex boarded buses and proceeded to Béthune after a largely uneventful few weeks. That same day a letter from Pte Peter Roney, the Bristol Rovers goalkeeper, was published in the *Sporting Chronicle*. Roney, who had transferred from the 17th Middlesex to the Machine Gun Corps (MGC) a few months earlier, was now playing for a MGC football team:

We have a first class Soccer team here – one that would make the City or Rovers a power in the land. I think they could hold their own with any selected team in England, and I will just give you their names, myself in goal, Weller (Everton), Jones (Blackpool), Connell (Ayr), Davidson (Middlesbrough), P. Allen (Clyde), Cunningham and Stringfellow (Portsmouth), Smith (Brighton & Bradford), Spencer (Clapton) and Nigh (Dundee). A gift from the Gods for any club manager. If the war was finished we might make a tour – this is, if they can be kept together – and we should not lose many matches.[3]

On reading this letter from 'his old friend' Pte John Stephenson, the Cardiff goalkeeper, wrote to the *Sporting Chronicle* listing the current 17th Middlesex team: John Stephenson (Cardiff City), goalkeeper; Pte Fred Whittaker (Millwall) and L/Cpl John Woodhouse (Brighton & Hove Albion), backs; Pte John Nuttall (Millwall), Cpl David Kenney (Grimsby Town) and Pte William Booth (Brighton & Albion), halfbacks; Pte John 'Jack' Dodds (Oldham Athletic), Cpl Jack Doran (Coventry City), Pte Alonzo Poulton (West Bromwich Albion), Pte Ernest Russ (Chelsea) and Pte Albert Holmes (Coventry City), forwards.[4] Pte Stephenson wrote that: 'I am certain that our team here wouldn't give Peter's much of a chance were we only to meet them'.[5] Even though there were only about 40 professional footballers still serving with the 17th Middlesex, the battalion team, trained by L/Cpl Pat Gallacher 'the old Spurs warrior', was still a formidable one. Every player was a professional footballer with the exception of Ernest Russ, a Chelsea amateur who had accompanied the Pensioners on a pre-war Continental tour.

On 22 June the 17th Middlesex relieved the 3/5th Lancashire Fusiliers in the front line, near Givenchy. One of the battalion's officers described the locality:

> There are no 'trenches' here in the true meaning of the word, only breastworks built of sandbags and raised 'duck-boards' to walk on. Behind us is open green country and lanes, somewhat pitted with shell holes it is true, but nevertheless quite fresh and green. All is very flat and old trenches grown over with grass and weeds and rushes are scattered around in parts – they are the German trenches captured by the Canadians in 1915. From this trench (which is called Richmond Terrace) a communication breastwork runs up to another. This is the front line. At night we have detached posts about 150 yards out in No Man's Land.[6]

This sector of front was quiet, but the arrival of the 2nd Division had not passed unnoticed. Within a couple of days the Germans increased their patrolling activity and their artillery and *Minenwerfer* became more troublesome. On 25 June, the same day on which the first large contingent of American soldiers arrived in France, the Germans mounted an unsuccessful raid on the 1st King's Liverpool, who were occupying trenches to the immediate right of the 17th Middlesex. The following evening the battalion was relieved by the 13th Essex and moved back into support. During this period in the trenches three soldiers, Ptes William Bisset, Tom Brooks and Thomas Aldridge lost their lives.

The 17th Middlesex moved back into the front line around Givenchy on the evening of 2 July. The trenches to the left of the 17th Middlesex were held by Portuguese troops. Germany had declared war on Portugal in March 1916, following Portuguese compliance with a British demand that the German ships interned in Portuguese ports be confiscated. Nicknamed 'Pork and Beans' by British soldiers, Portuguese troops had begun to arrive in France from February 1917 onwards, but had only recently been given their own section of the line.

In the early hours of 8 July the Germans launched a successful raid on the Portuguese. A heavy barrage was placed on the left flank of the 17th Middlesex in order to prevent any assistance being given to the Portuguese. Numerous shells fell on Cover Trench, Canadian Orchard, Shetland Road and Richmond Terrace. Cpl Walter Searle was in charge of a Lewis gun post in Canadian Orchard. Realising that No Man's Land was the safest place to be, Cpl Searle moved his men forward and established a new post. He then went out on a lone reconnaissance. Running into a party of eight Germans close to their wire, he threw grenades at them until they retired and returned to his men. Once the German barrage had died down, Cpl Searle withdrew his men from No Man's Land and reoccupied the original post in Canadian Orchard. The German bombardment had left four men dead and another ten wounded.[7] Cpl Walter Searle was subsequently awarded the Distinguished Conduct Medal for his conspicuous gallantry and devotion to duty.[8]

On 9 July the 17th Middlesex were relieved by the 13th Essex and marched back to Gorre Château. The next few days were spent reorganising and training. On 14 July it was the turn of the 17th Middlesex to relieve the 13th Essex. Despite periodic enemy shelling there were no fatalities during this spell in the trenches. On 19 July the battalion moved back into support. Three days later 2/Lt Frank Bower led a party of eight men out to No Man's Land and successfully destroyed a section of the German wire.

Back in the front line on the evening of 24 July, the 17th Middlesex were subjected to a heavy bombardment the following afternoon. Two men were killed during the strafe and nine men were wounded. Another man was killed during the night. The trenches were badly damaged. For the next couple of days working parties cleared away the debris and repaired the damage to the wire entanglements. On 30 July the 17th Middlesex were back in reserve at Gorre. Everyone was glad to be out of the trenches given the recent rain. The following morning the battalion visited the divisional baths. A platoon football contest took place in the afternoon.

Earlier that morning, the Battle of Third Ypres, more commonly known as Passchendaele, had started after a two-week bombardment in which over 4,500,000 shells had fallen on the German defences. Haig had long envisaged a sustained offensive in Flanders whereby the British would break out of the Ypres salient and advance on the key German rail junction at Roulers.[9] On two separate occasions already, at the beginning of 1916 and 1917, Haig had been forced to relinquish such plans in order to support the efforts of the French. By the end of the first day Gough's Fifth Army had advanced an average of 3,000yd at a cost of 30,000 casualties.

Prolonged spells of heavy rain made life very uncomfortable for the 17th Middlesex on moving back into the front line around Givenchy on 3 August. Six days later the battalion moved back into support at Windy Corner. Pte Walter Collop, who was wounded by a sniper, was the only casualty during this period in the front line. The implications of the foul weather were not lost on the officers and men of the 17th Middlesex. Capt Percy Barnfather wrote:

We are just having some excitement with Boche aeroplanes overhead at present. One thing you cannot get is very dull whilst in the trenches; you have always got something to occupy your mind with –

too much sometimes. Things seem to drag along in the old sweet way and there seems no end in sight at present.

The weather is greatly interfering with our operations. I don't think I have known an offensive yet that hasn't been accompanied by bad weather. Yesterday we had about the worst thunderstorm I have ever experienced, but even that does not silence the guns.[10]

On 15 August the 17th Middlesex relieved the 13th Essex in the front line at Givenchy. Three days later Sgt Frederick Ashman from Islington died of wounds. L/Cpl Bertram Oakley and L/Cpl William Gordon were both wounded, probably as a result of artillery fire. On 19 August Capt Cosmo Clark, who had recovered from the wound sustained at Guillemont the previous year, rejoined the battalion. He noted ruefully that 'Up here in the line there is an occasional face among the men that I recognise or rather they recognise me, but there aren't many of them left.'[11] After six days in the front line the 17th Middlesex moved back into reserve. The next few days saw the battalion engaged in training and recreational activities, including football and water polo matches. On 26 August a 17th Middlesex team played a football match against the 251st Tunnelling Company, winning 6–0. That evening the officers and men attended a concert in the divisional theatre.

On the evening of 27 August the 17th Middlesex moved up to the front line to relieve the 13th Essex. The weather was atrocious:

The weather hasn't been kind to us, for it started raining at midday and it has been steadily pouring ever since. We left our village at 9 o'clock and had a march of three hours in the rain, gradually passing from a nice little village to desolation and war . . . Then followed a long trudge through communication trenches to the front line. The Very lights as the rockets are called, and an occasional crack of a rifle, and burst of machine gun fire were the only intimation that there was a war on. The relief went very easily and the battalion we relieved trecked [sic] off back to occupy the old French Chateau [Gorre] we have vacated.[12]

There was no let up in the rain for the next couple of days. On

29 August there was a strong south-westerly wind blowing: 'Great gusts of wind are catching things up and sending them into the air, like feathers. Even steel helmets are being blown off the men's heads. However it has its consolations for the rain has stopped and the wet ground is drying up considerably.'[13]

On 30 August a company of Portuguese troops reported to Lt Col Kelly for instructional purposes. Reactions were less than favourable. Despite being 'very cheery and bright', one Portuguese officer was described as 'the fattest thing within four miles'. Apart from sporadic sniping and shelling, the next few days were uneventful. No casualties were sustained. On 3 September the 17th Middlesex were relieved by the 13th Essex in 'beautiful moonlight' and moved back into support at Windy Corner. Capt Clark wrote home that he 'was most relieved to get away from the line because the responsibility of a host of Portuguese under one was a bit trying. Their first time under fire and the little cooler evenings and nights made them appear so hopeless.'[14]

On 7 September the 17th Middlesex were relieved by the 23rd Royal Fusiliers and marched back to rest billets at Oblinghem. The Battalion War Diary recorded that the 'Men were in high spirits and sang all the way'.[15] Spirits were dampened somewhat when the battalion reached the village of Oblinghem: 'Innumerable streams of filthy water flowed through it and every house had an extremely fresh smelling cesspool in its garden.'[16] While the 17th Middlesex were billeted at Oblinghem, there was a change in command. On 9 September Lt Col George Kelly took his last muster parade before leaving to take over command of 2nd King's Royal Rifle Corps, which had been virtually destroyed by a recent German attack at Nieuport on the Belgian coast.

The new commanding officer was the 27-year-old Lt Col Ronald Stafford, whose grandfather, Sir Edward Stafford, had served three terms as Prime Minister of New Zealand. Born in Buenos Aires and educated at Temple Grove and Haileybury, Ronald Stafford was a talented sportsman, having captained the rugby and cricket teams at Jesus College, Cambridge. At the outbreak of war he had been working in the Egyptian Ministry of Finance. Returning to England, Stafford was commissioned in the 6th King's Royal Rifle Corps in March 1915 and was awarded a

Military Cross and a Distinguished Service Order the following year. He was already familiar to several officers of the 17th Middlesex, having seen service with the 1st King's Royal Rifle Corps of 99th Brigade. Capt Clark wrote to his parents that:

> We have got a new C.O. . . . The new chap has got the D.S.O. and the M.C. He is only 27, but very capable and knows his job. He relieved me at Montauban, down on the Somme in August 1916. He was then a captain. He remembered me, and we had a chat about our experiences. He has been in every 'do' since then and he told me nothing was as bad as our time around Delville. The young men and <u>not</u> middle aged or old 'uns are the best out here.[17]

The next few days were quiet for the 17th Middlesex. Out of the line, the usual routine of training and recreation resumed. A 6th Brigade football competition saw 'B' Company of the 17th Middlesex being awarded a trophy for having the best company football team in the brigade. Pte Alfred Cooper, a former apprentice in the office of the *Croydon Advertiser*, wrote home that 'We get a decent lot of sport out here when we are out of the line, football being the chief game; swimming gives pleasure to some. We also get some very good concerts, which make a very pleasant evening.'[18]

On 16 September Maj Gen Cecil Pereira presented medal ribbons to officers and men of the 17th Middlesex for acts of bravery. Capt Robert Templeman was awarded a Bar to his Military Cross, and CSM Lyndon Sandoe was awarded a Distinguished Conduct Medal. Military Medals were bestowed upon Sgt Herbert Austin, Pte George Barker, Pte Henry Young, and Pte Joseph Barry. That afternoon, a 17th Middlesex team played a match against XI Corps HQ, winning 5–1.

Two days later, the 17th Middlesex were back in the front line north of Givenchy, having relieved the 23rd Royal Fusiliers. German artillery was active over the next few days, but no fatalities were sustained. Early in the morning of 24 September the Germans mounted a raid on the 17th Middlesex. Just after 5 o'clock enemy shells rained down on Cover Trench, Richmond Terrace, Shetland Road and Pioneer Road. Under the cover of this bombardment a small party of the enemy slipped into the 17th

Middlesex lines 'just where the post for Canadian Orchard leaves Cover Trench. They were evidently a very short time in the trench and were seen by no-one owing to the mist, but bombs, boxes of explosives and boxes of machine gun ammunition were found in our trench.'[19] One man was missing and 13 other ranks were wounded. L/Cpl John Basham from Walthamstow, one of four badly-wounded men, would die the following day in Béthune. The missing soldier was L/Cpl Henry Hobbis from Coventry. Barely 19 years old, the unfortunate L/Cpl Hobbis had been dragged back to the German lines for interrogation.

The 17th Middlesex were relieved later that evening by the 13th Essex and marched back to Gorre. Over the next few days the battalion trained and played football, a suitable field having been procured and placed under the charge of L/Cpl Pat Gallacher. Despite the best endeavours of L/Cpl Gallacher and his helpers, such fields remained poor substitutes for football pitches, as Pte Jack Dodds, the Oldham Athletic outside-left, explained:

After a few weeks of trench work we arrive at some village for a few days and of course our first thought after a day or so of rest is to fix a game up. Very often a suitable ground is hard to find and to give you an idea the worst grounds at home are very often a croquet lawn to where we play. However our keenness gets over this, and then we play for four or five days running. In fact every man has had enough when our return to the trenches is necessary.

Sometimes we have teams waiting for us coming out of the line to try and lower our colours. So far none have managed, although we must have played over 50 games in this country. We have only once been extended, and that by the Argyll and Sutherland Highlanders whom we beat 1–0. This team included several Scottish players most prominent amongst them being Tom Logan of Chelsea.

We have played numerous battalions ASC and RAMC units and also the pick of different brigades and even divisions. All have been easily beaten and the one thing we are longing for now is an opportunity of trying ourselves once more as a battalion team against the boys at home, *après la guerre*, as the Frenchman says.[20]

On 29 September a divisional Lewis Gun competition took

place. It was won by No. 6 Platoon, 'B' Company, of the 17th Middlesex. That afternoon the battalion football team played a match against a team picked from the whole of the 2nd Division. In front of 2,000 spectators, the 17th Middlesex ran out 5–0 winners. The next day, after a church parade and a performance by the battalion band, Lt Col Stafford inspected and addressed a draft of 50 men who had just reported for duty. The Battalion War Diary recorded that they were 'a good lot, all have previous experience'.[21] Later that evening the 17th Middlesex went back into the front line at Givenchy. Over the next few days a further 53 reinforcements arrived. During this spell in the trenches four men were wounded, including the footballer Sgt Charles Stewart, whose former club, Croydon Common, had been the subject of a winding up order earlier in the year.

On 5 October the 17th Middlesex were relieved by the 3rd Worcesters and proceeded to Béthune, where the battalion was billeted in the tobacco factory. The next day another draft of 190 men arrived and the companies were reorganised into four platoons for the first time since the disaster at Oppy. On 7 October the 17th Middlesex marched 9 miles to the village of Burbure in pouring rain. The billets were poor, but the next day 'a good football field was found'.[22] Plenty of matches were played over the next few days, one game nearly ending in disaster:

> Players and onlookers were absorbed in the game when suddenly several loud explosions were heard right on top of them. Looking up they saw in the sky a couple of Boche planes which had unloaded several bombs and were beating a retreat. Fortunately, no one was hurt, and the game was immediately resumed and heartily enjoyed by players and spectators.[23]

On the afternoon of 14 October the 17th Middlesex played the 1st King's Liverpool at rugby, winning 16–0: 'A very excellent game when we played 13 men against 15.'[24] The following day the 17th Middlesex, along with the rest of 6th Brigade, paraded in a field outside Burbure, where they were inspected by Gen Sir Henry Horne, the commander of First Army. Later that evening 'B' Company put on a show. Capt Clark observed that:

The most interesting thing was to watch the tiny French kiddies who had managed to squeeze in between the burly sergeant door-keepers. The expressions of wonder and awe, as a Lancashire lad danced a clog dance, were wonderful to behold. The only time they laughed was when the company comedian came on dressed in the local butcher's clothes which they all recognised.[25]

On 17 October a 17th Middlesex team played another rugby match against the 1st King's Royal Rifle Corps: 'They turned out a team considerably heavier than ours, but we managed to keep them out by good tackling.'[26] The result was 6–0 victory for the battalion. Both tries were scored by Lt Fred Stansfeld, who had only recently rejoined the 17th Middlesex after recovering from his wounds sustained during the attack on the Redan Ridge. The following day another draft of 100 other ranks from the 18th Middlesex arrived. The Battalion War Diary commented that these reinforcements contained 'quite a good lot of men, who have seen a considerable amount of fighting around Arras and Ypres this year'.[27]

On 21 October a 17th Middlesex football team put nine goals past the 58th Casualty Clearing Station without reply. That same day the 6th Brigade Horse Show took place. The 17th Middlesex won three of the seven events: Best General Service Wagon, Best Limber, with the Best Charger award being won by Lt Col Stafford's horse 'Tommy'. The following afternoon there was a battalion sports day, which included races, blind-boxing and a tug-of-war. The highlight was undoubtedly the mule race, which was won eventually by Lt Fred Stansfeld:

There is nothing a Tommy likes to see more than an officer fall off a horse. None of the officers who got on the mules (which were bare-backed) knew how to ride. As soon as they got mounted, all the Tommies who were looking on, waved their arms and yelled. All the mules immediately bolted and after 20 yards only four of the fifteen officers were left on mules, the remainder were scattered about the course in various attitudes.[28]

In between the football matches, concerts and horse shows, the battalion practised musketry and underwent intensive training.

Various attack formations, which incorporated many of the lessons being learned in Flanders, were practised at company, battalion and brigade level. Particular emphasis was laid on the techniques of dealing with concrete pillboxes and other isolated strongpoints, which were now a key feature of German defensive tactics on the Western Front. The officers were kept especially busy, as Capt Clark recalled:

> In spite of the fact that we are not fighting at present, but miles back in a little quiet, peaceful village, time for writing seems to be less than when in the line. We have long days of training in the open air across fields and hills and at the end of the day I hardly ever have less than an hour and a half's writing and correspondence to deal with. A hundred and eighty men's food, clothing and pay to look after, not to mention arranging a training programme for the following day, and incidentally numerous letters from relatives of missing men – I have an average of about 3 per day of the latter![29]

The results of this period of training soon manifested themselves. By the end of the month many soldiers in the 2nd Division were able to fire 13 shots per minute, some individuals even achieving the pre-war standard of 15 aimed shots per minute. On 31 October Divisional HQ organised an inter-battalion rapid shooting competition. The 17th Middlesex team finished a creditable third. The team consisted of Sgt William Glenie (27 shots, 81 pts); Sgt William Hayes (22 shots, 66 pts); Sgt Bob Dalrymple (22 shots, 62 pts); and Cpl Frank Plaice (20 shots, 69 points).

For last couple of months the officers and men of the 17th Middlesex had speculated on the likelihood of their being sent to fight in the Ypres Salient. The Third Battle of Ypres was now entering its final stages, and it seemed that the battalion's time had come. On 5 November the three infantry brigades of the 2nd Division began to move northwards to join II Corps of Second Army. With a fighting strength of 40 officers and 987 other ranks, the 17th Middlesex left Burbure, arriving at Thiennes, south-west of Hazebrouck. The next day the battalion marched to its billets in a farm north of St Sylvestre-Cappel. The roads were so congested with traffic that the four companies had to march 100yd apart. On 7 November the 17th Middlesex proceeded to Houtkerque, a few miles north-west of Poperinghe. All ranks now expected to be involved in heavy fighting within a few days. Most of the officers and men were billeted in tents pitched on muddy ground. It had been a trying few days and the local inhabitants did not exactly make a favourable impression. Capt Clark wrote to his parents that:

We have been very busy for the last three days, marching, marching and still more marching. Each night we have stayed at a different village – strange to say in the neighbourhood which we traversed when the battalion first came to France. The weather is turning very wintry, dark grey clouds most days and a drizzly rain fanned by a nasty whining wind. Not exactly the most cheerful of weather. At present we are at a tiny village, which is very dirty and wet and we expect to remain here for some time . . .

My French is not much good to me up here because the people speak an extraordinary language which sounds like German. Also they behave like Germans to us. I suppose after three years of war they look upon us a great nuisance and forget we are their allies.[30]

The 17th Middlesex were not destined to serve in the lines around Ypres. From the outset the Flanders offensive had been plagued by long spells of prolonged rainfall. The incessant shelling had completely destroyed the drainage systems of the low-lying landscape, turning large parts of the battlefield into a treacherous morass. On 6 November the Canadian Corps had taken the shattered village of Passchendaele. Four days later, in torrential rain, the Canadian Corps and the 1st Division consolidated their hold on the Passchendaele Ridge. The Flanders campaign was effectively over. The British had advanced some 5 miles at a cost of 244,897 officers and men.[31]

The 17th Middlesex remained near Houtkerque for the next couple of weeks. Several rugby and football matches took place. One of these games saw the first team pitted against the second team at the nearby ground of 32 Squadron, Royal Flying Corps. Every player on the pitch had played professional football. The game ended in a 4–1 victory for the first team. During this period everyone's thoughts were dominated by the prospect of an impending move to Italy.

Following a crushing Austro-German victory over Italian forces at Caporetto in late October, Haig had been ordered to send out several divisions to help stabilise the situation. The 2nd Division was one of several units now earmarked for the Italian Front. Officers and men of the 17th Middlesex hurriedly wrote home asking for Italian maps and phrasebooks to be sent out at the earliest opportunity. In preparation for the journey, the officers were ordered to cut down their kit to 35lb. This was 'a great blow to the officers, most of whom are carrying about two hundred pounds in their valises'.[32] On 22 November news was received that there had been a change of plan. Italian phrasebooks would not be needed. Two days later the 17th Middlesex vacated the muddy billets at Houtkerque and began to entrain at Proven. Within a few days Capt Clark would write from a ruined village near Cambrai:

During the last six nights, I haven't slept in the same place for more than one night. At last we are settled for two or three nights at least. We are in tents in a thick wood and are jolly well off. We got here at four o'clock this afternoon and started to fix ourselves up. It's very interesting making yourself comfortable for the night out of odd bits of material. Everybody sets out to find what they can. My servant found a spring mattress for me out of a ruined house and has covered it with clean canvas. I hope it isn't lousy, though it is quite likely to be because the old Hun hasn't long left this place. Biscuit tins to wash in tomorrow. Stoves out of the ruined houses to keep the tent warm. Piles of wood from the wood to keep the fires going. Chairs from the ruined houses. It's great fun pinching all you can. The great thing is to get there first. Also, to keep what you have found. My cold is still pretty rotten but better than yesterday. I'm rather surprised I haven't got pneumonia after sleeping in the open the other night. By jove, it was cold. All my clothes in my valise and on me were soaked in snow and rain.[33]

1. BNL: *Croydon Advertiser*, 2 June 1917.
2. The resulting shock waves from the detonation of the mines were reportedly felt in the south of England.
3. BNL: *Sporting Chronicle*, 19 June 1917.
4. *Ibid.*, 3 July 1917.
5. *Ibid.*

6. Clark, C., *The Tin Trunk*, p. 82.
7. CWGC records show only three 17th Middlesex deaths on 8 July 1917: Pte Lewis Moore, Pte James Plumridge and Pte John Walker.
8. *London Gazette*, Issue 30251, 24 August 1917.
9. In several respects Flanders was the logical location for a major British offensive. It was close to the British lines of supply and, having been engaged in fighting there since 1914, the BEF was familiar with the ground.
10. BNL: *Croydon Advertiser*, 18 August 1917.
11. Clark, C., *The Tin Trunk*, p. 80.
12. *Ibid.*
13. *Ibid.*, p. 82.
14. *Ibid.*
15. TNA: WO 95/1361.
16. Clark, C., *The Tin Trunk*, p. 83.
17. Letter to Ellen Clark, 10 September 1917.
18. BNL: *Croydon Advertiser*, 15 September 1917.
19. TNA: WO 95/1361.
20. BNL: *Athletic News*, 6 November 1917.
21. TNA: WO 95/1361.
22. *Ibid.*
23. BNL: *Croydon Advertiser*, 3 November 1917.
24. TNA: WO 95/1361.
25. Clark, C., *The Tin Trunk*, p. 86.
26. TNA: WO 95/1361.
27. *Ibid.*
28. Clark, C. *The Tin Trunk*, p. 86.
29. *Ibid.*
30. *Ibid.*, p. 87.
31. German losses were officially admitted to be 217,000, but this figure did not include the lightly wounded.
32. Clark, C., *The Tin Trunk*, p. 90.
33. *Ibid.*, p. 92.

CHAPTER 14

CAMBRAI

The example set by Captain McReady-Diarmid
was beyond all praise
Lt Col Ronald Stafford

Following the German withdrawals in the spring of 1917, Gen Nivelle had proposed a simultaneous Franco-British operation in which the French would attack either side of St Quentin, while the British attacked the Hindenburg Line some 7 miles to the south-west of Cambrai. This proposal was acceptable to Haig; the Fourth and Fifth Armies, under Gen Rawlinson and Gen Gough respectively, were duly instructed to draw up plans for an attack on the Hindenburg Line between Banteux and Havrincourt. As a result of troops being moved northwards in readiness for the Flanders offensive, this sector of the front was taken over by the Third Army. Gen Sir Julian Byng, who had recently replaced Allenby as the commander of Third Army, continued to examine various proposals for an offensive in the Cambrai area.[1]

At the beginning of August Brig Gen Hugh Elles, commanding the Tanks Corps in France, and his chief staff officer, Lt Col J.F.C. Fuller, put forward a proposal for a 'hit-and-run' tank raid in which a large number of tanks would break through the Hindenburg Line and wreak havoc among the German gun batteries. Both men were eager to see tanks deployed effectively on suitable ground, believing that any attempt to use tanks in the mud around Ypres was doomed to failure. The relatively uncratered chalk downland around Cambrai would allow the tank to demonstrate its true capabilities.

Byng was enthusiastic about the prospects for a surprise tank attack, but decided to enlarge the scope of the proposed operation considerably. Fuller's original concept of a raid on the German gun line now became a full-blown attempt to break through the Hindenburg Line. GHQ was impressed with the Third Army's scheme, but felt that sufficient resources were not available to mount such an operation while the fighting raged around Ypres. By the middle of October, once it had become abundantly clear that the Flanders offensive would not fulfil its strategic objectives, Haig formally approved the Third Army's plans to launch an attack around Cambrai. Under a cloak of secrecy, operational planning for the tank attack gathered momentum.

On 26 October Byng outlined the plan at a conference of his corps commanders. That same evening Haig was ordered by the War Office to send two divisions immediately to Italy, following the Austro-German victory at Caporetto. Despite this unwelcome news, Haig remained adamant that it was in the best interests of Britain's allies that the Cambrai attack should proceed, writing to Lt Gen Lancelot Kiggell, his Chief of Staff that '. . . the Third Army offensive must go in, otherwise the enemy will be able, covered by the Hindenburg Line, to skin his front and attack – probably the French. That would put a stop to all reinforcements for Italy.'[2]

The plan was finalised on 13 November. On the centre and the right of the assault, III Corps were to secure the bridges over the St Quentin Canal at Masnières and Marçoing. The Cavalry Corps would then advance to isolate Cambrai, seizing the bridges over the River Sensée. On the left, IV Corps would capture the Flesquières Ridge and Bourlon Wood, a dense wood of some 600 acres on the crest of the Bourlon Ridge. The attack would be supported by a force of 378 Mark IV fighting tanks, 54 supply tanks, 32 tanks fitted with grapnels to clear lanes through the wire for the cavalry, 2 tanks carrying bridging equipment, 9 wireless tanks, and a tank loaded with telephone cable. In order to traverse the 12ft-wide trenches of the Hindenburg defences, tanks would carry fascines (large bundles of brushwood), each weighing 1¾ tons, which would be dropped into these trenches to form a bridge, allowing the tanks to cross.

Air support was to be provided by nearly 300 aircraft, which would attack enemy infantry, machine-gun posts and gun batteries. Through the use of aerial photography, sound-ranging and flash-spotting, the positions of German gun batteries would be accurately plotted without the need for pre-battle registration. Such methods would dispense entirely with the need for the

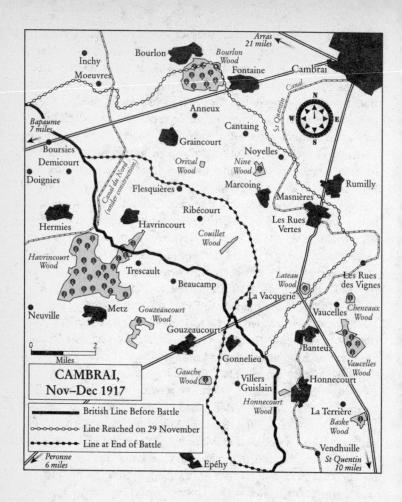

CAMBRAI,
Nov–Dec 1917

— British Line Before Battle
∘∘∘∘∘ Line Reached on 29 November
•••• Line at End of Battle

preliminary bombardment of enemy positions, which had previously served to give notice of British intentions. At Cambrai the guns would not open fire until Zero Hour.

The morning of 20 November was dull and misty. At 6.20 a.m. over 1,000 guns opened up on the German defences and artillery positions and the first wave of tanks crawled forward. At the same time the infantry began their advance along a frontage of 6 miles. By nightfall, at a cost of 4,000 casualties, the British had advanced 3 or 4 miles. Four thousand Germans had been taken prisoner and over 100 enemy guns captured or destroyed. When news of the victory reached England, church bells pealed in celebration for the first time in the war.

While the first day of the Battle of Cambrai had been a remarkable success, the attack had resulted in a 'break-in' rather than a 'break-through'. On the right of the assault, while III Corps had reached the St Quentin Canal and captured Marcoing, it had been unable to establish a firm footing on the eastern bank of the canal. On the left, IV Corps, having initially made good progress, had been held up at Flesquières, where German field guns had succeeded in knocking out 26 tanks. This check had serious ramifications in that it had prevented IV Corps from securing the vital objective of Bourlon Wood on the first day. A further concern was the fact that 179 tanks were out of action; the majority of which had succumbed to mechanical troubles rather than enemy action.

With Haig's approval, Byng issued orders that evening for operations to resume the next morning in an attempt to attain the untaken objectives of the previous day. The results of the day's fighting were bitterly disappointing. The attacks of III Corps made little progress in the face of stiffening enemy resistance, effectively putting an end to all hopes of the Cavalry Corps crossing the St Quentin Canal. To the north, the operations of IV Corps were barely more successful. The villages of Anneux and Fontaine were captured, but the advance had stalled in the face of heavy machine-gun fire from Bourlon Wood.

Haig now had a difficult decision to make. Having previously imposed a 48-hour deadline for the Cambrai offensive to realise its objectives, he was reluctant to halt operations with the Bourlon Ridge seemingly within his grasp, even though German reinforcements were already arriving on the battlefield. The capture of Bourlon Ridge would allow the British to dominate the western approaches to Cambrai, disrupting German communications across the entire sector. Such a clear-cut victory might also restore Haig's standing in the eyes of several influential politicians, who were becoming increasingly critical of his perceived methods. Accordingly, III Corps was instructed to maintain a defensive line along the St Quentin Canal, with its bridges prepared for demolition, while IV Corps was ordered to make every effort to secure the Bourlon Ridge.

On 22 November the preparations of IV Corps for an assault on the Bourlon Ridge were disrupted by German counterattacks, resulting in the loss of Fontaine. The main effort to capture the Bourlon Ridge took place the following day, supported by 92 tanks. Results were mixed. Although Bourlon Wood was captured by the 40th Division, the village of Bourlon, lying on the lower slopes to the north of the wood, remained in German hands and the defenders of Fontaine stubbornly resisted every attempt of the 51st Division to evict them. To the west, the 36th Division succeeded in occupying the greater part of Moeuvres, but was later forced back to the southern edge of the village.

On 24 November the Germans launched several counterattacks with the aim of recovering Bourlon Wood, but the troops of the 40th Division, fighting alongside dismounted cavalry units, held firm. Renewed British efforts to secure Bourlon village met with failure. On 26 November, the same day on which plans were hastily drawn up for another attack on Bourlon and Fontaine, the 2nd Division, now part of IV Corps, began the relief of the 36th Division in the trenches between Moeuvres and Bourlon Wood. In a heavy snowstorm, the 17th Middlesex left Doignies at 7.30 p.m. to relieve the 10th Royal Inniskilling Fusiliers in the front line between Lock No. 5 of the Canal du Nord to a point about 200yd south of the village of Moeuvres. The night was quiet apart from sporadic sniping and bursts of machine-gun fire.

Early on the morning of 27 November, the 62nd and the Guards Divisions attacked Bourlon Wood and Fontaine.[3] Both divisions made initial progress, but German resistance was too strong. The failure of these attacks marked the end of offensive operations. That afternoon Byng ordered IV Corps to close down operations, as 'the resources at the disposal of the Army do not permit of the offensive being continued any longer'.[4] Orders were duly given for the captured positions to be consolidated and improved lines of defence to be constructed. The closing down of offensive operations around Cambrai had left the British holding a pronounced salient, some 9 miles wide and 4 miles deep, from Bourlon Wood in the north to beyond Banteux in the south.

While the British were preparing to consolidate their gains, the Germans were busy making preparations of their own. Within

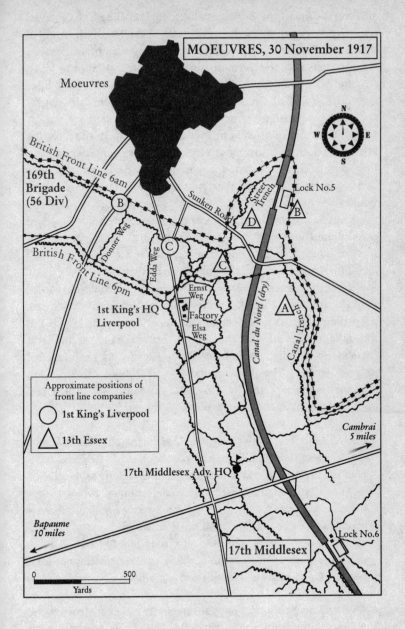

MOEUVRES, 30 November 1917

Moeuvres

British Front Line 6am

169th
Brigade
(56 Div)

Lock No.5

Sunken Road

Street Trench

Ⓑ

Ⓓ

British Front Line 6pm

Donner Weg

Ⓑ

Ⓒ

Edda Weg

Ⓒ

Ernst Weg

Factory

Elsa Weg

1st King's HQ
Liverpool

Canal du Nord (dry)

Canal Trench

Ⓐ

Approximate positions of
front line companies

◯ 1st King's Liverpool

△ 13th Essex

Cambrai
5 miles

17th Middlesex Adv. HQ

Bapaume
10 miles

Lock No.6

17th Middlesex

0   500

Yards

only a few days of the British attack being launched, the thoughts of Crown Prince Rupprecht, commander of the Northern Group of Armies, had turned to the possibility of a major counter-offensive. His plan was that the German 2nd Army would attempt to pinch out the British salient by attacking its shoulders. The first blow would be launched from the south-east by elements of General von Kathen's Busigny Group and General von Watter's Caudry Group. Their divisions were to advance westwards in the direction of Metz, and to capture Flesquières and Havrincourt Wood from the south. Once it became apparent that these attacks were making progress, another blow would fall between Moeuvres and Bourlon with General von Moser's Arras Group pushing southwards towards Flesquières and Havrincourt Wood. Opposed predominantly by tired and depleted British divisions, Rupprecht was confident that his counterstroke, which was to be launched on 30 November, would yield impressive results.

During the night of 27/28 November the 17th Middlesex worked hard to improve the makeshift defences south of Moeuvres, deepening trenches and clearing fire steps. Wiring parties worked throughout the night. The entire 6th Brigade sector was particularly ill-suited for defence. Lt Col Ronald Stafford labelled it 'a bit tricky'.[5] The problems largely arose from 6th Brigade's positions being bisected by the Canal du Nord, which had still been under construction at the outbreak of war:

The canal ran from south to north, not only through the 6th Brigade line, but also through the enemy's position east of Moeuvres, and from his trenches he was able to enfilade the bridges, so that they could not be used. In consequence, communication between the British troops east and west of the canal was most difficult and hazardous. The bed of the Canal du Nord was dry, and if a man wanted to cross it he had to slide down a slippery 20-foot wall and climb up the other side by means of a rope – while the enemy opened a galling fire on him with machine guns and rifles.[6]

Over the next couple of days strongpoints were constructed and supplies of ammunition brought forward. Officers and men alike took note of the fact that German artillery appeared to be registering their positions, which seemed to add credence to the widespread rumours of an imminent attack. Despite the increased shelling, the casualties of the 17th Middlesex were remarkably light: L/Cpl Cornelius Bradford, Ptes Henry Jeffery and Frank Owen were killed, and Pte Archibald Wilkin died of wounds. On the evening of 29 November the 17th Middlesex were relieved by the 1st King's Liverpool and moved back into support south of the Bapaume-Cambrai Road, 'A' Company of the 17th Middlesex being placed at the disposal of Lt Col David Murray-Lyon, the commanding officer of the 1st King's Liverpool.[7]

To the north, the divisions of General von Moser's Arras Group were making the final preparations for the forthcoming assault on the British positions between Moeuvres and Bourlon Wood. As part of the planned counterstroke, the German 49th Reserve Division, a predominantly Saxon division that had spent much of the war on the Eastern Front, was to drive in a southerly direction either side of the Canal du Nord. The Reserve Infantry Regiment 225 would attack west of the canal, while Reserve Infantry Regiment 226 would advance along its eastern bank.

At dawn on 30 November German artillery opened up a ferocious bombardment on the front lines of 6th Brigade. Among the shells that came crashing down were a number containing the dreaded mustard gas. By 8.30 a.m. large concentrations of hostile troops were reported all along the front between Moeuvres and Bourlon Wood. The 6th Brigade front was held by 13th Essex and 1st King's Liverpool. The 13th Essex held Canal Trench, Lock No. 5 and Street Trench, while the 1st King's Liverpool occupied the former support trench of the Hindenburg Main Position, south of Moeuvres. The 2nd South Staffords and the 17th Middlesex were in support.

At 9.20 a.m. the German infantry began to advance in large numbers against the Canal du Nord from the north and north-east. Half an hour later, German troops were seen forming up in Moeuvres. The 1st King's Liverpool sent up an SOS signal and divisional artillery opened fire.[8] The artillery response proved highly effective, tearing huge gaps in the advancing waves of German infantry, which also came under a withering fire from rifles, Lewis guns and heavy machine-guns.[9]

On the 6th Brigade front, the Germans concentrated their initial efforts on Lock No. 5 on the eastern bank of the Canal du Nord, which was defended by 'B' Company of the 13th Essex. The first wave of attacks were beaten off with a combination of rifle and Lewis-gun fire, 'B' Company virtually expending their entire supply of ammunition and grenades in doing so. About 10.20 a.m. German artillery sealed off Lock No. 5 with a box barrage, before launching another attack which forced its defenders to retire through the sunken road by the bridge into Canal Trench. 'C' Company of the 13th Essex, holding the line on the west bank, just south of the sunken road, were then attacked and forced back after a short, hard fight. The subsequent German occupation of Lock No. 5 and the sunken road left 'D' Company of the 13th Essex, holding a section of Street Trench on the western bank, completely stranded. Later that afternoon the surviving officers and sergeants would hold a council of war, at which it was resolved to continue to hold out throughout the night, even though 'D' Company had almost completely expended their supplies of ammunition.

To the left of the 13th Essex, the 1st King's Liverpool were also having a torrid time. At 10.25 a.m. a mass of German infantry rushed forward from the ruined houses of Moeuvres and practically wiped out 'B' Company of the 1st King's Liverpool on the left of 6th Brigade's front, west of the canal. The survivors, 2 officers and around 24 men, fell back along Donner Weg, one of the communication trenches linking the former front and support trenches of the Hindenburg Main Position, pursued by a large German bombing party. At the southern end of Donner Weg the Germans were checked and driven back to a point within 50yd of the original British front line, where a block was established. Soon after, the enemy attacked over open ground between Donner Weg and Edda Weg, but the extended lines of German infantry were torn apart by sustained Lewis Gun and rifle fire. Throughout the rest of the day German bombing parties would make several attempts to force their way down Donner Weg and Edda Weg, all of which would be beaten back.

The right front company of the 1st King's Liverpool, 'C' Company, were similarly overwhelmed through sheer weight of numbers. Swiftly following up their barrage, German troops had rushed their positions. The survivors of 'C' Company, 1st King's Liverpool, 2/Lt Scott and about a dozen men fell back and made a determined stand on an embankment in the vicinity of Ernst Weg before they were outflanked and forced back. By 11 a.m. large numbers of the enemy were seen to the north and east of Battalion HQ of the 1st King's Liverpool. German soldiers were also spotted entering the ruined factory buildings. For the next three-quarters-of-an-hour, there was desperate fighting, the defenders of Battalion HQ assisted by a carrying party of the 10th Duke of Cornwall's Light Infantry, who had just arrived with supplies of ammunition and grenades. Around noon Lt Fred Nunn and 'A' Company of the 17th Middlesex, having been sent up earlier that morning to support the 1st King's Liverpool, were ordered by Lt Col Murray-Lyon to clear Ernst Weg. Supported by Lewis Guns, Lt Nunn's attack was successful, driving the Germans back. Over 40 dead Germans were counted in the trench and 4 machine-guns captured. One of 'A' Company's Lewis guns had also succeeded in knocking out two *Flammenwerfer* at a range of over 600yd.

From their positions in support, the officers and men of the 17th Middlesex waited nervously for further orders. Lt Col Stafford had given the order for the battalion to 'Stand To' shortly after the opening of the enemy bombardment earlier that morning. Instructions were issued that each man should carry two grenades, and that packs should not be worn in order to improve mobility. Following reports that German infantry had crossed the sunken road, Lt Col Stafford had ordered Maj Percival Edwards to go forward and 'to counter-attack if necessary with C and D Companies'.[10] Just after 11 a.m. Capt Frank Gregory and 'C' Company were sent up to support the 1st King's Liverpool. Later that afternoon 'C' Company would take over the front line between Battalion HQ of the 1st King's Liverpool and Edda Weg.

While the fighting raged in the vicinity of Battalion HQ of the 1st King's Liverpool, a party of Germans had continued to drive southwards towards the Bapaume–Cambrai Road. It was clear to Maj Percival Edwards that immediate action was needed. Capt Allastair McReady-Diarmid and 'D' Company were ordered to counterattack. By 2 p.m. Capt McReady-Diarmid and 'D' Company had bombed the enemy back to a point, some 150yd west of the factory, where the counterattack had stalled due to a lack of grenades. Continuing the attack over open ground was an impossibility on account of the mass of wire lying about between the communication trenches. Twenty-seven Germans were taken prisoner by 'D' Company. Many more had been killed or wounded.[11]

Although the fighting continued at intervals throughout the remainder of the afternoon, no more ground was lost on 6th Brigade's front. By nightfall, south of Moeuvres the battered battalions of 6th Brigade had been forced back 100–300yd along a frontage of 800yd. East of the canal, the 99th Brigade had managed to hold virtually all of its positions. One of its officers, Capt Walter Stone of the 17th Royal Fusiliers, would be awarded a posthumous Victoria Cross for his actions during the fight. Under severe pressure, the 2nd Division had stood its ground.

On the left and right flanks of 2nd Division respectively, the 56th and 47th Divisions had similarly stood firm. Even though the strategically important crest of the Bourlon Ridge had been lost, the German counter-stroke at the northern shoulder of the salient had clearly failed in its objectives. To the south, the situation was markedly different. The Germans had broken through the British lines around the village of Villers Guislain. The situation would have been worse, but for a determined counterattack by the Guards Division which had regained Gouzeaucourt.

The casualties of the 17th Middlesex during the fighting of 30 November were remarkably light. Five other ranks had been killed, including Cpl George Poulter, a labourer from Fulham, who had enlisted in the 17th Middlesex on 28 May 1915. Another casualty was the RMO, Capt James Matheson, who was killed by an enemy shell while tending to the wounded. Educated at the Edinburgh Institution and Glasgow University, Capt Matheson had seen active service with the Royal Navy and in Mesopotamia before joining the 17th Middlesex on the Western Front. His grave was subsequently lost, but Capt Matheson is believed to have been buried in Hermies Hill British Cemetery, where today there is a special memorial bearing his name.

The wounded were dealt with by the Divisional Field Ambulances, which had worked tirelessly under constant shellfire.

The speedy evacuation of stretcher cases undoubtedly saved many lives that day:

> Wounded passed through in a steady stream, taxing our bearers, who had a long, hard carry of many relays, to the utmost. As a precaution against a block in evacuation and, if required, to afford breathing space to our bearers, a large tunnel at Lock 6, capable of accommodating some 30 to 40 stretchers, was placed in readiness. So steadily, however, were cases evacuated that there were never more than five or six cases there at one time. Evacuation was at first carried out by two bearer divisions in the line, and the third in reserve. By nightfall all three divisions had been used, and a party of 50 infantry were taken in on the rear relays, to allow one division to rest; and thereafter a rotation of 24 hourly reliefs of our bearers was carried out.[12]

To the immediate west of the Canal du Nord, the fighting continued into the night, as unsuccessful attempts were made by parties from the 1st King's Liverpool and the 2nd South Staffords to reach the isolated party of 13th Essex in Street Trench. At 9 p.m. Capt Fred Stansfeld and 'B' Company of the 17th Middlesex relieved Capt McReady-Diarmid and 'D' Company in the front line between the ruined factory and the Canal du Nord. 'D' Company moved back into close support. In the early hours of 1 December Lt Fred Nunn and 'A' Company were also relieved and moved back into support. At 4.45 a.m. a strong German bombing party, advancing down Edda Weg, was beaten back by CSM Jackson of the 1st King's Liverpool and a party from 'C' Company of the 17th Middlesex. An hour later Capt Frank Gregory and 'C' Company were relieved by two companies of the 2nd Highland Light Infantry and went back to dugouts south of the Bapaume–Cambrai Road. The left sector of 6th Brigade's front line was now held from left to right by the 1st King's Liverpool and 'A' Company of the 2nd Highland Light Infantry; the right sector by 'B' Company of the 17th Middlesex. Further forward, 'D' Company of the 13th Essex, stranded in Street Trench, were still holding out against the odds.

The intermixed battalions of 6th Brigade, west of the Canal du Nord, were in for another day of hard fighting. The Germans had brought up fresh troops to support Reserve Infantry Regiment 225 in its efforts to drive southwards down the western bank of the canal, the 2nd Highland Light Infantry War Diary recording that these reinforcements were 'men of high fighting quality and of considerable courage'.[13] Among their number was Leutnant Ernst Jünger of Fusilier Regiment 73, whose post-war writings are among the most striking accounts of the Great War. Around 7 a.m. 'D' Company of the 13th Essex were attacked by two companies of Fusilier Regiment 73. Forty minutes or so later 'D' Company, having held out for around 22 hours, capitulated. An account of the surrender and Jünger's subsequent encounter with the wounded company commander, Capt Herbert Jessop, in a dugout, can be found in *Storm of Steel*.[14]

From 8 a.m. onwards Capt Stansfeld and 'B' Company of the 17th Middlesex, who were holding the front line between the ruined factory and the Canal du Nord, were also subjected to a series of bombing attacks.[15] For the next few hours the fighting ebbed back and forth, but the officers and men of 'B' Company just about held their ground, launching immediate counterattacks to recover any section of lost trench. At 9 a.m. Lt Col Stafford sent three platoons of 'C' Company up to Advanced HQ of the 17th Middlesex with supplies of grenades and ordered the remaining platoon to reinforce the 1st King's Liverpool in the vicinity of Ernst Weg. About 11 a.m. an estimated three companies of German infantry were observed crossing a bank near the ruined bridge, south of Lock No. 5. Shortly afterwards another determined bombing attack was mounted on 'B' Company, supported by machine-guns firing from the vicinity of Lock No. 5.

It was not long before Capt Stansfeld and 'B' Company were struggling to hold their positions, particularly once the supply of grenades began to run low. Matters were not helped by the fact that several grenades sent up from the brigade dump proved to be utterly useless, owing to the fact that they had not been primed. The situation became so desperate that Pte Israel Colebourne, who would suffer shell shock as a result of his experiences that day, recalled that 'B' Company ended up 'using German stick bombs and anything lying about'.[16]

Barely 22 years old, Capt Stansfeld, described by Cpl Alexander Haggart as 'a brave man, almost recklessly so, and exceedingly popular', did his best to stem the German advance.[17] Lt Col Stafford would later refer to the 'magnificent example he set his men at a most trying time'.[18] Having jumped out of a trench to lead another counterattack across open ground, Capt Stansfeld was killed by a grenade, which exploded at his feet and left his body sprawled across the wire.[19] Sgt John Hogarth, who had become separated from his rifle, picked up his company commander's revolver to continue the fight. The 17th Middlesex War Diary commented that 'All B Company officers were now missing, the men tired and shaken'.[20]

Having run out of grenades, 'B' Company began to fall back. Parties of German bombers streamed southwards towards the Bapaume–Cambrai Road. Another party of the enemy began bombing westwards along Elsa Weg, threatening Battalion HQ of the 1st King's Liverpool. The situation was critical. From their positions in close support, Capt Allastair McReady-Diarmid and 'D' Company had a clear view of unfolding events. The divisional history records what happened next:

Captain A.M.C. McReady Diarmid of D Company, 17th Middlesex, seeing the position, called for volunteers from his company. Arming himself with a plentiful supply of bombs, he rushed forward and attacked the enemy. With extraordinary gallantry, and with such splendid bomb-throwing as was seldom seen, he gradually drove the enemy back up the trench down which his troops had forced their way. 'By throwing all the bombs himself,' said the Official Report, 'this officer killed and otherwise disposed of 94 of the enemy – 67 dead and 27 wounded were actually counted after the recapture of the trench, a feat which can hardly have been equalled in the past. Every foot of the 300 yards of lost trench was regained, and by his deliberate disregard of danger, his cheerfulness and coolness, Captain McReady-Diarmid inspired all who saw him, It was a marvellous performance, but alas! The gallant officer, having won back for his battalion the lost ground, was himself killed by an enemy bomb almost at the moment of his final triumph.'[21]

The efforts of Capt McReady-Diarmid and his men were ably supported by the Lewis guns of the 1st King's Liverpool and 2nd

Highland Light Infantry and a captured German machine-gun fired by 2/Lt James Armstrong of the 1st King's Liverpool, which had managed to silence the machine-guns firing from Lock No. 5. The German advance along Elsa Weg was also halted, primarily as a result of the actions of Capt Harrison of the 6th Brigade Trench Mortar Battery, who had rushed down a Stokes mortar to the junction of Elsa Weg and the main communication trench. Despite having only ten rounds of Stokes ammunition left, his rapid and accurate fire 'completely demoralised the enemy and silenced the Light M.G'.[22] Several German soldiers climbed out of Elsa Weg in a bid to escape and were cut down by Lewis guns.

Intermittent fighting continued for the rest of the day, but subsequent German bombing attacks made little progress. At 3.18 p.m. the 6th Brigade front was subjected to another heavy barrage. Enemy troops were reported to be massing once again in Moeuvres. An effective artillery response and massed fire from the British trenches brought the subsequent German advance to a peremptory halt, enemy artillery ceasing fire altogether around 5 p.m. After nightfall the exhausted men of 'B' and 'D' Companies of the 17th Middlesex were relieved by six platoons of the 2nd Highland Light Infantry and moved back to the Bapaume–Cambrai Road. Once again, the Germans had been thwarted in their efforts to break through the British lines in the vicinity of Bourlon. The situation had also begun to stabilise in the south. That evening Haig wrote in his diary: 'The splendid defence put up by the 2nd and the 47th Divisions around Bourlon and determination of the 29th and 6th Divisions on the Masnières front quite justifies a feeling of satisfaction.'[23]

The fighting of 1 December cost the 17th Middlesex the lives of 2 officers, Capts Fred Stansfeld and Allastair McReady-Diarmid, and 17 other ranks. Capt Fred Stansfeld, a keen sportsman, was one of the original officers of the 17th Middlesex, Educated at St Paul's School, Stansfeld had been admitted as a scholar to Pembroke College to read Mathematics for 1915, but had chosen instead to enlist in the Inns of Court OTC. Commissioned into the 17th Middlesex, he proceeded overseas with the battalion in November 1915. Following an accidental wounding in April 1916, Stansfeld had spent a period of convalescence in Salisbury, where he had met a nurse, Margaret Sutton. Wounded in the head on 13 November 1916, Stansfeld had been sent back to England for treatment and had married Margaret shortly before returning to the battalion in the autumn of 1917.

A few days after Capt Stansfeld's death, Margaret Stansfeld received a War Office telegram stating that her husband had been reported wounded and missing. A letter followed from Lt Col Stafford, which left little doubt that her husband was dead: 'He was a delightful companion, always cheerful and full of life, and I can assure you those qualities are worth a lot out here.'[24] Margaret refused to give up all hope. On 13 December she wrote to the War Office:

> The news is so terrible. I suppose that there is still some hope that he may be a prisoner in German hands. I feel certain you will wire me any news at once because my anxiety is great. I had a letter from his Lieutenant Colonel and it is a letter to be proud of, it speaks of the magnificent example the Captain set his men, during a dreadful attack.
>
> The Colonel says he has lost one of his most efficient officers in my husband. Please wire me any news because I shall await your final decision before giving up all hope.[25]

Subsequent reports from wounded soldiers of 'B' Company soon confirmed that Capt Stansfeld was indeed dead. For the rest of the war Margaret Stansfeld drove ambulances for the Red Cross. After the war it emerged that her husband's body had been found by the Germans on 15 December 1917 and had been buried to the east of the ruined sugar factory. His grave was never found and Capt Fred Stansfeld is today commemorated on the Cambrai Memorial to the Missing at Louverval.

Capt Allastair McReady-Diarmid is also commemorated on the Cambrai Memorial. This brave officer was known by three names during his lifetime: Arthur Malcolm Drew, Arthur McReady-Drew and Allastair Malcolm Cluny McReady-Diarmid. The third son of a civil servant, he was born plain Arthur Drew on 21 March 1888 in New Southgate. Educated in London, and for a short time at Victoria College in Jersey, he had shown little interest in his academic studies, excelling at cricket and athletics.

The *Victoria College Book of Remembrance* recorded that 'The outdoor life was his delight . . . He was a dead shot with a rifle, but such was his natural love of animals that, until the war, he had never fired at any living creatures. He knew the note of every wild bird.'[26]

His parents had wanted him to go to Cambridge and take Holy Orders, but by the age of 26 it would appear that Arthur Drew had yet to find his vocation in life. He had thought of going abroad, but the outbreak of war ensured that such plans never came to fruition. After a few months as an officer cadet in the University of London OTC, he was commissioned into the 4th Middlesex in March 1915 as 2/Lt Arthur McReady-Drew (McReady being his mother Fanny's maiden name), joining the battalion in France shortly afterwards. He was wounded not long after his arrival when a shell blew him off a fire step causing a serious internal injury, the extent of which was not immediately apparent. Returning to England for an operation a few weeks later, he would appear to have met Hilda Dainton, the daughter of a Dursley tinsmith, while convalescing from his wounds, although it is possible that they had, in fact, known each other before the outbreak of war. They were married by Special Licence at the Parish Church of St James in Dursley, Gloucestershire, on 20 September 1915. Ten days before the wedding, Arthur Drew changed his name by deed poll to Allastair Malcolm Cluny McReady-Diarmid. The exact reasons for this change of name are unknown.[27]

A few weeks after his marriage, McReady-Diarmid was back in France with the 4th Middlesex. On 23 June 1916 he was struck off battalion strength, possibly as a result of complications arising from his wounds the previous year, and returned to England. On 4 December 1916 he reported for duty with the 17th Middlesex and was promoted to the rank of Acting Captain on 26 October 1917. Only a few months before his death, Capt McReady-Diarmid had become a father, Hilda having given birth to a daughter, Alizon, on 24 May 1917.

Hilda McReady-Diarmid received the distressing news about her husband's death on 8 December 1917. A few days later, a letter arrived from Lt Col Stafford:

Your husband died the finest death that I have ever known a man die. He had personally led a bombing party up a trench and had driven back the enemy more than 300 yards. He was killed instantaneously at the moment of victory by a bomb, which hit him in the head. Your husband was entirely responsible for the repulse of the enemy at a most critical moment and nothing can be too much for him. His heroism is the talk of the Brigade. I am sure that he died happy. He had the true fighting spirit and his men would have followed him anywhere. His death has left a gap, which we will never be able to fill. Apart from his brilliant soldierly ability, he was a most charming companion in the mess. Always cheery and full of humour, he was always keeping our spirits up.

I cannot say how much I feel for you and your child. It is terrible to have lost such a husband. May God grant you strength to comfort you up in your sorrow. I can but offer you the sincerest sympathy of every officer and man in this battalion.

I very much regret to say that we were unable to recover your husband's body, as after he fell, his company were driven back a little way. The place where he was killed is just south of a village called Moeuvres, near Cambrai. The battalion has received high praise for its work in repelling the enemy attacks, but your husband stood out by himself among brave men.[28]

Among the other ranks of the 17th Middlesex who died on 1 December were Pte John Grubb, who had previously seen service with the 1/7th Middlesex, and two original enlistments in the Footballers' Battalions, Cpl Oscar Campbell, a warehouseman from Harringay, and Cpl Alfred Ramsey, a bookseller from Bayswater. Another soldier killed was Pte Walter Long, a former employee of the Direct Supply Mineral Water Co in Beckenham and a member of the Penge Lodge of the Ancient Order of Druids and the local Liberal Club. His wife was informed that 'The platoon was bombing the enemy out of a piece of trench, your husband was taking an active part when he was hit by a piece of German bomb; he died instantly. He will be much missed, as he was full of life, and gave many a good turn at our concerts'.[29]

Over the next two days the Germans renewed their efforts to break through the British lines south of Moeuvres, but the 6th

Brigade stood firm. On 2 December German artillery placed an effective barrage on the front and support lines of 6th Brigade. An hour later rifle fire was heard and 'B' Company of the 17th Middlesex was ordered to 'Stand To!' north of the Bapaume–Cambrai Road. The shellfire was 'intense and most accurate', causing heavy casualties and knocking out all the company's Lewis guns.[30] The number of fatalities would have been higher had it not been for the bravery of L/Cpl Albert Crouch, in charge of the company stretcher-bearers. Working throughout the bombardment, he ensured that all the wounded were speedily evacuated. For his 'extraordinary coolness and indifference to danger', L/Cpl Crouch would be awarded the Distinguished Conduct Medal.[31]

Among those killed during this bombardment were 32-year-old Cpl William Tallett, a pre-war territorial in the Royal West Kent Regiment, and Pte George Bouttell, an original enlistment in the 23rd Middlesex and a resident of Ardleigh in Essex. The following day saw two platoons of 'C' Company of the 17th Middlesex being sent up to assist the 2nd Highland Light Infantry, which was being troubled by enemy bombing parties in the vicinity of Donner Weg. Two men, Cpl William Graylin, a resident of Romford, and 19-year-old Pte Charles Neville from Watford, were killed.

On the evening of 4 December the 17th Middlesex moved back to Lebucquière, where the officers and men were billeted in an assortment of tents and huts. Stock could now be taken of the losses. Between 26 November and 3 December 1917, 3 officers and 47 other ranks had been killed, or had died of their wounds. Four officers, 2/Lts Percy Hislop, Ernest Francis, Claude Gann and William Tricker, and 138 other ranks had been wounded.[32] Only 11 of the other ranks killed have known graves. The remaining 36 men are commemorated, along with Capts Fred Stansfeld and Allastair McReady-Diarmid, on the Cambrai Memorial to the Missing, which commemorates more than 7,000 servicemen of the United Kingdom and South Africa who fell in the Battle of Cambrai in November and December 1917 and have no known grave.

The success of the German counterstroke in the south had left the British holding a vulnerable salient in the north. Holding the Bourlon salient would have undoubtedly proved 'difficult and dangerous' in the event of further attacks, so Haig ordered Byng to withdraw his troops to a new defensive line. By 7 December the withdrawal had been successfully completed, German attempts to push forward being disrupted by effective artillery fire. As the *Official History* would later comment: 'This was the closing scene of a boldly conceived offensive which failed in its strategic aims, but is of particular importance because it saw the development of new tactics destined to exercise so much influence on future warfare'.[33]

After such a promising start, the Cambrai offensive had fallen flat. The British had lost in excess of 40,000 men. German casualties were estimated to be in the region of 53,000. News of the German counterstroke and the subsequent evacuation of the Bourlon salient was greeted with disbelief back in Britain. The conclusion of previous British offensives on Western Front had never resulted in captured ground being handed back to the enemy. Such was the resulting political and public disquiet that four separate inquiries would take place.

Byng attributed blame to the lack of training of junior officers, NCOs and men, singling out the 'staunchness of the machine-gunners' for particular criticism.[34] Haig largely endorsed this view, but tempered Byng's criticisms by pointing out that many divisions were tired, and that they had been overwhelmed by superior numbers. Given his decision to persevere with efforts to secure the Bourlon Ridge, Haig had no option but to take full responsibility for the reverse, despite his belief that 'the enemy should not have succeeded in penetrating any part of our defence'.[35]

The determined stand of the 47th, 2nd and 56th Divisions along the Bourlon–Moeuvres front had played an important part in averting a major disaster, which would undoubtedly have occurred if the Germans had broken through at the northern shoulder of the salient. Within a few days the 17th Middlesex and the other units of the 2nd Division would receive messages of congratulation from Haig and their divisional commander, Maj Gen Pereira. Before making his recommendations for honours and awards, Lt Col Ronald Stafford wrote to Brig Gen Walsh on 5 December:

Generally, I wish to pay the highest possible tribute to the spirit of the men in the Battalion. They were very tired before Nov 30th, but they stuck to the work splendidly until 3rd Dec. They had practically no sleep and very little food and were most exhausted.

The work of the Company Commanders was also excellent. They all had to frequently act on their own initiative and they did all that could possibly be asked of them. The example set by Captain McReady-Diarmid was beyond all praise and it can have seldom happened that an individual has killed so many of the enemy. Captain Stansfeld and Lieut. Nunn also did splendidly and Captain Gregory with less opportunities carried out his orders with great ability and coolness. Particular praise must be awarded [to] 2/Lieut. Winship, the Battn. Signalling Officer. It was through him that wires lasted so well. He worked continuously in the thick of the enemy barrage and set a magnificent example to his men.

Major Edwards MC went up at 10 a.m. on the 30th and formed advanced Bn. HQ. He obtained an immediate grip of a difficult situation and subsequently was very largely responsible for the successful counter-attacks. His dispositions were excellent and he kept me very fully informed as to the situation.

The runners had to pass through enemy shelling time after time, but there was not a single case of a message not being promptly delivered. The stretcher bearers all worked extremely well and evacuation of the wounded was well and quickly carried out.[36]

As a result of the fighting at Cambrai, Lt Fred Nunn was awarded the Military Cross, 6 other ranks were awarded Distinguished Conduct Medals, and a further 12 men Military Medals. Among those awarded Distinguished Conduct Medals were L/Cpl Frank Berry, who had acted as Capt McReady-Diarmid's bayonet man, using his 'bayonet with very telling effect, clearing the trenches for three hundred yards of the enemy and inflicting very severe casualties on them', and Sgt William Glenie, who had driven back the enemy 'for several hundred yards, setting a magnificent example to all around him, who were inspired to the greatest efforts through his courage, endurance and splendid fighting spirit'.[37]

Already a holder of the Distinguished Conduct Medal, Cpl Joseph Hickman, 'a tiny man of unconquerable courage and, unfortunately, an equally unconquerable weakness for drink', was awarded the Military Medal.[38] L/Cpl Hickman had made a lasting impression on his commanding officer. Lt Col Stafford recalled, 'His gallantry and powers of leadership marked him out for promotion and promoted he often was even to the rank of sergeant, but as a result of drunkenness out of the line, he was as often reduced to the ranks.'[39]

There were also the actions of Capt McReady-Diarmid to consider. By 6 December, there was already talk of him being recommended for a posthumous Victoria Cross. On 12 December Brig Gen Richard Walsh concluded his report of 6th Brigade's recent operations with the following words:

> Amongst so many cases of gallantry and devotion to duty performed by individual Officers and Other Ranks, I wish to draw particular attention to the case of Lieut. (a/Captain) McReady-Diarmid, 17th Middlesex Regt., who unfortunately was killed in action on 1st December. This officer is reported to have killed and otherwise disposed of about 80 of the enemy, to his own hand, a feat which can hardly have been equalled in the past. His display of vigorous offensive action and the splendid example he set to those around him undoubtedly had invaluable effect in keeping back the enemy. His loss to his Battalion and the service is a very great one.[40]

On 17 December Maj Gen Cecil Pereira issued a Special Order of the Day, thanking the officers and men of 2nd Division for their recent efforts. He also chose to pay tribute to the bravery of Capt Allastair McReady-Diarmid along with a few other individuals who had distinguished themselves during the recent fighting. That same day Capt McReady-Diarmid's grieving father, Herbert Drew, wrote to the War Office, clearly dissatisfied with its response to a query regarding his son's surname. He clearly had no idea that his son had changed his name by Deed Poll the previous year:

> It was a War Office mistake to enter my son's name in the Army List as McReady-Diarmid, as you may see from his papers the change was made when he was in France & was done by request of his colonel to obviate confusion in orders owing to there being other officers named Drew in the Battalion. There was no legal change & I must ask you to

publish his proper name McReady-Drew, otherwise it will be no notification to his friends . . . I trust that there will be no further trouble in the matter. I hear unofficially that my son has been recommended for the Victoria Cross & I am therefore anxious that the true name should stand as in Gazette 1915.[41]

The War Office responded by sending a copy of the Deed Poll and there the correspondence ended. An examination of the relevant Army Lists fails to reveal a surfeit of officers called Drew who were serving in the Middlesex Regiment in 1915. It would appear that Capt McReady-Diarmid had neglected to tell his parents the real reasons behind the change of name.

Within a few months, the award of a Victoria Cross to Capt McReady-Diarmid was formally approved. The citation was published in the *London Gazette* of 15 March 1918. The fact that it made reference to his former name must have provided some solace to his parents and three brothers:

T./Lt. (A./Capt.) Allastair Malcolm Cluny McReady-Diarmid (formerly Arthur Malcolm McReady-Drew), late Midd'x B. For most conspicuous bravery and brilliant leadership. When the enemy penetrated some distance into our position and the situation was extremely critical, Captain McReady-Diarmid at once led his company forward through a heavy barrage. He immediately engaged the enemy, with such success that he drove them back at least 300 yards, causing numerous casualties and capturing 27 prisoners. The following day the enemy again attacked and drove back another company which had lost all its officers. This gallant officer at once called for volunteers and attacked. He drove them back again for 300 yards, with heavy casualties. Throughout this attack Captain McReady-Diarmid led the way himself, and it was absolutely and entirely due to his marvellous throwing of bombs that the ground was regained. His absolute disregard for danger, his cheerfulness and coolness at a most trying time inspired all who saw him. This most gallant officer was eventually killed by a bomb when the enemy had been driven right back to their original starting point.[42]

On 20 April 1918 Hilda McReady-Diarmid went to Buckingham Palace to receive her husband's medal from King George V. On 26

June 1920, she represented her husband at a Palace Garden Party for Victoria Cross winners. On Armistice Day 1929, their 12-year-old daughter Alizon, wearing her father's Victoria Cross, attended the service at the Cenotaph, where she assisted Earl Jellicoe in laying a wreath. In 1973 Hilda donated her late husband's medals to the Regimental Museum of the Middlesex Regiment, her daughter Alizon having predeceased her in 1966. Hilda never remarried and died in 1981 at the age of 91. Following the closure of the Regimental Museum, Capt McReady-Diarmid's medals passed to the National Army Museum. As part of its 150th anniversary celebrations in 2002, Victoria College named one of its houses Diarmid House in honour of one of its most distinguished former pupils.

1. Byng assumed command of the Third Army on 7 June 1917, following Allenby taking up command in Egypt and Palestine.
2. Miles, W., *Official History of the War, Military Operations: France & Belgium 1917*, vol. III, p 8.
3. On 27 November 1917, Lord Kinnaird, president of the FA, lost another son. Arthur, a lieutenant in the 1st Scots Guards, died of wounds sustained during the attack on Fontaine.
4. Miles, W. *Official History of the War, 1917*, vol. III, p 372.
5. IWM: 73/103/1.
6. Wyrall, E., *The History of the Second Division*, p. 490.
7. During the Second World War, Maj Gen David Murray-Lyon DSO, MC (1890–1975) commanded the 11th Indian Division in Malaya. He was taken prisoner after the fall of Singapore in 1942 and spent the rest of the war in captivity.
8. The defensive zones of fire for the British artillery had been arranged so that two-thirds of the gun batteries covered an entire section of front, the remaining third being superimposed over them. The key advantage of this arrangement was flexibility, as the superimposed gun batteries were able to turn their attention to emerging targets without leaving any gaps in the screen of fire.
9. By the end of the day the 16 heavy machine-guns of 6th Brigade Machine Gun Company, organised into 2 batteries of 8 guns each, had fired in excess of 100,000 rounds.
10. TNA: WO 95/1361.
11. Around the same time about 40 men from 'C' Company of the 13th Essex attempted to bomb up the communication trench from the block established by Lt Nunn and 'A' Company of the 17th Middlesex in Ernst Weg, but little headway was made. The 13th Essex War Diary records that the total strength of 'C' Company was only 2 officers and 15 men by 4 p.m.
12. Operations of 2nd Division Between Bourlon Wood and Moeuvres, 30 November–6 December 1917, in Wyrall, E., *The History of the Second Division*, p. 499.
13. TNA: WO 95/1347.
14. See Jünger, E. (tr. by Michael Hofmann), *Storm of Steel*, p. 209–10.
15. Jünger provides a vivid account of the fighting south of Moeuvres on 1 December 1917 in *Storm of Steel*, p. 210–17. It is highly probable that Jünger was involved in the bombing attacks on 'B' Company of the 17th Middlesex. Jünger himself was wounded in the head that day, keeping his perforated helmet as a souvenir. He died on 17 February 1998 at the age of 102.
16. TNA: WO 339/30402.
17. *Ibid*.
18. *The Pauline* (1918), p. 69.
19. Other accounts state that Capt Stansfeld was shot in the head.
20. TNA: WO 95/1361.

21. Wyrall, E., *The History of the Second Division*, p. 502–3.
22. *Ibid.*, p. 503.
23. Haig, D., *Douglas Haig: War Diaries and Letters*, p. 354.
24. TNA: WO 339/30402.
25. *Ibid.*
26. *The Victoria College Book of Remembrance*, p 162.
27. It is probable that the change of name was linked to parental disapproval of his marriage. There are several indications that his parents did not accept Hilda as a daughter-in-law. See Adams, G., 'The Curious Story of Captain Allastair McReady-Diarmid VC' (*Stand To!* No. 75; Jan 2006).
28. NAM: 9403-139.
29. *Beckenham Advertiser* (no date).
30. WO 95/1361.
31. *London Gazette*, Issue 30601, 26 March 1918.
32. Twenty-six year old 2/Lt Hislop, a bank cashier from Upper Clapton, would later die of his wounds at hospital in Rouen.
33. Miles, W. *Official History of the War, 1917*, vol. 3, p 305.
34. *Ibid.*, p 294.
35. *Ibid.*, p 295.
36. IWM: 73/103/1.
37. *London Gazette*, Issue 30601, 26 March 1918.
38. IWM: 73/103/1.
39. *Ibid.*
40. TNA: WO 95/1354.
41. TNA: WO 339/38513.
42. *London Gazette*, Issue 30578, 15 March 1918.

CHAPTER 15

THE FINAL WHISTLE

There is no team out here that can beat us
Sgt Fred Parker F/111 (Clapton Orient)

On 8 December 1917 the Chelsea match programme referred to an incident that was said to have occurred at a 4–3 home victory over Arsenal two weeks earlier, in which 'a discharged soldier, who had been dumb for months possibly from shell shock, recovered his speech after jumping and shouting "Goal" when Thomson scored the first goal which had been registered for five weeks'.[1] That same day the 17th Middlesex, with a fighting strength of 38 officers and 755 other ranks, were preparing to move up to the new front line. During the evening the battalion relieved the 17th Royal Fusiliers on the western bank of the Canal du Nord, Battalion HQ being situated in Lock No. 7. Morale was excellent given the battalion's performance in the recent fighting. No one expected any trouble. Of far greater concern to all ranks was the plummeting temperature. On completion of the relief, Capt Cosmo Clark wrote home that:

> We are up the line again – we arrived tonight. Things are pretty quiet
> and all goes well bar the weather. A persistent drizzly rain is making
> things unpleasant. I'm in a very deep German dug out, which has the
> remains of the German occupation about it (invading fleas). We are
> only hoping the Hun will come for us, so that we can hit him hard – I
> assure you we will do that. Nothing points to it however. All is quiet.[2]

It did not remain quiet for long. At 7.30 a.m. on 9 December a German raiding party with *Flammenwerfer* attacked the bombing posts held by men of 'A' Company and succeeding in knocking out one of the Lewis gun teams. Lt Col Stafford sent 'C' Company up to reinforce 'A 'Company and the Germans were driven off. As Capt Clark put it: 'The Hun tried to make an attack on us with liquid fire, but it soon fizzled out – both the attack and the *Flammenwerfer*.'[3] Continual bombing attacks took place for the remainder of the day. Ptes John Ashdown, Ernest Daniels and Sidney Ellis were killed and several others were wounded. The next day saw a heavy bombardment of Lock No. 7 and intermittent shelling of the front line. Another post on 'A' Company's front was raided by the Germans. Although wounded in the arm, Sgt William Glenie single-handedly drove the raiders back up the trench, before being taken prisoner.

On the evening of 11 December the 17th Middlesex were relieved by the 2nd South Staffords and moved back into support. Four men had been killed during the course of the day: Ptes George Dale, Colin Burchett, Clement Davies and Gershom Emsden, the latter two soldiers being only 19 years of age. The news of Pte Burchett's death must have hit his parents particularly hard. William and Eliza Burchett had already lost one of their sons, Arthur, a sergeant in the Coldstream Guards, in September 1914. Only a few days before the Armistice, they would lose another, Edwin, who was serving with the Wiltshire Regiment.

The front quietened over the next couple of days. An extensive programme of work was implemented: new shelters were built, fire bays cut into new trenches and further wire entanglements constructed. Behind the lines, cookhouses and officers' messes were erected. On 14 December the 17th Middlesex moved back to Velu Wood, where the battalion was billeted in tents which were covered by a thick layer of snow. The next few days were spent training and providing working parties. The weather remained bitterly cold.

On 20 December the 17th Middlesex relieved the 1st Royal Berkshires in the front line. During this spell in the trenches the enemy were quiet and there were no fatalities. Three days later, on relief by the 2nd South Staffords, 17th Middlesex moved back to Hermies in reserve, leaving 'B' Company in support. The next couple of days saw the majority of the battalion engaged in constructing a new Brigade HQ. The remainder were busy making concertinas for the troops in the front line. The decision was taken to postpone Christmas dinner until the 17th Middlesex were out of the line.

On Boxing Day the 17th Middlesex moved back into the front line, relieving the 13th Essex. Ptes William Hodby and Albert Tillett were killed later that evening, probably by shellfire. The next day German heavy guns pounded the front and support lines without response from British artillery. Five other ranks were killed and ten or so were wounded, two of whom later succumbed to their wounds. The next day a German shell caught a ration party carrying supplies up to 'A' Company. Ptes Warren Dore and Joseph Jones, an early enlistment in the 17th Middlesex from Edmonton, were killed and a further four wounded. On the evening of 29 December the battalion were relieved by the 2nd South Staffords and moved back into reserve, leaving 'A' Company in support.

On 2 January the 17th Middlesex relieved the 2nd South Staffords in the front line, north-west of Flesquières. Small groups of soldiers moved into No Man's Land in order to garrison a series of advanced posts. From left to right, these positions, situated a few hundred yards to the east of the Canal du Nord, were known as Stone, Scott and Sark Posts. Stone and Scott Posts were situated about 250yd from Hughes Switch, the British front line, Sark Post only 50yd. To the right of Sark Post lay Sap 'A', a trench that extended out a couple of hundred yards into No Man's Land from the British front line. Between Stone and Scot Posts a sunken road ran in a north-easterly direction towards the German lines.

At 4.20 p.m. on 3 January enemy trench mortars opened up on the positions of the 17th Middlesex. The bombardment was particularly severe on the occupants of Sark and Scott Posts. The defenders of Sark Post were driven out of their position by the accurate shelling, but were able to reoccupy the post before the attack started. Supported by heavy machine-gun fire, the enemy advanced using smoke bombs, several German soldiers wearing white suits in an attempt to camouflage themselves in the snow. Despite 2/Lt Ronald Murray throwing some 80 grenades at the enemy, the Germans eventually succeeded in driving back the defenders of Sap 'A' to a point within 25yd of Hughes Switch. A block was established with a Lewis gun, preventing any further enemy advance.

Scott Post was also attacked. Under the command of Sgt Arthur

Eldridge, 'who was reported to have put a very good fight', the garrison resisted fiercely, but was soon overwhelmed. The defence of Scott Post was hindered by the fact the Lewis gun had jammed, possibly as a result of damage sustained during the bombardment. The 17th Middlesex War Diary recorded that '11 of the garrison were wounded and 9 missing, believed killed, and the remaining six made their way back to the front line'.[4] Orders were then given for a counterattack to be launched by 'B' Company, assisted by 'D' Company:

A Lewis Gun was placed in Sunken Road . . . to fire down road and a party of 10 under an officer ordered to attack from the left and another party of same number from the right but owing to the strength of the enemy and the small number of men available to counter-attack no headway was made. Enemy had a party estimated at 200 lining the Sunken Road, large parties digging and wiring in and around Scott Post with a large covering party in front.[5]

On the extreme left of the battalion front, the garrison of Stone Post, under the direction of 2/Lt William Cousins, had managed to hold its positions, largely on account of effective Lewis gun fire. For the loss of only one man, heavy losses were inflicted on the enemy. The 17th Middlesex War Diary listed the total casualties as: 8 other ranks killed, 31 wounded, of whom 3 died later that evening, and 16 missing. At the time all of the missing were believed to have been killed, but the CWGC lists the names of only 14 soldiers whose date of death is given as 3 January 1918, suggesting that others from 17th Middlesex had been taken prisoner. Among the dead were Sgt Arthur Eldridge, originally from Erith in Kent, Sgt Norman Hughes, a holder of the Military Medal, and Pte Robert Steven, an original enlistment in the battalion and a resident of Wandsworth.

Later that evening the 17th Middlesex were relieved by the 10th Sherwood Foresters of 17th Division. The men marched back through communication trenches and along the bed of the Canal du Nord to the light railway near Hermies. There, the battalion entrained for Rocquigny, the last trainload departing shortly before dawn. Arriving at their billets in Beaulencourt later that morning, the men were disappointed to find that the camp was in a very poor condition, many of the Nissan huts being unlined and devoid of stoves. Capt Cosmo Clark described the severity of the weather conditions at this time:

It is biting cold. Thick snow covers everything and is really beautiful but we spend most of our time in knocking our feet together and blowing our fingers to get warm. This morning my wet shaving brush, sponge and brilliantine were as hard as steel. The condensed milk and mustard at breakfast were of the consistency of toffee.[6]

The next couple of days were spent refitting. Work was also done to make the huts more comfortable and bricks were collected to construct fireplaces. On 6 January the 17th Middlesex sat down to a belated Christmas dinner:

The men's dinner was a great success, and they enjoyed themselves immensely. Each Coy. had two dinners, and half the company sat down at each. The menu, which was plentiful and good, was as follows: ½ lb roast beef and ½ pork, potatoes and cabbage. Christmas pudding with white sauce followed. Oranges, apples, nuts, dates and a tot of rum finished up the feed. Each man had two pints of French beer to his dinner. They were all very happy with the prospect of three weeks' rest from fighting and the satisfaction of having fought hard and won a succession of fights. After dinner they all crowded fires and sang choruses and popular songs to the accompaniment of banjos, mouth organs and concertinas.[7]

On 8 January a battalion concert was planned to take place at the local YMCA hut that afternoon, when disaster struck: '. . . the stove fell over and the hut caught fire. As it was blowing hard at the time, and the hut was made of wood, the whole show was blazing in a minute. Fortunately only the band and the performers were in the building – the audience were to be admitted in about five minutes. 2 cornets and the padre's dog were the only casualties'.[8] In addition to the two cornets, the band lost their music stands and virtually all their sheet music. All the costumes belonging to the battalion troupe were also destroyed in the blaze.

Two days later, the 17th Middlesex marched to Bapaume to see a pantomime put on by the Royal Flying Corps: 'Cinderella was the story they had chosen, and it was a rattling good show. The fairy godmother was the only fly in the ointment. Her biceps and tattooed arms hardly fitted the part!'[9]

The weather took another turn for the worst over the next few days, interfering with training and the men's efforts to bank up the huts with earth for protection against German air attacks. Thaws and heavy rain left the camp and surrounding area ankle-deep in mud. On 16 January a draft of 2 NCOs and 40 other ranks joined the battalion, the majority of whom were only 19 years old. Lt Col Stafford welcomed them 'with a word on our traditions, which he bade them to live up to'.[10] Four days later the 17th Middlesex 'B' Team played a football match against the 13th Essex, winning 4–0.[11] On 24 January the 17th Middlesex marched to a camp in Etricourt, the 2nd Division having relieved the Royal Naval Division, near La Vacquerie. Two days later, a draft of 70 reinforcements arrived. These men were once again very different from the men who had previously made good the battalion's losses throughout 1916 and 1917, being described in the 17th Middlesex War Diary as 'lads who had just turned nineteen years old'.[12]

The 1917 offensives had taken their toll of British manpower. By the beginning of 1918, several divisions were well below strength and the British were scheduled to take over another 25 miles of line from the French. Haig had every reason to be concerned. His army was already over-extended and short of men. Following the cessation of hostilities on the Eastern Front, large numbers of German troops were being transferred to France and Belgium. By the spring of 1918 the Germans would enjoy a significant numerical superiority over the Allies on the Western Front. There was every chance that Germany would use this brief window of opportunity to launch a major offensive to win the war before American manpower could tip the balance in favour of the Allies.

While there were adequate numbers of reinforcements available in the UK to address the deficit in manpower, the War Cabinet was reluctant to hand them over to Haig. The Third Battle of Ypres had been the last straw for Lloyd George, whose prior misgivings about the Flanders offensive had proved to be well founded. In his view, the Allies would be better off waiting for the Americans to be ready in decisive numbers before launching another offensive. The decision was subsequently made to sanction only a partial reinforcement of the BEF in France, leaving it weaker in fighting troops that it had been in January 1917.

It was also decided to reduce the establishment strength of British divisions, but not the Dominion divisions, from 12 infantry battalions to 9, with the officers and men from the disbanded battalions being used to bring other battalions up to strength. It was stipulated that no regular, first-line territorial, or yeomanry units were to be broken up and that the most recently raised New Army and second-line territorial battalions were to be disbanded first. A list of 145 battalions was drawn up in January 1918, from which Haig had to select units for disbandment. In total 115 battalions would be disbanded with 38 battalions being amalgamated to form 19 battalions, and a further 7 being converted to Pioneer battalions. One of the battalions selected for disbandment was the 17th Middlesex.

On the evening of 31 January the 17th Middlesex relieved the 1st King's Liverpool in the front line, near La Vacquerie, having spent the preceding days training and providing working parties. Apart from occasional trench mortar activity, the next few days were quiet, and only one man lost his life, Cpl Arthur Hardy, a resident of Uxbridge. On 3 February the 17th Middlesex were relieved by the 1st King's Liverpool and moved back into support trenches near Villers-Plouich, where Lt Col Stafford was informed that the 17th Middlesex were to be disbanded, 'owing to the difficulties in obtaining reinforcements to keep all battalions up to establishment'.[13] He later wrote of everyone's reaction to this news: 'The whole Battalion was stunned when it heard the news of its disbandment, and many protests were made. The Divisional Commander too made strong representations as he told me the Battalion was one of the best in the Division. But it was of no avail . . .'[14]

Two other battalions of the 2nd Division were also selected for disbandment: the 13th Essex and the 22nd Royal Fusiliers. At least the majority of the officers and men of the 22nd Royal Fusiliers would stay within the 2nd Division, being divided between the 23rd and 24th Royal Fusiliers. Those of the 17th Middlesex and 13th Essex would have to be sent to different divisions entirely. It was a severe blow to morale, particularly for the relatively few officers and men who had been with their units from the beginning. As Maj Gen Pereira, commander of 2nd Division, commented: 'The old soldiers who have survived many a fight are very hard hit by this disbanding'.[15]

On the night of 6 February the 17th Middlesex were relieved by the 1st King's Liverpool and marched back to billets west of Metz, where preparations for disbandment were being overseen by the adjutant, Capt Thomas Carless. Writing 41 years after the event, Lt Col Stafford recalled his feelings at the final parade of the Footballers' Battalion:

> At the final parade of the Battalion, I said that whatever might happen in later life, I should never be so proud of anything as of having commanded the Footballers Battalion, and now after 41 years I know that I spoke truly. It was a splendid battalion and I can imagine that there were few New Army Battalions its equal. It did not bear unfavourable comparison with the 1st 60th [1st King's Royal Rifle Corps] apart from the lack of experienced senior N.C.O's. and the 1st 60th was generally considered to be the best battalion of that regiment.[16]

On 9 February the officers of the 17th Middlesex held a farewell dinner. The following day 15 officers and 300 other ranks of 'B' and 'D' Companies left to join the 13th Middlesex at Roisel, east of Peronne. On 12 February 15 officers and 300 other ranks were sent to the 21st Middlesex at Mercatel, south of Arras. This left 4 officers and around 100 other ranks, including about 40 men from the battalion transport. On 22 February most of the remainder were dispatched to the No. 6 Entrenching Battalion at Barastre. The transport drivers and horses of the 17th Middlesex would be incorporated within the newly formed 2nd Battalion, Machine Gun Corps in early March. At the time of the battalion's disbandment, there were only about 30 footballers still serving with the 17th Middlesex, including Pte Jackie Sheldon of Liverpool and Pte Tim Coleman of Nottingham Forest.

Even though the story of the 17th Middlesex had come to an end, the war still had several months to run. On 21 March 1918 Ludendorff launched the first of a series of offensives in a desperate last gamble to win the war. After a ferocious five-hour bombardment provided by over 6,000 guns, German troops advanced along a 40-mile front between the Rivers Sensée and Oise. The brunt of this assault, codenamed 'Operation Michael', fell on Gough's Fifth Army. By nightfall, British casualties were in the region of 38,000 men, of whom more than half had been taken prisoner. Over the next few days both the 13th and 21st Middlesex were involved in the desperate attempts to stem the German onslaught. Several former officers and men of the 17th Middlesex were killed, captured or wounded during this period. Within six days the Germans had advanced over 25 miles along a 50-mile front, but the sheer pace of the advance had ensured that their supply lines were becoming over-stretched, causing 'Michael' to lose momentum.

The next few months were a period of monumental crisis for the Allies, but Ludendorff's offensives failed to deliver a decisive German victory. The Allied armies had been badly battered, but they were undefeated. The last German offensive, launched on the Marne on 15 July, was stopped in its tracks by a determined French counterattack. It was the beginning of the end. The German army had lost over a million men since March and the success of Ludendorff's offensives had left his troops holding vulnerable salients, ill-prepared for defence.

Throughout the summer of 1918 the British steadily pushed the Germans back across north-eastern France, while the French and the Americans advanced to the south and south-east. By early September the Allied armies had clawed back most of the ground that had been lost earlier in the year. Fighting stubborn rearguard actions, the Germans fell back on the Hindenburg Line for the winter, but once its formidable defences were breached by Fourth Army on 29 September, Ludendorff realised that the war was lost. The fighting dragged on throughout October and into November. By now the German army was close to collapse and Germany tottered on the brink of revolution, but still the fighting continued. One of the last former members of 17th Middlesex to give his life for his country was 2/Lt Archie Aldridge MC, who died of wounds on 8 November. The son of a builder's foreman, Archie Aldridge had enlisted with his brother Charles at West Africa House on 8 February 1915 and, after recovering from wounds sustained at Oppy, had been commissioned into The Queen's (Royal West Surrey Regiment) in 1918.[17]

In the early hours of 11 November 1918 Germany signed an armistice. Later that morning, at 11 o'clock, the guns fell silent on the Western Front. By a strange quirk of fate, the British had reached Mons earlier that morning, the Belgian town where the 'Old Contemptibles' of 1914 had fired their first shots of the war. In the months following the cessation of hostilities, the slow process of demobilisation started and British POWs were repatriated, including Sgt Joe Mercer, who had been badly wounded in the shoulder at Oppy. The earliest memory of his young son would be of his father arriving back at the family home in Ellesmere Port and tossing him a football out of his kit bag. Not all the 17th Middlesex POWs made it home. Captured in September 1917, L/Cpl Henry Hobbis had survived his ordeal as a POW only to succumb to influenza while awaiting repatriation to England.

The losses of the respective combatants during the First World War were unprecedented in their magnitude. The British Empire had mobilised nearly 9 million men and women for war service, and had suffered over 3 million casualties. In the region of 2.5 million had been incurred on the Western Front, with nearly 750,000 losing their lives. It is difficult to be precise as to how many officers and men of the 17th Middlesex gave their lives for their country, as many were killed after the battalion's disbandment in February 1918, but it would appear that around 900 of the estimated 4,500 individuals who either enlisted in, or served with the 17th Middlesex at some stage of the First World War, lost their lives. Many others were left maimed or traumatised by the experiences, and struggled to readjust to civilian life. Comparatively few of the battalion's surviving professional footballers would ever be able to resurrect their careers at the top level.

In the years following the First World War professional football went from strength to strength.[18] In 1919 the Football League undertook an ambitious programme of expansion, enlarging both

Above: *A German trench near Guillemont, September 1916.* **(Julia Rhys)**

Below left: *Allen Foster of Reading, who died of wounds on 8 August 1916. 'If at any time the Reading club decide to erect marble monuments to players who in their opinion have been heroes, they will put up a life-sized statue of Foster at the entrance to Elm Park.'* **(David Downs)**

Below right: *Tommy Barber of Aston Villa. Wounded in the leg at Guillemont on 8 August 1916, Barber was the scorer of the winning goal in the 1913 FA Cup Final.* **(Colorsport)**

Above left: *At the outbreak of war Laurence 'Ivan' Horniman was studying to become a barrister.* (Michael Horniman)

Above right: *Sid Wheelhouse, captain of Grimsby Town: 'A model player both on and off the field who endeared himself to all who knew him.' His death in September 1916 caused much sorrow back in Grimsby.* (Colorsport)

Below left: *A shared 17th Middlesex grave in Euston Road Cemetery, Colincamps, with its original cross, c.1920.* (Tim Thurlow)

Below right: *John Lamb of Sheffield Wednesday who was wounded on the Somme during the autumn of 1916.* (Colorsport)

Above left: *Pte Albert Bourne, a farmhand from Kent, who was killed on 13 November 1916 during the attack on the Redan Ridge. In one of his last letters home, he wrote to his sister, Emily, 'Tell dad I should like to have a pint of O' English beer, it is some stuff out here, but we have to have what we can get.'* (**John Hickmott**)

Above right: *The grave of L/Sgt Archie Strike in Serre No. 1 Cemetery, another casualty of the fighting on 13 November 1916.* (**Authors' Collection**)

Below left: *Peter Roney of Bristol Rovers. The Rovers' goalkeeper, who scored a penalty in a match against QPR in 1910, was severely traumatised by his experiences on the Western Front with the 17th Middlesex and the Machine Gun Corps.* (**Mike Davage**)

Below right: *2/Lt John Paterson. An original 17th Middlesex recruit, Paterson later became the only British officer to be executed for murder in the field during the First World War.* (**TNA WO339/111890**)

Oppy, 28. April 1917 (im Hintergrund der Schloßpark)

Above: *A German photograph of Oppy taken on 28 April 1917. Oppy Wood lies in the background.* (**H.M. Hauschild GmbH**)

Below left: *2/Lt Bertie Wade, a former Scottish rugby international, who died a 'very gallant little gentleman' at Oppy on 28 April 1917.* (**John Luvian-Wade**)

Below right: *Bob 'Pom-Pom' Whiting. The former Brighton & Hove Albion and Chelsea goalkeeper lost his life tending to the wounded at Oppy on 28 April 1917.* (**Brighton & Hove Albion Collectors' and Historians' Society**)

Above: *A photograph purportedly taken at 8 a.m. on 28 April 1917, which shows German troops gathering in Oppy to counterattack the 17th Middlesex.* (**H.M. Hauschild GmbH**)

Below left: *Joe Mercer of Nottingham Forest. Wounded and captured at Oppy on 28 April 1917, Mercer never recovered from the effects of his war service.* (**Colorsport**)

Below right: *Capt Ernest Parfitt was wounded and captured at Oppy on 28 April 1917. He died a month later.* (**John Matthews**)

Above: *The 17th Middlesex football team in the autumn of 1917. Capt Percy Barnfather sent a copy of this photograph to the* Croydon Advertiser: *'What do you think of this little lot, unbeaten in France at football or fighting?' Front row, from left: Pte Jack Dodds (Oldham Athletic), Pte David Kenney (Grimsby Town), Capt Percy Barnfather (Croydon Common), Pte John Nuttall (Millwall), Sgt Charles Stewart (Croydon Common). Middle row: L/Cpl George Pyke (Newcastle Utd), Lt Bennett, Capt Cosmo Clark, Lt Col George Kelly, Capt Robert Templeman, Lt Claude Gann, Pte John Woodhouse (Brighton & Hove Albion). Back row: L/Cpl Jack Doran (Coventry City), L/Cpl Pat Gallacher (formerly Tottenham Hotspur), Pte John Spick, RSM Alfred Sabine, Pte Joe Webster (West Ham Utd), Sgt Alfred Hollanby, CSM Gibson (Nottingham Forest), Pte Gardiner.* **(Julia Rhys)**

Below: *A ruined bridge over the Canal du Nord, near Moeuvres, 28 November 1917.* **(IWM 6329)**

Above left: *Capt Fred Stansfeld, killed in action near Moeuvres on 1 December 1917.*
(Jane Jones)

Above right: *Capt Allastair McReady-Diarmid, who lost his life at 'the moment of victory'
near Moeuvres on 1 December 1917.* **(IWM Q80670)**

Below: *The Canal du Nord near Moeuvres, 28 November 1917. Royal Engineers are clearing
away a blown-up bridge.* **(IWM Q6331)**

Above left: *Allastair and Hilda McReady-Diarmid on their wedding day.* (Joan Harmston)

Above right: *Posthumous portrait of Capt Allastair McReady-Diarmid wearing a VC ribbon.* (Rupert Casey)

Below left: *The FA memorial tablet.* (Football Association)

Below right: *The Memorial to the Footballers' Battalions in Longueval shortly after it was unveiled by Greg Clarke, Chairman of the Football League, on 21 October 2010.* (Authors' collection)

divisions from 20 to 22 clubs. The next year a Third Division was created, all but one of its 22 clubs being former members of the Southern League. In 1921 it became the Third Division (South) when the Third Division (North) was formed, comprising 20 clubs from the Central League, the Cheshire League, the Lancashire Combination, the Midland League and the North Eastern League. Two years later the first FA Cup Final to be held at Wembley took place in front of an estimated 200,000 spectators.

A few months after the first Wembley final, the King's Colour of the 17th Middlesex was placed in a church built by the anti-slavery campaigner and parliamentarian, William Wilberforce: St Paul's Church in Mill Hill.[19] The following year Charles Clegg, the new president of the FA, unveiled a memorial tablet, commemorating all footballers, both amateur and professional, who fell in the service of their country during the Great War. Originally attached to the front wall of the FA offices in Russell Square, the tablet was of a simple design and quoted a passage from *A Discourse of a Discoverie for a New Passage to Cataia* by the Elizabethan soldier and explorer Sir Humphrey Gilbert (1537–83).

IN REMEMBRANCE

OF

THOSE WHO TOOK PART

IN THE NATIONAL GAME OF

ASSOCIATION FOOTBALL

AND GAVE THEIR LIVES

IN THE CAUSE OF RIGHT

AND JUSTICE

IN THE GREAT WAR

1914–18

Give me leave to live and die in this opinion, that he is not worthy to live at all who for fear of danger of death, shunneth his Country's service and his own honour.[20]

At the unveiling ceremony on 10 March 1924, Charles Clegg spoke of the sacrifice of both amateur and professional footballers, as well as the significant contribution of football to the war effort:

We have erected the War Memorial in remembrance of the heroic part taken by so many of our players in the late war.

When war was declared in 1914 there were approximately three-quarters of a million players in membership with The Football Association. Vast numbers of these players joined one of the Branches of the Services – the Royal Navy, the Army, and the Air Force. Many made the Great Sacrifice. Many others were disabled.

On the Amateur side of the Game, of which there were approximately 20,000 Clubs, football ceased to be played. The players were away at training or overseas.

On the professional side, of which there were only about 400 clubs, only such matches were played as were deemed to be expedient as a means of relief both to the mind and body, and these by players who were in training at Home Depots, engaged on munition or other essential work, or on furlough from overseas. Although adversely criticized, the action received general approval.

Three Battalions were formed, known as The Football Battalions - the 17th, 23rd and 27th Middlesex Regiments.

Association football was the means of raising many thousands of pounds for the 'comforts' of its own men and for the relief and sustenance of the families of the players who were killed in the War, and of the men who were wounded. Some £25,000 altogether was so raised. Whilst the Armies were in conflict, a vast quantity of goods, and other 'comforts', were sent to the Front.

The Football National War Fund has distributed some thousands of pounds to the bereaved and the maimed. The Fund is still in existence and contributes to this good cause.

From this it will be seen that the Memorial which we have erected is only a small acknowledgement of the sacrifices of our heroes during the terrible struggle through which we have passed, and we hope and trust that none of us will have to pass through a similar trial in future.[21]

Football had clearly subordinated itself to 'the greater game'. From their inception, the 17th Middlesex had been at the forefront of the game's contribution to the war effort, many of its recruits joining the battalion in order to defend the honour of the game. The 17th Middlesex had assisted with recruitment and fought in some of the bloodiest engagements of the First World War. Of perhaps greater importance still were the countless football matches on active service, in which battalion teams played against other units of the BEF in France, allowing everyone to forget briefly the horrors of the trenches, and to recall better times.

Many had doubted whether professional footballers could ever form an effective fighting unit. Such views were not just confined to the Home Front, as Maj Frank Buckley recalled: 'Some of the *quidnunes* in the brigade were doubtful about the quality of the battalion when first grouped at The Front, but the footballers proved themselves valiant among the valorous and most rigid in their observance of all regulations.'[22] The spirit of the professional players, amateurs and 'club enthusiasts' within the ranks of the battalion made a lasting impression on everyone who encountered it. As Col Henry Fenwick himself commented only a few months after the 17th Middlesex had proceeded overseas on active service:

I knew nothing of professional footballers when I took over this battalion. But I have learnt to value them. I would go anywhere with such men. Their esprit de corps was amazing. This feeling was mainly due to football – the link of fellowship which bound them together. Football has a wonderful grip on these men and on the Army generally.[23]

The final word on the 17th Middlesex should perhaps be left to Maj Frank Buckley. He was speaking of the professional footballers, but the same could be said of all the officers and men who served with the 17th Middlesex: 'I feel I cannot say too much for them, always cheerful and willing, and the first to volunteer for anything.'[24]

1. BNL: *The Chelsea F.C. Chronicle*, 8 December 1917.
2. Clark, C., *The Tin Trunk*, p. 94.
3. *Ibid.*
4. TNA: WO 95/1361.
5. *Ibid.*
6. Clark, C., *The Tin Trunk*, p. 100.
7. *Ibid.*
8. Letter to parents, 13 January 1918.
9. Clark, C., *The Tin Trunk*, p. 102.
10. TNA: WO 95/1361.
11. The last recorded match played by the 17th Middlesex football team in France took place on 27 January 1918 against the 1/1st Northumberland Yeomanry. The game ended in a 5–0 victory for the battalion.

12. TNA: WO 95/1361.
13. *Ibid.*
14. IWM: 73/103/1.
15. Wyrall, E., *The History of the Second Division*, p. 523.
16. IWM: 73/103/1.
17. His brother Charles survived the war.
18. Interestingly, the same could not be said for public schools' football. The 'sad and rapid defection' from football to rugby in many public schools accelerated in the years following the First World War. A factor in this shift was undoubtedly the widely held perception that rugby players had answered their country's call more readily than footballers in 1914.
19. The King's Colour has deteriorated to such an extent that it is no longer on display in St Paul's Church, which was the Chapel of the Middlesex Regiment for a number of years.
20. The Memorial Tablet was later moved to the entrance hall of the FA offices at 22 Lancaster Gate in 1929. It can be found today at the National Museum of Football in Preston.
21. Green, G., *History of the Football Association 1863–1953*, p.294. The officers and men of the Footballers' Battalions now have their own memorial.   On 21 October 2010 Greg Clarke, Chairman of the Football League, unveiled a memorial to the officers and men of the 17th and 23rd Middlesex in the village of Longueval. The necessary funds for the memorial were raised at collections held at Football League matches. The campaign was led by Phil Stant, a veteran of the Falklands War and a former professional footballer.
22. BNL: *Athletic News*, 18 September 1916.
23. BNL: *Sporting Chronicle*, 20 September 1916.
24. *The Villa News and Record*, 30 August–1 September 1919, p. 13.

EPILOGUE

After the war, former officers and men of the 17th Middlesex held annual reunion dinners in London on the evening of the FA Cup Final. In 1938 the reunion dinner took place on 30 April. It was held at the Bedford Corner Hotel on Tottenham Court Road, Preston North End having defeated Huddersfield Town 1–0 earlier that day. Tickets were priced at 5s, with subsidised tickets made available for former members who would otherwise have been unable to attend on financial grounds. It was a source of considerable satisfaction for Col Fenwick that the dinner was attended by 152 officers and men.

At the 1939 reunion dinner there were only about 80 former members of the battalion present. Earlier that day Maj Buckley's widely fancied Wolverhampton Wanderers team, having finished runners-up to Everton in the Football League, had been surprisingly beaten 4–1 by a workmanlike Portsmouth side in the FA Cup Final. No reunion took place the following year. The world had plunged once more into a terrible war, in which several former members of the 17th Middlesex served their country a second time, many as ARP Wardens or members of the Home Guard.

As soon as Britain had declared war in September 1939, the FA moved swiftly to ensure the game was not subjected to the vitriol of 1914. The football season was suspended immediately, but it was not long before a regional competition and a Football League Cup were set up. The FA assisted the war effort by working alongside a range of bodies, including the War Office, the Armed Forces, the Red Cross and the Central Council of Physical Education. At nearly 200 football grounds up and down the country, over 40,000 men participated in a Fitness for Service campaign organised jointly by the FA and Central Council of Physical Recreation. Provided that the game did not undermine the war effort, the authorities were keen to ensure that as much football as possible was played. The 'people's game' was needed to maintain the morale of civilians at home, as well as that of officers and men serving their country overseas. And it did . . .

Extra Time

Abbs, Charles William Christmas (1887–1956)
Charles Abbs spent the remainder of the war in various POW camps. After the war, he worked as a fishmonger in the family business and later became the chairman of Runton FC. He also served as a local parish councillor for many years.

Bailey, Walter George 'Joe' (1890–1974)
Joe Bailey ended the war as a highly decorated officer. As a result of his bravery and leadership during the fighting of 1918, Bailey was awarded the Distinguished Service Order, the Military Cross and two Bars. His fellow officers held Bailey in such high esteem that they selected him to fetch the battalion's Colours from England and take them to Germany after the Armistice. After the war Bailey resumed his footballing career, scoring Reading's first ever Football League goal against Newport on 28 August 1920. A week later he scored the club's first Football League hat-trick. Having finished top scorer for the season with a tally of 18 goals, Bailey left the club to coach cricket at Warwick School, still playing non-league football. During the Second World War, Bailey was a company commander in the Dorset Home Guard: 'If there had been a battle, I was never in any doubt that we should have given Jerry a sticky time.'

Barber, Thomas (1886–1925)
Tommy Barber did not return to the Western Front on account of the serious leg wounds sustained at Guillemont. By the end of the war he was working in a Glasgow munitions factory and had been admitted to hospital suffering from pleurisy. Despite being told by doctors that he would never play football again, Barber spent brief spells at a number of clubs, including Crystal Palace and Walsall, before succumbing to tuberculosis.

Barnfather, Percy (1879–1951)

In March 1918 Barnfather married Evelyn Harris, the daughter of a former Croydon Common director. After the war he made four appearances for Merthyr Town during the 1919/20 season. He later worked as a clerical officer in the Ministry of Supply. He died of stomach cancer and was buried in Croydon Cemetery. At the time of the Croydon Common's winding up in 1917, Barnfather had made more appearances (286) and scored more goals (88) for the Robins than any other player during the club's short history.

Bartholomew, Frederick (1885–1979)

Fred Bartholomew made only a few appearances for Reading after the war, but by the time he hung up his boots in 1923 the popular defender had played in every position for the club, including that of goalkeeper. After a three-year stint on the coaching staff, Bartholomew became the groundsman at Elm Park, a position that he occupied until 1957. After his retirement, 'Old Bart' continued to watch the team that he had faithfully served for 53 years.

Bell, Edward Inkerman Jordan (1886–1918)

While serving on the staff of 99th Brigade, Edward Bell was killed by an enemy shell, near Albert, at 5.35 p.m. on 24 March 1918. A few months after his death, he was gazetted a Bar to the Military Cross that he won at Delville Wood. On 25 October 1918 his widow Edith, whom he had married shortly before the battalion had proceeded overseas three years earlier, gave birth to a son, to whom she gave the forenames, Edward Inkerman Jordan.

Buckley, Franklin Charles (1882–1963)

On demobilisation, Buckley ventured into football management and went on to become one of the most famous managers in the history of the game, notwithstanding the fact that none of his sides (Norwich City, Blackpool, Wolves, Notts County, Hull City, Leeds Utd and Walsall) ever won a major honour. As a manager, Buckley was renowned as a strict disciplinarian and for his ability to unearth young talent, numbering players such as Stan Cullis and Billy Wright among his finds. A pioneer of modern training methods, Buckley caused a media furore by stipulating that his

Wolves players undergo a course of 'monkey gland' injections to improve fitness ahead of the 1939 FA Cup Final against Portsmouth. For the rest of his career in football, Frank Buckley was known simply as 'The Major'.

Carter, William Henry 'Harry' (1880–1951)

Harry Carter finished the war as a lieutenant-colonel, having been awarded Bars to his Military Cross and Distinguished Service Order. He served as a brigadier-general in the Army of Occupation before reverting to his substantive rank of captain in the peacetime Army. Leaving the Army with a gratuity of £1,500 in 1922, Carter set up a poultry farm and then a taxi business, but both ventures failed. He later found work as a motorcycle mechanic and a steel erector. In later life, problems arising from a First World War wound resulted in the amputation of his foot.

Clark, John 'Cosmo' (1897–1967)

Having transferred to the 13th Middlesex in February 1918, Cosmo Clark was awarded a Military Cross for his actions during the German offensives and was wounded in the leg during the Advance to Victory in October 1918. After the war he resumed his artistic studies and married fellow artist Jean Wymer in 1924. He went on to become a successful painter in both oils and watercolours and was best known for his depictions of London scenes. During the Second World War he served as the Deputy Chief Camouflage Officer in the Ministry of Home Security between 1939 and 1942 before being appointed Director of the Rural Industries Bureau the following year, a position that he would hold until his retirement in 1963. Awarded the CBE in 1955, he was elected a full member of the Royal Academy of Arts three years later.

Cock, John Gilbert 'Jack' (1893–1966)

Despite being reported killed at one stage, Jack Cock survived the war. He resumed his career at Chelsea in 1919, scoring 21 goals in 25 League appearances in his first season. He also represented the Football League against the Scottish League, and played in a Victory International against Wales. Becoming the first

Cornishman to be capped by England in a 1–1 draw against Ireland in October 1919, Cock scored after only 30 seconds. An athletic player, good in the air, and able to shoot accurately with both feet, he consistently scored goals throughout the 1920s for Everton, Plymouth Argyle and Millwall. He later rejoined Millwall as manager in 1944, a club for whom he had scored 92 goals in 135 appearances. Four years later, he retired from the game, and became licensee of the White Hart Pub at New Cross. A snappy dresser with a fine tenor voice, Cock appeared as himself in a film, *The Winning Goal* (1920), and featured in another football film, *The Great Game* (1930), alongside a young Rex Harrison.

Coleman, John George 'Tim' (1881–1940)

After the war, Tim Coleman played briefly for Tunbridge Wells Rangers before becoming player-manager of the Maidstone Utd reserves for the 1920/21 season. He later moved abroad to the Netherlands, where he coached Enschede (a predecessor of modern-day club FC Twente) to the national championship in 1926. In 1940, at the height of the Blitz, it was reported that 'J.G. Coleman, 59 - a labourer' had died, as a result of a fall from the roof of an electricity generating station in London, while repairing bomb damage.

Daly, Arthur Crawford (1876–1936)

Maj Gen Arthur Daly returned to the Western Front to command 33rd Brigade before assuming command of the 24th Division until April 1919. By the cessation of hostilities, Daly had been mentioned in despatches on seven occasions. Between 1925 and 1927 he was Inspector-General and Military Adviser in Iraq.

Fenwick, Henry Thomas (1863–1939)

After the war Col Fenwick took a keen interest in the lives of former members of the battalion, playing an active role in the organisation of the 17th Middlesex reunion dinners. In July 1939, having attended what would turn out to be the last dinner, he arrived in South Africa and proceeded to Bulawayo for a six-week trip. On 30 August he was found dead in a compartment of the Rhodesia-Capetown Express. The following year former members of the battalion placed a notice in the 'In Memoriam' column of *The Times*:

> FENWICK – COLONEL H.T. FENWICK C.M.G., D.S.O., M.V.O., who died in South Africa on Aug 30th 1939, is remembered with gratitude and admiration by all members of the 17th (Footballers) Battalion, Middlesex Regiment.

Foxcroft-Jones, Robert

Foxcroft-Jones survived the war. In 1924 he told a prospective purchaser of his business that 'he had a regular commission in 10th Hussars prior to the war and rose to the rank of Brigadier-General in Salonika and also served in the South African War'.

Glenie, William (1888–1927)

After his capture south of Moeuvres in December 1917, William Glenie lost the use of his right arm as a result of ill treatment while a prisoner of war. On his discharge from the army in 1919, he proceeded to Australia, but returned to England the following year, settling in Sittingbourne, Kent. On 5 December 1927, Glenie was lopping a tree on his allotment when a branch gave way. He fell 25ft to the ground and fractured his spine. The old soldier clung onto life in Rochester Hospital for three weeks before finally succumbing to his injuries. He left a widow and a 6-year-old daughter.

Grantham, Charles Fulford 'Johnnie' (1857–1938)

After the war, Col Grantham devoted much time to the activities of the British Legion, serving as chairman of its South-Eastern Area for over 15 years.

Hickman, Joseph John

The small man with the 'unconquerable weakness for drink' transferred to the 21st Middlesex on the disbandment of the 17th Middlesex. Over the next few months, Cpl Hickman DCM, MM, distinguished himself on several occasions, and was gazetted two Bars to his Distinguished Conduct Medal, one of only nine soldiers to achieve this distinction during the First World War. Lt Col

Stafford recalled that, 'The last I heard of him was in December 1918 when I read a newspaper article headed "Hero in Trouble". It was Hickman in London. He was drunk and had fought two policemen. He was about 5ft 6in in height and lightly built. Policemen are bigger than that.'

Horniman, Laurence 'Ivan' (1893–1963)

After the war Ivan Horniman embarked on a successful legal career. In 1925 he edited the 13th edition of *Wharton's Law Lexicon*, and became a King's Counsel in 1947. Retiring to Dorset, he served on the committee of the Somersetshire Archaeological & Natural History Society.

Joynson-Hicks, William (1865–1932)

Joynson-Hicks was created a baronet in 1919. The following year he toured Sudan, Sri Lanka and India, where a visit to Amritsar convinced him that Brig Gen Dyer's actions the previous April, when he had ordered troops to open fire on a large crowd with catastrophic results, were entirely justified. On the fall of Lloyd-George's Coalition government in 1922, Joynson-Hicks held various ministerial appointments under Bonar-Law and Baldwin until Labour formed its first government in January 1924. When the Conservatives returned to power later that year, Joynson-Hicks was appointed Home Secretary, a post he occupied until his retirement from the House of Commons in 1929. As Home Secretary, he gained a reputation as a puritanical reactionary through his efforts to suppress nightclubs and other perceived threats to 1920s society. In 1927 he was at the forefront of opposition to the proposed new version of the *Book of Common Prayer*, which was viewed by many as an attempt to reintroduce pre-Reformation ideas into the Church of England. His greatest political legacy was perhaps his contribution to the cause of women's rights, when remarks made without Cabinet authority led to the Representation of the People Act 1928, which lowered the voting age for women from 30 to 21. In 1929 Joynson-Hicks was elevated to the peerage, becoming 1st Viscount Brentford.

Keenor, Fred (1894–1972)

Fred Keenor was one of the few players in the 17th Middlesex to achieve success on the football field after the war. He played for Wales in the Victory internationals, and scored in the first game of Cardiff City's inaugural Football League season. In 1924 he captained Wales to the Home International Championship. Three years later he led the Cardiff team to a 1–0 victory over Arsenal in the FA Cup final, still the only occasion on which the FA Cup has left England. Released from the club in 1931, Keenor went on to play for Crewe Alexandra for three seasons before ending his career in non-League football at Oswestry, later becoming player-manager of Tunbridge Wells Rangers. One of the all-time greats of Welsh football, Keenor returned to Cardiff in 1958, working as a storekeeper for a local building firm.

Maclaine, Kenneth Douglas Lorne (1880–1935)

After the war Maclaine of Lochbuie became the manager of a theatrical company, but was forced to relinquish his career due to a heart condition brought about by his war service. Following a lengthy legal battle, ownership of the Lochbuie estate passed out of his hands and he was never able to realise his dream of building a residential home for destitute clansmen. On the occasion of his marriage at St Margaret's, Westminster, in 1920, Lochbuie wore Bonnie Prince Charlie's waistcoat. His grandson is the 26th Maclaine of Lochbuie.

McCormick James (1883–1935)

Despite feigning madness and attacking a German officer in an unsuccessful attempt to be repatriated, James McCormick survived the war. He played again for Plymouth Argyle before emigrating to Ladysmith, British Columbia, in May 1920, where he captained the local football team and coached their youth side.

Mercer, Joseph Powell (1890–1927)

Joe Mercer's health never recovered from his war experiences. He took a job as a bricklayer and tried to resurrect his footballing career with non-League side Tranmere Rovers. His health continued to fail, forcing his retirement from the game after Tranmere Rovers' inaugural Third Division (North) season in

1921/22. Within a few years he was dead. His son, also called Joe, grew up to become one of the most respected figures in English football both as a player and a manager.

Nixon, Wifred (1882–1985)
Despite undergoing considerable hardships in a succession of POW Camps, Nixon survived the war. He returned to Craven Cottage, making only a handful of appearances for Fulham. He later became one of the longest-lived professional footballers. On the occasion of his 100th birthday, Nixon was invited to Craven Cottage to attend Fulham's match against Burnley in October 1982. Having flown down from his native north-east, he was taken ill shortly before kick-off and spent the afternoon in Charing Cross Hospital.

Norris, Henry George (1865–1934)
On the resumption of football in 1919, when the Football League decided to expand the First Division from 20 to 22 clubs, Norris managed to convince the Management Committee that Arsenal should replace their rivals, Tottenham Hotspur, in the First Division, even though Arsenal had only finished 5th in the Second Division of 1914/15. Norris was also responsible for appointing the legendary Herbert Chapman as Arsenal manager in 1925, but he was destined to miss out on the club's glory days. Barely two years after Chapman's appointment, Norris was discovered to have made illegal payments to obtain players and was banned from all involvement with the game.

Parker, Frederick George (1885–1949)
'Spider' Parker returned to Clapton Orient after the war. Having made a total of 350 League and FA Cup appearances for the O's, Parker left the club to manage Folkestone Town in 1922. In later life, the first man to enlist in the 17th Middlesex reportedly worked as a railway porter at King's Cross Station.

Paterson, John Henry (1890–1918)
While in command of a 1st Essex working party near Zillebeke, on 26 March 1918, 2/Lt Paterson disappeared into thin air. On 3 July two military policemen, Sgt Collison and L/Cpl Stockton,

challenged a British officer with a young French woman at Pont de Coulogne, near Calais. After first claiming to be 2/Lt Barford of the Essex Regiment, the officer admitted that he was, in fact, 2/Lt John Paterson. For some inexplicable reason Paterson was allowed to have tea with the French woman in a house while the military policemen waited outside. Nearly two hours late Paterson came out of the house and fired at least two shots from his revolver, wounding both himself and Sgt Collison, who died shortly afterwards. Finally apprehended later that month, Paterson faced a General Court Martial on 11 September, charged with murder, desertion and five counts of forgery. Found guilty of murder, Paterson was sentenced to death and was shot by a firing squad on 24 September 1918. Second Lieutenant John Paterson was the only officer in the British army to be executed for murder in the field during the First World War.

Pyke George (1893–1977)
After demobilisation George Pyke played a few games for Durham City before returning to Newcastle Utd. Playing for the reserve team in the North Eastern League, Pyke proved himself to be a natural goalscorer. Despite interest from several Football League clubs, Pyke elected to remain in his native north-east. Moving to Blyth Spartans in 1922, he scored a total of 136 goals for the club before his retirement from the game in 1927.

Roney, Peter (1887–1930)
Having transferred to the Machine Gun Corps, Peter Roney survived the war. Like many former servicemen, he struggled to put the war behind him. In 1919 it was reported that Roney had undergone 'such experiences during the war that he is unlikely to be heard of again in professional football'. After the war he had brief spells with Albion Rovers and Ayr Utd, but Roney was by now a broken man. On 12 November 1921 a special collection for him was held at a Football League Division Three (South) fixture between two of his former clubs, Bristol Rovers and Norwich City. The appeal raised the sum of 10 guineas. On his death certificate, Roney was still listed as a professional footballer even though he had not played a first-class game for several years.

Sheldon, John 'Jackie' (1887–1941)

In June 1919 the FA Council elected to 'favourably consider' applications from suspended 'players, officials and others connected with the game' to mark the end of hostilities. The diminutive right-winger successfully applied to have his ban lifted, and went on to make a further 72 appearances for Liverpool. A broken leg finished his career in 1921.

Stafford, Ronald Sempill Seymour Howard (1890–1972)

After the war Lt Col Stafford resumed his career with the Egyptian Civil Service. In 1926 he took up a position with the Ministry of the Interior in Iraq. Following the 1933 massacre of Christian Assyrians in Iraq, Stafford resigned his post and returned to England. Shortly afterwards he wrote a graphic account of events, entitled *The Tragedy of the Assyrians*. In 1936 Stafford joined the BBC, where he was primarily concerned with plans for Civil Defence. Now back in England, he was able to attend the last three 17th Middlesex reunion dinners: 'It was quite delightful to meet them all again.' On the outbreak of war in 1939 he was appointed Defence Director. From 1942 onwards he held various regional posts in the BBC, ending up as director of the South West Region. He retired from the BBC in 1952 and died 20 years later after a short illness at his home near Plymouth.

Tull, Walter Daniel John (1888–1918)

After service with the 23rd Middlesex on the Western Front and in Italy, 2/Lt Walter Tull was killed in action near Favreuil on 25 March 1918. On 11 July 1999 a memorial was erected to Tull by one of his former clubs, Northampton Town. The memorial bears the following words:

Through his actions W.D.J. Tull ridiculed the barriers of ignorance that tried to deny people of colour equality with their contemporaries. His life stands testament to a determination to confront those people and those obstacles that sought to diminish him and the World in which he lived. It reveals a man, though rendered breathless in his prime, whose strong heart still beats loudly. This memorial marks an area of reflective space as a Garden of Remembrance.

Wall, Frederick (1858–1944)

Frederick Wall was knighted in 1930. Retiring four years later, he was rewarded for his services to the FA with a golden handshake of £10,000. He is perhaps best known today for being the man who declined invitations for England to participate in the World Cup. Wall is also believed to have been responsible for the introduction of the singing of *Abide With Me* at the FA Cup Final.

Woodward, Vivian John (1879–1954)

After the war Vivian Woodward played for local side Clacton Town during the 1919/20 season. On 15 September 1920 he appeared for Chelsea in a match against an Army team to raise funds for former officers. The game ended in a 2–0 victory for Chelsea, Woodward scoring both goals. Having given up his architectural practice, Woodward then became a dairy farmer in Essex and was a director of Chelsea from 1922 to 1930. During the Second World War he was an ARP warden. By 1949 Woodward was in poor health. He was moved to a nursing home in Ealing, where his care was overseen by a committee specially set up by the FA. In 1953 he told a visiting journalist and Robert Baxter, a former private in the 17th Middlesex, that 'no one who used to be with me in football has been to see me for two years. They never come – I wish they would'.

APPENDIX II

A PROFESSIONAL FOOTBALLER'S CONTRACT

IN 1914: CHARLES ABBS (F/289)

——————————————

Date: **August 15**th **1914**[1]

THE

NORWICH CITY

FOOTBALL CLUB LIMITED

AND

CHARLES ABBS

AGREEMENT
for hire of a Player.

1. Text in bold represents handwritten text.

AN AGREEMENT made the 15th day of August 1914 between **Jack Burton Stansfield** of **Norwich** in the County of **Norfolk**, the Secretary of and acting pursuant to Resolution and Authority for and on behalf of the **Norwich City Football** Club Limited of **Norwich** in the County of **Norfolk** (hereinafter referred to as the Club) of the one part and **Charles Abbs** of **East Runton** in the County of **Norfolk**, Professional Football Player (hereinafter referred to as the Player) of the other part WHEREBY it is agreed as follows.

1. The Player hereby agrees to play in an efficient manner and to the best of his ability for the club during the season of 1914- 1915.

2. The Player shall attend the Club's ground or any other place decided upon by the Club for the purposes of or connection with his training as a Player pursuant to the instructions of the Secretary, Team Manager, or Trainer, of the Club or of such other person or persons as the Club may appoint.

3. The Player shall do everything necessary to get and keep himself in the best possible condition prior to and during the season aforesaid so as to render the best possible service to the Club and will carry out all the training and other instructions of the Club through its representative officials.

4. The Player shall observe and be subject to all the Rules, Regulations and Bye-laws of the Football Association, the Southern League, the English Football League Board and any other Association, League, or Combination of which the Club or the Southern League shall be a member.

1. If the Player shall prove palpably inefficient or shall be guilty of serious misconduct or breach of the disciplinary Rules of the Club, the Club may on giving 14 days' notice to the said Player terminate this Agreement and dispense with the services of the Player (without prejudice to the Club's right for transfer fees) in pursuance of the Rules of all such Associations, Leagues, and Combinations of which the Club may be a member.

2. In consideration of the observance by the said Player of the terms, provisions and conditions of this Agreement, the said **James [sic] Burton Stansfield** on behalf of the Club hereby agrees that the said Club shall pay to the said Player the sum of **£1 - 10 - 0** per week, from **September 1st 1914** to **April 30th 1915.**

The **Norwich City FC Limited agree to pay for season contract between Cromer & Norwich and agree to pay him 10% extra when playing in Southern League Teams.**[2]

As Witness the hands of the said parties the day and year aforesaid.

Signed by the said _____   *James Burton Stansfield*

    and **James Burton Stansfield**   *Charles Abbs*

In the presence of **JN Alderson**
(OCCUPATION) **Civil Service Clerk**
(ADDRESS) **18 Doris Rd, Norwich**

2. This additional clause meant that Abbs would play for Cromer FC with his wages being paid by Norwich City. In the event of Abbs being selected to represent Norwich City in the Southern League, he would be paid an additional 10s per week while playing in the team.

APPENDIX III

A BRIEF CHRONOLOGY OF THE GAME 1863–1914

1863 The Football Association is formed at a meeting held in the Freemason's Tavern, Holborn, by Metropolitan clubs in an attempt to codify the rules of football.

1871 Fifty clubs are affiliated to the FA.
Seven members of the FA meet at the offices of the *Sportsman* to discuss a proposal by Charles Alcock, secretary of the FA, to set up a knock-out competition for members.

1872 Wanderers beat Royal Engineers 1–0 in the first FA Challenge Cup Final, played at the Kennington Oval.
First England *v* Scotland International takes place at the West of Scotland Cricket Club. The match ends in 0–0 draw.

1873 Scottish Football Association is formed.

1875 First crossbars are introduced.

1876 Football Association of Wales is formed.

1878 Whistles are used by referees for the first tine.

1880 Irish Football Association is formed.

1881 Old Carthusians defeat Old Etonians to win the FA Cup, the last occasion on which the final is contested by two amateur teams.

1882 N.L. Jackson, assistant secretary of the FA and a bitter opponent of the professionalism widely rumoured to becoming prevalent in the game, sets up the Corinthians for the best amateur players of the day.
Introduction of the two-handed throw-in.
Lord Kinnaird captains Old Etonians to victory over Blackburn Rovers in the FA Cup Final.

1883 Blackburn Olympic beat Old Etonians to win the FA Cup, ending domination of the competition by southern amateur teams.

1884 London club Upton Park lodge a formal complaint that Preston North End had fielded a professional side in FA Cup match. FA expels Preston from the competition. Football is plunged into crisis as 31 clubs, predominantly from Lancashire and the Midlands, threaten to break away to form a rival British Football Association.

1885 To avoid a disastrous split, the FA legalises payment of players, but seeks to 'manage' professionalism by attaching stringent conditions. Clubs are allowed only to pay players if they had either been born, or had lived for a two-year period within a six-mile radius of the ground. Professionals must also be registered annually. Professionals and ex-professionals are barred from sitting on FA Committees.

1886 The first acknowledged professional to play for England, James Forrest, has to wear a different-coloured shirt from the rest of the team in a match against Scotland following complaints from Scottish officials.

1888 Football League is founded at a meeting in Manchester by 12 clubs from the north and Midlands.
1,000 clubs are affiliated to the FA.

1889 Old Etonian Sir Francis Marindin resigns as FA president following the abolition of the two-year residence qualification for professionals. He is succeeded by Lord Kinnaird, a member of the FA committee since 1869.

1891 Goal nets are introduced.
Penalty kick is introduced. Several amateurs resent playing under a rule that assumes a player could intentionally set out to commit a foul.
'Retain and transfer' system is introduced. This system prevents a professional footballer from playing for another club on the expiry of his contract if his club chooses not to release him.
Woolwich Arsenal become the first professional southern side

1892 The Second Division of the Football League is set up.
Goodison Park becomes the first major purpose-built football ground.
Players and officials are banned from placing bets on matches.

1893   The *Athletic News Annual* claims that professional footballers are being paid an average wage of £3 per week during the season and £2 a week during the summer months.

The FA sets up the FA Amateur Cup in response to criticism that it appears only concerned with the professional game.

Referees' Association is founded.

1894   Frederick Wall becomes FA secretary.

Southern League is formed. Initial members include Reading, Millwall Athletic and Luton Town. The league proves vital to the development of the professional game in southern England. Several of its clubs would eventually join the Football League.

1898   Football League teams are automatically promoted and relegated for first time.

1900   Following reports that the top professional players are being paid up to £8 per week, the FA introduces a maximum wage of £4, which comes into effect the following season.

Madame Tussauds unveils a waxwork of a professional footballer for the first time. (Arthur Turner of Southampton.)

1901   First FA Cup Final is filmed.

Tottenham Hotspur of the Southern League become the last non-Football League team to lift the FA Cup.

1902   First £500 transfer (Alf Common, from Sheffield United to Sunderland).

1903   Amateur sides, predominantly those derived from public schools, set up their own cup competition, named after Arthur Dunn, an Old Etonian and England International who was injured during the 1883 FA Cup Final against Blackburn Olympic.

1904   Fédération Internationale de Football Association (FIFA) is founded.

1905   First £1,000 transfer (Alf Common, Sunderland to Middlesbrough).

10,000 clubs are affiliated to the FA.

1907   *Daily Mail* becomes first newspaper to provide photographic coverage of football matches.

Amateur clubs break away from the FA to form the Amateur Football Association. The AFA recruits over 500 clubs, mainly from the south of England. Although never recognised by FIFA, the AFA is recognised as a governing body of football by organisations sympathetic to its amateur ideals, such as the Rugby Football Union and the Hockey Association.

Association Football Players Union (AFPU) is formed at the Imperial Hotel, Manchester. Previous attempts to establish a players' union in 1893 and 1898 failed due to a lack of recognition and support. Its primary objectives are the abolition of the 'retain and transfer' system and the maximum wage.

1908 Football tournament features in the London Olympic Games. Great Britain defeats Denmark to win Gold Medal.

FA acts to curb soaring transfer fees by setting a maximum fee of £350. The scheme proves unworkable and is abandoned after only a few months.

First FA Charity Shield match, played by Manchester United, Football League champions, and Queen's Park Rangers, Southern League champions.

1909 After a series of disputes with the FA, the AFPU leads its members to the brink of a national strike.

1910 6,800 professional footballers are registered with the FA. Of this number, only 573 are in receipt of the maximum wage.

1912 Goalkeepers are no longer permitted to handle the ball anywhere in their half of the pitch.

Great Britain beat Denmark again to win Gold Medal at the Stockholm Olympic Games.

First £2,000 transfer (Danny O'Shea, West Ham Utd to Blackburn Rovers).

AFPU unsuccessfully challenges the legality of the 'retain and transfer' system in the English courts.

1914 Amateur Football Association returns to the FA as an affiliated society.

Severely weakened by its inability to bring an end to the 'retain and transfer' system, membership of the AFPU has declined from about 1,300 in 1908 to about 400.

Top players earning £5 per week.[1]

Clubs from the north and the Midlands still dominate the English game. Out of the 40 Football League clubs, only Arsenal, Bristol City, Chelsea, Clapton Orient, Fulham and Tottenham Hotspur are from the south.

King George V presents the FA Cup at the Final.

OFFICERS AND MEN OF THE 17TH MIDDLESEX DURING THE FIRST WORLD WAR

The following officers and men are believed to have either enlisted in, or served with, the 17th Middlesex at some stage of the First World War. Ranks shown are generally the highest attained while serving with the Middlesex Regiment. Where known, dates of death and cemetery/ memorial details are given for those who lost their lives between 1 January 1915 and 31 December 1921. Such details have also been included for several individuals who were serving with other units at the time of their deaths. Unless stated, all cemeteries/memorials are in France. Further information concerning casualties/cemeteries can be found on the website of the Commonwealth War Graves Commission: www.cwgc.org

Among the sources that have been used to compile this list are: the 17th Middlesex War Diary, the medal rolls of the Middlesex Regiment and several other regiments and corps, *Soldiers Died in the Great War*, Red Cross Lists, Medal Index Cards, Monthly Army Lists, army service records, Absent Voter Lists, annotated photographs of the 17th Middlesex, various national and local newspapers, and the records of the Commonwealth War Graves Commission. A further 60 or so names have been added since the publication of the hardback edition of this book in 2008. In the event of discrepancies between sources, a decision has been made as to the most likely interpretation. The list itself is by no means complete, and the authors would welcome details of any omissions. While every reasonable effort has been made to ensure the accuracy of this list, the authors cannot accept responsibility for any matters arising from it.

Surname	Rank	Forenames	Prefix	Number	Date of Death	Cemetery/Memorial
ABBITTS	Pte	Leonard Foster	F	95		
ABBOTT	Pte	J				
ABBOTT	Pte	Henry Thomas	G	18097	1 Dec 1917	Cambrai Memorial
ABBS	Pte	Charles	F	289		
ABEAR	Pte	John Leonard	F	129	28 Apr 1917	Lievin Communal Cemetery Ext.
ABEL	Pte	Walter Watson	TF	207997		
ABERCROMBY	2/Lt	John Stevenson			29 Apr 1917	Aubigny Communal Cemetery Ext.
ABRAHAM	Pte	Marks	G	14681		
ABRAHAMS	Pte	George	F	96		
ADAMS	Pte	Arthur Otto	TF	203861		
ADAMS	Pte	Benjamin	F	322	23 Aug 1916	Northampton (Towcester Road) Cemetery (UK)
ADAMS	Pte	Frederick	G	44153	25 Dec 1918	Staines (St Mary) Churchyard Ext. (UK)
ADAMS	Pte	George	F	372	28 Jul 1916	Thiepval Memorial
ADAMS	Pte	Joseph	F	1388	22 Jan 1916	Guards Cemetery, Windy Corner
ADAMS	Pte	Joseph	G	1034		
ADAMS	Pte	William G	PW	6344		
ADCOCK	Sgt	Francis Orlando	F	321	28 Mar 1916	Heston (St Leonard) Churchyard (UK)
AGNEW	Pte	George William	G	10018		
AINGER	Pte	Alfred	F	1368		
AINGER	Pte	Sidney	G	44032		
AINGER	Pte	William T	F	1287		
ALBRECHT	Sgt	Frank Louis	F	323	8 Aug 1916	Delville Wood Cemetery
ALCOCK	Sgt	Charles William	F	1013		
ALCOCK	Pte	Henry James	G	18382		
ALDERSON	Pte	Horace John	F	1825		
ALDIS	Pte	Allan Cecil	G	87390		
ALDRIDGE	Cpl	Archie Horace	F	597	8 Nov 1918	St. Sever Cemetery Ext.
ALDRIDGE	Pte	Charles	F	596		
ALDRIDGE	Pte	Thomas	G	44028	26 Jun 1917	Niederzwehren Cemetery (Germany)
ALEXANDER	Pte	F				
ALEXANDER	Pte	Jerimiah Soames	G	19335		
ALISOP	Pte	William	G	43601		
ALLEN	L/Cpl	Cyril Charles Hodgson	F	800		
ALLEN	Pte	Edgar John	G	24065		
ALLEN	2/Lt	JL				
ALLEN	Pte	John	F	1681		
ALLEN	Pte	John Charles	F	1104		
ALLEN	Cpl	Joseph H	TF	205257		
ALLEN	Pte	William Alfred	G	12567	8 Aug 1916	Contalmaison Chateau Cemetery
ALLSOPP	Pte	William F	G	8684		
ALLSWORTH	Pte	William G	G	11532		
ALMOND	Pte	Percy Arthur	G	43696		
AMBROSE	Pte	Edward	G	2303		
AMES	Sgt	Joseph William	G	13410		
AMMER	Pte	Sidney	F	1191		
AMOS	Pte	Arthur	G	43603		
AMOS	Pte	Edward Alfred	L	16002		
AMY	Pte	John Leonard	G	43941	17 Feb 1917	Regina Trench Cemetery
ANDERSON	Pte	Archibald Roseveare	F	87		
ANDERSON	Pte	Charles	G	27860		
ANDERSON	Pte	Edward Joseph	G	34772	28 Apr 1917	Arras Memorial
ANDERSON	Cpl	Frank	F	78		
ANDERSON	Pte	George	G	41651	28 Apr 1917	Arras Memorial
ANDERSON	Pte	George Harry	F	420		
ANDERSON	Pte	James Edward	G	44129		
ANDREW	Pte	Alfred	F	1386		
ANDREW	Pte	Cyril Pentreath	G	12295		
ANDREWS	Pte	Charles Clotton	G	86520		
ANDREWS	Pte	Edward James	G	5094		
ANDREWS	Pte	Fred William	G	11733		
ANDREWS	Pte	George	F	250		
ANDREWS	Pte	John Thomas	G	20220		
ANDREWS	Pte	William Edward	TF	203029		
ANGOOD	Pte	Sidney George Harold	F	650		

Surname	Rank	Forenames	Prefix	Number	Date of Death	Cemetery/Memorial
ANGRAVE	Pte	Herbert	G	34141		
ANSELL	Pte	Edward Frederick	G	89012		
ANSELL	Pte	Frank Morgan	G	43604	13 Nov 1916	Serre Road No.2
ANSTEY	Pte	Frank	F	1510	18 Sep 1916	Euston Road Cemetery
APPLETON	Pte	Bernard	G	24460		
APPLETON	Pte	William James	G	34859		
ARCHER	Pte	Albert	G	20265	10 Dec 1917	Etaples Military Cemetery
ARCHER	Pte	George	G	25969		
ARCHER	Pte	James William	G	34263	28 Apr 1917	Arras Memorial
ARGENT	Pte	Albert	F	1492		
ARKELL	Pte	Arthur Charles	F	1270		
ARKMAN	Sgt					
ARNETT	Pte	Frederick George	F	324	29 Nov 1917	Tyne Cot Memorial (Belgium)
ARNOLD	L/Cpl	Arthur	G	43873	25 Apr 1917	Aubigny Communal Cemetery Ext.
ASH	L/Cpl	John Frederick	F	554		
ASHALFORD	Pte	George Henry	G	28304	14 Oct 1918	Honnechy British Cemetery
ASHBY	Pte	GE	G	87045		
ASHBY	Pte	George Robert	F	374		
ASHBY	Pte	Sidney	PW	6053		
ASHDOWN	Pte	John Frederick	TF	203030	9 Dec 1917	Arras Memorial
ASHELFORD	Pte	George	G	28304		
ASHLEY	Pte	Edward	F	268		
ASHLEY	Pte	George Edward	G	87045		
ASHMAN	Sgt	Frederick Charles	G	15406	18 Aug 1917	Gorre British and Indian Cemetery
ASHTON	Pte	Walter	G	41030		
ASKEW	Pte	Adolphus James	G	42637		
ASTON	Pte	Clement	G	20557		
ASTON	Pte	Harry	G	16256		
ATKINS	Sgt	William Frederick	F	1062		
ATKINS	Pte	Thomas William	G	16534		
ATTEW	Pte	Ernest Edward	F	1232		
ATTHEWS	Sgt	Henry W	G	53095		
ATTRIDGE	Pte	Amos	G	43602	13 Nov 1916	Serre Road No.2
ATTRYDE	Sgt	Henry John	F	775		
ATTWELL	L/Cpl	Leonard Alfred	G	27933	28 Apr 1917	Arras Memorial
AUSTEN	2/Lt	William Henry Ambrose			13 Nov 1916	Serre Road No. 1
AUSTIN	Pte	Charles	F	1244	22 Jun 1917	Ypres (Menin Gate) Memorial (Belgium)
AUSTIN	Sgt	Herbert Oliver		1321		
AUSTIN	Pte	Stanley Edward	F	375		
AVERY	Pte	Robert A	G	12246		
AXTELL	Pte	Norman Wilfred	G	34184		
AYARD	Pte	Wallace	G	43551		
AYLOTT	Pte	Albert Henry	G	22791		
AYLOTT	Pte	Arthur	PS	3618	29 Sep 1918	Villers Hill British Cemetery
AYRTON	Cpl	George H	G	34024		
AYSHFORD	Cpl	Reginald	G	43860		
BACKLER	Pte	Abner Charles	G	24518	13 Nov 1916	Thiepval Memorial
BACON	Cpl	Charles	G	26273		
BACON	Sgt	John Sidney	F	79		
BACON	Pte	Herbert William	G	34088	28 Apr 1917	Arras Memorial
BADRICK	Pte	George Ford	F	325	10 Aug 1916	Islington Cemetery and Crematorium (UK)
BAGNALL	Pte	AJ	PW	4539		
BAGNALL	Pte	Frederick John	F	1149		
BAILEY	Pte	George	PW	5857		
BAILEY	Pte	George William	G	50844		
BAILEY	Pte	James	F	326		
BAILEY	Sgt	James Alfred	F	112		
BAILEY	Cpl	Walter George	F	290		
BAILEY	Cpl	William Arthur	PS	3746		
BAILEY	Pte	William Frederick	F	1484		
BAKE	2/Lt	Noel			10 Apr 1918	Loos Memorial
BAKER	Pte	David Edward	G	87137		
BAKER	Pte	DJ	F	197		
BAKER	Pte	Ephraim	G	43687	13 Nov 1916	Thiepval Memorial

Surname	Rank	Forenames	Prefix	Number	Date of Death	Cemetery/Memorial
BAKER	Pte	Francis George	F	1936	24 Sep 1918	St. Sever Cemetery Ext.
BAKER	Pte	Harry James	G	2655		
BAKER	Pte	James Alfred	G	34265	22 Feb 1917	Thiepval Memorial
BAKER	Pte	Sidney	G	34084		
BAKER	Pte	Sidney Heil	G	40870	3 Jan 1918	Arras Memorial
BAKER	Pte	William	PW	372	9 Apr 1918	Ploegsteert Memorial (Belgium)
BAKER	Pte	William	F	1657		
BAKER	Sgt	William James	F	521	22 Oct 1916	Sucrerie Military Cemetery
BALCHIN	Pte	Amos Fred	PW	5759		
BALDERSON	Pte	Norman	F	130	28 Jul 1916	Thiepval Memorial
BALDWIN	Sgt	Fred Barnardo Thomas	G	2937		
BALDWIN	Pte	Thomas George	F	563	22 Oct 1916	Thiepval Memorial
BALDWIN	Pte	William	S	6760		
BALES	Pte	Edward Dennis	PW	6378		
BALL	Sgt	Arthur	F	8		
BALL	2/Lt	Edward Ralph				
BALL	Pte	George William	F	899	8 Aug 1916	Delville Wood Cemetery
BALL	Cpl	James A	F	601		
BALLANTYNE	Sgt	James Douglas	F	677		
BANHAM	CSM	Stanley Alfred	F	896		
BANKS	Pte	Albert	G	30312		
BANKS	Pte	Leonard	TF	202895		
BANKS	2/Lt	George Francis Hampton				
BANKS	Pte	Levi	PW	3708	1 Dec 1917	Cambrai Memorial
BANTING	Cpl	W	F	2594		
BARBER	Pte	Thomas	F	852		
BARBER	Pte	William	F	113		
BARBY	Pte	Sydney Thomas	G	41872		
BARDEN	Pte	Benjamin	PW	2387		
BAREHAM	Pte	Arthur James	G	44126	13 Nov 1916	Mailly Wood Cemetery
BARHAM	Pte	Herbert	G	87046		
BARHAM	Pte	William James	G	43934		
BARKER	Pte	Ernest Edward	G	34143	13 Aug 1917	Gaza War Cemetery (Israel)
BARKER	L/Cpl	George	F	3187		
BARKER	2/Lt	HW				
BARKER	Pte	James William	G	12335	28 Jul 1916	Delville Wood Cemetery
BARKER	Pte	William	G	43695		
BARKER	Pte	William	L	14073		
BARNES	Pte	William Henry	G	27429	13 Apr 1918	St. Sever Cemetery Ext.
BARNETT	Sgt	Alfred Edward		102557		
BARNETT	Pte	James William	PW	6626		
BARNETT	L/Cpl	Ernest	G	43554	13 Nov 1916	Thiepval Memorial
BARNFATHER	Capt	Percy	F	39		
BARRATT	Pte	William A	S	7888		
BARRETT	Pte	F	F	1513		
BARRETT	Pte	George Charles	G	11994	29 Jul 1917	Ypres (Menin Gate) Memorial (Belgium)
BARRETT	Pte	Herbert Frederick	F	988		
BARRETT	Sgt	James William	L	16580		
BARRETT	QMS	Richard Exham Moore	F	269		
BARRY	Pte	Joseph	F	2425		
BARTHOLOMEW	Pte	Charles	G	34267		
BARTHOLOMEW	C/Sgt	Frederick	F	291		
BARTLETT	Pte	Frederick John	G	29205		
BARTLETT	Pte	Harry Abel	F	1229	10 Oct 1918	St. Aubert British Cemetery
BARTON	Pte	Jabez	G	40190		
BARTON	Pte	Thomas Arnold	F	1298		
BARTRAM	L/Cpl	Francis William	G	43544	28 Apr 1917	Arras Memorial
BASHAM	L/Cpl	John Leonard	G	34206	25 Sep 1917	Bethune Town Cemetery
BASHFORD	Pte	Henry	PW	6623		
BASS	Pte	Horace Oliver	PW	6256	11 Apr 1918	Mesnil Communal Cemetery Ext.
BASSETT	Pte	Edward John	F	319		
BASTARD	Pte	Bertie A	F	1090		
BASTIN	Pte	Benjamin	G	34030	28 Apr 1917	Arras Memorial
BASTON	Pte	George William	G	19766	25 Mar 1918	Arras Memorial
BATES	Pte	Charles	TF	20125		

Surname	Rank	Forenames	Prefix	Number	Date of Death	Cemetery/Memorial
BATES	Pte	Frederick	G	20095		
BATES	Pte	Henry Spencer	F	1473		
BATES	Pte	Sydney	G	2098		
BATES	Sgt	Walter	L	983		
BATEY	Pte	Jasper Matthews	F	60	23 Oct 1916	Cambrin Military Cemetery
BATTEN	Pte	Ernest George	G	44125		
BAUCKHAM	Pte	Percival James	G	34086	28 Apr 1917	Arras Memorial
BAVIN	L/Cpl	Robert Edwin	G	37529	1 Dec 1917	Grevillers British Cemetery
BAXTER	Pte	Albert Cecil	F	700	28 Jul 1916	Thiepval Memorial
BAXTER	Pte	Ernest George	G	43675	22 Aug 1918	Serre Road No.2
BAXTER	Pte	John Ronald	F	882		
BAXTER	Pte	Robert Joseph	G	41417		
BAXTER	Pte	William Stanley	F	114	26 Mar 1918	Arras Memorial
BAYFORD	Pte	Alfred Charles	G	34393		
BEAL	Cpl	Edward Henry	G	75774		
BEAN	Cpl	Walter Henry Pearson	F	2153		
BEANEY	Pte	George	TF	293276		
BEANEY	Pte	Moses	F	2598		
BEAR	Sgt	Herbert Charles	F	233		
BEARD	Pte	Bertie Edward	G	34335		
BEARD	Sgt	Irwin Ellis	F	232		
BEARD	Pte	Josiah Charles Smith	G	43672	13 Nov 1916	Serre Road No.2
BEARDALL	Pte	George	F	251		
BEARE	Pte	Ernest Arthur	G	43699		
BEARTON	Pte	Edwin	PW	5781		
BEAUMONT	Pte	Horace	PS	3489		
BEAUMONT	2/Lt	Roy J				
BEAVERSTOCK	Pte	William George	F	1227		
BEAVIS	Sgt	Jonathan Thomas	F	180		
BECK	Pte	Ernest	F	252	13 Nov 1916	Thiepval Memorial
BECK	Pte	George Robert	PW	6413		
BECK	L/Cpl	Harry A	F	824		
BECK	Pte	Robert	G	42643		
BECKETT	Sgt	Frederick Edwin	F	443		
BECKETT	Pte	Henry William	G	43999	17 Apr 1917	Cologne Southern Cemetery (Germany)
BEDFORD	Pte	Geo Joseph	L	16770		
BEDFORD	Pte	Robert Francis	F	327	31 May 1917	Duisans British Cemetery
BEDWELL	Pte	Albert Victor	G	44008	13 Nov 1916	Thiepval Memorial
BEECH	Sgt	George	F	12		
BEGENT	Pte	Charles Edward	F	164	10 Oct 1916	Thiepval Memorial
BEGGS	2/Lt	James			9 Apr 1918	Ploegsteert Memorial (Belgium)
BELCH	L/Cpl	James John	F	1014	27 Jul 1916	Thiepval Memorial
BELL	Pte	Arthur Edward	TF	242773		
BELL	L/Cpl	Charles	F	292		
BELL	Capt	Edward Inkerman Jordan			24 Mar 1918	Albert Communal Cemetery Ext.
BELL	Pte	Frederick	G	34089		
BELL	Pte	James	F	1094		
BELL	Pte	Samuel	G	29090		
BELLAMY	Pte	Henry	L	15267		
BELL-WEDGE	Pte	William George	F	1557	8 Jun 1915	Paddington Cemetery (UK)
BELSEY	Pte	James Thomas	G	43703		
BELSOM	Pte	George Henry	PW	6420		
BELTON	Pte	Frederick Ernest	F	234		
BENCE	Pte	Henry Herbert	F	883	23 Jun 1916	Tancrez Farm Cemetery (Belgium)
BENNETT	Pte	GW	TF			
BENNETT	Lt					
BENNETTS	Cpl	Richard	F	198		
BENSBERG	Sgt	Francis Caspar	F	1166	1 Oct 1916	Thiepval Memorial
BENT	Pte	Harry	G	44130		
BENTLEY	Pte	Francis George	F	583		
BENTLEY	Pte	George Frederick William	F	1835		
BERKSHIRE	Pte	George Alfred	G	20040		
BERRY	Pte	Alfred Benjamin	G	34207	28 Apr 1917	Arras Memorial
BERRY	Pte	Charles	G	43552		

Surname	Rank	Forenames	Prefix	Number	Date of Death	Cemetery/Memorial
BERRY	Pte	Edward W	G	42644		
BERRY	Pte	Ernest	F	131		
BERRY	Cpl	Frank Percy	G	42642		
BERRY	Cpl	George	L	15317		
BERRY	Pte	Joseph James	G	34090		
BERRY	Sgt	OW				
BERWICK	Pte	Albert Christopher	G	44040		
BEST	Pte	Edward	PS	1709		
BETHEL	Pte	Arthur	F	1987		
BEW	Pte	Walter H	F	181		
BICKERDIKE	Pte	Norman Campbell	PS	3246		
BIGGS	Pte	Charles Ernest	F	270		
BIGGS	Pte	Josiah Clifford	F	2079		
BIGWOOD	Pte	Walter Edward	G	43939		
BILLINGS	Pte	Alfred H. A.	G	11926	27 Nov 1916	Willesden New Cemetery (UK)
BINGHAM	Pte	Alfred Edward	G	19875	2 Dec 1917	Achiet-Le-Grand Communal Cemetery Ext.
BIRCH	Pte	GL		104130		
BIRCHFIELD	Pte	William Ernest	F	461		
BIRCHLEY	Pte	Tom	F	948		
BIRD	Pte	Ernest Henry	PS	3721	28 May 1917	Reninghelst New Military Cemetery (Belgium)
BIRD	Pte	Percy	G	17562		
BIRD	Pte	Walter Charles	F	2459		
BIRD	Pte	William George Charles	G	15192		
BISHOP	Pte	Fred George	G	34269		
BISHOP	2/Lt	RS				
BISHOPP	Pte	Henry	G	43689	28 Apr 1917	Arras Memorial
BISSELL	Pte	Frederick C	F	1353		
BISSETT	Pte	Charles William	G	34390	22 Jun 1917	Brown's Road Military Cemetery
BLABER	Pte	Bertie Harry	G	43973	13 Nov 1916	Thiepval Memorial
BLACK	Pte	Ernest Stanley	G	77560		
BLACKALLER	Pte	Charles	G	12090		
BLADES	Pte	George Albert	F	328	2 Jun 1916	Barlin Communal Cemetery Ext.
BLAIR	Sgt	Jeffrey Douglas	F	943	13 Nov 1916	Mailly Wood Cemetery
BLAKE	Pte	Alfred James	G	12447	13 Nov 1916	Thiepval Memorial
BLAKE	Sgt	Bertie Newton	G	25268		
BLAKE	Pte	Charles Henry	G	41652		
BLAKE	Pte	Harold Ewart	G	20657	24 Mar 1918	Rocquigny-Equancourt Road British Cemetery
BLAKE	Pte	William Bertie	G	44021		
BLAKEY	CSM	George William	F	320		
BLAKEY	L/Sgt	William	F	826	28 Jul 1916	Delville Wood Cemetery
BLAND	Sgt	Charles John	F	1119		
BLAND	Pte	John Arthur	F	1245	28 Apr 1917	Arras Memorial
BLATCH	Sgt	Arthur James	F	782		
BLAY	Pte	Charlie	F	873		
BLAYNEY	Pte	Llewellyn HJ		16150		
BLOOMFIELD	Pte	Frederick	PW	1576		
BLOUNT	Pte	Ernest J	F	1773		
BLOWS	Pte	Walter	G	11629		
BLUFFIELD	Pte	Horace Frank	G	94031	29 Sep 1918	Tottenham Cemetery (UK)
BLUNDELL	Pte	John	G	87042		
BLUNT	Pte	Walter	F	1537	28 Jul 1916	Thiepval Memorial
BLYTH	Pte	James Henry	G	34025		
BLYTHE	Pte	David	F	1120		
BODY	Pte	John	F	450	14 Aug 1917	Monchy British Cemetery
BOLTON	Pte	Henry Edward	G	34208	3 Jan 1918	Arras Memorial
BONATHAN	2/Lt	Frank Stanley			28 Apr 1917	Arras Memorial
BONES	Pte	Samuel	G	34394	28 Apr 1917	Arras Memorial
BONIFACE	Pte	Alfred	F	80		
BONIFACE	Pte	Arthur William	G	44054		
BOON	Pte	John Owen	F	1315		
BOON	Pte	William Richard	G	26525		
BOOTH	Pte	William	F	13		
BOOTH	Pte	Peter	G	42640	7 Jan 1918	Rocquigny-Equancourt Road British Cemetery

Surname	Rank	Forenames	Prefix	Number	Date of Death	Cemetery/Memorial
BOREHAM	Pte	Stephen George	G	24949		
BORTHWICK	Pte	John JB	F	14		
BOSTON	Pte	Frederick	F	1053		
BOSTRIDGE	Pte	William	G	28489		
BOSWORTH	Pte	Leonard Thomas	F	2534	24 Jan 1918	Warmington (St Mary) Churchyard (UK)
BOTTING	Pte	Reginald	G	43709		
BOTTING	Pte	William Isaac	G	44101	13 Nov 1916	Mailly Wood Cemetery
BOUFFLER	Pte	James George Charles	G	34028	11 Sep 1917	Chocques Military Cemetery
BOULT	Pte	Stephen	G	43928		
BOURNE	Pte	Albert Ernest	G	43945	13 Nov 1916	Serre Road No.2
BOUTTELL	Pte	George Frederick	F	2526	2 Dec 1917	Moeuvres Communal Cemetery Ext.
BOWCOCK	Pte	Walter William	G	34087	28 Apr 1917	Arras Memorial
BOWDEN	Pte	Edward	F	182		
BOWEN	Cpl	Walter William	F	1548		
BOWER	2/Lt	Frank George				
BOWERMAN	L/Cpl	Ernest	F	1076	20 Sep 1916	Couin British Cemetery
BOWLER	Pte	George Henry	F	27		
BOWLER	Pte	James	F	61		
BOWLER	Pte	Leonard Christopher	F	332		
BOWLES	Pte	Percy	G	34334		
BOWMAN	Cpl	Frederick John	F	867	5 May 1917	Heston (St Leonard) Churchyard (UK)
BOXALL	Pte	Frank	PW	4941		
BOXALL	Cpl	Henry Ivo	F	516		
BOYCE	Pte	Charles	G	13382		
BOYCE	Pte	Ernest	F	1876	8 Aug 1916	Thiepval Memorial
BOYCE	Sgt	George Francis	F	488		
BOYD	Pte	William	G	34033	31 Jul 1917	Ypres (Menin Gate) Memorial (Belgium)
BOYLETT	Pte	Albert Ernest	L	16671		
BOYS	Pte	Ernest Alfred	G	11205		
BRACKING	Pte	Samuel	G	27424		
BRACKLEY	Pte	Herbert George	G	32805	24 Aug 1917	Bedford House Cemetery (Belgium)
BRADBURY	Pte	Frederick	G	43678		
BRADFORD	Pte	James	G	87436		
BRADFORD	L/Cpl	Cornelius William	PW	6408	28 Nov 1917	Cambrai Memorial
BRADLEY	Pte	Albert Harry	TF	203902		
BRADLEY	Pte	Bertie John	F	561	27 Feb 1916	Calais Southern Cemetery
BRADLEY	Pte	James	G	11078		
BRADLEY	Pte	Lawrence Edward	G	5412		
BRADLEY	Capt	MG				
BRADSTREET	2/Lt	Lionel Arthur			1 Jun 1916	Cabaret-Rouge British Cemetery
BRADY	Pte	John	F	215		
BRAINE	Cpl	Ernest	G	11279		
BRAINS	Pte	Ernest Arthur	PW	5468		
BRAND	Pte	Ernest	F	1082		
BRANDON	Pte	Sidney Herbert	G	34091		
BRANDON	Pte	Walter George Alfred	F	1627	11 Jul 1916	Boulogne Eastern Cemetery
BRANNAN	Pte	James	PW	4582		
BRANT	L/Sgt	Walter James	F	377		
BRAYBROOK	Pte	Ernest Henry	G	34392		
BREAKELL	Pte	John	F	1550		
BREMNER	Pte	Herbert George	G	1702	28 Apr 1917	Arras Memorial
BRENNAN	Pte	J	PW	3582		
BRERETON	Cpl	James	F	1341		
BRERETON	Pte	John William	F	1316	8 Aug 1916	Thiepval Memorial
BRETT	Pte	Frederick William	F	795		
BRETT	Pte	Frederick	G	51418	2 Dec 1917	Cambrai Memorial
BREWER	Sgt	Thomas Henry	F	378		
BREWER	Pte	William John	F	452	1 Aug 1916	Quarry Cemetery, Montauban
BRIAN	Pte	Thomas Robert	G	9875		
BRICKETT	Sgt	F	F			
BRIDGE	Pte	Alfred John	G	24517		
BRIDGER	Pte	William	G	32942		
BRIDGETTE	Pte	Sydney Frederick	G	9988		
BRIERLEY	Pte	G				
BRIGHT	Pte	Leonard Charles	G	34032		
BRIGNALL	Pte	Horace George	PS	1716		

Surname	Rank	Forenames	Prefix	Number	Date of Death	Cemetery/Memorial
BRITTON	Pte	Arthur	F	271		
BRITTON	Pte	James	F	703		
BRITTON	Pte	Walter	G	19377		
BROAD	Pte	Henry Walter	F	1065		
BROAD	Pte	Thomas	G	94007		
BROCKLEHURST	L/Cpl	John P	F	2843		
BROOK	Pte	Sidney Leonard	L	16668		
BROOKER	Pte	Leonard	G	89101		
BROOKS	Cpl	Albert Edward	F	331		
BROOKS	Pte	Alfred	L	13530		
BROOKS	Pte	Redvers John Charles	F	330		
BROOKS	Pte	Tom	G	44131	22 Jun 1917	Brown's Road Military Cemetery
BROOKS	Pte	William Edgar	G			
BROOM	Pte	Harry	F	379		
BROUGHTON	CQMS	Jonathan H	F	3		
BROWN	Lt	Archibald Henry				
BROWN	Cpl	Charles	G	43981		
BROWN	Pte	Charles	G	50434		
BROWN	Cpl	Charles William	F	674		
BROWN	Pte	David Jonathon	G	34332		
BROWN	L/Cpl	Ernest	F	333	17 Aug 1916	St. Sever Cemetery Ext.
BROWN	Pte	Fred Arthur Henry Peter	F	1219		
BROWN	Pte	Frederick	TF	202423		
BROWN	Pte	George Charles	TF	203033		
BROWN	Cpl	George Henry	G	14844		
BROWN	Pte	Henry	F	495		
BROWN	Pte	Leonard	G	43697		
BROWN	Pte	Robert	G	42641		
BROWN	Pte	Robert GT	G	87644		
BROWN	Sgt	Sidney	G	34085		
BROWN	Pte	Tom William	G	27391		
BROWN	Pte	Victor Stephen	G	34395		
BROWN	Pte	William Arthur	G	75606		
BROWN	Pte	William Henry	G	43949		
BROXUP	Sgt	George Frederick	F	1059		
BRUNTON	2/Lt	Edward Benjamin D			13 Nov 1916	Thiepval Memorial
BRYAN	Pte	James Alfred	PS	2675		
BRYANT	Pte	Bert	F	1175		
BRYANT	Pte	Walter	F	380		
BRYANT	Pte	Walter H	G	50027		
BUCHAN	Pte	Alfred	L	13314		
BUCHAN	Pte	Alfred	G	71213		
BUCHANAN	Pte	David	G	39030		
BUCK	Pte	Ernest Frederick	G	43669	14 Nov 1916	Varennes Military Cemetery
BUCKINGHAM	Pte	Harry William	F	3043		
BUCKLEY	Maj	Franklin Charles				
BUDD	Pte	James	G	33466		
BUDD	L/Sgt	Edward Henry	G	44075	2 Dec 1917	Cambrai Memorial
BUGG	Pte	Albert W	G	15845		
BUGGY	Pte	Charles Edward	F	890	22 Aug 1918	Gommecourt British Cemetery No. 2
BULGER	Pte	George HF	F	1551		
BULL	Pte	Alfred	G	2114	15 Jul 1916	Thiepval Memorial
BULL	Pte	Ernest	G	32391		
BULL	Pte	George A	F	1293		
BULL	Sgt	William Henry	F	833	17 Sep 1916	Euston Road Cemetery
BULLEN	Pte	Alfred	G	34331	21 Feb 1917	Thiepval Memorial
BULLEN	Pte	Charles Felix	PW	6393		
BULLEN	Pte	Walter	G	33330		
BULLEN	Pte	William James	G	44123	13 Feb 1917	Contay British Cemetery
BULLOCK	L/Cpl	Frederick Edwin	F	629		
BULMAN	Pte	Edward J	G	1122		
BUNCH	Pte	Albert Edward	G	34209		
BUNKER	Pte	Herbert Arnold	G	44044	31 Aug 1918	H.A.C. Cemetery
BUNKER	Pte	Sydney	G	34029	6 Feb 1917	Contay British Cemetery
BUNTING	Pte	Tom	F	382		
BUNYAN	Pte	Charles	F	1050		

Surname	Rank	Forenames	Prefix	Number	Date of Death	Cemetery/Memorial
BURBEDGE	Pte	Albert	F	1372		
BURCHETT	Pte	Colin	G	48086	11 Dec 1917	Lebucquiere Communal Cemetery Ext
BURDEN	Pte	John Edward	G	44045	5 Mar 1917	Contay British Cemetery
BURGESS	Pte	William	L	9071		
BURGESS	Pte	James Richard	G	87643	1 Dec 1917	Cambrai Memorial
BURGOYNE	Capt	Alan Hughes				
BURKWOOD	Pte	Victor Collyer	G	34271		
BURLEY	L/Cpl	Albert Henry	F	623	8 Aug 1916	Thiepval Memorial
BURMAN	Pte	Joseph	G	27757		
BURRAGE	Pte	Alfred	G	43712		
BURRELL	Pte	Frederick	G	34078		
BURROWS	Pte	John Martin	F	3296		
BURROWS	L/Cpl	Frederick Arthur	F	924	28 Apr 1917	Arras Memorial
BURTON	Pte	John Frederick	F	562		
BURTON	Pte	Joshua	G	44133		
BURTON	Pte	William	G	43556		
BURTON	L/Cpl	William Herbert	F	821		
BURTON	Pte	William	G	34210	28 Apr 1917	Arras Memorial
BUSBY	Pte	H				
BUSBY	Pte	Walter Howard	F	996		
BUSH	Sgt	Henry V	L	12429		
BUSHELL	Cpl	Clifford	G	34026		
BUSHELL	Pte	Richard	G	34083		
BUTCHER	Pte	Albert Reginald	G	87405		
BUTCHER	Cpl	Ernest Frank	F	199	8 Aug 1916	Thiepval Memorial
BUTCHER	Pte	James	G	16556		
BUTLER	Cpl	Albert Victor	F	62	13 May 1916	Bruay Communal Cemetery
BUTLER	Pte	Charles	F	1575		
BUTLER	Pte	CW				
BUTLER	Pte	Francis Charles	G	34082		
BUTLER	Pte	John Dennis	F	63		
BUTLER	Cpl	Sidney Bartholomew	F	99	12 Aug 1916	Heilly Station Cemetery
BUTLER	Cpl	Walter	L	12811		
BUXTON	Pte	Charles	G	44079	13 Nov 1916	Serre Road No.2
BUZEE	Pte	William	G	12151	23 Apr 1917	Arras Memorial
BYE	Pte	SJ	G			
BYFIELD	RSM	Arthur Charles	L	13763		
BYFORD	Pte	Charles William	G	29825	22 Mar 1918	Roye New British Cemetery
CAFFREY	Pte	Harold Joseph	G	86324		
CALEY	Pte	Henry Charles	G	43482		
CALLARD	Cpl	Harry William	F	422	30 Jul 1916	Delville Wood Cemetery
CALNAN	Sgt	Timothy	F	1088		
CAMPBELL	L/Cpl	Oscar Clare	F	3276	1 Dec 1917	Cambrai Memorial
CAMPION	Pte	Basil Theodore	G	21835		
CANE	Pte	Frederick Arthur	G	44118		
CANNING	Pte	Michael Thomas	G	20732		
CANSDALE	Pte	George H	G	50726		
CAPON	Pte	Alfred		6742		
CARDON	Cpl	Maurice Jules	G	26052		
CARLESS	Capt	Thomas Frederick G				
CARLINE	Pte	John	F	1307		
CARPENTER	Pte	Harry T	F	694		
CARR	Pte	Ernest	F	584		
CARR	Pte	Henry	G	87180		
CARRUTHERS	Sgt	Henry Albert	F	509		
CARRUTHERS	2/Lt	Percy G				
CARSWELL	Pte	Hamilton	F	473	6 Aug 1916	Thiepval Memorial
CARTER	Cpl	Edwin Richard	G	43545		
CARLESS	L/Cpl	H	F			
CARTER	Pte	Herbert	G	34097	7 Mar 1917	St. Sever Cemetery Ext.
CARTER	Pte	JH		104936		
CARTER	Pte	Walter Charles	PW	5747	3 Dec 1917	Tincourt New British Cemetery
CARTER	Maj	William Henry				
CARTLIDGE		William				
CARVEY	Pte	Arthur	G	50522		
CASEY	Pte	John	F	1210		
CASEY	Pte	William	G	11231		

Surname	Rank	Forenames	Prefix	Number	Date of Death	Cemetery/Memorial
CASTLE	Pte	John Thomas	PW	5474		
CATCH	Pte	Leonard C	TF	293731		
CATER	CSM	Arthur Cecil	F	59	8 Aug 1916	Thiepval Memorial
CATES	Pte	James	G	18245	5 Nov 1918	Awoingt British Cemetery
CATON	Pte	Frank	G	34093	28 Apr 1917	Arras Memorial
CATTERMOLE	Pte	Jesse T	G	43607		
CAVE	Pte	George H	G	8706		
CAWDERY	Pte	Frederick Alexander	F	973		
CAWTE	Pte	Richard Stephen	F	1168	3 Aug 1917	Arras Memorial
CHADBURN	Pte	Albert	G	42649		
CHADDER	Pte	Reginald Charles	G	443	28 Jul 1916	Thiepval Memorial
CHADWICK	Pte	Alfred	F	254		
CHALCROFT	Pte	Charles Edward Lovell	F	2190		
CHALKLEN	Cpl	John Britton	G	42629		
CHALLIS	Pte	Charles	G	43959		
CHALMERS	Pte	Colin Ward	PS	1216		
CHALMERS	Pte	David	F	910		
CHAMBERLAIN	Pte	Charles John	G	34093	23 Feb 1917	Thiepval Memorial
CHAMBERS	Pte	George	G	44065	28 Apr 1917	Roclincourt Military Cemetery
CHAMBERS	Pte	Herbert Charles	G	43483		
CHAMBERS	Pte	Sydney	G	34040	9 May 1917	Niederzwehren Cemetery (Germany)
CHAMBERS	Pte	Thomas William	G	7776		
CHAMP	Pte	George James	PS	3185		
CHANDER	Pte	George	F	1196		
CHANDLER	2/Lt	Francis Philip				
CHANDLER	L/Cpl	Frank	F	81	8 Aug 1916	Thiepval Memorial
CHANTLER	Pte	Godfrey	G	40302	24 Jul 1918	St. Amand British Cemetery
CHANTLER	Pte	John Hohmann	G	87072		
CHAPLIN	Pte	James	G	5532		
CHAPLIN	Pte	James	PW	5532		
CHAPLIN	2/Lt	William				
CHAPMAN	Pte	Charles Albert	G	34037		
CHAPMAN	Sgt	Charles Godfrey	F	684		
CHAPMAN	Pte	George	G	50547		
CHAPMAN	Pte	Harold Victor	G	43879		
CHAPMAN	L/Cpl	Henry	F	1079		
CHAPMAN	Pte	Henry James Edward	G	34339	28 Apr 1917	Arras Memorial
CHAPMAN	Pte	Walter	F	1441		
CHAPMAN	Pte	Walter James	F	183		
CHARGE	Pte	William	G	15061		
CHATTERSON	Pte	William Henry	F	334		
CHEESEMAN	Pte	George	F	457		
CHEESLEY	L/Cpl	Frederick	F	1413	28 Jul 1916	Delville Wood Cemetery
CHERON	Pte	George Augustus	G	1765		
CHESHIRE	Pte	Frank Henry	G	34212		
CHESNAYE	Pte	Ernest	F	1581	1 Oct 1916	Thiepval Memorial
CHEW	Pte	Edward Joseph	G	34399	28 Apr 1917	Arras Memorial
CHILD	Pte	Francis Harvey	F	1601		
CHILDS	L/Cpl	Albert	G	27431	3 Jan 1918	Arras Memorial
CHILDS	2/Lt	Arthur				
CHILDS	Pte	Charles	G	43670		
CHILDS	Pte	Ernest Edward	G	34340	23 Apr 1917	Roclincourt Military Cemetery
CHOWN	Pte	George Newman	G	4527		
CHRISTMAS	2/Lt	Leslie Frederick			13 Nov 1916	Serre Road No. 1
CHRISTY	Pte	Joseph Thomas	G	42648	1 Dec 1917	Cambrai Memorial
CHURCH	Pte	Henry Arthur	G	43662		
CHURCHILL	Cpl	Charles	G	20157		
CLAPTON	Pte	Leonard	G	34038	30 Nov 1917	Niederzwehren Cemetery (Germany)
CLARE	Pte	Henrie Nugent	G	50380	27 Dec 1917	Hermies Hill British Cemetery
CLARE	Pte	John Edward	F	1015		
CLARK	Cpl	A				
CLARK	Pte	Albert	F	1086		
CLARK	Pte	Alfred William	G	44074	13 Nov 1916	Thiepval Memorial
CLARK	Pte	Arthur James	F	1577		
CLARK	Pte	Charles	G	44073	13 Nov 1916	Serre Road No.2
CLARK	Pte	Frank Rome	G	29962	28 Apr 1917	Arras Memorial
CLARK	Pte	Frederick William	F	82		

Surname	Rank	Forenames	Prefix	Number	Date of Death	Cemetery/Memorial
CLARK	Pte	George Ernest Frederick	G	44050	28 Apr 1917	Arras Memorial
CLARK	Pte	George William	L	14057		
CLARK	Pte	Henry George	PW	5210	30 Jul 1916	Thiepval Memorial
CLARK	Pte	Henry William	PS	3196	13 Sep 1916	Couin British Cemetery
CLARK	Pte	Herbert	G	43682		
CLARK	Capt	John Cosmo				
CLARK	Pte	Norman	F	1869	1 Jun 1916	Cabaret-Rouge British Cemetery
CLARK	Cpl	Richard	F	100	10 Nov 1916	Abbeville Communal Cemetery Ext
CLARK	Pte	Thomas	G	34100	22 Apr 1917	Roclincourt Military Cemetery
CLARK	Pte	William	G	43674		
CLARKE	Pte	Alfred	G	586		
CLARKE	L/Cpl	C	L	14033		
CLARKE	RSM	Charles	F	383		
CLARKE	Pte	Charles	G	44073		
CLARKE	L/Cpl	EW				
CLARKE	Pte	Frank	F	1255		
CLARKE	Pte	George Edward	F	454		
CLARKE	Cpl	George William	F	695		
CLARKE	Pte	Henry Augustus	F	2509	25 Oct 1918	Heestert Military Cemetery (Belgium)
CLARKE	Pte	Herbert Victor	G	6190	1 Jul 1916	Thiepval Memorial
CLARKE	Pte	John Charles	G	28215	25 Mar 1918	Arras Memorial
CLARKE	Pte	Lucas	G	44132	8 Jul 1917	Gorre British and Indian Cemetery
CLARKE	Cpl	Reginald	F	3250		
CLARKE	Pte	Thomas Alfred	F	1167	8 Aug 1916	Thiepval Memorial
CLARKE	Pte	William John	F	1917	1 Oct 1917	Tyne Cot Memorial (Belgium)
CLARKSON	Pte	William	F	1130		
CLATWORTHY	Pte	Maurice William	F	1639	1 Jul 1916	Thiepval Memorial
CLAXTON	Pte	Henry Charles	G	34092	28 Apr 1917	Arras Memorial
CLAYTON	Pte	Frederick Walter	G	3350		
CLEAVER	Pte	John Stanley	G	43692	13 Nov 1916	Thiepval Memorial
CLEMENT	L/Cpl	James	F	1238		
CLEMENTS	Pte	Harry	G	26360		
CLEMENTS	Pte	Horace	G	43693		
CLEMENTS	L/Cpl	John	F	1514	18 Sep 1916	Euston Road Cemetery
CLEMENTS	Pte	John Alfred	G	8562		
CLEMENTS	Pte	Richard	G	8674	28 Apr 1917	Arras Memorial
CLIFFORD	Pte	Andrew	G	92827		
CLIFFORD	Pte	John Charles	G	43608		
CLIFFORD	Pte	William Robert	G	43883	13 Nov 1916	Serre Road No.2
CLIFTON	Pte	Charles	G	44016	22 Apr 1917	Roclincourt Military Cemetery
CLIMO	Pte	Frederick	G	41640	16 Aug 1917	Tyne Cot Memorial (Belgium)
CLOSE	Pte	Raymond	F	1434	1 Jul 1916	Thiepval Memorial
COBB	Lt	Rhodes Stanley				
COBB	Pte	John	F	510		
COBBOLD	Pte	William	G	44013		
COCK	L/Sgt	John Gilbert	F	1418		
COCKELL	Pte	James	G	2217	9 Apr 1918	Ploegsteert Memorial (Belgium)
COCKS	2/Lt	Edward Louis			8 Aug 1916	Thiepval Memorial
CODD	Pte	Thomas	F	1476		
COE	Pte	George Henry	G	34338		
COEN	Pte	Charles J. Lawrence	TF	202852	28 Apr 1917	Arras Memorial
COHEN	Pte	Joseph Harris	G	12306		
COLAM	L/Cpl	Charles	F	1326	28 Jul 1916	Delville Wood Cemetery
COLDHAM	Pte		TF			
COLE	Pte	Arthur James	G	25937	13 Nov 1916	Serre Road No.2
COLE	Pte	Frederick William	G	34398	22 Feb 1917	Thiepval Memorial
COLE	Pte	George David	F	116		
COLE	Pte	William	G	34060	18 Feb 1917	Aveluy Communal Cemetery Ext.
COLE	Pte	William George	TF	203035	28 Apr 1917	Arras Memorial
COLE	2/Lt	William Walter Stratford				
COLEBOURNE	Pte	Israel		4583	3 Aug 1920	Derby (Nottingham Road) Cemetery (UK)
COLEMAN	Pte	John George	F	904		
COLES	Pte	Harvey H	G	43924	13 Nov 1916	Serre Road No. 1
COLLARD	Pte	Walter	G	34095	1 Dec 1917	Cambrai Memorial

Surname	Rank	Forenames	Prefix	Number	Date of Death	Cemetery/Memorial
COLLETT	L/Cpl	Thomas Edwin	F	670	28 Jul 1916	Delville Wood Cemetery
COLLIER	L/Cpl	Charles H		3357		
COLLINS	Pte	Albert	TF	202288	28 Apr 1917	Arras Memorial
COLLINS	Pte	Alfred H	G	34276		
COLLINS	Pte	Alfred Henry	G	34276		
COLLINS	Sgt	F				
COLLINS	Pte	George Walter	F	1409	16 Jan 1918	Rethel French National Cemetery
COLLINS	Pte	Jack Peter	F	1319		
COLLINS	Pte	James	F	1281		
COLLINS	Pte	John	F	642		
COLLINS	Pte	William	G	44039		
COLLIS	Lt	Herbert				
COLLISON	Cpl	George	F	1252	13 Nov 1916	Thiepval Memorial
COLLOP	Pte	Walter	F	1347		
COLQUHOUN	2/Lt	D				
COLYER	Pte	John Tempest	F	1210		
COMBLY	Pte	Henry	G	24509		
COMER	Pte	Thomas Henry	G	86240		
COMLEY	Pte	Thomas	F	992		
COMM	Pte	Sidney	G	34049		
CONNAH	Pte	William	F	2834		
CONNELL	Pte	Richard	G	44089		
CONNOLLY	L/Cpl	James Henry	F	875	8 Aug 1916	Delville Wood Cemetery
CONNOLLY	Pte	Joseph Patrick	F	1209		
CONSTABLE	Pte	Thomas Harold	G	41638		
COOK	Pte	Alfred Jubilee	G	42645		
COOK	Pte	Arthur	F	1521		
COOK	Sgt	Charles Wallington	F	335		
COOK	Pte	Henry C.	G	44098		
COOK	Pte	HW				
COOK	Sgt	William F	F	1271		
COOK	Pte	William T	F	471		
COOMES	Pte	Lucien Ernest	G	43943	2 Dec 1917	Achiet-Le-Grand Communal Cemetery Ext.
COOP	Pte	William George	F	887	23 Oct 1916	Thiepval Memorial
COOPER	Pte	Albert Edward	G	43558		
COOPER	Pte	Alfred G	G	43610		
COOPER	Pte	Arthur	G	34144		
COOPER	Pte	Ernest	G	44112	28 Nov 1916	Redhill (St John) Churchyard (UK)
COOPER	Pte	Frank	F	944		
COOPER	Pte	Frederick	G	41667		
COOPER	L/Cpl	Harold	F	217		
COOPER	Pte	Henry	F	1596	28 Jul 1916	Delville Wood Cemetery
COOPER	Sgt	Leslie Charles	L	13352		
COPE	Sgt	Jack Henry Bennett	F	336	8 Aug 1916	Thiepval Memorial
COPE	Pte	Richard Ernest	F	272		
COPELAND	Pte	Francis Mount	G	89024		
COQUET	Sgt	Ernest	F	44		
CORDELL	Pte	James George	G	26539		
CORNISH	Pte	Percy John	F	1003		
CORNISH	Pte	Robert Fenton	G	37530	23 Apr 1917	Heninel-Croisilles Road Cemetery
COTTRELL	Pte	James	G	21405	26 Jul 1917	Gorre British and Indian Cemetery
COURTNEY	Pte	Alfred Allen	TF	202905		
COURTNEY	Cpl	Frederick William C	G	50740		
COUSINS	2/Lt	William George				
COUTURIER	Pte	George	F	184		
COUTURIER	Pte	Michael	F	185		
COUZENS	Pte	Alfred	G	44085		
COVENEY	Pte	Thomas Charles	F	859		
COVERLY	Cpl	Albert Edward	G	42632		
COWARD	Pte	Thomas Wilford	G	42647		
COWELL	L/Sgt	Albert	G	7241	16 Mar 1917	Thiepval Memorial
COWLING	Pte	Joseph	G	34397		
COX	Pte	Charles	F	798		
COX	Pte	Frederick Williams	F	2803		
COX	Pte	George	G	70711	24 Jun 1917	Reninghelst New Military Cemetery (Belgium)

Surname	Rank	Forenames	Prefix	Number	Date of Death	Cemetery/Memorial
COX	Pte	James Fred	G	50741		
COX	Pte	Thomas	G	44135		
COX	Pte	Wallace H	F	148		
COX	Pte	Walter John	F	3193		
COX	Pte	William Frederick	G	43930	28 Apr 1917	Arras Memorial
COX	Pte	William George	G	34712	28 Apr 1917	Arras Memorial
COZENS	Pte	Thomas A	G	43654		
CRABB	Pte	Henry William	G	27321	3 Jan 1918	Arras Memorial
CRAFT	Pte	Cecil Edward	G	40919	21 Mar 1918	Pozieres Memorial
CRAFT	Sgt	James	G	42646		
CRANE	Pte	Ernest	G	10352	7 May 1917	Wandsworth (Earlsfield) Cemetery (UK)
CRANSHAW	2/Lt	N				
CRAPP	Pte	John Henry	F	1824		
CRAWFORD	Pte	William James	G	34918		
CRAWLEY	L/Cpl	Victor Austin	F	558	28 May 1917	Reninghelst New Military Cemetery (Belgium)
CRAWT	Pte	George	G	44116	24 Jan 1917	Unicorn Cemetery
CRESSEY	Pte	William Arthur	G	43652		
CRIPPS	Pte	William Edward	F	2458		
CRISP	Pte	Horace Walter	L	19256		
CRISP	Pte	Albert Edward	G	41653	28 Apr 1917	Arras Memorial
CRITCHLEY	Pte	Stanley Osmond	G	86005		
CROCKETT	Pte	Alfred Gladstone	G	34036		
CROFTS	Pte	Albert	G	6318		
CROKER	Sgt	Henry Frederick	L	13369	13 Nov 1916	Serre Road No. 1
CRONER	Pte	William	G	41777		
CROOK	Cpl	Ernest	G	42627		
CROPLEY	Sgt	Arhur	PW	6412		
CROSS	Pte	Aubrey Edward	F	1064	27 Jul 1916	London Cemetery & Ext.
CROSS	Pte	Frederick James	PW	6210	31 May 1917	Arras Memorial
CROSS	Pte	Herbert John	F	1063		
CROSSLEY	Pte	Arthur	F	294		
CROSWELLER	Pte	WJ				
CROUCH	L/Cpl	Albert George	F	1291	16 Nov 1918	Awoingt British Cemetery
CROUCHER	Pte	Arthur	G	44037		
CROUCHER	Pte	William George	G	43557		
CROWTHER	Pte	Albert James	F	862	27 Jul 1916	Thiepval Memorial
CROWTHER	Pte	George Leslie	F	1475		
CROWTHER	Pte	James	G	87047		
CROWTHER	Cpl	John Thomas	F	615	13 Nov 1916	Thiepval Memorial
CRUMMACK	Pte	John	F	1556		
CUBLEY	Pte	Frederick James	F	83		
CUDE	Cpl	Gordon William	G	43606		
CULLINGFORD	Pte	Albert Joseph	TF	205054		
CUMMINGS	Pte	Stephen	F	493	13 Aug 1916	Tancrez Farm Cemetery (Belgium)
CUNDELL	Pte	Charles	G	94019	7 Apr 1918	Etaples Military Cemetery
CUNNINGHAM	Pte	Arthur John	F	505		
CUPPY	Pte	James George	G	12273		
CURD	Pte	Charles	F	1441		
CURL	Pte	Thomas William	G	1587	9 Apr 1918	Ploegsteert Memorial (Belgium)
CURL	Pte	William Charles	F	3226	31 Jul 1917	Ypres (Menin Gate) Memorial (Belgium)
CURRINGTON	Pte	Albert George	G	27432		
CURTIS	Pte	Arthur	G	34041		
CURTIS	Capt	CW				
CURTIS	Pte	Edwin H	G	87073		
CURTIS	Pte	Joseph	F	485	31 Jan 1916	Chocques Military Cemetery
CURTIS	Pte	Walter Thomas	G	34094		
CUSICK	Pte	Charles James	F	1501		
CUTLER	Pte	John Charles	F	764		
CUTTS	Pte	Harry	G	34035		
DAINTON	Pte	Stanley F	G	10452		
DALE	Sgt	Cyril	F	1143		
DALE	Pte	George Francis	TF	205069	11 Dec 1917	Lebucquiere Communal Cemetery Ext
DALEY	Pte	William	F	1246	8 Aug 1916	Delville Wood Cemetery
DALGARNO	Capt	John Hunter				
DALLY	Pte	H	F	1036		

Surname	Rank	Forenames	Prefix	Number	Date of Death	Cemetery/Memorial
DALTREY	Sgt	James	F	337		
DALRYMPLE	Sgt	Robert Rodie	F	267		
DAMARY	Pte	William Charles	F	660		
DAMEREL	Pte	Edwin John	G	86357		
DANIELLS	Sgt	Joseph	F	647	30 Mar 1918	Pozieres Memorial
DANIELS	Pte	Charles Thomas	G	44104		
DANIELS	Pte	Frank Edward	G	87026		
DANIELS	Sgt	William	F	7		
DANIELS	Pte	Ernest James	G	34217	9 Dec 1917	Arras Memorial
DANN	Pte	Charles Herbert	G	42668		
DARLEY	Pte	Alfred Edward	G	89029		
DART	Pte	Doug John	G	11969		
DASHPER	Pte	Henry Cecil	F	1509		
DAUGHTERS	Pte	Henry	F	1047		
DAURIS	Pte	George Walter	F	620		
DAVENPORT	Pte	Frederick Pendel	F	458	26 Mar 1918	Pozieres Memorial
DAVEY	Pte	Edward Robert Huntley	F	386		
DAVEY	Sgt	Ernest Alfred	F	1505	31 May 1917	Arras Memorial
DAVIDSON	Pte	John E		5910	18 Sep 1916	Euston Road Cemetery
DAVIES	Pte	Charles	F	1289	21 Mar 1916	Etaples Military Cemetery
DAVIES	Pte	Clement Hugh	G	86328	11 Dec 1917	Lebucquiere Communal Cemetery Ext
DAVIES	L/Cpl	Daniel	G	42650		
DAVIES	Pte	David	G	2743	28 Apr 1917	Arras Memorial
DAVIES	Pte	Sydney Ernest	G	87058		
DAVIES	Pte	William E.	G	44036	13 Nov 1916	Mailly Wood Cemetery
DAVIES	Pte	William Ernest	F	607	27 Sep 1918	La Targette British Cemetery
DAVIES	Pte	William Victor	F	1169	28 Apr 1917	Arras Memorial
DAVIS	Pte	Benjamin Isaac	F	673		
DAVIS	Pte	Charles Henry	G	87075		
DAVIS	Pte	George William	G	18606	9 Dec 1917	Etaples Military Cemetery
DAVIS	Cpl	James	G	27477		
DAVIS	Pte	John James	F	980	8 Aug 1916	Thiepval Memorial
DAVIS	Pte	John	F	1211		
DAVIS	Pte	Leonard	G	11464		
DAVIS	Pte	Samuel George	F	295		
DAVIS	Pte	Thomas William	TF	203041	28 Apr 1917	Arras Memorial
DAVIS	Pte	William Marshall	PW	5761	10 Aug 1917	Ypres (Menin Gate) Memorial (Belgium)
DAWKINS	Pte	Arthur	G	9831	8 Aug 1916	Thiepval Memorial
DAWKINS	Pte	Arthur Edward	G	43559	13 Nov 1916	Thiepval Memorial
DAWSON	Pte	Walter A	G	51009		
DAY	Sgt	Charles J		10241		
DAY	Pte	David Benjamin	G	43596		
DAY	Pte	Edward	F	834		
DAY	L/Cpl	Thomas John	F	146		
DEADMAN	L/Cpl	Alfred Charles	G	9684		
DEADMAN	Pte	Alfred Joseph	F	1096	1 Aug 1916	Quarry Cemetery, Montauban
DEAN	Pte	Thomas Henry	F	1377		
DEAN	Pte	Henry	F	455	14 Nov 1916	Forceville Communal Cemetery and Ext.
DEARMAN	Pte	John Alfred	F	101		
DEAVILLE	Cpl	Leslie Joseph James	F	501		
DEE	Pte	Richard W	F	690		
DEESON	Cpl	Fred William	TF	204646		
DELLER	Pte	Charles	PW	6441		
DENHAM	Sgt	Alfred Stewart	G	7525		
DENHAM	Pte	Frederick Cyril	F	1568		
DENN	Pte	William Henry	F	1058	26 Sep 1916	Thiepval Memorial
DENNIS	Pte	Robert	F	1267		
DENNIS	Cpl	Victor George	L	15847	30 Aug 1918	Shrine Cemetery
DENNY	Pte	Ernest	G	43852		
DENTON	Pte	Reginald Gordon	PS	1453	3 Jan 1918	Arras Memorial
DERISLEY	L/Cpl	Herbert	F	28	1 Jun 1916	Cabaret-Rouge British Cemetery
DERMOTT	Pte	Walter	PS	2312		
DETTMER	Pte	Arthur Edwin	G	43691		
DEVERELL	Pte	Arthur Henry	G	20132		
DEWEY	Pte	Percy	G	26965		

Surname	Rank	Forenames	Prefix	Number	Date of Death	Cemetery/Memorial
DEXTER	Pte	Charles	F	15	27 Jun 1917	Derby (Nottingham Road) Cemetery (UK)
DICK	2/Lt	Norman Brabazon			28 Apr 1917	Arras Memorial
DICKSON	Pte	William Hare	G	89009		
DIGGON	Pte	Harold Rose	G	27445	25 Mar 1918	Arras Memorial
DILLNUTT	Pte	William Charles	F	256		
DIMMICK	Pte	Sidney	F	1429		
DINES	Pte	William George	G	34218		
DIPROSE	Pte	Reginald	G	7679		
DISS	Pte	Stanley A.	G	43972	23 Mar 1918	Vaulx Hill Cemetery
DIVERS	Pte	William	PW	5916		
DIXON	Pte	Fred	G	34189		
DIXON	Pte	John Hainsworth	PS	1428	30 Jul 1916	Heilly Station Cemetery
DOBSON	Pte	Edward	F	507		
DODDS	Pte	John Thirlwell	F	1466		
DODSON	Pte	Ralph George	F	1172	12 Aug 1917	Artillery Wood Cemetery (Belgium)
DODSON	Pte	William Robert	G	40875		
DOHERTY	Pte	George	G	9874		
DORAN	Cpl	John	F	706		
DORE	Pte	Warren Keith	G	87074	28 Dec 1917	Hermies Hill British Cemetery
DOUGLAS	Pte	Frederick	F	809		
DOUGLAS	Pte	George Edward	F	1895		
DOUGLAS	Sgt	William	F	832		
DOWDESWELL	Pte	Thomas Albert	F	1182		
DOWLING	Pte	Harry	G	34219		
DOWNEY	Pte	William Benjamin	F	1083	17 Feb 1917	Regina Trench Cemetery
DOWSETT	Cpl	Daniel William	F	1478	31 May 1916	Cabaret-Rouge British Cemetery
DOXSEY	Pte	Albert Lawrence	F	3228	13 Nov 1916	Serre Road No. 1
DRACKETT	L/Cpl	William	L	15142	9 Jun 1917	Niederzwehren Cemetery (Germany)
DRAGE	Pte	William	G	44151		
DRAIN	Pte	Alfred George	G	34043	24 Mar 1918	Arras Memorial
DRAKE	Pte	Alexander	F	165		
DRAKE	Cpl	Thomas G	F	149		
DRANE	Pte	Robert H	F	1497		
DRAPER	Sgt	Harold	PS	1506		
DREW	Pte	Walter	G	44105		
DRIVER	Pte	James	G	15153		
DRURY	Pte	Arthur	G	24865		
DRURY	CSM	Albert Edward	F	339	15 Nov 1916	Varennes Military Cemetery
DUBERRY	Pte	F				
DUBERY	Pte	Charles William	G	50429		
DUCKETT	Pte	William Thomas	F	577	12 Aug 1917	Gorre British and Indian Cemetery
DUDLEY	Pte	Charles	G	94040		
DUFFELL	Pte	James William	F	1123		
DUFFILL	Pte	Thomas William	G	32789		
DUKER	Pte	Archibald	F	1054	13 Nov 1916	Thiepval Memorial
DUMAN	2/Lt	CN				
DUNCAN	2/Lt	Arthur Seymour			9 Apr 1918	Le Grand Beaumart, British Cemetery
DUNLOP	Pte	Alexander	F	1649		
DUNN	Pte	Arthur Charles	G	44047	13 Nov 1916	Thiepval Memorial
DUNN	Pte	Horace Norman	G	42651		
DUNN	Pte	James	G	6205		
DUNN	Pte	John	F	64		
DUNN	Pte	Richard George	F	469		
DUNNETT	Pte	John T	F	423	11 May 1917	Duisans British Cemetery
DUNTON	2/Lt	Samuel Harry				
DURRANT	Pte	Ezekiel	F	1397	9 Aug 1916	Thiepval Memorial
DURSTON	Pte	Frederick John	F	11		
DYER	Pte	Albert Edward	G	34282		
DYER	Pte	Charles Henry	G	12		
DYER	Pte	Edward	G	26507		
EADY	Pte	William Thomas	PW	5954	17 Apr 1917	Monchy British Cemetery
EADY	Pte	Harold	G	34003	28 Apr 1917	Arras Memorial
EAGAR	Pte	Horace William	F	3298		
EARL	Pte	Herbert Arthur	F	218		
EARLES	Pte	Thomas George	G	43907	13 Nov 1916	Serre Road No.2
EARWICKER	Sgt	Charles Edward Lovell	G	4966		

Surname	Rank	Forenames	Prefix	Number	Date of Death	Cemetery/Memorial
EASTAUGH	Pte	Albert Edward	PS	3658	11 Apr 1917	Boulogne Eastern Cemetery
EASTAUGH	Pte	Henry	G	34220		
EASTER	Pte	James	G	21300		
EASTERFORD	Pte	Alfred Allen	TF	203901	2 Dec 1917	Cambrai Memorial
EASTMAN	Sgt	Charles	G	57032		
EASTMAN	Sgt	Clement	S	7794	26 Mar 1918	Etaples Military Cemetery
EASTMEAD	Pte	Stanley James	G	50424		
EASTWOOD	Pte	Frederick John	F	1357	8 Aug 1916	Thiepval Memorial
EATON	Pte	Henry Frederick	F	1264		
EATON	Pte	William Whitmore	G	20148		
ECAILLE	Pte	Frederick James Eugene	G	26309	4 Jan 1918	Rocquigny-Equancourt Road British Cemetery
EDDIES	Pte	Alfred	G	86302	25 May 1918	Pernes British Cemetery
EDE	Pte	Henry C	F	1179		
EDIS	Pte	Arthur Henry	PW	5484	24 Aug 1918	Vis-en-Artois Memorial
EDMUNDS	Pte	Harold	G	43896		
EDWARDS	Cpl	Alfred	F	1379	4 Nov 1918	Villers-Pol Communal Cemetery Ext
EDWARDS	Pte	FH	F	815		
EDWARDS	Pte	Hubert George	G	34101		
EDWARDS	Pte	James H	F	565		
EDWARDS	Pte	John Bennett	F	641		
EDWARDS	L/Cpl	John Rees	G	2913	28 Apr 1917	Arras Memorial
EDWARDS	Pte	Leonard	F	3111		
EDWARDS	Pte	Mark	G	44122	9 Feb 1917	Niederzwehren Cemetery (Germany)
EDWARDS	Maj	Percival George				
EELES	Pte	William	F	257		
EGGERTON	Pte	John	PW	6400		
ELDRIDGE	Pte	Fred Leonard	PS	3616		
ELDRIDGE	Sgt	Arthur	G	579	3 Jan 1918	Ribecourt Road Cemetery
ELLEN	Pte	James William	F	817		
ELLINGHAM	Cpl	Ernest	G	15204	3 Jan 1918	Arras Memorial
ELLIOTT	Lt	Arthur Foord				
ELLIOTT	Sgt	Charles	F	1000	29 Jul 1916	Thiepval Memorial
ELLIOTT	Pte	Charlie	F	102		
ELLIOTT	L/Cpl	George	F	151		
ELLIOTT	2/Lt	Leslie Grant				
ELLIS	Pte	Alfred John Roland	G	44106		
ELLIS	Pte	Arnold	G	12202	8 Aug 1916	Delville Wood Cemetery
ELLIS	Sgt	Ernest Broad	G	6723		
ELLIS	Sgt	Frederick George Henry	G	43885		
ELLIS	Pte	Frederick William	G	44000		
ELLIS	Pte	Sidney George	G	33134	9 Dec 1917	Arras Memorial
ELMER	Pte	Chris	G	34221		
ELPHINSTONE	Capt	Alexander				
EMBERSON	Pte	James Walter	G	14095		
EMBERSON	Pte	Mark	G	34190		
EMERY	Sgt	Alfred John	L	10005		
EMERY	Pte	Samuel Lewis	G	9576		
EMSDEN	Pte	Gershom James	G	87374	11 Dec 1917	Arras Memorial
ENGLAND	Pte	Thomas James	L	21184		
ENGLAND	Pte	William Alfred	G	6719	13 Nov 1916	Thiepval Memorial
ENGLEBURTT	2/Lt	John Francis				
EVANS	Pte	Albert Edward	G	43635		
EVANS	Pte	Archibald George	G	26308	28 Apr 1917	Arras Memorial
EVANS	Lt	Bernard			8 Apr 1917	Ontario Cem, Sains-Les-Marquion
EVANS	Lt	E Dudley				
EVANS	Pte	Emile	G	22785		
EVANS	Pte	Henry Fred	G	29274		
EVANS	Cpl	Nolan	F	29		
EVANS	Pte	Thomas	F	1194		
EVANS	Pte	Thomas	F	2740	7 Jun 1917	Arras Memorial
EVE	Pte	Arthur	G	34222	28 Apr 1917	Arras Memorial
EVERETT	Pte	Fred	G	34147		
EVERETT	Pte	Frederick George	G	34401	27 Dec 1917	Hermies Hill British Cemetery
EVERETT	L/Cpl	Harry James George	F	523		
EVERETT	Sgt	Samuel	G	34341	28 Apr 1917	Arras Memorial

Surname	Rank	Forenames	Prefix	Number	Date of Death	Cemetery/Memorial
EXLEY	CSM	Richard	G	14324		
FAIRHALL	Pte	Charles Elsey	F	1318		
FALCONER	Pte	William Joseph	F	598		
FARAWAY	Pte	Charles	G	34345		
FARMER	Pte	Ernest William	G	34450	28 Apr 1917	Arras Memorial
FARMSARY	Pte	Thomas Henry	F	1100		
FARNFIELD	Pte	Harry	G	2621		
FARR	Pte	Hedley	G	20105	8 Aug 1916	Thiepval Memorial
FARRANT	Cpl	Archie Raymond	G	34102	15 Nov 1919	Hornchurch (St Andrew) Churchyard (UK)
FARRELL	Pte	Percy George Croxbye	F	1702		
FARROW	Sgt	Albert James	PW	6859	14 Apr 1918	Tyne Cot Memorial (Belgium)
FARROW	Pte	Richard Ronald Frank	G	25574		
FATHERS	Pte	Joseph Arnold	F	3219	8 Aug 1916	Thiepval Memorial
FAULKNER	Pte	Fred	TF	205166		
FAULKNER	Pte	Charles John	G	87010	4 Dec 1917	Tincourt New British Cemetery
FEARY	Pte	Fred John	PW	6384		
FEATHERS	Pte	Albert James	F	1052		
FEATHERSTONE	Pte	Edward George	F	1153	23 Jun 1916	Bailleul Communal Cemetery Ext.
FELSTEAD	Pte	Albert	G	34285		
FELTON	Lt	Richard				
FENSON	L/Cpl	Charles R	F	792		
FENWICK	Pte	George	F	1454		
FENWICK	Col	Henry Thomas				
FERRIS	Pte	Frederick	F	940		
FICKLING	Pte	Albert Ernest	G	9858		
FIDLER	Pte	Joseph Edward (Joe)	F	296		
FIELD	Sgt	Herbert James	F	1285		
FIELD	Pte	John W	F	166		
FIELD	Pte	Sydney J	G	43612	13 Nov 1918	Etaples Military Cemetery
FILTNESS	Pte	Alfred	G	34045		
FINCH	Pte	Harry William	G	23399		
FINCH	Pte	Robert William	G	34223	10 Oct 1918	Beaulencourt British Cemetery
FINCH	Pte	Theophilus	G	34105	31 Jan 1917	Contay British Cemetery
FINDLEY	Pte	William Thomas	TF	203365		
FINLAY	Pte	B	TF			
FISH	Pte	George William	G	19405		
FISHER	Pte	Albert Edward	F	797	18 Sep 1916	Euston Road Cemetery
FISHER	L/Cpl	Arthur	F	341		
FISHER	Pte	George Alfred	G	34182		
FISHER	Pte	Herbert	G	34346	17 Feb 1917	Regina Trench Cemetery
FISHER	Pte	Joseph Templeton	G	34224		
FISHER	L/Cpl	Thomas	F	599		
FLANAGAN	Pte	James	F	880	29 Jul 1916	Delville Wood Cemetery
FLANDERS	Sgt	Harry Cecil	G	34287		
FLANNERY	Pte	Thomas	F	790		
FLEMING	L/Sgt	James	G	41666	1 Dec 1917	Cambrai Memorial
FLETCHER	Pte	Frank	PW	5472		
FLETCHER	Pte	Richard William Roby	F	849	30 Jul 1916	Corbie Communal Cemetery Ext.
FLEXEN	Pte	Ernest William	PS	2595		
FLINT	2/Lt	Charles	F	575		
FLINT	Pte	Fred Percy Francis	G	34225		
FLORENCE	Pte	John	G	87057		
FLOWERS	Pte	John	G	41639		
FLOWERS	Pte	Philip James	PW	6415		
FLYNN	Sgt	J				
FLYNN	Pte	James Joseph	F	1087		
FOARD	Pte	Ernest	G	44127		
FOGARTY	Pte	Arthur	G	2594		
FOGDEN	Pte	Edward James	F	1327		
FOLLETT	Pte	Edward	F	1250	31 Jul 1917	Ypres (Menin Gate) Memorial (Belgium)
FOORD	Pte	Edward John	F	30		
FOOT	Pte	Ernest James	PW	5403	10 Oct 1917	Tyne Cot Memorial (Belgium)
FOOT	Sgt	Joseph Edward	F	545		
FORD	Sgt	Daniel Joseph	F	449		
FORD	Pte	George Edward	F	45		

Surname	Rank	Forenames	Prefix	Number	Date of Death	Cemetery/Memorial
FORD	Pte	John Charles	F	784		
FORD	Sgt	Walter Edward	L	10805		
FORESTER	Pte	Ernest	F	773		
FORT	Pte	Fred	G	24498		
FOSTER	Sgt	Alfred Thomas	PS	3495		
FOSTER	Pte	Allen	F	297	8 Aug 1916	Corbie Communal Cemetery Ext.
FOSTER	Pte	Edward	G	42652		
FOSTER	Pte	Ernest J	G	50728		
FOSTER	Pte	James	F	1367		
FOSTER	Pte	John	G	34883	23 Apr 1917	Heninel-Croisilles Road Cemetery
FOUNTAIN	Pte	Herbert John	G	43990	17 Dec 1918	Benwick Cemetery (UK)
FOWLER	Pte	Albert John	G	34004		
FOWLER	Pte	David Henry	F	1004		
FOWLER	2/Lt	Gordon Henry Ashton				
FOWLER	Pte	John	G	6791	3 May 1917	Arras Memorial
FOX	Pte	Alfred	G	27965	20 Sep 1918	Villers Hill British Cemetery
FOX	Pte	John	G	87501		
FOX	Pte	Leslie	S	6435		
FOX	Pte	Sydney James Fox	G	41668		
FOXCROFT-JONES	Capt	Robert Evan				
FRANCIS	Pte	Eric Stanley	F	1410	9 Jun 1917	Etaples Military Cemetery
FRANCIS	2/Lt	Ernest John				
FRANCIS	Pte	Frederick	G	11597		
FRANCIS	Pte	Guy	G	1874		
FRANCIS	Pte	Samuel	F	1401		
FRANKLIN	Pte	Herbert	PS	2218		
FRANKLIN	Pte	Oscar	G	12545	8 Aug 1916	Thiepval Memorial
FRANKLIN	Pte	William	F	342		
FRAPWELL	Pte	Harry Charles	F	1295	26 Sep 1916	Thiepval Memorial
FRASER	L/Cpl	Edgar Harold	F	1161		
FREE	Pte	Ernest Alfred	L	14011		
FREE	Pte	Salvo Clifford	G	34044		
FREEMAN	Pte	Arthur John	G	44091	23 Apr 1917	Chili Trench Cemetery
FREEMAN	Pte	William Henry	G	86920		
FREEMAN	Pte	William	F	759	25 Jul 1916	Carnoy Military Cemetery
FRESHWATER	Pte	George Henry	G	33083		
FRETTER	Pte	Albert	F	1480		
FRETTER	Cpl	Charles F	F	1261		
FREWIN	Pte	George William	F	103		
FRISBY	Pte	Walter	G	43931		
FRITH	Pte	Robert William	F	65		
FRITZ	Pte	Albert Edward	F	816		
FROST	Pte	Bertie Stockwell	F	855		
FROST	Pte	John	G	34764		
FROST	Pte	Reuben	TF	202135	3 May 1917	Arras Memorial
FROST	Cpl	Sidney	G	34402		
FROST	Pte	Thomas	F	1338	29 Sep 1918	Villers Hill British Cemetery
FROST	L/Cpl	Edward Morgan	F	808	26 Apr 1915	Woodgrange Park Cemetery (UK)
FULLER	Pte	Albert George	G	34405		
FULLER	Pte	Alfred	F	3171		
FULLER	Pte	Alfred Peter	F	644		
FULLER	2/Lt	EA				
FULLER	Pte	Fred Henry	PW	5866	20 Nov 1917	Potijze Chateau Grounds Cemetery (Belgium)
FULLER	Pte	Frederick	F	1625		
FULLER	Pte	Reuben	G	34103		
FULLER	Pte	William George	G	34344		
FUNNELL	Pte	Percy William	TF	242764		
FURLONG	L/Cpl	Percival James	F	273	13 Nov 1916	Thiepval Memorial
FURNEAUX	L/Cpl	Philip	F	794	28 Apr 1917	Arras Memorial
FURNER	Cpl	William	L	12108	27 May 1918	Soissons Memorial
FURNESS	Pte	Frederick	F	1562		
FURYER	Pte	Ernest George	PW	5044		
FUTER	Sgt	Thomas March	G	692		
GAGE	Pte	George	G	34226		
GAINSFORD	Pte	Percy George	G	10812		

Surname	Rank	Forenames	Prefix	Number	Date of Death	Cemetery/Memorial
GALE	Pte	William	F	658		
GALLACHER	Pte	Hugh	F			
GALLACHER	L/Cpl	Patrick	F	298		
GALLEY	2/Lt	William James	F	2771		
GALPIN	Pte	Albert Victor	G	43650		
GAMMAGE	Pte	Walter Edward	G	34523		
GAMMON	Sgt	Jack	F	1262		
GANDY	Pte	Peter	F	539		
GANN	2/Lt	Claude George				
GARATY	Pte	Ernest	G	34289		
GARBETT	Pte	Joseph Arthur	TF	207946		
GARDINER	Pte	Frederick	G	34412	6 May 1917	Etaples Military Cemetery
GARDINER	L/Cpl	J				
GARDINER	Pte	John Frederick	F	672		
GARDINER	Pte	Sydney Ernest	F	1457		
GARDINER	Pte	Thomas	PW	2858	10 Oct 1918	Etaples Military Cemetery
GARDNER	Pte	Frederick James	F	167		
GARDNER	Pte	Frederick Stephen	F	85		
GARDNER	Pte	George Russell	G	92833		
GARDNER	Sgt	Gerald Francis Claude	F	1164		
GARDNER	Pte	Stephen Harold	TF	203888	2 Dec 1917	Cambrai Memorial
GARNELL	Pte	Robert Edward	G	2264		
GARNER	Pte	Sidney John	G	43613		
GARNSEY	Pte	Sidney	F	3210	27 Jul 1916	A.I.F. Burial Ground
GARRETT	Pte	Bert Lewis	G	43164		
GARRETT	Cpl	Ernest Albert	G	34048	28 Apr 1917	Arras Memorial
GARRETT	Pte	William Thomas	G	20688		
GARROD	Pte	Arthur	F	525		
GARROD	Pte	George Thomas	L	12359		
GARTON	Pte	Frederick Jones	G	78730		
GARVEY	Pte	Thomas	G	33268	30 Nov 1917	Cambrai Memorial
GATHERCOLE	Pte	George Mansfield	G	24421	31 Aug 1916	Puchevillers British Cemetery
GAUL		W	F			
GAUNT	Pte	Edward	PW	5061		
GAYLOR	Sgt	Alex Victor	G	34351		
GAYLOR	Pte	Norman Herbert	G	34409		
GAZE	Pte	Charles	G	8825		
GEARY	Pte	Alfred	PS	2819		
GEDDES	Pte	David	G	43926		
GEE	Pte	John	F	1609		
GEE	L/Cpl	W	G	86304		
GERRISH	L/Cpl	Walter Herbert	G	42654		
GERRISH	Pte	William Webber	F	936	8 Aug 1916	Thiepval Memorial
GIBBENS	Sgt	William	G	1922		
GIBBS	Pte	Robert Henry	G	42633		
GIBBS	Pte	Ernest Yeoman	F	3254	11 Aug 1916	St. Souplet British Cemetery
GIBSON	Sgt	Henry	F	26		
GIBSON	Pte	Joseph	F	119		
GIBSON	2/Lt	Percy Montague	F	3756	6 Sep 1918	Heilly Station Cemetery
GIBSON	CSM	Thomas	F	287		
GIBSON	Pte	Thomas James	G	42653		
GIFFEN	Pte	George	TF	266914		
GIFFEN	Pte	Percy Albert	PS	2257		
GILBERT	Pte	Fred William	S	7608		
GILBOY		Bertram T	F			
GILES	Pte	Alfred Thomas	TF	205134		
GILES	Pte	Harry	F	1150	29 Oct 1918	Hautmont Communal Cemetery
GILES	Pte	Stewart	F	854	27 Jul 1916	Thiepval Memorial
GILFILLAN	Pte	George Leach	G	34407		
GILL	Cpl	Ernest	F	132		
GILL	L/Cpl	Thomas E	G	50421		
GILLETT	Pte	Frederick L	G	87517		
GILLETT	Pte	William Hamilton	G	43645		
GILLHAM	Pte	James Alfred	TF	203855		
GILLHAM	Pte	Thomas	G	86615	1 Dec 1917	Cambrai Memorial
GILLING	Pte	Albert Edward	F	258		
GILMORE	Sgt	Edward B	L	12711		

Surname	Rank	Forenames	Prefix	Number	Date of Death	Cemetery/Memorial
GIRDWOOD		David	F			
GISBY	Pte	Harold Victor	F	1580	23 Jul 1919	Kelvedon (St Mary) Churchyard Ext. (UK)
GLANFIELD	Pte	George	G	24419	26 Jul 1917	Gorre British and Indian Cemetery
GLENIE	Sgt	William	L	9107		
GLOVER	Pte	Edward John	F	1218		
GLYNN	Pte	Arthur	G	14472		
GODDARD	Pte	Albert Charles	F	344		
GODDARD	Pte	William	F	237	8 Aug 1916	Thiepval Memorial
GODDARD	L/Cpl	William James	G	43680	28 Apr 1917	Arras Memorial
GODERSON	Pte	Frederick	G	50759		
GODFREY	Pte	Ernest	G	43560		
GODMAN	Pte	Arthur James	G	34107		
GODWIN	Pte	Ernest	G	11473		
GODWIN	L/Cpl	Leonard Gerald	F	1106		
GOFBERRY	Pte	Harold	F	2057	1 Aug 1916	Abbeville Communal Cemetery
GOLBORN	Pte	William J	F	916		
GOLDHAWK	Pte	Harry	F	2723		
GOLDMAN	L/Cpl	Joseph	G	14548	13 Nov 1916	Thiepval Memorial
GOLDSMITH	Pte	Sidney	G	33464		
GOLDSTEIN	Pte	M	G			
GOLDTHORPE	Pte	Joe	F	1184		
GOOD	Pte	Charles Isaac	F	1180		
GOODBODY	Pte	Albert	F	635		
GOODCHILD	2/Lt	Joseph E				
GOODCHILD	Pte	William	G	9385		
GOODING	Pte	Charles	G	7535		
GOODING	Pte	Cyril Victor	F	701		
GOODLAKE	Pte	Walter William	G	44161		
GOODMAN	Pte	Joseph	G	14548		
GOODMAN	Pte	Walter	G	34228	22 Apr 1917	Walthamstow (Queen's Road) Cemetery (UK)
GOODWIN	L/Cpl	Frederick	F			
GORDON	Pte	William Alex	TF	203045		
GORMER	Pte	James	G	34348	21 Feb 1917	Thiepval Memorial
GOULD	Pte	WE	F	1691		
GOULD	Pte	William Charles	G	34291		
GOULD	Cpl	Alfred	F	3467		
GOULDING	Pte	Edward Charles	F	1452		
GOULDING	Pte	John	F	186		
GOVER	L/Cpl	William	F	578	15 Oct 1915	Vermelles British Cemetery
GOVETT	2/Lt	Horace Edward				
GOWALD	Pte	William	PW	5905		
GOWER	Pte	Charles		2311		
GRAINGER	Pte	Reginald	F	1407		
GRAINGER	Pte	William Arthur	F	388		
GRANT	L/Cpl	Charles Thomas	F	1351		
GRANT	Pte	George	G	34559		
GRANT	Pte	George Edward	G	34050	15 Nov 1918	Berlin South-Western Cemetery (Germany)
GRANTHAM	Col	Charles Fulford				
GRAY	Pte	Alfred Edmund	F	238		
GRAY	Pte	Arthur	G	26362		
GRAY	Pte	Charles Andrew	F	468		
GRAY	Cpl	David	F	300		
GRAY	Pte	Frederick Charles	F	152		
GRAY	Pte	Joseph	TF	242797	26 Mar 1918	Arras Memorial
GRAY	Pte	William John	PS	3627		
GRAYLIN	L/Cpl	William James	G	42358	3 Dec 1917	Cambrai Memorial
GREATOREX	Pte	George	F	86		
GREEN	Pte	Albert	G	44119		
GREEN	Pte	Albert Edward	G	34350		
GREEN	Pte	Albert Victor	L	13706		
GREEN	Pte	Alfred		19310		
GREEN	Pte	Charles Edward	TF	203188	28 Apr 1917	Arras Memorial
GREEN	Pte	Charles William	G	22038	22 Mar 1918	Arras Memorial
GREEN	Pte	E				

Surname	Rank	Forenames	Prefix	Number	Date of Death	Cemetery/Memorial
GREEN	Pte	George	G	43866		
GREEN	Pte	Hayden (Adrian)	F	541		
GREEN	Pte	HE				
GREEN	Pte	James	TF	241326	12 Oct 1918	Romeries Communal Cemetery Ext.
GREEN	Pte	John Stuart	G	50723		
GREEN	Pte	Joseph William	TF	203188		
GREEN	Pte	Stanley Arthur	F	1140		
GREEN	Pte	Walter Thomas	G	34408		
GREENWOOD	L/Cpl	Charles L	G	43646	28 Apr 1917	Arras Memorial
GREENWOOD	Pte	James Edward Samuel	G	13305		
GREENWOOD	Cpl	Thomas	G	92834		
GREER	Pte	Henry Arthur	TF	207945	5 Nov 1918	Swindon (Radnor St) Cemetery (UK)
GREETHAM	Pte	Bernard	PS	2044		
GREETHAM	Pte	Leonard Charles	G	86454		
GREGORY	Capt	Frank				
GREGORY	Pte	John	F	67		
GREGORY	Pte	Joseph Anthony	F	440		
GREGORY	Pte	Walter	G	34411		
GREGSON	Cpl	Alfred Edmund	F	912		
GREY-MACKSEY	Lt	J				
GRICE	Pte	William Edward	TF	203048		
GRIEF	Pte	John Edward	G	44017		
GRIFFEN	Pte	Albert E	F	1336		
GRIFFITHS	Pte	Frank	G	43657	28 Apr 1917	Arras Memorial
GRIFFITHS	Pte	John	G	92836	29 Nov 1917	Lebucquiere Communal Cemetery Ext
GRIGG	Pte	A				
GRIGGS	Pte	Bert	PW	5386		
GRIMMITT	Pte	Josiah	F	1961		
GRIMSEY	Pte	Charles	G	43562		
GRIMWOOD	Pte	Arthur George	G	20951		
GRINHAM	Pte	George Stanford	PS	2621	4 Jul 1916	Zouave Valley Cemetery
GROHMANN	Sgt	Harold Ernest	G	18359		
GROMM	Pte	Leopold Joseph	G	36603		
GROOM	Pte	George Alfred	TF	203049		
GROUND	Pte	Stanley Ernest	G	43718		
GROVER	Pte	Reginald	G	12277	8 Aug 1916	Thiepval Memorial
GROVES	Pte	Albert	F	1443		
GROVES	Pte	Fred Alfred	G	34352		
GRUBB	Pte	John England	TF	207948	1 Dec 1917	Cambrai Memorial
GUEST	2/Lt	John Aloysius			27 Jul 1916	Thiepval Memorial
GULLIVER	Pte	John	G	44134		
GUNDRY	Pte	Harold Herbert	F	389	28 Jul 1916	Thiepval Memorial
GUNN	Pte	George William	F	3129		
GUNNING	Pte	John	G	92837		
GURR	Pte	Albert	G	89562		
HACKETT	Pte	Stephen	G	44156		
HACKETT	Pte	Walter	F	2144		
HADLER	Pte	Frederick Harry	PS	2411		
HAGERTY	Pte	James Edward	F	274		
HAGGART	Cpl	Alexander	G	90727		
HAGGERTY	Pte	Joseph Peter	F	153		
HAILSTONE	Pte	Louis	G	34110		
HAINSBY	Pte	Arthur	F	1278		
HALGATE	Pte	Joseph	G	73919		
HALL	Pte	Charles H		3434		
HALL	Pte	George Frederick	F	1516		
HALL	Pte	Henry Arthur	F	1692	5 Oct 1916	Thiepval Memorial
HALLAM	Pte	William R	F	932		
HALSE	L/Cpl	George F	G	15273		
HAM	Pte	Bertie	G	92838		
HAMILTON	Pte	Robert Ernest	TF	203051	10 Oct 1918	St. Aubert British Cemetery
HAMILTON		Sidney	F			
HAMILTON	Pte	SJ	G	1445		
HAMMON	Pte	Herbert Brockfield	G	34292		
HAMMOND	Pte	Henry John	F	3104		
HAMMOND	Cpl	Sidney	G	50743		
HAMMOND	Pte	William Francis Edwin	F	711	8 Aug 1916	Thiepval Memorial

Surname	Rank	Forenames	Prefix	Number	Date of Death	Cemetery/Memorial
HAMPSON	Pte	Harry	F	1817		
HAND	Pte	Lawrence	F	1469	18 Jun 1917	Hazebrouck Communal Cemetery
HANKINS	Pte	William Alfred	L	8186	28 Apr 1917	Arras Memorial
HANNEY	Sgt	Terence Percival	F	1613		
HANSON	Pte	Ben	F	1081	28 Jul 1916	Thiepval Memorial
HARAGAN	Pte	Alfred Frederick	F	857		
HARBOURN	CSM	Henry William	F	822		
HARDING	Pte	Arthur Percy	F	1075		
HARDING	Pte	Robert Joseph	F	976	29 Jan 1916	Chocques Military Cemetery
HARDMAN	2/Lt	CW				
HARDOUIN	Pte	Victor Cyril	G	50729	30 Apr 1917	Aubigny Communal Cemetery Ext.
HARDY	L/Cpl	Arthur James	G	43858	3 Feb 1918	Rocquigny-Equancourt Road British Cemetery
HARDS	Pte	Harold	F	1432		
HARE	Pte	George	G	12601		
HARE	Cpl	William H	F	1414		
HARGREAVES	Pte	Richard Allan	F	1620		
HARMAN	Pte	Charles Edward	PS	2442		
HARMAN	Pte	John	PW	6278	26 Apr 1917	Etaples Military Cemetery
HARMAN	Pte	John William	G	27325		
HARPAM	Pte	George	G	15780		
HARPER	Pte	Ernest	F	618		
HARPER	Pte	John	G	11229		
HARRESTON	Pte	Fred	PW	5867		
HARRINGTON	Pte	Sidney	TF	203187		
HARRINGTON	Pte	Harry	G	34231	28 Apr 1917	Arras Memorial
HARRIS	Pte	A				
HARRIS	Pte	Charles James	PW	6258		
HARRIS	Pte	Charles Leonard	G	43706	30 Nov 1917	Cambrai Memorial
HARRIS	Cpl	Frederick John	G	10033		
HARRIS	Pte	George James William	G	28150		
HARRIS	Sgt	J	F	76		
HARRIS	Pte	Leon	F	1363		
HARRIS	Sgt	Mark Henry	F	1135		
HARRIS	Pte	Stanley George	G	34076		
HARRISON	Pte	Edward	G	34775		
HARRISON	Pte	Edward	F	1269		
HARRISON	Pte	Herbert Phillips	PS	3195		
HARROBIN	Pte	James Alfred	F	1361		
HARROLD		Patrick	F			
HARROLD	Pte	Henry George	F	240	28 Jul 1916	Thiepval Memorial
HART	Pte	Frederick	F	1563	23 Oct 1918	Le Cateau Communal Cemetery
HART	Pte	Thomas	F	574		
HART	Cpl	William Henry	PW	4974		
HARTLEY	Pte	Ernest	F	571	27 Jan 1916	Guards Cemetery, Windy Corner
HARTY	Pte	Finibar P	G	43564	28 Apr 1917	Arras Memorial
HARVEY	Pte	Christopher A		5868		
HARVEY	Pte	Harry	F	871		
HARVEY	Pte	Leonard	F	1187		
HASNIP	Pte	Albert Conrad	G	44114		
HASSELWOOD	Pte	William	G	87077	12 Apr 1918	Duhallow A.D.S. Cemetery (Belgium)
HATHAWAY	Sgt	Edgar	G	50722		
HATTON	Pte	George	F	214		
HAWES	Pte	William	G	24435		
HAWKES	Pte	Sidney	G	44095		
HAWKINS	Pte	Arthur	G	43701		
HAWKINS	Pte	Charles	G	44051	13 Nov 1916	Thiepval Memorial
HAWKINS	Sgt	Frederick William	F	1254		
HAWKINS	Pte	John Frank Cyril	G	43565		
HAWKINS	Pte	Lionel Frank	G	12281	17 Sep 1916	Thiepval Memorial
HAY	Maj	CR				
HAY	2/Lt	Douglas Woulfe			29 Sep 1918	Villers Hill British Cemetery
HAY	Pte	Thomas Arthur	F	1594		
HAYDEN	Pte	Richard	F	392		
HAYDON	Pte	Edwin John	G	22122	23 Apr 1917	Orchard Dump Cemetery
HAYES	Pte	John Robert	F	2463	26 Sep 1916	Suzanne Military Cemetery No. 3
HAYES	Sgt	Thomas Henry	F	860	23 Nov 1917	Charlton Cemetery, Greenwich (UK)

Surname	Rank	Forenames	Prefix	Number	Date of Death	Cemetery/Memorial
HAYES	Sgt	William Dennis	L	13680	1 Dec 1917	Cambrai Memorial
HAYLES	Pte	Howard	G	43922	28 Apr 1917	Arras Memorial
HAYLETT	Pte	William	F	154		
HAYNES	Pte	Archibald	F	393		
HAYNES	2/Lt	George James			16 Jun 1918	Arras Memorial
HAYNES	Pte	William	F	595		
HAYWARD	Maj	Arthur Gracie				
HAYWARD	L/Cpl	Ben Thomas	F	1174	8 Aug 1916	Delville Wood Cemetery
HAZELWOOD	Pte	Alexander		27684		
HEAD	Pte	John	F	222		
HEADY	Pte	Richard William	G	94006		
HEALEY	Pte	Ernest Robert	G	34108		
HEALEY	Pte	Stephen Ernest	G	43690	13 Nov 1916	Thiepval Memorial
HEARN	Pte	Fred	G	13156		
HEDGER	Pte	Reginald Victor	F	979		
HEDGES	Pte	Stephen William	G	43600		
HELLER	Cpl	Thomas	F	770	28 Jul 1916	Thiepval Memorial
HEMBERGER	Pte	Franz Joseph	F	920	6 Aug 1916	Bernafay Wood British Cemetery
HEMBLEY	Pte	George William		15214		
HEMMINGS	Sgt	George Edward	L	6130		
HEMMINGS	Pte	Percy F	F	1544		
HEMMINGTON	Pte	Alfred Edward	G	32795		
HENDERSON	2/Lt	Alfred Roche			28 Apr 1917	Arras Memorial
HENDERSON	2/Lt	William Fraser			8 Aug 1916	Thiepval Memorial
HENDRIKS	Pte	George	PS	3290	8 Aug 1916	Thiepval Memorial
HENDRY	2/Lt	William			27 Jul 1916	Thiepval Memorial
HENNESSEY	Cpl	Daniel	G	40724		
HENNESSEY	Pte	Alfred James	F	1449	13 Nov 1916	Thiepval Memorial
HERBERT	Pte	James	L	16876		
HERBERT	Pte	Thomas Samuel	SR	7251	27 May 1918	Soissons Memorial
HERBERT	Cpl	William Stephen	F	768		
HERRING	Pte	Henry	G	43647		
HESLINGTON	L/Cpl	Gordon	F	2037	28 Apr 1917	Arras Memorial
HESTER	L/Sgt	Charles	G	5280	28 Apr 1917	Arras Memorial
HEWETT	Pte	George	F	624		
HEWETT	Cpl	Thomas C	F	961		
HEWING	Pte	WH	F			
HEWITT	L/Cpl	Albert James	F	863		
HEWITT	L/Cpl	Alexander	F	1138		
HEWITT	Pte	Augustus George	F	1610		
HEWITT	Pte	Thomas Charles	F	961		
HICKMAN	L/Sgt	Joseph J	F	3055		
HICKMAN	Pte	John Ernest	G	92839	2 Dec 1917	Hermies Hill British Cemetery
HIGGS	Pte	Charles		6294		
HIGGS	Pte	Walter Arthur	F	223		
HILDERLEY	Pte	Percy John	F	1134	08 Nov 1916	Thiepval Memorial
HILL	Pte	Frank	F	1837		
HILL	Pte	Frederick Thomas	G	42655		
HILL	Pte	Percy	G	92840		
HILL	Pte	Walter Edward	G	86802		
HILL	2/Lt	Sydney Arthur George				
HILLARD	Pte	James Fred	G	86608		
HILLIER	Pte	Henry	G	43886		
HILLMAN	Cpl	Henry	G	1416		
HILLS	Pte	George Arthur	G	98840		
HILLS	Pte	Thomas	G	10757		
HILLS	Pte	George Ernest	G	43717	13 Nov 1916	Serre Road No.2
HINCE	Pte	Alfred William	L	15563		
HIND	Pte	Horace	F	1365		
HINGE	Pte	Augustus John	F	2012	21 Jun 1916	Bordon Military Cemetery (UK)
HINTON	Pte	Albert Frederick Charles	F	969	7 Aug 1918	Niederzwehren Cemetery (Germany)
HISGROVE	Pte	Albert	F	845		
HISLOP	2/Lt	Percy Robert			7 Dec 1917	St. Sever Cemetery Ext.
HITCHEN	Pte	Raymond	PS	2640		
HITCHING	Pte	Benjamin P	G	44087	28 Apr 1917	Arras Memorial
HITCOX	Pte	Harold	F	71		
HOAD	Lt	Walter				

Surname	Rank	Forenames	Prefix	Number	Date of Death	Cemetery/Memorial
HOBBIS	Pte	Henry James	G	42656	5 Jan 1919	Les Baraques Military Cemetery
HODBY	Pte	William	TF	204488	26 Dec 1917	Hermies Hill British Cemetery
HODDER	Pte	Lionel W	F	774		
HODDER	Pte	Thomas	F	594		
HODGE	Pte	Horace Sidney	G	86512		
HODGES	Pte	Frederick	PS	2869		
HODSON	Pte	Alfred Thomas George	F	1103		
HOEY	Pte	John	F	1275		
HOGARTH	Pte	Henry	F	301		
HOGARTH	Sgt	John	G	9281		
HOGGER	Pte	Richard William	F	1362	5 May 1918	Berlin South-Western Cemetery (Germany)
HOGSFLESH	Pte	William	G	44120		
HOLBARD	Pte	Charles	G	17588	13 Nov 1916	Thiepval Memorial
HOLFORD	Pte	Thomas	G	10005		
HOLGATE	Pte	Joseph	G	73919		
HOLIDAY	Pte	William	TF	203052		
HOLLAND	Sgt	Alfred Budd	F	1302		
HOLLAND	Pte	Charles	F	3150		
HOLLAND	Pte	Frederick	G	21841	18 Sep 1916	Euston Road Cemetery
HOLLAND	Pte	Frederick Victor	F	699	31 Jan 1916	Bethune Town Cemetery
HOLLAND	Pte	William Francis	F	787		
HOLLETT	Pte	Alfred Harry	F	777		
HOLLIBRAND	Pte	Charles	G	87449		
HOLLIDAY	Cpl	Charles Frederick	G	11367	12 Aug 1916	St. Sever Cemetery Ext.
HOLLIDAY	Pte	William	TF	203052	28 Apr 1917	Arras Memorial
HOLLINDRAKE	Cpl	H				
HOLLINGSWORTH	Cpl	Harold	G	34295		
HOLLINGSWORTH	Cpl	Leslie Wiliam	G	34233	28 Apr 1917	Arras Memorial
HOLLOWAY	Pte	Robert	G	27106		
HOLLOWOOD	Sgt	Walter	PS	1484	2 Dec 1917	Cambrai Memorial
HOLLY	Pte	Sydney Harry	G	50732	24 Mar 1918	Arras Memorial
HOLMES	Pte	Albert	F	708		
HOLMES	L/Cpl	Norman	F	1617		
HOMENT	Pte	William J	G	43702		
HOMEWOOD	L/Cpl	S	G			
HONIGBAUM	Pte	Louis	G	42657	·	
HOOK	Pte	Frederick	F	865		
HOOPER	Pte	Arthur John	G	20127	8 Jul 1917	Gorre British and Indian Cemetery
HOOPER	Sgt	Harold	G	43615		
HOOPER	Sgt	John Joseph	F	668		
HOPKINS	Pte	Herbert Hopkins	F	1523		
HORLEY	L/Cpl	William John	F	696		
HORLOCK	Pte	Charles Ernest	F	578		
HORLOCK	Pte	George	G	44077	15 Oct 1918	Duisans British Cemetery
HORNBY	Capt	Richard Arthur			9 Apr 1918	Ploegsteert Memorial (Belgium)
HORNIMAN	Capt	Laurence Ivan				
HORWOOD	Pte	Edward	F	1308	8 Aug 1916	Thiepval Memorial
HOUGHTON	2/Lt	DL				
HOULTON	Pte	Henry George	G	44066	13 Aug 1917	Cologne Southern Cemetery (Germany)
HOUSE	Pte	Allen Victor	PS	2391	13 Aug 1917	Mendinghem Military Cemetery (Belgium)
HOUSTON	Pte	David	F	1283	·	
HOUSTON	L/Cpl	Robert	F	47	13 Nov 1916	Thiepval Memorial
HOWARD	Pte	Benjamin	G	10557	28 Jul 1916	Thiepval Memorial
HOWARD	Pte	Charles	F	133		
HOWARD	Pte	Charles William	F	426	1 Aug 1916	Quarry Cemetery, Montauban
HOWARD	Sgt	Edwin	G	1247		
HOWARD	Pte	Harry	G	32578		
HOWARD	2/Lt	John Gulliver				
HOWARD	Pte	Sidney	G	921		
HOWE	Pte	Alfred	G	11305		
HOWE	Pte	Henry Josiah	F	866		
HOWE	Sgt	Percy Frederick	G	15487		
HOWE	Pte	Thomas Henry	G	86618		

Surname	Rank	Forenames	Prefix	Number	Date of Death	Cemetery/Memorial
HOWE	Cpl	William Frederick	G	34235	3 Jun 1917	Cologne Southern Cemetery (Germany)
HOWELL	Pte	Sidney	F	499		
HOWELL	Pte	William Henry	L	11464		
HOWELL	Pte	Frank	F	576		
HOWELL	Pte	Frank	F	576	27 Jan 1916	Guards Cemetery, Windy Corner
HOY	L/Cpl	George Samuel	G	42629		
HUBBARD	Pte	Harry	F	187		
HUBBARD	Pte	Robert William	F	903	6 Aug 1916	Bernafay Wood British Cemetery
HUDSON	Pte	Charles James	G	29466		
HUGALL	Cpl	Jimmy	F	16		
HUGGETT	Pte	Sydney	G	27427		
HUGHES	2/Lt	Harry Halmshaw				
HUGHES	Pte	John	F	1400		
HUGHES	Pte	Harry	F	276		
HUGHES	Pte	Henry Jones	F	2733	28 Apr 1917	Arras Memorial
HUGHES	Pte	John	F	2835		
HUGHES	Sgt	Norman Walter	G	41538	3 Jan 1918	Ribecourt Road Cemetery
HUGHES	Pte	Sidney Herbert	F	1570		
HUGHES	Pte	William Thomas	G	87506		
HUMPHREY	Pte	Holl Roger	PW	5773	28 Apr 1917	Arras Memorial
HUMPHREY	Pte	Reginald George	F	1487	1 Aug 1916	Quarry Cemetery, Montauban
HUMPHREYS	Pte	Harry David	G	6206		
HUMPHREYS	Pte	Walter	G	9019		
HUMPHREYS	Sgt	William Henry	G	14437		
HUMPHRIES	CSM	Arthur John	G	42006		
HUMPHRIES	Pte	Percy	F	828		
HUMPHRIES	Pte	Richard	G	43614		
HUNT	Pte	Fred John	G	34053		
HUNT	Cpl	Harold Stuart	G	43550		
HUNT	Pte	Henry	F	1048		
HUNT	Sgt	Henry	F	1851		
HUNT	Pte	Leslie Joseph	F	995		
HUNT	Pte	Sidney	TF	241522	10 Jun 1917	Ypres (Menin Gate) Memorial (Belgium)
HUNT	Pte	Thomas Frederick	G	34356	28 Apr 1917	Arras Memorial
HUNT	Pte	Walter George	F	1588		
HUNT .	L/Cpl	William Frederick	F	526		
HUNTER	Pte	Joseph	F	945		
HUNTER	Pte	Robert Henry	G	34298		
HURLEY	Pte	Herbert L	F	774		
HURMAN	L/Cpl	Francis Bertie	F	959	28 Apr 1917	Arras Memorial
HURRAN	Pte	Thomas	F	589		
HURST	Pte	Frederick	F	1002		
HURST	Sgt	S				
HUSSEY	Pte	William Herbert	G	12706		
HUSTWITT	Pte	Cyril Charles	G	34413		
HUTCHINGS	Pte	Harry Robert	G	15143	8 May 1918	Tyne Cot Memorial (Belgium)
HUTCHINSON	Pte	George John	G	43595		
HUTHWAITE	Pte	James Alfred	F	224	21 Apr 1918	Ypres Reservoir Cemetery (Belgium)
HUTSON	Pte	William Asdail	G	25333		
HYATT	Pte	Thomas	F	2665		
HYDE	Pte	George	G	87134		
HYDE	Pte	John William	G	3201		
ILES	Pte	Thomas	F	1069		
ING	Pte	Alfred Henry	F	1288		
ING		Joseph Charles	F			
ING	Pte	Richard Gilbert	G	41405		
INGRAM	Pte	John Edward	G	43913	13 Nov 1916	Thiepval Memorial
INNS	Pte	Edward James	F	1115		
INWOOD	Sgt	Frederick	L	11571	29 Sep 1918	Villers Hill British Cemetery
IREMONGER	Pte	Harold	F	302		
IRONS	Pte	Richard Barker	F	2533		
ISAACS	Pte	David Samuel	G	952		
ITTER	Sgt	William Henry	G	585		
JACKMAN	Pte	Walter	G	33963		
JACKSON	Sgt	Charles	F	949		

Surname	Rank	Forenames	Prefix	Number	Date of Death	Cemetery/Memorial
JACKSON	Cpl	Edwin	F	2052		
JACKSON	Pte	Edwin William	G	42639		
JACKSON	Sgt	Frederick Herbert James	F	807		
JACKSON	2/Lt	HG				
JACKSON	Pte	Philip John	F	1572		
JACKSON	Pte	Thomas	F	394		
JACKSON	Pte	Sam	G	3007	27 Dec 1917	Hermies Hill British Cemetery
JACOBS	Pte	Henry Robert	G	44136	9 Apr 1918	Rue-du-Bois Military Cemetery
JACOBS	Pte	John A	F	395		
JACQUES	Pte	Ronald Alfred	G	89554	22 Mar 1918	Roye New British Cemetery
JAGGER	Pte	Hubert	PS	3010		
JAGGER	Pte	Thomas	F	527		
JAGO	Sgt	James HV	F	396		
JAMES	Pte	Frederick Richard James	F	671		
JAMES	Pte	George William	G	28357		
JAMES	Pte	Ivo	G	43891		
JAMES	Pte	James	F	1767		
JAMES	Cpl	Sidney	F	470		
JAMES	Pte	T				
JAMES	Pte	Thomas Frederick	G	6454		
JAMES	Pte	William Bernard	G	87035		
JANSON	Pte	Leonard	F	1420	19 Jun 1916	Tancrez Farm Cemetery (Belgium)
JARMAN	Pte	Frank	F	1416		
JARVIS	Pte	Herbert Peter	G	30135	10 Jun 1917	Roclincourt Military Cemetery
JARVIS	Pte	John Charles	F	1213		
JEE	Pte	Herbert Victor	F	1247		
JEFFERY	Pte	Ronald G	F	460		
JEFFERY	Pte	Henry Alfred	G	87079	27 Nov 1917	Cambrai Memorial
JEFFORD	Pte	Sidney Joseph	F	188		
JEFFS	Pte	Percy	G	44111		
JEFFS	Pte	William Francis	F	3217	6 Aug 1916	Thiepval Memorial
JEMPSON	Pte	Albert Edward	G	41645		
JENKINS	Pte	Edward	F	1746	3 May 1917	Arras Memorial
JENKINS	Pte	Ephriam Job	G	43616	13 Nov 1916	Serre Road No. 1
JENKINS	L/Sgt	Frederick John	G	5387	28 Apr 1917	Arras Memorial
JENKINS	Pte	Leonard Frederick	F	1569		
JENKINS	Pte	William	G	42659		
JENKINSON	Pte	Albert Victor	F	885		
JENNER	Pte	H	G			
JENNINGS	Pte	Edward	F	1340		
JENNINGS	Sgt	Frederick Thomas	L	10427		
JENNINGS	L/Cpl	James	F	1620		
JERMY	Pte	Harry Holland	F	189		
JERRAM	Pte	Sidney John	F	1297		
JERRAM	Pte	Herbert Arthur	F	1296	8 Aug 1916	Dantzig Alley British Cemetery
JIGGINS	Pte	Frederick	G	29952		
JINMAN	Pte	Albert Victor	G	21235		
JOHNS	Pte	GE	G			
JOHNSON	Pte	Albert G	F	553		
JOHNSON	Pte	Charles	F	968		
JOHNSON	Pte	Edward A	F	662		
JOHNSON	Pte	Harry	G	9534		
JOHNSON	Cpl	James	F	592		
JOHNSON	Pte	James Henry	F	200		
JOHNSON	Pte	John	PW	5488	3 May 1917	Arras Memorial
JOHNSON	Pte	John	G	43567		
JOHNSON	Pte	Joseph	F	1927	23 Oct 1916	Thiepval Memorial
JOHNSTON	Pte	Frederick George	F	585		
JOHNSTONE	Pte	Alan	PS	1918		
JONAS	Pte	William	F	32	27 Jul 1916	Thiepval Memorial
JONES	Pte	Albert	L	9612		
JONES	Pte	Edward	F	398		
JONES	Pte	EJ				
JONES	L/Cpl	George Frederick	F	819		
JONES	Pte	Henry Thomas	F	1068	13 Nov 1916	Thiepval Memorial

Surname	Rank	Forenames	Prefix	Number	Date of Death	Cemetery/Memorial
JONES	Pte	John Henry	F	1282	26 Mar 1918	H.A.C. Cemetery
JONES	Sgt	John Robert	G	15573		
JONES	Pte	Joseph Henry	F	171	28 Dec 1917	Hermies Hill British Cemetery
JONES	Pte	Reg Henry	TF	207944		
JONES	Pte	Robert	G	21002		
JONES	L/Cpl	Robert George	F	397		
JONES	Pte	Stanley James	F	1499		
JONES	Pte	Sydney Ernest	F	2272		
JONES	Pte	Thomas Russell	G	76163		
JONES	Pte	William Harry	F	656		
JONES	Cpl	William James	G	11415		
JORDAN	Cpl	AJ	G	50851		
JORDAN	Pte	Albert	G	28359		
JORDAN	Pte	Alfred Edmund	PS	1529	23 Mar 1918	Arras Memorial
JORDON	Pte	Daniel	G	9941		
JORDON	Pte	Thomas	F	845		
JOSEPH	Cpl	George Albert	F	1221		
JUFFKINS	Pte	George	G	44159		
JUPP	Sgt	William Herbert	G	43938		
KAY	Pte	James Livesey	F	1006		
KEASLEY	Pte	Arthur	G	43686		
KEATES	Pte	Harry	PW	2142		
KEATES	Pte	Thomas	PW	1547		
KEENOR	Sgt	Frederick Charles	F	653		
KEEVIL	Pte	John	TF	207943	25 Mar 1918	Arras Memorial
KEEN	Pte	William	F	1066		
KEIRLE	Pte	William Frederick	F	926	6 Aug 1916	Thiepval Memorial
KELLETT	Pte	George Abraham	F	637		
KELLEY	Pte	Thomas	F	1084		
KELLON	Pte	Frederick William	F	1471		
KELLY	Lt-Col	George				
KELLY	Pte	James P	F	474		
KELLY	Pte	Thomas	PW	687		
KEMP	Pte	Sydney Victor	G	28965		
KEMPSTER	2/Lt	Stephen Alec			8 Jun 1917	Roclincourt Military Cemetery
KENDALL	Pte	Alfred James	F	682		
KENNARD	Sgt	Leonard John	F	104	13 Nov 1916	Thiepval Memorial
KENNEWELL	Pte	Lewis Edwin	F	346	26 Sep 1916	St. Sever Cemetery
KENNEY	Cpl	David	F	911		
KENT	Cpl	Harold	G	50926		
KENTFIELD	Pte	Edward Saffal	G	41406		
KERRISTON	Pte	A				
KERRY	Pte	Robert Sidney Arthur	G	21992		
KESSACK	Capt	James O'Connor			13 Nov 1916	Thiepval Memorial
KEY	Pte	Charles	F	134		
KEY	Pte	Roland	TF	205043		
KIBBLE	Pte	Arthur	G	43974	13 Nov 1916	Serre Road No.2
KIDD	Pte	Harold George	G	43707	26 Apr 1917	Aubigny Communal Cemetery Ext.
KILLICK	Pte	Amos	PW	6347		
KILROY	Pte	Leonard Samuel	F	559	4 Apr 1917	West Norwood Cemetery (UK)
KIMMINS	Pte	James		7635		
KING	Pte	Arthur	PS	3649	28 Apr 1917	Arras Memorial
KING	2/Lt	BH				
KING	Pte	Charles George	F	602		
KING		Edward	F			
KING	2/Lt	Edward S				
KING	Pte	Joshua	F	2495		
KING	L/Cpl	Sidney Edward	F	1472	15 May 1917	Wimereux Communal Cemetery
KING	Pte	Sidney W		5756		
KING	Pte	Thomas Alfred	TF	203055		
KINGHAM	Pte	T	G			
KINGTON	Sgt	Arthur	F	616	13 Nov 1916	Serre Road No. 1
KINGWELL	Pte	Charles	G	1749	8 Aug 1920	Wandsworth (Streatham) Cemetery (UK)
KIRK	Pte	Albert	G	43955	28 Apr 1917	Arras Memorial
KIRKUM	Pte	John	G	87048		
KIRKWOOD	Pte	Joseph Josiah	F	48		

370

Surname	Rank	Forenames	Prefix	Number	Date of Death	Cemetery/Memorial
KITCHENMASTER	Pte	Charles	F	925		
KITCHING	Pte	Albert	F	1095	28 Jul 1916	Delville Wood Cemetery
KITTERIDGE	Pte	Leonard Thomas Richard	F	1543	8 Aug 1916	Thiepval Memorial
KLOSS	Pte	Nathaniel	G	1317		
KLUST	Pte	Ernest George	G	89000		
KNAPP	Pte	William	G	18399	3 Dec 1917	Grevillers British Cemetery
KNAPTON	Pte	Bernard	F	2437		
KNIGHT	Sgt	George	L	16555		
KNIGHT	Pte	George Albert William	L	16533		
KNIGHT	Pte	William George	F	537		
KNOCK	Pte	Bertram	G	75485		
KNOCK	Pte	George Ernest	G	43568		
KOOP	2/Lt	Charles				
KOSH	Pte	Arthur Herbert	G	21727	28 Apr 1917	Arras Memorial
KRUG	Pte	William Alfred	F	68		
LACAM	Pte	Charles Alfred	F	1394		
LACEY	Pte	Abraham John	PS	3146		
LACEY	Cpl	Reginald	F	1040	8 Aug 1916	London Cemetery & Ext.
LADYMAN	Cpl	Arthur	F	1578		
LAIDLAW	Pte	John	F	1234		
LAING	L/Cpl	William Danick	F	697	9 Aug 1916	Thiepval Memorial
LAKER	Pte	William	F	399	28 Jul 1916	Thiepval Memorial
LAMB	Pte	Ernest Frederick	G	51057		
LAMB	Pte	John	F	1702		
LAMBARD	Pte	Edward	F	163		
LAMBERT	Cpl	George Thomas	L	15111		
LAMBERT	Pte	Leonard Wilson	G	50731		
LANDER	Pte	William Montague	G	43546		
LANDYMORE	Pte	Leonard	G	41670		
LANE	Pte	Harry	TF	203879		
LANE	L/Cpl	James	F	758	28 Jul 1916	Thiepval Memorial
LANE	Pte	William Charles	G	21984	2 Dec 1917	Cambrai Memorial
LANGHAM	Pte	George	G	32943	9 Jun 1917	Ypres (Menin Gate) Memorial (Belgium)
LANGHAM	Pte	Reginald Sydney	F	512		
LANGLEY	Pte	Harry	G	43906	28 Apr 1917	Arras Memorial
LANGSTONE	Pte	Frederick	G	44102		
LANGTREE	Pte	Alec Robert	G	26543		
LAST	2/Lt	Basil Herbert			23 Apr 1917	Highland Cemetery, Roclincourt
LAVENDER	Pte	Edward	G	43889		
LAVENDER	Pte	Henry	G	32354		
LAVER	Pte	Bertie	F	2914	19 Dec 1916	Etaples Military Cemetery
LAW	Pte	William	G	23913		
LAW	Pte	William Bradshaw	G	43925		
LAWES	Pte	William	F	1231		
LAWFORD	Pte	Henry George	G	87043		
LAWFORD	Pte	James	F	503		
LAWLEY	Cpl	Leonard	G	43644		
LAWNER	Pte	Arthur C	G	43871		
LAWRENCE	Pte	Charles	F	528		
LAWRENCE	Pte	Charles George	G	44052		
LAWRENCE	Pte	Ernest Robert	G	27970	6 Jun 1917	Arras Memorial
LAWRENCE	Pte	Frank	G	43852		
LAWRENCE	Pte	Henry C	F	844		
LAWRENCE	Pte	Sidney Charles	F	105		
LAWS	Pte	Charles	G	1592		
LAWS	Pte	William	G	20896		
LAWSON	Pte	Arthur Charles	G	20686	29 Sep 1918	Villers Hill British Cemetery
LAY	Pte	Joseph	TF	204972		
LAY	Pte	Joseph Thomas	L	20576		
LAYE	Pte	Albert	G	43618	28 Apr 1917	Arras Memorial
LAYTON	Pte	Howard A	F	1196		
LEACH	Pte	Henry Walter	L	14813	27 May 1918	Soissons Memorial
LEACH	L/Cpl	Ernest Cecil	F	428	8 Aug 1916	Delville Wood Cemetery
LEACH	Pte	Wilfred Arthur	F	1494		
LEAR	Pte	Ernest	G	4522		

Surname	Rank	Forenames	Prefix	Number	Date of Death	Cemetery/Memorial
LEATHERS	Pte	Charles	G	44080		
LEAVER	2/Lt	Stanley Horace			9 Apr 1918	Ploegsteert Memorial (Belgium)
LEAVER	Pte	William John Tom	G	34589		
LEDGER	Pte	William	G	50745		
LEE	Pte	Daniel	F	1415		
LEE	2/Lt	Edgar Charles			1 Jun 1916	Cabaret-Rouge British Cemetery
LEE	Sgt	James Fred	L	7930		
LEE	Pte	Thomas	F	966		
LEE	Pte	Thomas	F	400		
LEGGE	Pte	Harold	F	1600		
LEGOOD	Pte	Harry	G	87044		
LEIGH	Pte	Matthew Joseph	F	1970		
LEMARQUAND	Pte	Joseph Henry	G	20768		
LENEY	Pte	Frederick	F	1060		
LENSH	Pte	Frederick	G	89055		
LEONARD	Pte	Alfred Cook	F	155	30 Jul 1916	Corbie Communal Cemetery Ext.
LETTS	Pte	Charles Henry	G	44113	21 Feb 1918	Cabaret-Rouge British Cemetery
LEVENE	Pte	Harry	G	18620		
LEVERETT	Pte	Albert	G	43619		
LEVERETT	Sgt	Sidney Robert	G	49210		
LEVERINGTON	Pte	James William	G	94034		
LEVETT	Pte	Charles Victor	G	27361		
LEVETT	Pte	Francis George	G	24512	28 Apr 1917	Arras Memorial
LEVEY	Pte	William Henry	TF	202916	1 Oct 1917	Denain Communal Cemetery
LEVY	Pte	Ben	F	348	1 Jan 1918	Giavera British Cemetery (Italy)
LEVY	Pte	Gabriel Dabiel	PS	1845		
LEVY	Pte	Isaac	F	172		
LEWES	Pte	Herbert Sidney	F	1292		
LEWINDON	Pte	Joseph William	F	638	24 Apr 1918	Pozieres Memorial
LEWIS	Pte	Frank	F	1215		
LEWIS	Pte	Frederick Charles	L	16678	1 Dec 1917	Cambrai Memorial
LEWIS	Pte	John Lee	F	1158	28 Apr 1917	Arras Memorial
LEWIS	Pte	Maurice James	G	43923	16 Nov 1916	Warlincourt Halte British Cemetery
LEWIS	Pte	Thomas	G	92844		
LEY	Pte	Andrew Stephen	G	44049		
LIDDIARD	Pte	Alfred	G	8564		
LIGHT	Sgt	Charles Francis	F	349		
LIMEHOUSE	Pte	Frederick William	G	43917		
LINCOLN	Pte	Maurice	F	3471		
LINDLEY	Pte	Frank Louis	F	17		
LINDSEY	Cpl	Douglas Wilson	F	1522		
LING	Pte	Frederick George	F	1411	28 Jul 1916	Thiepval Memorial
LINKSON	Pte	Oscar Horace Stanley	F	1723	8 Aug 1916	Thiepval Memorial
LINSELL	Pte	William John	G	53021		
LINWOOD	Pte	William	F	1378	28 Jul 1916	Thiepval Memorial
LISSENDEN	Pte	Charles William	G	9547		
LITTLE	Pte	Francis Thomas	F	1224		
LITTLEJOHN	Pte	Joseph	G	14185		
LLOYD	Pte	Fred William	TF	204495		
LLOYD	L/Cpl	Owen	F	1109	20 Sep 1917	Cement House Cemetery (Belgium)
LLOYD	L/Cpl	Thomas	F	150		
LOADER	Pte	Walter Frederick	G	43932		
LOMAS	Pte	Herbert	F	1435		
LONG	Pte	William Harry	F	582		
LONG	2/Lt	John Thomas				
LONG	Pte	Walter Victor	G	43957	1 Dec 1917	Cambrai Memorial
LONSDALE	Pte	Thomas Stewart	F	906		
LOVATT	Pte	Horace	PW	6410		
LOVE	Pte	George Francis	PS	2560		
LOWDEN	Sgt	Herbert Walter	G	34081		
LOWE	Pte	CJ	F	2559		
LOWE	Pte	James Thurey	F	1467		
LOWE	Pte	William Frederick	F	799		
LOWE			F			
LUCAS	Pte	James S	G	43665	28 Apr 1917	Arras Memorial
LUCK	Pte	Alfred	G	43713		
LUCK	Pte	Charles	F	1468		

Surname	Rank	Forenames	Prefix	Number	Date of Death	Cemetery/Memorial
LUCK	Pte	Frank	F	1385		
LUCKETT	Pte	Charles Thomas	G	86650		
LUDLOW	Pte	Ernest	G	43854		
LUFF	Pte	Bernard William Henry	G	11485		
LUKER	Pte	Charles William	F	120	16 Apr 1918	Meteren Military Cemetery
LUXFORD	Pte	Fred Alfred	TF	203058		
LYON	Pte	William		5876	18 Sep 1916	Euston Road Cemetery
MACDONALD	Pte	James	F	106	11 Dec 1915	Cambrin Churchyard Ext.
MACINTYRE	2/Lt	Robert				
MACKLIN	Pte	Richard Hubert	F	1417		
MACLAINE	Maj	Kenneth Douglas Lorne				
MACMASTER	Cpl	John Balshaw	TF	203132		
MACMILLAN	2/Lt	Roland John				
MADDISON	Pte	George William	F	1035		
MAIDENHALL	Pte	George Henry	G	50746		
MAIDMENT	L/Sgt	Albert Frederick George	G	43656	13 Nov 1916	Thiepval Memorial
MAIN	L/Cpl	A				
MAINWOOD	Pte	Harry Cecil	PS	3455		
MAJOR	L/Cpl	Charles Arthur	F	1325		
MALISON	Pte	William Victor	G	15063		
MANDALL	Pte	Robert	PW	5852	28 Apr 1917	Arras Memorial
MANDERSON	Pte	David	F	350		
MANKTELOW	Pte	William	G	41436		
MANN	Pte	Frank	F	709		
MANN	Pte	Vernon Charles	G	12292	28 Jul 1916	A.I.F. Burial Ground
MANSFIELD	Pte	Charles Smith	G	24515		
MANTON	Pte	Thomas	G	19881	28 Apr 1918	Islington Cemetery and Crematorium (UK)
MARCHANT	Lt	Ernest William				
MARDELL	Cpl	Sydney	F	636		
MARIGOLD	L/Cpl	Frederick	G	2976	28 Apr 1917	Arras Memorial
MARKS	Pte	Abraham	F	1077	28 Jul 1916	Delville Wood Cemetery
MARLOW	Pte	Harry	G	44139	2 Apr 1918	Caix British Cemetery
MARLOW	2/Lt	Robert William				
MARRIAN	Pte	Arthur Wilfred	PS	2496		
MARSH	Pte	Albert	TF	201931		
MARSHALL	Pte	John	F	843		
MARSHALL	Pte	Richard George	G	20263		
MARTIN	Pte	Albert C	F	1408		
MARTIN	Pte	Francis	F	908		
MARTIN	Pte	George	G	43975		
MARTIN	Sgt	James John	L	11289		
MARTIN	Pte	John	G	34900		
MARTIN	Sgt	William John	L	13243		
MARTIN	L/Cpl	Herbert William	G	8850	28 Apr 1917	Arras Memorial
MARVEN	Pte	Charles	F	1586		
MASKELL	Sgt	Edward	F	1028	13 Nov 1916	Thiepval Memorial
MASON	Pte	Frank Clifford John	PS	2538	24 Aug 1916	Euston Road Cemetery
MASON	Pte	George Frederick	L	16500		
MASON	Pte	George William	PW	3798		
MASON	Cpl	James Henry	G	87038	7 Oct 1918	Brown's Copse Cemetery
MASON	Pte	Sidney	G	43569		
MASON	Pte	William	F	446		
MASSON	Pte	Mark	G	9973		
MATHESON	Capt	James McDonald			30 Nov 1917	Hermies Hill British Cemetery
MATTHEWS	Cpl	Cecil James	F	989		
MATTHEWS	Pte	Frederick John	G	43623	13 Nov 1916	Serre Road No.2
MATTHEWS	Pte	William	F	1490		
MATTHEWS	Pte	William Charles	G	43944		
MAXIM	Pte	G				
MAXTED	Pte	Albert Edward	F	685		
MAXTED	Pte	Ernest	G	41443		
MAXWELL	Pte	Ernest	G	12104		
MAXWORTHY	Pte	Herbert James	G	12472		
MAY	Pte	Bertie David	G	29002	24 Mar 1918	Arras Memorial
MAY	Pte	Charles	F	625		

Surname	Rank	Forenames	Prefix	Number	Date of Death	Cemetery/Memorial
MAY	Pte	George	G	12550	8 Aug 1916	Thiepval Memorial
MAY	L/Cpl	John Charles	F	861		
MAYGER	Pte	Edward	G	43688		
MAYHO	Pte	John		8821		
MAYNARD	Sgt	Leonard Harry	F	121		
MAYNARD	Pte	Robert J		24410		
McCLUSKEY	Pte	Philip	F	351		
McCOLL	Pte	Duncan	G	92846	9 Dec 1917	Grevillers British Cemetery
McCORMICK	Sgt	James	F	286		
McDONALD	Pte	Frank	G	92847		
McDONALD	L/Sgt	George William	F	303		
McDONNELL	Pte	Thomas	F	1463		
McFADDEN	CSM	Richard	F	162	23 Oct 1916	Couin British Cemetery
McFADYEN	Pte	James	G	87081		
McKAY	Pte	Frederick Charles	F	3225	10 Sep 1916	Doullens Communal Cemetery Ext. No. 1
McKEE	Pte	William	PS	3472		
McKELVEY	Sgt	George Henry James	G	34199	28 Apr 1917	Arras Memorial
McKENHAM	Pte	George	F	1474		
McKENNA	Pte	Edward Patrick	L	9347		
McKENNA	L/Sgt	Francis	G	42661		
McKENNA		Thomas	F			
McKENNA	Pte	Thomas Patrick		177840		
McLAUCHLAN	Pte	Joseph	F	19		
McMANUS	Pte	Patrick	L	16391		
McMANUS	2/Lt	Terence Joseph			23 Dec 1919	Eastbourne (Ocklynge) Cemetery (UK)
McMILLAN	Pte	Alexander	G	24492	28 Apr 1917	Arras Memorial
McREADY-DIARMID	Capt	Allastair Malcolm Cluny			1 Dec 1917	Cambrai Memorial
MEACHAM	Pte	George	F	2790		
MEAD	Pte	David William	F	1277		
MEAD	Pte	Harold John	G	18622		
MEALE	Pte	Henry	F	1334		
MEANEY	Pte	Patrick	G	94035		
MEDCALF	Pte	Alfred William	G	20211		
MEIGH	Pte	John	F	190		
MENDELSON	Pte	Bert	G	43921		
MEPHAM	Pte	Jesse	G	27894	2 Dec 1917	Grevillers British Cemetery
MERCER	Sgt	Joseph Powell	F	10		
MERISON	Pte	George Alfred	G	34525		
MERKELT	Pte	Albert	F	918		
MERRICK	Sgt	Charles	F	196	15 Mar 1919	Bedfont Church Cemetery (UK)
MERRION	Pte	Horace Richard	F	3200		
MERRIOTT	Cpl	Fredrick John	F	1621		
MESSENGER	Pte	James Benjamin	F	1631		
MESSENGER	Pte	Walter	SR	6841	15 Aug 1916	Abbeville Communal Cemetery
METCALF	Pte	Walter	G	92824		
MEYER	Sgt	Joseph	F	1236		
MICHIE	Pte	Harry	F	352		
MICKLEBURGH	Pte	William Charles	F	278		
MIDDLETON	Pte	George William	F	18		
MIDDLETON	Pte	William	F	279	29 Sep 1918	Villers Hill British Cemetery
MIDDLETON	Pte	William	F	36		
MIDDLETON	Pte	William James	F	3305	3 May 1917	Arras Memorial
MILEHAM	Pte	Albert	G	50683	6 May 1918	Red Farm Military Cemetery (Belgium)
MILES	Pte	Jesse	F	1102		
MILLER		Bill	F			
MILLER	Pte	Edward Stanley	F	1465		
MILLER	Pte	Leo Bernard	F	1430		
MILLER	Pte	Richard Arthur	F	1442		
MILLER		Stanley	F			
MILLING	Capt	Thomas				
MILLINGTON	Pte	Alfred	F	2900		
MILLS	Pte	FB				
MILLS	Cpl	Frank	G	43621		
MILLS	Pte	George Thomas	PW	5612		
MILLS	Pte	Leonard	G	43961		

Surname	Rank	Forenames	Prefix	Number	Date of Death	Cemetery/Memorial
MINISTER	Pte	Alfred William Philip	G	44015	13 Nov 1916	Thiepval Memorial
MINSTER	Pte	George Edward	F	1129		
MITCHAM	L/Cpl	Thomas James	F	487	28 Jul 1916	Thiepval Memorial
MITCHELL	Pte	Chris Henry	G	78696		
MITCHELL	L/Cpl	Harry	F	202		
MITCHELL	Pte	Harry	PW	6023		
MITCHELL	Pte	James	F	654		
MITCHELL	Pte	Sidney		19311		
MITCHELL	Pte	William	G	43914		
MITCHELL	Pte	William John	F	1628		
MOLD	Pte	Harry	G	44140		
MONEYPENNY	Pte	George Francis	TF	203189	28 Apr 1917	Arras Memorial
MONK	L/Cpl	Edward	L	13481	22 Feb 1917	Thiepval Memorial
MONKS	Pte	Robert C	F	1124		
MOON	Pte	William Ernest	G	50943	4 Dec 1917	St. Sever Cemetery Ext.
MOORE	Cpl	Harold George	TF	207937	9 Apr 1918	Rue-Petillon Military Cemetery
MOORE	Pte	John	TF	235493		
MOORE	Pte	Lewis Gustave	G	29979	8 Jul 1917	Gorre British and Indian Cemetery
MOORE	Pte	Reginald Thomas	F	631		
MOORE	Pte	Thomas	L	8927		
MOORE	Pte	Thomas Arthur	G	77344		
MOORE	Sgt	William	G	10881		
MOORE	L/Cpl	William Herbert	F	933	27 Jul 1916	Thiepval Memorial
MORGAN	Pte	Ernest Walter	G	7007		
MORGAN	Sgt	John Noble	F	403		
MORGAN	Pte	William Herbert	F	1801	28 Jul 1916	Thiepval Memorial
MORRIS	Pte	Charles Frederick	PS	3522	21 Jun 1917	Perth Cemetery (China Wall) (Belgium)
MORRIS	Lt	J				
MORRIS	Pte	Myer	G	89056		
MORRIS	Sgt	Samuel	F	304		
MORRIS	Pte	Sidney James	F	225	8 Aug 1916	Thiepval Memorial
MORTIMER	Pte	Henry	G	43929	28 Apr 1917	Arras Memorial
MORTIMER	Pte	James John	G	43570	28 Apr 1917	Arras Memorial
MORTIMER	Pte	John H	L	12815		
MORTON	Pte	Charles	G	43622		
MORTON	Pte	Horace	G	8102	2 Aug 1917	Oak Dump Cemetery (Belgium)
MOSS	Pte	Albert	G	34716		
MOSS	Pte	Christian	F	529	28 Jul 1916	Thiepval Memorial
MOSS	Pte	Frank Herbert	G	43683		
MOSS	Pte	James W	PW	6419		
MOSS	Pte	William	G	94016		
MOTTRAM	Pte	Samuel Roberts	PS	3206	24 Apr 1917	Aubigny Communal Cemetery Ext.
MOULD	Pte	Percy	F	955		
MOULOS	Pte	Richard	PW	6280		
MOUNTENEY	Pte	Arthur	F	1531		
MOUNTJOY	Cpl	Bertie Arthur	G	10798		
MOUTRIE	Pte	Albert Edward	F	930		
MOYSE	L/Cpl	Frederick Arthur	G	43900	28 Apr 1917	Arras Memorial
MULLABY	Pte	Sidney James	G	26320	6 Aug 1917	Cologne Southern Cemetery (Germany)
MULLETT	Pte	William Henry	G	41448	24 Mar 1918	Arras Memorial
MULLINS	Pte	Sydney Jesse	G	6984		
MUMMERY	Pte	Charles James	PS	2586		
MUNDAY	L/Cpl	Albert Edward	G	44058	28 Apr 1917	Arras Memorial
MUNDEN	Pte	Horace Charles	G	42634		
MUNKS	Pte	John	F	1419		
MUNSON	Pte	W		625		
MURCH	Pte	Albert Reginald	G	43935		
MURCOTT	Pte	Arthur	F	593		
MURKIN	Pte	Harry E	F	688		
MURPHY	Pte	Bernard William	F	1190		
MURPHY	Pte	John	L	5090	11 Oct 1917	Voormezeele Encl. No. 1 and No. 2 (Belgium)
MURPHY	Pte	William	F	1223		
MURRAY	2/Lt	Athole Montague				
MURRAY	2/Lt	Ronald James				
MURRILL	Pte	Sidney Arthur	F	838	8 Aug 1916	Delville Wood Cemetery

Surname	Rank	Forenames	Prefix	Number	Date of Death	Cemetery/Memorial
MURRILL	Pte	Walker Thomas	F	897		
MURROCK	Pte	Frederick William	G	44068	13 Nov 1916	Thiepval Memorial
MUSPRATT	Pte	Walter	G	34878		
MUTTICK	Pte	Edward	G	26359		
MYERS	Pte	Jack	G	8168		
MYLAM	Pte	Edwin George	G	43620		
NABBS	L/Cpl	William Henry Frederick	F	572	28 Jul 1916	Delville Wood Cemetery
NASH	Pte	Frederick Thomas	G	53020		
NASH	Pte	Walter	G	43719		
NASH	Pte	William	G	24444		
NASH	L/Cpl	Harry	L	14834	28 Apr 1917	Arras Memorial
NATION	Pte	Edwin Richard	F	1558	31 Jul 1917	Ypres (Menin Gate) Memorial (Belgium)
NAUGHTON	Pte	Alfred Edward	F	1248	28 Jul 1916	Thiepval Memorial
NEAL	Pte	Frederick George	G	43985		
NEALE	Pte	Herbert	F	135		
NEEDHAM		Archibald	F			
NEEDLEY	Pte	Noel	F	1073		
NEIGHBOUR	Pte	Walter C. P.	G	42635		
NELDER	Pte	Harold Robert Francis	G	40629		
NELLER	Pte	Walter George	G	24525	13 Nov 1916	Serre Road No. 1
NEVILLE	Pte	John Alfred	G	43624		
NEVILLE	Pte	Frederick Charles	G	10980	3 Dec 1917	Cambrai Memorial
NEWBATT	L/Cpl	Derrick	G	43857	28 Apr 1917	Arras Memorial
NEWBERY	Pte	Alfred Robert	G	7834		
NEWBOLD	Pte	Sydney J		27436		
NEWELL	Pte	Edward	F	3072		
NEWELL	Pte	Edward	PW	6112		
NEWELL	Pte	John William	G	43909	13 Nov 1916	Serre Road No.2
NEWITT	Pte	Henry John	G	86514	1 Oct 1918	Hooge Crater Cemetery (Belgium)
NEWMAN	Pte	Cecil Thomas	G	33828		
NEWMAN	Pte	Henry J	TF	241143		
NEWSTEAD	Pte	William	F	543		
NEWTON	Pte	Frederick	TF	201208		
NEWTON	Pte	Tom	F	69		
NIXON	Pte	Wilfred	F	1731		
NOON	Pte	Thomas Alfred	G	8301		
NORGARD	Pte	Percy Lionel Eric	F	531		
NORKETT	Pte	Alfred Albion	F	466		
NORMAN	Pte	Charles Ernest	G	89059		
NORMAN	Pte	Frederick	G	24170		
NORMAN	L/Cpl	Joseph	F	405	9 Jun 1917	Bus House Cemetery (Belgium)
NORMAN	Pte	William	F	157	13 Nov 1916	Serre Road No.2
NORRIS	Pte	Albert H	G	4528		
NORTH	Cpl	Walter Charles	PS	2583		
NOTTINGHAM	Pte	James Walter	G	11304		
NOYLE	Pte	George	F	191	8 Aug 1916	Thiepval Memorial
NUNN	Pte	Charles Francis	G	12076	3 Apr 1918	Ploegsteert Memorial (Belgium)
NUNN	Capt	Frederick James				
NUTTALL	Pte	John	F	49		
OAKHAM	Pte	Frederick	F	1524		
OAKLEY	L/Cpl	Bertram	G	42628		
OAKLEY	Pte	George Robert	F	1260		
O'BRIEN	Pte	George Christopher	F	1242		
OCKENDEN	Pte	Victor	G	40541		
O'CONNOR	Pte	Edward Bernard Ignatius	F	1565		
O'DELL	Pte	Alfred	G	20940		
OFFEN	Pte	Herbert George	G	53024		
OFFORD	2/Lt	Norman				
OGLEY	Pte	William	F	938		
OLDACRE	Pte	Edmund	F	1381		
OLDING	Pte	Alfred	G	23261		
OLDROYD	Pte	Henry Joseph	F	990	25 Jul 1916	Thiepval Memorial
O'LEARY	Pte	Michael James	F	1684	5 Oct 1918	Kirechkoi-Hortakoi Military Cemetery (Greece)

Surname	Rank	Forenames	Prefix	Number	Date of Death	Cemetery/Memorial
OLIVE	Pte	Harold	F	712	8 Aug 1916	Thiepval Memorial
OLIVER	Cpl	Ebenezer	G	41450		
OLIVER	Pte	William	F	3351		
OLIVER	Pte	William John	F	34		
OLIVER	Pte	Leslie	F	137	13 Nov 1916	Serre Road No.2
OLNEY	Pte	John	G	43888		
ONIONS	Pte	William Henry	G	89060		
ORGAR	Pte	George Bertie	G	50432	1 Oct 1918	Lijssenthoek Military Cemetery (Belgium)
ORME	Pte	Joseph H	F	94		
ORMSTON	Pte	Harry	G	53023		
ORROW	Cpl	John	F	406	28 Apr 1917	Arras Memorial
ORSMAN	Pte	Archibald Bernard	G	26406	28 Apr 1917	Arras Memorial
OSBORN	Cpl	Frederick Charles	G	41632	28 Apr 1917	Arras Memorial
OSBORN	Pte	Leonard	G	34121		
OSBORN	Pte	Thomas John	G	22794	1 Apr 1918	Highgate Cemetery (UK)
OSBORN	Pte	William	G	43912		
OSBORNE	Pte	James Arthur Evans	G	19660		
OSBORNE	Pte	Percy	G	43936	13 Nov 1916	Serre Road No.2
OSEY	Pte	Robert	TF	242379	3 Jan 1918	Arras Memorial
OSMOND	2/Lt	WH				
OSMOND	Pte	Sidney	G	26551	28 Apr 1917	Arras Memorial
O'SULLIVAN	Pte	Sidney	F	1714		
O'TOOLE	Pte	John	G	48926		
OTTAWAY	Pte	George	G	27275		
OTTER	Pte	Raymond Ernest		2222		
OWEN	Pte	Alfred John	G	53022		
OWEN	Cpl	Allen Viler	F	281	8 Aug 1916	Thiepval Memorial
OWEN	Pte	Frank Harold	TF	207939	28 Nov 1917	Cambrai Memorial
OWEN	Pte	Harry	G	24301		
OWEN	Pte	Lloyd	F	1109		
OWEN	Pte	Walter	F	1806	8 Aug 1916	Delville Wood Cemetery
OXENBOULD	Lt	Maurice				
PACK	Pte	Alfred Leonard	G	41452		
PADMORE	2/Lt	Arthur				
PAGDEN	Pte	William G	PS	1991		
PAGE	Pte	Henry Saunders	G	44054		
PAGE	Pte	Richard	F	1220		
PAGE	Pte	William Alfred	G	43629		
PAGE	L/Cpl	William	F	634	13 Nov 1916	Serre Road No. 1
PAGET	Pte	Arthur William	G	19202		
PAIN	L/Cpl	George Thomas	F	659	13 Nov 1916	Thiepval Memorial
PALK	Pte	William Frederick	G	53028		
PALMER	Pte	Albert W R	G	53031		
PALMER	Lt	Arthur Baillie Bentinck				
PALMER	Pte	Burt	G	50733		
PALMER	Pte	Ernest George	TF	203891		
PALMER	Pte	George	F	676		
PALMER	Pte	William	F	646		
PALMER	Pte	Robert	G	43997	13 Nov 1916	Serre Road No.2
PARDOE	Cpl	Herbert William	G	5	28 Apr 1917	Arras Memorial
PARFITT	Capt	Ernest			28 May 1917	Niederzwehren Cemetery (Germany)
PARGETER	L/Sgt	George Leslie	F	407		
PARIS	Sgt	William S	F	1108		
PARKER	Pte	Arthur Stanley	PS	3454		
PARKER	Pte	Edward John	F	1459	15 Sep 1916	Thiepval Memorial
PARKER	Pte	Frederick Lewis	G	41456		
PARKER	Pte	Frederick Moses	TF	203059	28 Apr 1917	Arras Memorial
PARKER	Sgt	Frederick William	F	111		
PARKER	Pte	Herbert V	TF	203514		
PARKER	Pte	Sidney George	G	53025		
PARKER	Lt	Spencer Furlong				
PARKINSON	Pte	Frederick	F	1406	7 Aug 1916	Thiepval Memorial
PARKS	Pte	Ernest	F	540		
PARNELL	Pte	Charles William	F	1451		
PARROTT	Pte	Frederick	F	429		
PARROTT	Pte	Frederick George	G	43625		

Surname	Rank	Forenames	Prefix	Number	Date of Death	Cemetery/Memorial
PARRY	Pte	Hugh	G	13195		
PARSONS	Pte	Ernest Samuel	G	12171		
PARSONS	Pte	Frederick	G	28399		
PARSONS	Capt	Oswald				
PARSONS	Pte	Richard	G	43720		
PARTRIDGE	Pte	Harry	G	8397		
PATEMAN	Pte	John Henry	G	43628		
PATERSON	Pte	John Henry	F	1239	24 Sep 1918	Terlincthun British Cemetery
PATTENDER	Pte	Stephen	TF	202260		
PATTERSON	L/Cpl	Albert	F	1547	28 Jul 1916	Thiepval Memorial
PAVEY	Pte	Samuel	F	353		
PAYNE	Pte	Charles Henry	G	53032		
PAYNE	Pte	Frederick Thomas	G	18323		
PAYNE	Pte	Frederick William	G	41427		
PAYNE	Pte	Herbert	G	44014		
PAYNE	Pte	Sidney George	G	53033	15 Oct 1918	Orchard Dump Cemetery
PAYTON	C/Sgt	William T	F	1567		
PEACH	Pte	Stanley Fred	G	43996	13 Nov 1916	Thiepval Memorial
PEACOCK	Pte	E				
PEARCE	Pte	Albert E	G	53027		
PEARCE	L/Cpl	Charles	F	679		
PEARCE	Pte	George W	F	1382		
PEARCE	Pte	Sydney Tabox	G	44097		
PEARCE	Pte	George Frederick	G	43708	28 Apr 1917	Arras Memorial
PEARLESS	Pte	Reginald Frank	F	985	1 Jun 1916	Cabaret-Rouge British Cemetery
PEARSE	Pte	Frank Worthington	G	1382		
PEARSE	Pte	George Henry	F	1382		
PEARSON	Pte	Arthur	G	86546	23 Oct 1918	Montay British Cemetery
PEARSON	L/Cpl	Thomas Henry	F	20		
PECK	Pte	Reginald William	G	40920	22 Sep 1917	Tyne Cot Memorial (Belgium)
PEGG	Pte	George William	TF	205164		
PELL	Pte	Herbert Wilfrid	PS	2301		
PELLING	Pte	Percy	G	43965	13 Nov 1916	Thiepval Memorial
PENFOLD	Pte	Edward Bert	PS	3520		
PENFOLD	Pte	Sidney John	G	50734		
PENGELLY	Pte	Percy Harris	F	1371		
PENN	Cpl	William Wise	F	213		
PENNIFER	Pte	Henry John	F	70	24 Mar 1918	Pozieres Memorial
PENNY	L/Cpl	Thomas Herbert	G	29983	22 Apr 1917	Arras Memorial
PERCIVAL	Pte	Harold Valentine	G	43572		
PERRIMAN	Pte	Frederick	G	44046	13 Nov 1916	Thiepval Memorial
PERRISS	Pte	Albert Edward	G	32822		
PERRY	Pte	Ernest	G	17419		
PERRY	Pte	George Henry	L	16673		
PERRY	Sgt	William Charles	F	354		
PESTELL	Pte	Alfred Lawrence	G	43979	25 Apr 1917	Aubigny Communal Cemetery Ext.
PETCHEY	L/Cpl	S				
PETERKIN	Pte	Sidney Ernest	G	50747		
PETERS	Pte	Alfred Leslie	F	1159		
PETERS	Cpl	Arthur	PS	1804		
PETERS	Pte	Charles William	F	923	8 Jul 1918	Cologne Southern Cemetery (Germany)
PETERS	L/Cpl	Richard Stephen	F	1149		
PETHEN	Pte	Robert William	PS	1892		
PETLEY	Pte	William	F	1151		
PETRIE	Pte	John Henry	F	1005		
PETTITT	Pte	Ernest William	G	41657		
PETTITT	Cpl	Louis	G	43851	20 Jul 1918	Bully-Grenay Communal Cemetery British Ext.
PHILLIMORE	Pte	William Alfred	F	645		
PHILLIPS	Pte	Francis Leslie	F	1266		
PHILLIPS	Pte	JH	F	1694		
PHILLIPS	Pte	John Leonard	G	6951		
PHILLIPS	Pte	Reginald Alfred	F	158		
PHILLIPS	Pte	Richard	G	12361	8 Aug 1916	Thiepval Memorial
PHILPOT	Pte	Arthur	G	18418	8 Aug 1916	Thiepval Memorial
PHILPOTT	Pte	Alfred G	F	612		

Surname	Rank	Forenames	Prefix	Number	Date of Death	Cemetery/Memorial
PHIPP	Pte	Leonard W	G	89550	23 Mar 1918	Arras Memorial
PICKETT	Pte	Charles Frederick	PW	3533	27 Dec 1917	Hermies Hill British Cemetery
PIERCE	Pte	Alfred John	G	43960		
PIERSON	Pte	Albert James	G	44128	13 Nov 1916	Serre Road No. 1
PIKE	Pte	Arthur	G	42669		
PILBROW	Cpl	Alfred Davis	F	934		
PILE	Pte	William George	F	430		
PILGRIM	Sgt	Frederick Charles	L	10753		
PIMM	Pte	Harry	G	28989		
PINNER	Pte	Robert	G	44070		
PIPER	Pte	Charles Clarence	G	89271		
PIPER	Pte	Edward Alfred	F	964	11 Oct 1918	Wellington Cemetery Rieux-en-Cambresis
PIPER	Pte	Frederick	PW	6080		
PITCHER	Pte	Clifford Arthur	G	42232		
PITFIELD	Pte	William	TF	203554		
PITTS	Pte	Charles A	F	1178		
PLAICE	Cpl	Frank R	G	13804		
PLATT	Pte	Stephen F	G	68868		
PLAYLE	Pte	Bertie Charles	G	13208		
PLEDGER	Pte	William George	PS	1782		
PLOWMAN	Pte	Cuthbert Charles	F	431		
PLUMB	Pte	Harry	G	53029		
PLUMLEY	Pte	George	G	28407	12 Oct 1918	St. Aubert British Cemetery
PLUMRIDGE	Pte	Joseph Thomas	G	42636	8 Jul 1917	Gorre British and Indian Cemetery
PLUTHERO	Pte	Arthur	F	1310	13 Nov 1916	Serre Road No.2
POLDING	Pte	Norman	G	43630		
POLLARD	Pte	Samuel F		355		
POLLEY	Pte	Percy	F	356	28 Jul 1916	Thiepval Memorial
POLLEY	Pte	William Henry	G	43956	13 Nov 1916	Thiepval Memorial
POND	Pte	Charles H	TF	201480		
PONTIN	Pte	Walter Avery	PS	2890	12 Apr 1918	Aveluy Wood Cemetery
POOLE	Pte	Daniel M	F	1133		
POOLE	Pte	George A	G	41465		
POOLEY	Pte	Charles	G	33738		
POORE	Pte	Harry	PS	3543	23 Mar 1918	Delsaux Farm Cemetery
POORE	Pte	James	G	44053		
POPE	Pte	Alfred Thomas	G	43980		
POPE	Pte	Henry Albert	G	34429		
POPLE	Cpl	William Charles	F	1553		
POPPLEWELL	Pte	Thomas John	G	27327		
PORTER	Pte	John Clark	PW	5994		
PORTER	Pte	Walter Frederick	G	41647	28 Apr 1917	Arras Memorial
POSSELL	Pte	Arthur Alfred	F	763		
POSTLE	Pte	Robert	G	44002		
POSTLETHWAITE	Pte	William Ben	G	34369		
POTTER	Pte	Ernest James	F	588	26 Mar 1918	Arras Memorial
POTTER	Pte	Lionel	G	43890	28 Apr 1917	Arras Memorial
POTTER	Cpl	Sidney Robert	G	25120		
POTTER	Sgt	Walter Victor	F	586		
POTTER	L/Cpl	William	F	587	8 Aug 1916	Thiepval Memorial
POTTS	Sgt	John	G	10727		
POTTS	Pte	Robert	G	18653		
POULTER	Pte	Frederick William	PS	1868		
POULTER	Cpl	George Arthur	F	1571	30 Nov 1917	Cambrai Memorial
POULTON	Pte	Alonso	F	1602		
POWELL	Pte	Frederick William	F	566		
POWELL	Pte	Alfred Ernest	G	43592	22 Oct 1916	Sucrerie Military Cemetery
POWELL	Pte	Gordon Henry	G	40667	2 Dec 1917	Cambrai Memorial
POYTON	Pte	Leonard William	G	53030		
PRATT	Sgt	Charles Henry	G	19810	13 Nov 1918	Luton General Cemetery (UK)
PRATT	Pte	WH	G			
PRECIOUS	Pte	Clifford Maxwell	PS	3210		
PRENDERGAST	Pte	Charles	G	44071	22 Aug 1918	Berlin South-Western Cemetery (Germany)
PRENDERGAST	Pte	John	PW	4332		
PRENTICE	Pte	Charles	F	1114		

Surname	Rank	Forenames	Prefix	Number	Date of Death	Cemetery/Memorial
PRENTICE	Pte	HA	G			
PRENTICE	Pte	Henry	L	21506		
PRESS	Pte	Alfred Charles	F	1162		
PRESTRIDGE	Pte	Frederick	F	3003		
PRETLOVE	Pte	William	G	4977		
PRETT	Pte	Sydney	G	20144		
PRETYMAN-NEWMAN	Maj	John Robert B				
PREVOST	Pte	Percy Victor	F	1080		
PREW	Sgt	Herbert	G	965	3 Jan 1918	Arras Memorial
PRICE	Pte	Charles W	F	1304		
PRIEST	Pte	EL		5572		
PRIEST	Pte	George Albert	PS	2616		
PRIME	Pte	Frederick	F	935	8 Oct 1918	Lijssenthoek Military Cemetery (Belgium)
PRINCE	Pte	Francis	G	27261		
PRINCE	Pte	Herbert	G	92855		
PRINT	Pte	Sidney	G	1306	4 Jun 1915	Greenwich Cemetery (UK)
PRIOR	Pte	Alfred Murray	PW	5107	28 Apr 1917	Arras Memorial
PROCTOR	Pte	Albert Herbert Wilkie	G	50428		
PRYOR	Pte	William Thomas M	PS	3666		
PULLEN	Pte	Henry	F	993		
PULLINGER	Pte	Albert John	G	23739		
PULMAN	Pte	George	G	53025		
PURCHASE	2/Lt	NS				
PURDAY	Pte	James William	G	53034		
PURKISS	CSM	Albert Edward	F	1566	1 Feb 1917	Dickebusch New Military Cemetery (Belgium)
PURLE	Pte	Herbert Charles	F	1311		
PUSEY	Pte	Sidney Herbert	F	408		
PUTNAM	Pte	William Arthur	G	41664		
PUTTICK	Pte	Harold	G	2354		
PYBUS	Pte	Arthur	G	52265		
PYE	Pte	Frederick	F	409		
PYKE	Pte	George Woolston	F	921		
QUAYLE	Pte	Robin Hartby	G	42670		
RADFORD	L/Cpl	Sydney John	F	1503	27 Jul 1916	Thiepval Memorial
RADLEY	Pte	Percy Albert	G	24160		
RAMSDEN	Pte	George	PW	4781	1 Dec 1917	Cambrai Memorial
RAMSEY	L/Cpl	Alfred John	F	877	1 Dec 1917	Cambrai Memorial
RAMSEY	Pte	Sidney	PW	5017		
RANDALL	Pte	Charles Henry	F	1587		
RANN	Pte	David William	G	26324		
RANN	L/Cpl	Ernest	F	881		
RANSOM	Pte	Walter	F	1240		
RANSON	Sgt	John Leonard	F	719	9 Dec 1917	Grevillers British Cemetery
RANSON	Pte	Thomas	G	40365	29 Apr 1917	Aubigny Communal Cemetery Ext.
RAPSON	Pte	Harry	F	3164		
RATCLIFF	Pte	Thomas	F	21		
RATCLIFFE	Pte	William	G	42663		
RAVEN	Pte	Thomas Alfred	G	34020	29 Sep 1918	Terlincthun British Cemetery
RAVEN	Pte	William	G	43946		
RAW	Pte	Joseph Henry	F	23		
RAWLINGS	Pte	Percy James	G	34852		
RAWLINSON	Cpl	George William	G	13730		
RAWORTH	Pte	Thomas	G	2622		
RAY	Pte	George Henry	TF	203860		
RAY	Cpl	Lionel Evelyn Walter	F	692		
RAYMOND	Pte	Frederick Charles	G	43978	28 Apr 1917	Arras Memorial
RAYNER	Pte	Vincent	G	21373		
RAYSON	Pte	Sidney Joseph	F	492	28 Jul 1916	Thiepval Memorial
READ	Pte	Charles EG	F	483		
READ	Cpl	Harold	F	410		
READ	Capt	Stanley			28 Apr 1917	Arras Memorial
REASON	Pte	Harry	F	689		
REDKNAP	Pte	George Henry	F	1051		
REDMAN	Pte	Percy Rosslyn	G	43597		

Surname	Rank	Forenames	Prefix	Number	Date of Death	Cemetery/Memorial
REED	Pte	Adrian	G	53037	24 Mar 1918	Bac-du-Sud British Cemetery
REED	Pte	Albert Victor	TF	203061	2 Dec 1917	Cambrai Memorial
REED	Sgt	Christopher	L	10397		
REED	L/Cpl	Claude Walter	G	43599	13 Nov 1916	Thiepval Memorial
REED	Cpl	Horace Arthur	F	632		
REED	Pte	John A	F	1355		
REED		William	F			
REEN	Pte	George	G	33675	27 Dec 1917	Hermies Hill British Cemetery
REEVE	Pte	Christopher William G	G	44157		
REEVES	Pte	Albert Edward	F	1241		
REEVES	Pte	William James	L	16155		
REID	Pte	Frederick Charles	G	43577		
REID	Pte	John Malcolm	G	85272	1 Dec 1917	Hermies Hill British Cemetery
RELF	Pte	William Henry	G	44062		
REUCROFT	Pte	George Robert	G	86314		
REYNOLDS	Sgt	Albert Edward Henry	G	41474		
REYNOLDS	Pte	Alfred	G	41785		
REYNOLDS	Pte	Ernest	F	203		
REYNOLDS	Pte	W				
REYNOLDS	Pte	William	F	433		
RHOADES	Pte	George	G	50735		
RHODES	Pte	Frederick Arthur	F	1072		
RHODES	L/Sgt	George Frederick	F	492	14 Sep 1916	North Sheen Cemetery (UK)
RICE	Pte	Joseph	G	53039		
RICHARDI	Pte	William	F	1554		
RICHARDS	Pte	Alfred Charles	G	86312		
RICHARDS	Pte	Fred Clariss	G	29639	28 Apr 1917	Arras Memorial
RICHARDS	Pte	Horace	G	24079		
RICHARDSON	Pte	Reginald Herbert	G	24514	21 Aug 1918	Bagneux British Cemetery
RICHARDSON	Pte	Frederick	G	43903	7 Oct 1916	Thiepval Memorial
RICHMOND	Pte	George Alfred	F	1605		
RICKETT	Pte	Charles		27406		
RIDGERS	Pte	Frank	G	43704		
RIDGEWAY	Pte	Edward	G	22094		
RIDLEY	Pte	George Thomas	F	282		
RIDLEY	Pte	James	F	412		
RIDOUT	Sgt	Arthur Brian	F	555		
RIDSDALE	Pte	James	F	1204		
RIGGS	Pte	William	F	552		
RILEY	Pte	Alfred William	G	44011	28 Apr 1917	Arras Memorial
RIPLEY	Pte	Harry	G	50423		
RIPLEY	Pte	William Stanley	F	630	10 Mar 1917	Sunderland (Mere Knolls) Cemetery (UK)
RIPPIN	Pte	Arthur Harold	TF	203063	2 Jan 1919	Unknown (UK)
RITCHIE	Pte	R				
RIVERS	Pte	Arthur	G	44149		
RIVETT	Pte	Joseph Henry	G	46450	4 Dec 1917	Grevillers British Cemetery
RIXON	Pte	Charles	G	2707	13 Nov 1916	Serre Road No.2
ROADS	Pte	Thomas William Goddard	G	43877		
ROBERTS	Pte	Alfred Edward	G	82206		
ROBERTS	Pte	Arthur	G	6678		
ROBERTS	L/Cpl	Arthur Charles	F	750		
ROBERTS	Pte	Herbert John	F	986		
ROBERTS	Pte	Hugh Pierce	F	51		
ROBERTS	Pte	William	TF	204511		
ROBERTSON	Pte	George	F	858		
ROBERTSON	2/Lt	George MW				
ROBERTSON	CQMS	James	F	432		
ROBINS	Sgt	Henry	G	4576		
ROBINSON	Pte	AE	F	605		
ROBINSON	Pte	Bert	G	44142		
ROBINSON	Pte	Christopher Henry	G	32536	2 Dec 1917	Cambrai Memorial
ROBINSON	Pte	Walter	F	1477		
ROBINSON	Pte	William	G	18413		
ROBSON	Pte	Frederick	F	35		
ROBSON	Cpl	William Barter	G	11142		

381

Surname	Rank	Forenames	Prefix	Number	Date of Death	Cemetery/Memorial
RODMAN	Pte	Benjamin	F	1061		
ROE	Pte	Albert William	G	53038		
ROE	L/Cpl	Arthur	F			
ROE	L/Cpl	James John	G	44029	13 Nov 1916	Thiepval Memorial
ROE	Sgt	Walter George	F	179		
ROFFEY	Pte	George Thomas	G	50749	28 Apr 1917	Arras Memorial
ROGERS	Pte	Albert Victor	F	3535	4 Apr 1918	Crucifix Corner Cemetery
ROGERS	Pte	Archie	G	50750	30 Dec 1917	Grevillers British Cemetery
ROGERS	Pte	Arthur Tom	TF	202921		
ROGERS	Pte	Frederick Richard	G	14250		
ROGERS	Pte	Henry G	G	24773		
ROGERS	C/Sgt	John	F	305		
ROLFE	Pte	Albert Edward	G	53036		
ROLFE	L/Cpl	Walter Herbert	G	20343	23 Mar 1918	Arras Memorial
ROLING	Pte	Horatio Harry	G	27265		
ROLLASON	Capt	Thomas				
ROLPH	Pte	Henry W	PW	756		
ROMAIN	Pte	Charles Frederick	F	24		
RONAN	L/Cpl	Patrick	F	962	13 Nov 1916	Mailly Wood Cemetery
RONEY	Pte	Peter	F	306		
ROPER	Pte	Sidney George	G	41669		
ROSE	Pte	Arthur	F	2642		
ROSE	Pte	Harry Alfred	PS	3052		
ROSE	Pte	Herbert George	F	122		
ROSE	Pte	Thomas John	G	36653		
ROSE	Pte	Walter	F	1192		
ROSIER	Pte	Stanley Janes Fred	G	94004		
ROSIER	Cpl	William Frederick	G	9822		
ROSS	Pte	Ernest J	F	1603		
ROSS	Pte	Frank Albert Victor	PS	1544		
ROSS	2/Lt	Roderick O'Connor				
ROSS	Pte	T				
ROSS	Pte	Wallace Edgar	TF	203064	28 Apr 1917	Arras Memorial
ROSSITER	L/Cpl	Ernest	F	173		
ROTHE	2/Lt	Sidney Ernest Orme			13 Nov 1916	Thiepval Memorial
ROUSE	Pte	John	G	44022	1 Aug 1917	Ypres (Menin Gate) Memorial (Belgium)
ROUSE	Pte	John Alfred	G	21399		
ROUSE	Pte	William Francis	G	43574		
ROUSSELL	Pte	Charles John	G	21153		
ROUTLEDGE	Pte	Ralph	F	22		
ROWE	Pte	Alfred	G	44033		
ROWE	Pte	Arthur	G	43631		
ROWE	Pte	Harry Gordon	G	26383	4 Jan 1918	Ruyaulcourt Military Cemetery
ROWE	Pte	Walter Ernest	G	43663		
ROWLAND	L/Sgt	George Frederick	F	837	28 Apr 1917	Arras Memorial
ROWLAND	Pte	Thomas	F	1493		
ROWLAND	Pte	Walter Riches	G	43716	28 Apr 1917	Arras Memorial
ROWLATT	Pte	William Ernest	G	43576	13 Nov 1916	Mailly Wood Cemetery
ROWLEY	Pte	Rupert Charles	G	11232	28 Jul 1916	Thiepval Memorial
ROWSELL	Pte	Charles John	G	21153	28 Jul 1916	Thiepval Memorial
ROWSELL	Sgt	Walter Henry	F	1506		
ROWSELL	Pte	William Austin	F	465	22 Mar 1918	Queens Cemetery, Bucquoy
RUBENSTEIN	Pte	Julius	G	24705		
RUCKMAN	Pte	George	PS	3531		
RUDD	Pte	Joseph W	F	1517		
RUFF	Pte	John Leonard	TF	203065		
RUMBLE	Pte	Herbert William	G	44034	13 Nov 1916	Serre Road No.2
RUNDLE	Pte	Henry Osgood	G	43902		
RUSHBRIDGE	Sgt	Edward	F	358		
RUSKIN	Pte	Mark	F	123		
RUSS	Pte	Ernest John	F	1603		
RUSSELL	Pte	Charles Albert	F	359		
RUSSELL	Pte	Fred Joseph	G	6856		
RUSSELL	Pte	George James	F	1268		
RUSSELL	Pte	Walter	G	43575		
RUSSELL	Pte	William John	G	43894	28 Apr 1917	Arras Memorial

Surname	Rank	Forenames	Prefix	Number	Date of Death	Cemetery/Memorial
RUTHERFORD	Pte	Thomas William	G	42662		
RYAN	Pte	George Edward	G	89067		
RYAN	Pte	James	F	360		
SABERTON	Sgt	Gordon E	F	982		
SABINE	RSM	Alfred J	F	542		
SADLER	Pte	Ernest George	G	34836		
SALISBURY	Pte	Alfred Henry	G	44108	13 Nov 1916	Serre Road No.2
SALISBURY	Pte	William Thomas	F	226	2 Nov 1918	South Ealing Cemetery (UK)
SALMON	Pte	Albert Charles	F	1152		
SALMON	Pte	Charles	G	43548	9 Apr 1918	Ration Farm Military Cemetery
SALTER	Pte	John	G	13506	8 Aug 1916	Thiepval Memorial
SALTER	Capt	William			8 Aug 1916	Thiepval Memorial
SAMSON	2/Lt	Evelyn Hoper Andrew				
SAMUEL	Pte	George Henry	F	953		
SANDERS	Pte	Edgar Wilfred	G	43878		
SANDERS	Lt	Herbert Were				
SANDFORD	Pte	Alfred T		6087		
SANDIFORD	Sgt	Albert	G	53051		
SANDOE	CSM	Lyndon	F	627		
SANGWIN	Pte	Richard Cain	G	43547	21 Nov 1916	Puchevillers British Cemetery
SANTER	Pte	William	PW	6109	28 Apr 1917	Arras Memorial
SAPSWORTH	Pte	William John	TF	203454	28 Apr 1917	Arras Memorial
SARGENT	Pte	John	F	2434	8 Aug 1916	Thiepval Memorial
SASIENI	Pte	Harry	G	26651		
SATTERTHWAITE		Joseph				
SAUNDERS	Pte	Arthur	G	41486	22 Mar 1918	Arras Memorial
SAUNDERS	L/Cpl	Arthur George	G	50736	28 Jun 1918	Terlincthun British Cemetery
SAUNDERS	Pte	Charles Alfred William	G	43583		
SAUNDERS	Pte	Charles Herbert	G	53052	12 Apr 1918	Tournai Communal Cemetery Allied Ext. (Belgium)
SAUNDERS	Pte	Edward	G	38901		
SAUNDERS	Pte	Harry Jack	G	53055		
SAUNDERS	Pte	John	F	434		
SAUNDERS	L/Cpl	Thomas P	F	192		
SAUNDERS	Pte	Thomas Warwick	PS	3402		
SAUNDERS	Pte	William Ernest	F	801		
SAVAGE	Pte	William John	F	570		
SAVILLE	Pte	Albert James	G	44006	14 Jan 1918	Tournai Communal Cemetery Allied Ext. (Belgium)
SAVILLE	Pte	Harry	G	3664	27 Mar 1918	Pozieres Memorial
SAWLEY	Pte	Frederick George	G	53043		
SAWYER	Cpl	Albert Reginald	G	43634		
SAWYER	Pte	William George Adrian	G	53056		
SAXTON	Pte	Robert William	G	41633		
SAYERS	Pte	Elgar James	G	44150	27 May 1917	Berlin South-Western Cemetery (Germany)
SCAMMELL	Pte	Edward	F	621	21 Sep 1917	Tyne Cot Memorial (Belgium)
SCEATS	Pte	George Phillip	G	43580	13 Nov 1916	Thiepval Memorial
SCHNIDER	Pte	Edward Benedict	G	87056		
SCOPES	Pte	Frederick William	TF	203905	28 Nov 1917	Cambrai Memorial
SCOPES	Pte	Walter Stephen	G	44009	24 Mar 1918	Arras Memorial
SCOTLAND	Lt	William Wilkie				
SCOTT	Pte	Albert Henry	F	496		
SCOTT	Pte	Alexander	TF	203066	16 Dec 1918	Berlin South-Western Cemetery (Germany)
SCOTT	Pte	George	F	1583	16 Aug 1916	St. Souplet British Cemetery
SCOTT	Cpl	Harry William	PS	3356		
SCOTT	Pte	Richard	TF	203904		
SCOTT	Pte	Simon Wye	F	1688		
SCOTT	Sgt	Thomas	PW	535		
SCOTT	Pte	Walter George	G	94023		
SCRIVENER	Pte	Robert	G	53040		
SCUDDER	Pte	R				
SCUDDER	L/Cpl	Thomas Edward	G	44086	28 Apr 1917	Arras Memorial
SEABY	Pte	Arthur Harry	F	3045		
SEACH	Pte	Albert Charles	F	246		
SEAGRIEF	Pte	Edgar John	TF	203067	23 Apr 1917	Arras Memorial

Surname	Rank	Forenames	Prefix	Number	Date of Death	Cemetery/Memorial
SEALS	Pte	Walter	F	1258		
SEAMER	2/Lt	Charles				
SEAR	Cpl	Herbert George	F	1331	27 Jul 1916	Thiepval Memorial
SEARLE	Cpl	Walter	L	13112		
SEARSON	Sgt	Sydney G	F	1444		
SEARSTON	Pte	John Henry	G	89072	10 Dec 1917	Grevillers British Cemetery
SEBRIGHT	Lt	John Harold Knowles				
SECRETT	2/Lt	Albert George			28 Apr 1917	Arras Memorial
SEED	Cpl	Angus Cameron	F	25		
SEERS	Pte	Charles Arthur	G	43951		
SEERS	Pte	Joseph	G	12227	28 Jul 1916	Delville Wood Cemetery
SELBY	Pte	WH				
SELLEY	Pte	Cecil Howard	F	1590	29 Jul 1916	Corbie Communal Cemetery Ext.
SELWOOD	Pte	Sidney Leonard	G	76562		
SENG	Pte	Reuben Armadale	G	43954		
SETON	Pte	Harold Claude	PS	2111		
SETTERS	Cpl	Percy	L	12085		
SEVENOAKS	2/Lt	Ernest Tebbot				
SEWELL	Pte	Albert Henry	F	1682		
SEWELL	L/Cpl	John Wright	F	361		
SHACKLOCK	Pte	William	F	227		
SHADBOLT	Pte	Richard Thomas	F	193		
SHAMBROOK	Pte	Ernest	TF	20874		
SHANKS	Pte	William	F	139		
SHARMAN	Pte	Samuel Richard	G	9707		
SHARP	Pte	John	G	44155		
SHARP	Cpl	Richard H	TF	240307		
SHARP	Sgt	William	G	41663		
SHARPE	Pte	William	F	228	28 Apr 1917	Orchard Dump Cemetery
SHAVE	Pte	George Underwood	G	20843		
SHAW	Pte	Albert George	G	50425		
SHAW	Sgt	Henry Harry	F	1243		
SHAW	Pte	Horace Walter	S	7039		
SHAW	Pte	John Thomas	G	38559		
SHAW	Pte	Sidney	G	89075	30 Nov 1917	Cambrai Memorial
SHAWE	Pte	Dudley Chestly	F	260	4 Nov 1917	Rethel French National Cemetery
SHEATE	Pte	Charles Thomas	G	32537	28 Apr 1917	Arras Memorial
SHEFFIELD	Pte	Edwin	PS	3602		
SHELDON	Pte	John	F	1695		
SHELLEY	Pte	John Robson	F	362		
SHELLEY	Pte	Michael	F	2137		
SHELTON	Pte	George Isaac	G	87375		
SHENTON	Pte	Henry	G	43898		
SHEPARD	Pte	Albert Edward	F	812	18 Jan 1916	Bethune Town Cemetery
SHEPHARD	Pte	Thomas James	G	27215		
SHEPHERD	Cpl	Ernest Richard	L	7630		
SHEPHERD	Pte	Thomas	PW	5471	23 Oct 1916	Wandsworth (Earlsfield) Cemetery (UK)
SHEPPARD	Pte	Albert	PW	6010		
SHERMAN	Pte	Albert	PS	2695		
SHERRING	Pte	William Edward Frank	G	42672		
SHERWELL	Pte	Sidney	G	20934		
SHERWOOD	Pte	Ernest	F	1952		
SHIPP	Pte	Walter	G	43632		
SHIPPERLEY	Pte	S				
SHIPSTONE	Pte	Leonard		3846		
SHIRLEY	Pte	Ernest	G	43908		
SHIRLEY	Pte	James William	G	24859		
SHOPLAND	Pte	A		36342		
SHORE	Sgt	Frederick	F	1585		
SHURETY	Pte	Thomas Charles	F	856		
SHUTER	L/Cpl	Horace	G	41658		
SIBUN	Pte	James	F	580		
SILCOCKS	Pte	Edward Lionel Redbury	F	996	28 Apr 1917	Arras Memorial
SILK	Pte	Alfred	TF	201936		
SILVEYER	Pte	Edwin Albert	F	846		
SIMMONDS	L/Cpl	Charles William	F	1093	27 Jul 1916	Thiepval Memorial

Surname	Rank	Forenames	Prefix	Number	Date of Death	Cemetery/Memorial
SIMMONDS	Cpl	Henry George	G	29026		
SIMMONDS	Sgt	John Charles	G	86607		
SIMMONDS	Pte	Thomas William	G	29500	11 Oct 1917	Niederzwehren Cemetery (Germany)
SIMMONS	Pte	George	TF	203872		
SIMS	Pte	Ernest	F	36		
SIMS	Pte	Frederick	F	1011		
SIMS	Pte	Reginald	F	840	28 Jan 1916	Bethune Town Cemetery
SIMS	Pte	Roland	F	963		
SIVIL	Pte	Thomas	G	40447		
SKEELS	Cpl	H	G	10677		
SKERRY	2/Lt	James Beadnell			1 Jun 1916	Cabaret-Rouge British Cemetery
SKILTON	Pte	Albert	G	24442		
SKINNER	L/Cpl	Alfred Albert	G	41634		
SKINNER	Pte	Frank	G	41492		
SLADE	Pte	George Fred	TF	203858	28 Apr 1917	Arras Memorial
SLADE	Pte	Harold Stanley	F	901	31 May 1918	Hammersmith Old Cemetery (UK)
SLADE	Pte	Henry	G	87041		
SLADE	Pte	George Frederick	TF	203858	28 Apr 1917	Arras Memorial
SLANEY	Pte	Fred Albert	G	29629		
SLATER	Pte	Fred	F	1031		
SLAUGHTER	Pte	Ernest	TF	203875		
SLEEP	Pte	Emmanuel Charles	TF	202491		
SLY	Pte	Samuel James	G	42630		
SMALL	Pte	Walter	G	21290		
SMART	Sgt	Francis William	F	229		
SMART	Pte	James Douglas	G	43549		
SMELT	Pte	Frank	G	43722	28 Apr 1917	Arras Memorial
SMITAERMAN	Pte	John	G	44043		
SMITH	Pte	Albert	G	44025		
SMITH	Pte	Alexander Albert V	G	34375		
SMITH	Pte	Alfred	G	43633		
SMITH	Pte	Alfred William	F	678	25 Jul 1916	Carnoy Military Cemetery
SMITH	Pte	Arthur C	PS	2085		
SMITH	Pte	Charles Alfred	G	43578	22 Oct 1916	Sucrerie Military Cemetery
SMITH	Pte	Cyril	F	52		
SMITH	Pte	D				
SMITH	Pte	Edward	G	10867		
SMITH	Pte	EJ				
SMITH	Pte	Ernest	G	53047		
SMITH	Pte	Frank	G	80538		
SMITH	Pte	Frederick William	G	53049		
SMITH	Pte	George	G	34932		
SMITH	Pte	George Crossley	F	1770		
SMITH	Pte	George Thomas	G	23747		
SMITH	Pte	George W	F	464		
SMITH	Pte	Harry	F	1141		
SMITH	Pte	Harry	G	21024	17 Sep 1916	Thiepval Memorial
SMITH	Pte	Henry	G	44154		
SMITH	Pte	John Frederick Wyndham	F	363	19 Apr 1918	Conde-Sur-L'Escaut Communal Cemetery
SMITH	CSM	Joseph	F	308	13 Nov 1916	Serre Road No. 1
SMITH	Cpl	Leonard William	PS	2077		
SMITH	Pte	Maurice	L	16128	28 Apr 1917	Arras Memorial
SMITH	Pte	Percy William	G	43671	13 Nov 1916	Serre Road No.1
SMITH	Pte	Robert Leslie	G	86638	12 Oct 1918	Romeries Communal Cemetery Ext.
SMITH	Cpl	Samuel	F	262	17 Sep 1916	Thiepval Memorial
SMITH	Pte	Sidney	F	818		
SMITH	Pte	Sidney Lawrence				
SMITH	Pte	Walter Thomas	PW	6086		
SMITH	Pte	William	G	94022		
SMITH	Pte	William	G	44152	13 Nov 1916	Serre Road No. 2
SMITH	Pte	William Herbert	G	53055		
SMITH	L/Cpl	William James	F	1185		
SMITHERMAN	Pte	John	G	44043	13 Nov 1916	Thiepval Memorial
SMYTHE	L/Cpl	Charles William	G	43869		
SNARE	Pte	Alfred Robert	F	1606		
SNELGROVE	Pte	Alfred	G	92859		

Surname	Rank	Forenames	Prefix	Number	Date of Death	Cemetery/Memorial
SNELL	L/Sgt	Charles Andrew	G	43555		
SNOWDEN	Pte	George Thomas	G	53054		
SNOWDEN	Pte	Harry Christopher	G	42673		
SOLE	Pte	Albert		5878		
SOMERVILLE	Pte	Phillip French	F	913		
SONGHURST	Pte	Thomas	TF	242683		
SONGI	Pte	Albert Edward	G	32308		
SOUTHEY	Pte	Frank	G	21919		
SOUTHGATE	Pte	Francis James	G	53057		
SOUTHWELL	Pte	Alfred George	PS	1882	18 Sep 1916	Euston Road Cemetery
SOUTHWOOD	Pte					
SPAIN	Pte	Harry Collard	G	27365	9 Apr 1918	Ploegsteert Memorial (Belgium)
SPARKES	Pte	Albert	L	9370		
SPARY	Pte	Ernest	G	24987		
SPENCER	Pte	Francis Henry Best	F	53		
SPENCER	Pte	Fred Talbot	G	43668		
SPENCER	Pte	Joseph	F	1479		
SPENCER	Pte	Thomas	PW	1762		
SPICK	Pte	John Henry	F	310		
SPINKS	Pte	George William	G	52364		
SPIRES	Cpl	Horace Edward	G	33980		
SPITTLE	Cpl	William Arthur	F	54		
SPITTLE	Pte	George William	G	40978	28 Apr 1917	Arras Memorial
SPONG	Cpl	Arthur John	F	810		
SPONG	L/Cpl	Lancelot Edwin		7778		
SPRANGE	Pte	Arthur	G	43948	22 Oct 1917	Tyne Cot Memorial (Belgium)
SPURGEON	Pte	Henry	F	868	28 Apr 1917	Arras Memorial
STACE	Pte	Harold James	G	53041		
STACEY	Pte	Sidney	PW	5908		
STAFFORD	Lt Col	Ronald Semphill SH				
STAGG	2/Lt	John Reginald			17 Sep 1916	Euston Road Cemetery
STALEY	Pte	Ernest HW	F	891		
STALLWOOD	Pte	William Alfred	G	41496		
STANDEVEN	Pte	Samuel	F	1584		
STANFORD	Cpl	Fred Victor	G	29716		
STANNARD	Pte	Edward	F	999		
STANNARD	Pte	Frederick Elias	G	43864		
STANNARD	Pte	Sidney William	G	27407	31 May 1918	Bully-Grenay Communal Cemetery British Ext.
STANSFELD	Capt	Frederick Noel			1 Dec 1917	Cambrai Memorial
STAPLETON	Cpl	Arthur Edward	L	14708		
STAPLETON	Pte	Leonard	G	53044		
STATHAM	Pte	W				
STEAD	Pte	George	G	6854		
STEADMAN	Pte	William J	F	3103		
STEELE	Pte	George Robert	PW	2637		
STEER	Pte	James	PW	5762		
STENNING	Pte	Ernest Frederick	G	50770		
STENNING	Pte	Frederick	G	37585		
STENNING	Pte	Henry	TF	203876	17 Apr 1918	St. Sever Cemetery Ext.
STEPHENS	Cpl	Henry John	TF	242354		
STEPHENSON	CSM	Alexander	F	2		
STEPHENSON	Pte	Henry D	G	53045		
STEPHENSON	Pte	William	F			
STEPHENSON	Pte	John	F	442		
STERNE	L/Cpl	Frank	G	12041	28 Apr 1917	Arras Memorial
STEVEN	Pte	Robert	F	364	3 Jan 1918	Ribecourt Road Cemetery
STEVENS	Pte	Charles William	G	53059		
STEVENS	Pte	Joseph George	G	34919		
STEVENS	Pte	Thomas James	F	161		
STEVENS	Pte	William Frederick	F	1546	7 Jun 1917	Ypres (Menin Gate) Memorial (Belgium)
STEVENS	Pte	Edward Arthur	F	869	27 Jul 1916	Thiepval Memorial
STEVENSON	L/Cpl	John William	G	92860	26 Aug 1918	Bucquoy Road Cemetery
STEVENSON	Pte	William Cornelius	TF	266937		
STEWARD	L/Cpl	Walter	G	36535		
STEWART	Pte	Albert George	F	1332		

Surname	Rank	Forenames	Prefix	Number	Date of Death	Cemetery/Memorial
STEWART	Pte	Alexander	F	37		
STEWART	Sgt	Charles Harold	F	310		
STEWART	Pte	Donald Ernest	F	1039		
STEWART	Pte	James	TF	207936		
STEWART	Pte	William	F	707		
STIFF	Pte	William	G	44010		
STILE	Pte	George	G	37699	4 Jan 1918	Wimereux Communal Cemetery
STILL	Cpl	Harry	G	9468		
STOKES	Pte	Frederick James	PW	6104	27 Dec 1917	Grevillers British Cemetery
STONE	Pte	Arthur B	G	87467		
STONE	L/Cpl	Edward John	F	538		
STONE	Pte	Frederick George	F	1305	14 Aug 1916	Abbeville Communal Cemetery
STONE	Sgt	Henry	G	43863		
STONE	Pte	Joseph	G	43940	13 Nov 1916	Serre Road No. 2
STONE	Pte	William	G	21945	30 Nov 1917	Cambrai Memorial
STONES	L/Cpl	Cecil J		2022		
STOPPS	Pte	Albert E	F	1233	15 Sep 1916	Thiepval Memorial
STORER	Pte	Jack	G	5638	28 Apr 1917	Arras Memorial
STRATTON	Sgt	Frederick Walter James	F	107		
STREET	Sgt	Percy William Becker	F	174		
STRIKE	Sgt	Archibald Victor	F	311	13 Nov 1916	Serre Road No. 1
STRONG	Pte	J				
STRONG	Pte	John William Plowright	G	44117		
STRONG	Pte	George	PS	2537	24 Aug 1916	Auchonvillers Military Cemetery
STROUD	Pte	Albert Edward	F	1938	16 Aug 1916	La Neuville British Cemetery
STRUTTON	Pte	John	F	1841		
STUART	Sgt	William	L	12768		
STUBLEY	Pte	Albert	G	43711	13 Nov 1916	Serre Road No.2
STUCKEY	L/Cpl	William Thomas	F	1450	12 Aug 1916	Corbie Communal Cemetery Ext.
STUDD	Pte	Ernest Frederick	PW	5206		
STUDDS	Pte	Charles	F	2721		
STURT	Pte	Charles Aubrey	G	92863	3 Jan 1918	Arras Memorial
STUTTERS	Pte	Percy Guy	G	43589		
SULLIVAN	Pte	Eugene	F	975	8 Aug 1916	Thiepval Memorial
SULLIVAN	Pte	Frederick R	F	1389		
SULLIVAN	Pte	Patrick	S	6950		
SUMMERS	Pte	Edwin Alexis	F	436		
SUMMERS	Pte	Percy	F			
SUMPTION	Pte	Reginald	G	86315		
SURRIDGE	Pte	Herbert William Castle	G	53050	9 Apr 1918	Ploegsteert Memorial (Belgium)
SURRIDGE	Pte	John James	G	44146		
SURRY	Cpl	Fred JT	G	26094		
SUSSEX	Sgt	William	G	7123	2 Dec 1917	Cambrai Memorial
SUTTERS	Pte	Thomas A R	G	53042		
SWAIN	Pte	Charles Albert	F	752	24 Apr 1921	Tottenham Cemetery (UK)
SWAIN	Pte	Frederick J	G	47709		
SWALL	Pte	Leonard	G	89006	10 Dec 1917	Halifax (Stoney Royd) Cemetery (UK)
SWANN	Pte	Ernest Dawson	G	43681	13 Nov 1916	Mailly Wood Cemetery
SWANN	Cpl	Thomas William	F	283	28 Apr 1917	Arras Memorial
SWATTON	Sgt	William John	F	780		
SWEET	Pte	Arthur	G	41659	28 Apr 1917	Arras Memorial
SWIFT	Pte	Edward Charles	TF	203896		
SWIFT	L/Cpl	James Henry	F	1038		
SYKES	Pte	Joseph Thomas	G	8711		
TABOR	Pte	William Charles	F	617		
TACK	Pte	William	F	2605		
TACKLEY	Sgt	William	G	9251		
TAIT	Pte	Alexander	F	175		
TALBOT	Pte	Arthur Henry	PW	5900		
TALBOT	Pte	Archibald C	F	125		
TALLETT	Cpl	William	G	41660	2 Dec 1917	Cambrai Memorial
TAMPLIN	Pte	William	G	42674	3 Jan 1918	Arras Memorial
TANNER	Pte	William	F	914		
TANNER	Pte	William Charles Edward	G	42280		
TANSEY	Pte	Frank	PS	2990		
TAPPING	Pte	Victor Albert	F	603	8 Aug 1916	Thiepval Memorial

Surname	Rank	Forenames	Prefix	Number	Date of Death	Cemetery/Memorial
TARGETT	Pte	George	G	53062		
TARLING	Pte	Harold William	TF	203398		
TARRANT	Pte	Alan Douglas F	F	917		
TATTERSALL	2/Lt	H				
TAYLOR	L/Cpl	Albert Edward	G	43636	1 Dec 1917	Tincourt New British Cemetery
TAYLOR	L/Cpl	Alfred PE	F	1358		
TAYLOR	Cpl	Arthur George	L	14929		
TAYLOR	Pte	Frank Albert	F	1146		
TAYLOR	Pte	Frank Albert	F	2151	4 Jul 1916	Zouave Valley Cemetery
TAYLOR	Pte	George C	F	1056		
TAYLOR	Sgt	George James	F	546		
TAYLOR	Pte	Harry	PS	2973		
TAYLOR	Pte	John	F	1349		
TAYLOR	Pte	Joseph	F	1099	17 Oct 1918	Orchard Dump Cemetery
TAYLOR	Sgt	Joseph Thomas	F	1007		
TAYLOR	Pte	Mills	G	44060		
TAYLOR	Pte	TA	F	591		
TAYLOR	Pte	William	G	43586		
TEASDALE	Pte	George	G	92864		
TEBBUTT	Pte	Bryan	F	957		
TEMPLEMAN	Capt	Robert Henry				
TERNIVICK			F			
TERRY	Pte	Charles	G	41635	28 Apr 1917	Arras Memorial
TESTER	Pte	Cyril Henry	F	1230		
TETLEY	Pte	Ernest	G	2841	3 Jun 1916	Cabaret-Rouge British Cemetery
TEULON	Pte	Arthur Cyril	F	195	3 Dec 1917	Tincourt New British Cemetery
THAINE	Pte	Leslie Angus	F	206	7 Sep 1916	Euston Road Cemetery
THANE	Pte	George William Victor	F	90		
THOMAS	Pte	Henry Graham	F	141		
THOMAS	Pte	Herbert		27435		
THOMAS	Pte	Joseph	F	752		
THOMAS	Pte	William James	F	713		
THOMPSON	Pte	Benjamin	F	971		
THOMPSON	Pte	George	G	44061		
THOMPSON	Pte	Harry Vernon	G	43587		
THOMPSON	L/Cpl	Herbert	F	265	8 Aug 1916	Thiepval Memorial
THOMPSON	Pte	J				
THOMPSON	QMS	Joseph Alfred	F	285		
THOMPSON	Pte	Percy Langham	PS	2065		
THOMPSON	Pte	Peter	G	26395		
THOMPSON	Pte	Stewart V	F	1922		
THOMPSON	Pte	William	F	1468		
THOMPSON	Pte	William Basil	F	543		
THOMPSON	Pte	William Henry	G	44088	24 Sep 1918	Mont Huon Military Cemetery
THORNE	2/Lt	Tom Holt				
THORNE	2/Lt	William John				
THORNTON		HV	F			
THORPE	Pte	Arthur	PS	3499	28 Apr 1917	Arras Memorial
THORPE	Pte	James	G	25074		
THREADKELL	Pte	Herbert Edward	G	39550	1 Apr 1918	St. Sever Cemetery Ext.
THURBON	Pte	Sydney Victor	G	9978	26 Mar 1918	Puchevillers British Cemetery
THURSTON	Pte	Henry Joseph	F	970	8 Aug 1916	Delville Wood Cemetery
TIBBATTS	Pte	Samuel	PW	5033		
TICKLER	Lt	Arthur				
TIGHE	Cpl	Charles Vincent	F	453		
TILBROOK	Pte	William Walter	F	416		
TILBURY	Pte	George Thomas	TF	203897		
TILLETT	Pte	Albert	L	16181	26 Dec 1917	Hermies Hill British Cemetery
TILLING	Pte	Edward Arthur	F	263		
TILLEY	Pte	Arthur William	F	72		
TIMMINS	Pte	James	G	53064		
TIMMS	Pte	William James	G	40927	25 Mar 1918	Arras Memorial
TIPPING	Pte	Joseph	PW	5563	28 Apr 1917	Arras Memorial
TITCHENER	Pte	David	F	793		
TOBY	Pte	John	G	53060		
TODD	Pte	James	F	1907		
TODD	Sgt	Sidney	G	87426		

Surname	Rank	Forenames	Prefix	Number	Date of Death	Cemetery/Memorial
TOFT	Pte	Christopher	G	12338		
TOMKINS	Pte	Albert James	F	38		
TOMKINS	Pte	Sidney	F	776	24 Mar 1918	Pozieres Memorial
TOMPKINS	Pte	George	F	1284	1 Jun 1916	Cabaret-Rouge British Cemetery
TONGUE	Pte	Ernest	F	415		
TOOKEY	Pte	Walter Charles	F	519	17 Feb 1917	Regina Trench Cemetery
TOOMEY	Sgt	Albert	G	44855		
TOOVEY	Pte	Ernest	F	1529		
TOOZE	Capt	AL				
TOWLER	RSM	Christopher		92850		
TOWNLEY	Pte	Shelah	G	44147		
TOWNS	Pte	Arthur Lovis	G	29976	2 Aug 1918	Tournai Communal Cemetery Allied Ext. (Belgium)
TOWNSEND	Pte	Ernest Scott	PS	3383		
TOWNSEND	Pte	Horace Brookes	F	691		
TOYE	Pte	Henry Alexander	F	3123		
TRAVERS	Pte	William Richard	F	247		
TREADWELL	Pte	Arthur	G	23103	9 Apr 1918	Ploegsteert Memorial (Belgium)
TRENDELL	Pte	Thomas J	F	557		
TRIBE	Pte	Percy	G	27256		
TRICE	Sgt	Arthur W	F	884		
TRICKER	2/Lt	William				
TRIGGS	Pte	Percy Ernest	F	704	9 Sep 1916	Netley Military Cemetery (UK)
TROUGHTON	Pte	Frank	PW	6050	28 Apr 1917	Arras Memorial
TRY	L/Cpl	Charles Augustus	G	43859	28 Apr 1917	Arras Memorial
TUBB	Pte	Arthur	G	92561		
TUCK	2/Lt	Henry Malpas			26 Oct 1918	Moorseele Military Cemetery (Belgium)
TUCK	Pte	Frederick Albert	L	16186	13 Nov 1916	Thiepval Memorial
TUCKER	Pte	Henry Valentine	G	26515		
TUDDENHAM	Pte	Walter	G	32706		
TUFFIN	Pte	Frederick Henry	F	176		
TUGWELL	L/Sgt	Charles S	F	91		
TULL	2/Lt	Walter Daniel	F	55	25 Mar 1918	Arras Memorial
TULLETT	Pte	Harry	G	43677	13 Nov 1916	Thiepval Memorial
TURMEAU	Pte	Henry	G	33714		
TURNER	Cpl	Arthur	F	313	28 Mar 1918	Pozieres Memorial
TURNER	Pte	Arthur Alfred	G	27526		
TURNER	Pte	Charles	F	177		
TURNER	Pte	Frederick G	F	417		
TURNER	Pte	James William	F	1624		
TURNER	Pte	Richard	G	21056		
TURNER	Pte	William	G	35055	22 Sep 1917	Achiet-Le-Grand Communal Cemetery Ext.
TURTON	Pte	Harry	G	43916		
TURVEY	Pte	Fred	G	34079	16 Aug 1917	Tyne Cot Memorial (Belgium)
TUSTIN	Pte	Henry	F	2521		
TWINLEY	Sgt	George James	G	9234		
TYE	Pte	Frederick	G	44027		
TYLER	Pte	Alfred John	F	56		
TYLER	Pte	Burt Elverdine	F	590	17 Aug 1917	Chingford Mount Cemetery (UK)
TYLER	Pte	Charles Brunger	G	86518		
UNDERHILL	Pte	Charles	G	43637		
UPEX	Pte	Dick	F	73		
UPTON	Pte	ATG				
USHER	Pte	Albert	G	6921		
USHER	Pte	William	G	43983		
VAINES	Pte	Leslie William John	F	675		
VANT	Pte	Stanley Herbert	G	41636		
VAUGHAN	Pte	John Edgar	F	437		
VEDY	L/Cpl	Louis George	TF	262917		
VERNON	Pte	Walter Robert	G	50431		
VERSEY	Pte	Francis	L	15808	24 Mar 1918	Arras Memorial
VERYARD	Pte	William Thomas	G	13166	28 Apr 1917	Arras Memorial
VINCENT	Pte	Alfred	F	609		
VINCENT	Pte	Ernest A	G	2655		
VINCENT	Pte	Percy W	PS	3364		
VINE	Pte	Ernest Frederick	F	1008		

Surname	Rank	Forenames	Prefix	Number	Date of Death	Cemetery/Memorial
VINE	L/Cpl	John James	F	829		
VINEY	Pte	John	G	33303		
WADE	Lt	Albert Luvian			28 Apr 1917	Arras Memorial
WADE	2/Lt	Gordon Standley			13 Nov 1916	Varennes Military Cemetery
WADHAM	L/Cpl	James	F	1078		
WADHAM	CSM	Joseph	F	715	27 Jul 1916	Thiepval Memorial
WADSWORTH	Pte	Percy Beaumont	G	44072		
WAIGHT	Pte	Charles William Henry	F	532		
WAKE	L/Cpl	Harry John	F	418	28 Jul 1916	Thiepval Memorial
WAKEFORD	Pte	John	G	43969		
WAKELIN	Pte	Thomas Henry	F	611		
WALDEN	Pte	William Albert	F	1356		
WALKER	Pte	Charles Edgar	PW	6153	28 Apr 1917	Arras Memorial
WALKER	Pte	Frank	TF	201812	28 Apr 1917	Arras Memorial
WALKER	Pte	Hugh Horace	F	1027		
WALKER	Pte	John	G	53048		
WALKER	Pte	John	PS	3772	17 Feb 1917	Regina Trench Cemetery
WALKER	Pte	John	G	11921	25 Jul 1917	Gorre British and Indian Cemetery
WALKER	Pte	Joseph	PW	4493		
WALKER	Cpl	William Thomas	G	50751		
WALL	Capt	Anthony Herbert W				
WALL	Pte	Arthur	F	1181		
WALL	Pte	Charles Henry	F	1225		
WALL	Pte	Henry	G	11707		
WALL	Sgt	Stanley George	F	142		
WALLDER	Pte	Walter Joseph	F	533	24 Mar 1918	Arras Memorial
WALLER	Pte	Dennis	F	2907		
WALLER	Pte	Harry		14294	15 Jun 1920	New Southgate Cemetery (UK)
WALLINGTON	Pte	Harold Victor	G	43594		
WALLOND	2/Lt	William John			22 Mar 1918	Pozieres Memorial
WALSH	Maj	James R				
WALSH	Pte	John Whittaker	G	42681		
WALSH	Sgt	Joseph	G	8735		
WALTERS	Pte	Charles	G	25597		
WALTHO	Pte	Harry Reginald	F	1787	30 Jul 1916	Thiepval Memorial
WANSTALL	Pte	Charles Frederick	PS	3395		
WARBRICK	L/Cpl	William Ernest	F	1137		
WARBURTON	Pte	Frederick J	F	981		
WARBY	Pte	Alfred John	G	29504		
WARD	Pte	Albert Charles	F	1276		
WARD	Pte	Albert Horace	TF	242735		
WARD	Pte	Charles	F	209		
WARD	Pte	Charles John	TF	203451	8 Nov 1918	Blaugies Communal Cemetery (Belgium)
WARD	Pte	Leonard William	G	44007		
WARD	Pte	William	TF	241489		
WARD	Pte	William Arthur	F	1604		
WARD	Pte	William Stanley	PS	3286		
WARDLEY	Pte	Eli	F	939	6 Aug 1916	Bernafay Wood British Cemetery
WARNE	Pte	Thomas William	G	43685		
WARNER	Pte	George	G	24347		
WARNER	Pte	James William	G	34016		
WARNER	Pte	Sidney C	F	1121		
WARNER	Pte	Charles Frederick	G	51231	2 Dec 1917	Grevillers British Cemetery
WARREN	Cpl	Alfred J	F	367		
WARREN	Pte	Arthur	G	44023		
WARREN	Pte	George Henry	F	210	28 Apr 1917	Arras Memorial
WARREN	Pte	Henry Edwin	F	2585	3 May 1917	Arras Memorial
WARREN	Pte	James	G	44092	28 Apr 1917	Arras Memorial
WARREN	Pte	William C	F	710		
WASS	L/Cpl	Horace Wilson	F	1019	11 May 1916	Loos British Cemetery
WATERS	Pte	Alfred Stanley	G	27426		
WATERS	Cpl	Arthur	F	1462		
WATERS	Pte	Cecil John	TF	202168	23 Jan 1918	Boulogne Eastern Cemetery
WATERS	Pte	Charles Henry	G	40460	26 Sep 1918	Thilloy Road Cemetery
WATERS	Pte	Thomas James	PS	3647		
WATKINS	Pte	Arthur William	G	98804		

Surname	Rank	Forenames	Prefix	Number	Date of Death	Cemetery/Memorial
WATKINS	Pte	Walter	G	12697		
WATLING	L/Cpl	John Emanuel	F	1136		
WATSON	Pte	James	F	1538	15 Sep 1916	Thiepval Memorial
WATSON	Pte	Robert	G	44035	13 Nov 1916	Thiepval Memorial
WATSON	Pte	Matthew Hanley	F	438	2 Jun 1916	Cabaret-Rouge British Cemetery
WATSON	Sgt	Robert James	F	5		
WATTS	Sgt	Alfred James	G	43640		
WATTS	Pte	Archibald	G	41194		
WATTS	Pte	Edwin Charles	F	997		
WATTS	L/Sgt	Ernest James	F	534		
WATTS	Pte	John	G	41514		
WAYLAND	Pte	Herbert Charles	G	43655	13 Nov 1916	Thiepval Memorial
WEARY	Pte	Alfred	G	87525	12 Dec 1917	Lebucquiere Communal Cemetery Ext
WEATHERLY	Pte	Alfred James	G	27463		
WEBB	Pte	Cecil Edwin	G	26911		
WEBB	Sgt	Charles	PS	630		
WEBB	Pte	Charles	G	29550	11 May 1918	Chorleywood Road Cemetery (UK)
WEBB	L/Cpl	Edger Sidney	G	43897		
WEBB	Pte	Frederick James	G	6031	7 Dec 1917	Tyne Cot Memorial (Belgium)
WEBB	Pte	Frederick Rowland	G	43927	13 Nov 1916	Thiepval Memorial
WEBB	Cpl	George Herbert	F	673		
WEBB	Pte	Harry	TF	203857		
WEBB	RSM	James	F	475		
WEBB	Pte	John William	G	44107		
WEBB	CQMS	Joseph	F	1144		
WEBB	Cpl	Reginald John	F	1165		
WEBB	Pte	Thomas	G	44067	28 Apr 1917	Arras Memorial
WEBB	Pte	William	F	2298	27 Jul 1916	Thiepval Memorial
WEBB	Pte	William Henry	F	1352	28 Apr 1917	Arras Memorial
WEBDALE	Pte	John E	F	1509		
WEBSDALE	Pte	Cecil Charles	G	5025		
WEBSTER	Pte	Joseph	F	314		
WEEDON	Pte	Charles Albert	F	1507		
WELCH	Cpl	Sidney Charles	F	419	8 Aug 1916	Thiepval Memorial
WELCH	Pte	William John	F	633	25 Jul 1916	Thiepval Memorial
WELDON	Pte	William	F	1396	27 Oct 1916	Voormezeele Encl. No. 3 (Belgium)
WELLER	Pte	Arthur Charles	G	41516		
WELLER		S	F			
WELLER	Pte	William	F	1404		
WELLS	Pte	Joseph Arthur	G	29805		
WELLS	Pte	William	L	16168		
WELLS-HOLLAND	Capt	Henry				
WELSH	CSM	George Edward	L	12872		
WELSTEAD	Lt	Eric Marion				
WENDON	Pte	Percy	G	89001		
WENSLEY	Pte	George Henry	F	1542	7 Jun 1917	Ypres (Menin Gate) Memorial (Belgium)
WESLEY	Pte	George Arthur	G	43911		
WEST	Pte	Alfred	F	851		
WEST	Pte	Edward Henry	G	50738	24 Mar 1918	Arras Memorial
WEST	Pte	George Benjamin	G	42675		
WEST	L/Cpl	Joseph	G	43804	13 Nov 1916	Serre Road No.2
WEST	Pte	Percy	F	1097		
WEST	L/Cpl	William Frederick	F	804		
WESTACOTT	Pte	Frank Searle	F	248		
WESTERMAN	Pte	George	F	937	6 Aug 1916	Bernafay Wood British Cemetery
WESTON	Pte	Robert John	F	927		
WHEATLEY	L/Cpl	B				
WHEATLEY	Pte	Edward Henry	F	535		
WHEELER	Pte	Albert Edward	F	1170		
WHEELER	Pte	Arthur	F	556		
WHEELER	Cpl	Arthur	TF	203184	28 Apr 1917	Arras Memorial
WHEELER	Pte	Ernest	TF	203071	28 Apr 1917	Arras Memorial
WHEELER	Pte	GE				
WHEELER	Pte	James	G	24731	22 Mar 1918	Pozieres Memorial
WHEELER	Pte	John Frederick	F	212		

Surname	Rank	Forenames	Prefix	Number	Date of Death	Cemetery/Memorial
WHEELER	Pte	John Thomas	F	1107		
WHEELER	Pte	Thomas V	F	1171		
WHEELER	Pte	William	G	10897		
WHEELER	Sgt	William Thomas	G	26521		
WHEELHOUSE	L/Cpl	Sidney	F	909	19 Sep 1916	Couin British Cemetery
WHEWELL	Pte	John William	G	42676		
WHILES	Cpl	Sidney	G	42664		
WHITBREAD	Pte	James Henry	G	44081		
WHITCHURCH	Pte	HF				
WHITE	L/Cpl	Albert George	F	508		
WHITE	Pte	Charles Samuel	F	463	14 Mar 1917	Thiepval Memorial
WHITE	2/Lt	Cyril Arthur			28 Apr 1917	Arras Memorial
WHITE	Cpl	Frederick Edward	F	608	28 Apr 1917	Arras Memorial
WHITE	Pte	Frederick James	F	1375		
WHITE	Pte	James	F	983		
WHITE	Pte	John James	F	1589		
WHITE	Pte	Reginald				
WHITE	Pte	George	F	1427	28 Jul 1916	Thiepval Memorial
WHITEHEAD	Pte	Edgar Reginald	G	18223	18 Sep 1916	Euston Road Cemetery
WHITEHEAD	Pte	George	G	41637		
WHITEHEAD	Pte	Leslie	F	439	1 Jun 1916	Cabaret-Rouge British Cemetery
WHITEHEAD	L/Cpl	Philip Thomas	F	823	14 Sep 1917	Reninghelst New Military Cemetery (Belgium)
WHITELEY	Pte	Alfred	G	27409		
WHITING	Pte	Alfred	G	43641		
WHITING	Pte	Alfred Thomas	F	1595		
WHITING	Pte	David William	F	640	8 Aug 1916	Thiepval Memorial
WHITING	Cpl	Edward Jervis	G	53046		
WHITING	Pte	Robert	F	74	28 Apr 1917	Arras Memorial
WHITING	CSM	William Henry	L	16932		
WHITLEY	Pte	James	F	842		
WHITTAKER	Pte	Fred	F	786		
WHITWORTH	Pte	George	F	315		
WHITWORTH	Pte	William	PS	2886		
WHYMAN	Pte	William George	G	33907		
WICK	Pte	Harry Joseph	G	26420		
WICKENDEN	Pte	Stanley William	G	50754	28 Apr 1917	Arras Memorial
WICKENS	L/Cpl	Frank	G	43872		
WICKENS	Pte	William	G	43084		
WICKS	L/Cpl	Edward	F	1032	1 Feb 1916	Bethune Town Cemetery
WIGG	Pte	Ernest H	F	977		
WIGGINS	Pte	William H	PW	4681		
WILCOCK		George Harrie				
WILD	Pte	Sidney James	TF	207934		
WILDE		J	F			
WILDMAN	Pte	William	G	20712		
WILEMAN	Sgt	Arthur Harold	F		28 Apr 1918	Tyne Cot Memorial (Belgium)
WILKES	CSM	Frederick	F	520		
WILKES	Pte	George Samuel	G	42666	27 Dec 1917	Rocquigny-Equancourt Road British Cemetery
WILKIN	Pte	Archibald James	G	34385	28 Nov 1917	Hermies Hill British Cemetery
WILKINSON	Pte	Albert	G	43723	28 Apr 1917	Arras Memorial
WILKINSON	Pte	Frederick Edgar	PS	3774		
WILKINSON	Pte	Richard Mills	G	42677		
WILKINSON	Pte	Thomas Frederick G	F	1322		
WILKINSON	Capt	William Durham				
WILKINSON	Pte	William Frederick	F	108	13 Nov 1916	Thiepval Memorial
WILLATS	Pte	Albert	G	34059		
WILLCOX	Pte	Bernard C	F	368		
WILLEATTS	Pte	Frederick William	F	1335		
WILLETT	Pte	John Thomas	PW	5481		
WILLEY	Pte	W				
WILLGOSS	Pte	Ernest William James	G	41399		
WILLGOSS	Pte	William	G	43642	10 Oct 1918	St. Aubert British Cemetery
WILLIAMS	Pte	Allen James	F	1303		
WILLIAMS	Pte	EH	G	17211		
WILLIAMS	Pte	Frederick	G	129		

Surname	Rank	Forenames	Prefix	Number	Date of Death	Cemetery/Memorial
WILLIAMS	Pte	Gilbert	F	1663	10 Aug 1917	Ypres (Menin Gate) Memorial (Belgium)
WILLIAMS	Cpl	Horace Cyril	G	43962		
WILLIAMS	Pte	John William	F	57	5 Jun 1916	Arras Memorial
WILLIAMS		Reginald	F			
WILLIAMS	Cpl	William H	F	2140		
WILLIAMSON	Pte	Ernest Clarke	F	40		
WILLIAMSON	Pte	Herbert John	G	44018		
WILLIS	L/Cpl	Albert Edward	F	1874	13 Nov 1916	Serre Road No.2
WILLIS	Pte	Mancer	G	44048	13 Nov 1916	Thiepval Memorial
WILLISON	Pte	James Thomas	G	20856		
WILLMOTT	Pte	Robert	PW	5811		
WILLS	Pte	Jesse	G	27276		
WILSON	Pte	Albert	F	1539	31 Jul 1917	Ypres (Menin Gate) Memorial (Belgium)
WILSON	Pte	Albert	G	34774		
WILSON	Pte	Arthur	F	494		
WILSON	Pte	Charles	F	233		
WILSON	L/Cpl	Charles	F			
WILSON	Pte	Charles Albert	F	802	29 Jul 1916	Dive Copse British Cemetery
WILSON	Pte	Frederick Rob	TF	204531		
WILSON	Pte	Horace Henry	G	11999		
WILSON	Pte	John William	F	1456		
WILSON	Sgt	Joseph Thomas	F	2424		
WILSON	Pte	Robert James	F	3304		
WILSON	Cpl	Stephen Fawcett	G	42683		
WILSON		T	F			
WILTSHIRE	Pte	Alfred Dennis	G	87039		
WINDIBANK	Pte	Jack	G	50755	29 Apr 1917	Douai Communal Cemetery
WINDSOR	Pte	Thomas	F	1608		
WING	L/Cpl	Frederick Charles	F	231		
WINGATE	Pte	George Alfred	PW	4842	11 Jan 1918	Rocquigny-Equancourt Road British Cemetery
WINGHAM	Pte	George Albert	G	43971		
WINGROVE	Pte	Joseph	F	75		
WINSHIP	Lt	Ernest Roland				
WINSLADE	Pte	Percy Stephen	G	43638		
WINSLOW	Pte	Arthur David	G	43895		
WINTER	Pte	Walter Kerval Everett	F	771		
WITHERINGTON	Pte	Robert	G	42665		
WITHERS	Pte	Philip John	G	43705		
WOOD	L/Cpl	Albert Edward	G	43884		
WOOD	Cpl	Albert John	G	43893		
WOOD	Pte	Albert William George	G	34444	24 Aug 1918	Douchy-les-Ayette British Cemetery
WOOD	Pte	DA				
WOOD	Pte	Frank	G	44057		
WOOD	Pte	General Gordon	G	41662		
WOOD	Pte	George	TF	242505		
WOOD	Pte	George Frederick	PS	3497		
WOOD	Pte	Lawrence	G	43639		
WOOD	Cpl	Norman Arthur	F	663	28 Jul 1916	Thiepval Memorial
WOOD	Cpl	Percy Frank	G	42682		
WOOD	Pte	Sidney	G	41648	28 Apr 1917	Arras Memorial
WOOD	Pte	Terence	F	266		
WOODCRAFT	Pte	Harry	G	44026	17 Feb 1917	Courcelette Cemetery
WOODERSON	Pte	William George Henry P	L	15360		
WOODHEAD	Pte	Joseph William	TF	203185	16 Apr 1917	Anzin-St Aubin British Cemetery
WOODHOUSE	L/Cpl	John	F	41		
WOODMAN	Pte	George	S	5233		
WOODS	Pte	Charles TG	G	45070		
WOODS	Pte	Ernest	G	43861	28 Apr 1917	Arras Memorial
WOODS	Pte	Reuben	G	43998		
WOODS	L/Cpl	SR				
WOODS	Pte	William John	G	32654		
WOODWARD	L/Sgt	Maurice	F	316		
WOODWARD	Capt	Vivian John				

Surname	Rank	Forenames	Prefix	Number	Date of Death	Cemetery/Memorial
WOODWARD	Pte	Wilfred G	TF	292661		
WOOLDRIDGE	Pte	George Thomas	G	42631		
WOOLER	Pte	Frederick John	G	24041		
WOOLETT	Pte	Henry	PS	3558		
WOOLF	Pte	Albert Arthur	G	50756	28 Apr 1917	Arras Memorial
WOOLGER	Pte	Henry George	F	482	28 Jul 1916	Delville Wood Cemetery
WOOLNOUGH	L/Cpl	Albert J	G	44019		
WOOSTER	Pte	Frederick	F	811		
WOOSTER	Pte	WC				
WORLD	Cpl	William John	G			
WRAGG	Pte	Granville	F	1022		
WRAIGHT	Pte	Percival Arthur	F	93		
WRAMPLING	Pte	Raynham James	F	109		
WRAY	Pte	Edward	G	24110	13 Nov 1916	Thiepval Memorial
WRENCH	Pte	William	G	11247		
WRETHAM	Pte	David George	G	47282		
WRIGHT	Pte	Alfred Edward	F	364		
WRIGHT	L/Cpl	Elias	F	951	20 Mar 1917	Dernancourt Communal Cemetery Ext.
WRIGHT	Cpl	Frederick	F	870		
WRIGHT	Pte	G				
WRIGHT	Pte	George William	G	44099	24 Aug 1918	Vis-en-Artois Memorial
WRIGHT	Pte	Henry Albert	F	1828	13 Nov 1916	Serre Road No.2
WRIGHT	Pte	Howard C F	G	50757		
WRIGHT	Pte	James	G	42679		
WRIGHT	Pte	John Victor James	F	1359		
WRIGHT	Pte	Percy Walter	G	44148		
WRIGHT	Pte	Thomas	F	110	28 Jul 1916	Thiepval Memorial
WRIGHT	Pte	Thomas Daniel	F	915		
WRIGHT	Sgt	Walter	F	462		
WRIGHT	Pte	William	F	1345		
WRIGHTSON	Pte	Leonard Sladden	G	7523	3 Jan 1918	Arras Memorial
WYETH	Cpl	Arthur Henry	F	1012		
WYNNE	Cpl	James Walter	F	741	13 Nov 1916	Serre Road No.2
YARWOOD	Pte	Willliam Arthur	G	44082		
YEAMAN	Pte	Peter	G	42688		
YEATMAN	Pte	Frank Ernest	G	12280		
YEOMAN	Pte	William John	TF	241304		
YEOVAL	Sgt					
YOUELL	Pte	Arthur	G	87384		
YOUNG	Pte	Arthur George	TF	203075	28 Apr 1917	Arras Memorial
YOUNG	Pte	George	TF	241516		
YOUNG	L/Cpl	H	G			
YOUNG	Pte	Henry	G	43901		
YOUNGS	Pte	SB	G	44012		
YOXALL	Pte	Frederick	G	42687		

BIBLIOGRAPHY AND SOURCES

Bank of England Archives (BoE)
Minutes of the Court of Directors.

British Newspaper Library, Colindale (BNL)
Newspapers
*Andover Advertiser and North West Hants Gazette, Athletic News,
Beckenham Advertiser, Berkshire Chronicle, Bexley Heath, Bexley &
District Times and Dartford Chronicle, Birmingham Daily Post, Croydon
Advertiser, Daily Record and Mail, Dorset Daily Echo, East Grinstead
Observer, Enfield Gazette, Evening Argus, Football Post* (Nottingham),
*Fulham & West Kensington Gazette, Fulham Chronicle, Grimsby News,
Hackney and Kingsland Gazette, Manchester Football News, Mansfield
Chronicle, Middlesex County Times, Morning Post, Nottingham Evening
Post, Salisbury Times, The Scotsman, Sporting Chronicle, Sportsman,
Surrey Times and County Express, Surrey Weekly Press, Sutton-in-Ashfield
and Shirebrook Gazette, The Times, Tottenham & Edmonton Weekly
Gazette, West London & Fulham Times, West London Observer, Western
Evening Herald, Western Weekly Mercury.*

Club Programmes
*The Albion News and Official Programme; The Arsenal F.C. Official
Programme; The Villa News and Record: Official Journal of the Aston
Villa Football Club; The Chelsea F.C. Chronicle: Official Programme;
Oriental Notes: The Official Organ of the Clapton Orient Football Club Ltd;
The Everton and Liverpool Official Football Programme; The Cottagers'
Journal: Official Journal of the Fulham Football Club; Official
Programme of the Huddersfield Town Football Club; Tottenham Hotspur
Football and Athletic Club Limited; Official Programme of the West Ham
United Football Company.*

Dulwich College Archives (DCA)
Papers relating to Lt A.L. Wade.

Football Association (FA)
Football Association and Council Minutes.

Imperial War Museum, Department of Documents (IWM)
Papers relating to Maj W.G. Bailey (74/127/1) and Lt Col R.S.S.H. Stafford. (73/103/1)

Liddle Collection, Brotherton Library,
University of Leeds (LC)
Papers relating to Pte Wilf Nixon (POW 047) and Pte Fred Hodges (POW 048).

National Army Museum, Department of Archives,
Photographs, Film and Sound (NAM)
Papers relating to Capt J.G. Howard (1999-03-95-2) and Capt A.M.C. McReady-Diarmid (9403-139).

Private Collections (PC)
Papers relating to Capt J.C. Clark, Maj K.D.L. Maclaine, Sgt J. McCormick, and Capt E. Parfitt. Capt. L.I. Horniman's annotated copy of *The History of the Second Division*.

The National Archives (TNA)
WO 95 (Unit War Diaries): 17th Middlesex, 2nd South Staffords, 13th Essex, 1st King's Liverpool, 1st King's Royal Rifle Corps, 2nd Highland Light Infantry, 17th Royal Fusiliers, 23rd Fusiliers, 176th Tunnelling Company, 8th East Surreys, 6th Brigade, 2nd Division; **WO 339, WO 374, AIR 76** (Officers' records of service); **WO 363, WO 364** (Other ranks' service records); **WO 329** (Rolls for 1914–15 Star, British War Medal, Victory Medal and Silver War Badge); **WO 161** (POW interviews – other ranks).

Books, Articles and Other Sources
Adams, G., 'The Curious Story of Captain Allastair McReady-Diarmid VC', *Stand To!* No. 75, January 2006

Alexander, J., *McCrae's Battalion* (Edinburgh, Mainstream, 2003)

Anon, *List of British Officers taken Prisoner in the various Theatres of War between August 1914 and November 1918* (London, Messrs Cox & Co, 1919)

——, *A Short History of the Middlesex Regiment* (Aldershot, Gale & Polden Ltd, 1919)

——, *Histories of 251 Divisions of the German Army Which Participated in the War 1914–1918* (London, London Stamp Exchange, 1989)

Ashworth, T., *Trench Warfare 1914–1918: The Live and Let Live System* (London, Macmillan, 1980)

Association of Football Statisticians, *War Reports 1915–1919* (AFS, *c.*1982)

Babington, A., *Shell-Shock: A History of the Changing Attitudes to War Neurosis* (London, Leo Cooper, 1997)

Bailey, J., *Not Just on Christmas Day – An Overview of Association Football in the Great War* (Upminster, 3–2 Books, 1999)

Barrie, A., *War Underground: The Tunnellers of the Western Front* (London, Tom Donovan, 1988)

Basson, S., *Lucky Whites and Spireites: Who's Who Chesterfield F.C.* (Harefield, Yore Publications, 1998)

Bidwell. S. and Graham, D., *Firepower: British Army Weapons and Theories of War 1904–1945* (London, Allen & Unwin, 1982)

Book of Remembrance of Victoria College (Jersey, 1920)

Borough of Hove, Municipal War Record, Roll of Honour

Bourne, J., 'Two British Officers of the Great War', *The Response: An Occasional Magazine of the Northumberland & Durham Branches of the W.F.A.*, No. 11, 2000

Brown, T., *Football League: Results & Dates:* vol. I (Nottingham, Tony Brown, 2002)

——, *Football League: Results & Dates:* vol. II (Nottingham, Tony Brown, 2002)

——, *Football League: Results & Dates:* vol. IV (Nottingham, Tony Brown, 2002)

Burrows, J., *The Essex Regiment: 9th, 10th, 11th, 13th & 15th Battalions* (Southend-on-sea, John H. Burrows & Sons, 1935)

Butler, B., *The Official History of the Football Association* (London, Queen Anne Press, 1991)

Byrne, S. and Jay M., *Bristol Rovers Football Club: The Definitive History 1883–2003* (Stroud, Tempus, 2003)

Carder, T. and Harris, R., *Albion A–Z: A Who's Who of Brighton & Hove Albion F.C.* (Brighton, Goldstone Books, 1997)

Chausseaud, P., *Rats Alley: Trench Names of the Western Front 1914–1918* (Stroud, Spellmount, 2006)

Clark, C., *The Tin Trunk – Letters and Drawings 1914–1918* (London, F.S. & J. Rhys, 2000)

Consolidation of Trenches, Localities and Craters After Assault and Capture, With a Note on Rapid Wiring (London, General Staff, War Office, 1916)

Cooper, M., *Pompey People: Portsmouth F.C. Who's Who 1899–2000* (Harefield, Yore Publications, 2000)

Corns, C. and Hughes-Wilson J., *Blindfold and Alone: British Military Executions in the Great War* (London, Cassell, 2001)

Cox, R., Russell, D. and Vamplew, W., *Encyclopedia of British Football* (London, Frank Cass, 2002)

Cron, H., *Imperial German Army 1914–18, Organisation, Structure, Orders-of-Battle* (Solihull, Helion, 2002)

Cull, I., *China Dragon Tales: The 1st Battalion of the Royal Berkshire Regiment in the Great War* (Salisbury, Wardrobe Museum Trust, 2004)

Davage, M., *Glorious Canaries 1902–1994* (Norwich, Norwich City FC, 1994)

Davies, G. and Garland. I., *Who's Who of Welsh International Soccer Players* (Bridge Books, 1991)

de Ruvigny, Marquis, *The Roll of Honour: A Biographical Record of Members of His Majesty's Naval and Military Forces who Fell in the Great War,* 5 vols. (1922)

Die-Hards: Journal of the Middlesex Regiment (1922–1966)

Downs, D., *100 Greats – Reading Football Club* (Stroud, Tempus, 2000)

Dudley Ward, C., *The Fifty-Sixth Division: 1st London Territorial Division 1914–1918:* (London, John Murray, 1921)

Edmonds, Sir J., *Official History of the War, Military Operations: France & Belgium 1916,* vol. I (London, HMSO, 1932)

——, *Official History of the War, Military Operations: France & Belgium 1918,* vol. I (London, HMSO, 1935)

Dykes, G., *Latics Lads: The Official Who's Who of Oldham Athletic 1907–2002* (Harefield, Yore Publications, 2002)

Ellis, J., *Eye Deep in Hell: The Western Front 1914–18* (Harmondsworth, Penguin, 2002)

Falls, Capt. C., *Official History of the War, Military Operations: France & Belgium 1917*, vol. I (London, Macmillan, 1940)

Field Service Pocket Book (London, General Staff, War Office, 1914, reprinted with amendments 1916)

Futter, A., *Who Killed the Cock Robins? The History of Croydon Common F.C. 1897–1917* (Croydon, Alan Futter, 1990)

Gilbert, M., *First World War* (London, Harper Collins, 1995)

Gliddon, G., *The Battle of the Somme: A Topographical History* (Stroud, Sutton Publishing, 1994)

——, *VCs of the Great War: Cambrai 1917* (Stroud, Sutton Publishing, 2004)

——, *VCs of the Great War: The Somme* (Stroud, Sutton Publishing, 1994)

Green, G., *History of the Football Association 1863–1953* (London, Naldrett Press, 1953)

Grieve, Capt W. and Newman, B., *Tunnellers* (London, Herbert Jenkins, 1936)

Haig, D. (eds Sheffield, G. and Bourne, J.), *Douglas Haig: War Diaries and Letters 1914–1918* (London, Weidenfeld & Nicolson, 2005)

Hansard HC, vol. 78

Harding, J., *For the Good of the Game: The Official History of the PFA* (London, Robson Books, 1991)

——, *Living to Play: From Soccer Slaves to Socceratti* (London, Robson, 2003)

Hare, Sir S., *The Annals of the King's Royal Rifle Corps*, vol. 5 (London, John Murray, 1932)

Harris, R., Billie: The Nevill Letters 1914-1916 (London, Julia Macrae, 1991)

Hart, P., *The Somme* (London, Weidenfeld & Nicholson, 2005)

Hesketh-Prichard, H., *Sniping in France* (London, Leo Cooper, 1994)

Hayes, D., *Who's Who of Cardiff City* (Derby, Breedon Books, 2006)

Hart's Annual Army List, Special Reserve List and Territorial Force List for 1915 (London, John Murray, 1915)

Holley, D. and Chalk, G., *Alphabet of the Saints* (Leicester, ACL & Polar Publishing, 1992)

Holmes, R., *Tommy: The British Soldier on the Western Front 1914–1918* (London, Harper Collins, 2004)

——, *The Western Front* (London, BBC Worldwide, 1999)

Hussey, Brig Gen A. and Inman, Maj D., *The Fifth Division in the Great War* (London, Nisbet, 1921)

Inglis, S., *League Football and the Men Who Made it 1888–1988* (London, Willow Books, 1988)

——, *Soccer in the Dock: A History of British Football Scandals 1900–1965* (London, Willow Books, 1985)

Jacobs, N., *Vivian Woodward: Football's Gentleman* (Stroud, Tempus, 2005)

James, E., *British Regiments 1914–1918* (London, Samson Books, 1978)

James, G., *Football With a Smile: The Authorised Biography of Joe Mercer* (Leicester, ACL & Polar Publishing, 1993)

Jenkins, S., *They Took the Lead* (London, DDP, 2005)

Jerrold, D., *The Royal Naval Division* (London, Hutchinson, 1923)

Joannou, P., *The Black 'N' White Alphabet: A Complete Who's Who of Newcastle F.C.* (Leicester, Polar, 1996)

Johnson, J., *Stalemate: The Great Trench Warfare Battles of 1915–1917* (London, Arms & Armour, 1995)

Jones, J., *A History of the South Staffordshire Regiment 1705–1923* (Wolverhampton, Whitehead Bros, 1923)

Jones, T., *Watford Football Club Illustrated Who's Who* (Twickenham, TGJ, 1996)

Joyce, M., *Football League Players' Records 1888–1939* (Nottingham, Soccer Data Publications, 2006)

Jünger, E. (tr. Michael Hofmann), *Storm of Steel* (London, Allen Lane, 2003)

Kaufman, N., *The Men Who Made Leyton Orient Football Club* (Stroud, Tempus, 2002)

Kingsford, C., *The Story of the Duke of Cambridge's Own (Middlesex Regiment)* (London, Country Life, 1916)

Lamming, D., *Who's Who of Grimsby Town AFC* (Beverley, Hutton Press, 1985)

——, *An English Internationalist's Who's Who* (Beverley, Hutton Press, 1990)

Lindsay, R., *Millwall: A Complete Record 1885–1991* (Derby, Breedon Books, 1991)

Lloyd, G., *C'mon City! A Hundred Years of the Bluebirds* (Bridgend, Seren, 1999)

London Gazette

Marks, J., *Heroes in Hoops: QPR Who's Who 1899–2003* (Harefield, Yore Publications, 2003)

Mason, T., *Association Football and English Society 1863–1915* (Brighton, Harvester Press, 1980)

Matthews, T., *Who's Who of Aston Villa* (Edinburgh, Mainstream, 2004)

——, *Who's Who of West Bromwich Albion* (Derby, Breedon Books, 2005)

Maude, A., *The 47th (London) Division 1914–1919* (London, Amalgamated Press, 1922)

McCarthy, C., *The Somme: The Day-by-Day Account* (London, Brockhampton Press, 1998)

McLaren, S. (ed.), *'Somewhere in Flanders'. A Norfolk Padre in the Great War: The War Letters of The Revd Samuel Frederick Leighton Green MC, Army Chaplain 1916–1919* (Dereham, Larks Press, 2005)

Messenger, C., *Call To Arms: The British Army 1914–18* (London, Weidenfeld & Nicolson, 2005)

Middlebrook, M., *The First Day on the Somme* (London, Allen Lane, 1971)

——, *Your Country Needs You* (Barnsley, Pen & Sword, 2000)

Miles, Capt. W., *Official History of the War, Military Operations: France & Belgium 1916*, vol. II (London, HMSO, 1938)

——, *Official History of the War, Military Operations: France & Belgium 1917*, vol. III (London, HMSO, 1948)

Monthly Army Lists 1914–1918

Mortimer, G., *Who's Who of Derby County* (Derby, Breedon Books, 2004)

Myerson, G., Fighting for Football: From Woolwich Arsenal to the Western Front: The Lost Story of Football's First Rebel (London, Aurum Press, 2009)

Nannestad, I., '"The Charge at Football is Good, That with the Bayonet Finer" The Formation of the Footballers' Battalion

1914', *Soccer History*, Issue 1, April 2002

Nicholls, J., *Cheerful Sacrifice: The Battle of Arras 1917* (London, Leo Cooper, 1990)

O'Moore Creagh, G., *The VC and DSO Book*, 3 vols (London, Standard Art Book Co, 1924)

Ollier, F., *Arsenal: A Complete Record 1886–1990* (Derby, Breedon Books, 1990)

O'Neill, H.C., *The Royal Fusiliers in the Great War* (London, Heinemann, 1922)

Oxford Dictionary of National Biography (Oxford, Oxford University Press, 2004)

Prior, R. and Wilson, T., *Command and Control on the Western Front: The Military Career of Sir Henry Rawlinson 1914–1918* (Oxford, Blackwell, 1992)

Quirke, P., *The Major: The Life and Times of Frank Buckley* (Stroud, Tempus, 2006)

Robinson, M., *Football League Tables 1888–2003* (Cleethorpes, Soccer Books Ltd, 2003)

Rollin, J., *Soccer at War 1939–45* (London, Headline, 2005)

Russell, D., *Football and the English* (Preston, Carnegie Publishing, 1997)

Sanders, R., Beastly Fury: The Strange Birth of British Football (London, Bantam Press, 2009)

Sands, Revd N., *The Men Who Made Crystal Palace Football Club* (Stroud, Tempus, 2005)

Saunders, A., *Weapons of the Trench War 1914–1918* (Stroud, Sutton Publishing, 1999)

Sedunary, A., *Heaven on Earth: Official History of Reading FC 1871–2003* (Harefield, Yore Publications, 2003)

——, *Royals Remembered: Official Who's Who of Reading F.C 1920–2001* (Harefield, Yore Publications, 2001)

Seton Hutchinson, G., *The Thirty-Third Division in France and Flanders 1915–1919* (London, Waterloo, 1921)

Sewell, E., *Rugby Football Internationals' Roll of Honour* (London, TC & EC Jack, 1919)

Sharpe, G., *Free the Manchester One* (London, Robson, 2003)

Sheffield, G., *Forgotten Victory* (London, Headline, 2001)

Sheldon, J., *The German Army on the Somme 1914–1916* (Barnsley, Pen & Sword, 2005)

Simkins, P., *Kitchener's Armies: The Raising of the New Armies 1914–1916* (Manchester, Manchester University Press, 1988)

Stenton, M. and Lees, S., *Who's Who of British Members of Parliament*, Vol. III, 1919–1945 (Brighton, Harvester Press, 1979)

Soldiers Died in the Great War, CD-ROM version 1.1 (Uckfield, Naval & Military Press, 1999)

Taylor, H., *Jix: Viscount Brentford* (London, Stanley Paul, 1933)

Taylor, P. and Smith, D., *The Foxes Alphabet* (Leicester, Polar Publishing, 1995)

Terraine J., *Douglas Haig: The Educated Soldier* (London, Hutchinson, 1963)

The Pauline (St Paul's School Magazine)

Vamplew, W., *Pay Up and Play the Game: Professional Sport in Britain 1875–1914* (Cambridge, Cambridge University Press, 1988)

Vasili, P., *Colouring Over the White Line: The History of Black Footballers in Great Britain* (Edinburgh, Mainstream, 2000)

Vasili, P., Walter Tull (1888-1918) Officer, Footballer: All the Guns in France Couldn't Wake Me (London, Raw Press, 2009)

Van Emden, R., *Boy Soldiers of the Great War* (London, Headline, 2005)

Veitch, C., "Play Up! Play Up! and Win the War", Football, the Nation and the Great War 1914–15', *Journal of Contemporary History*, vol. 20, No. 3, July 1985

Wall, F., *50 Years of Football 1884–1934* (reprinted, Cleethorpes, Soccer Books Ltd, 2006)

War Office, Manual of Military Law (London, HMSO, 1914)

Ward, F., *The 23rd (S) Battalion Royal Fusiliers (First Sportsman's): A Record of Its Services in the Great War 1914–1919* (London, Sidgwick & Jackson, 1920)

Westlake, R., *English and Welsh Infantry Regiments* (Staplehurst, Spellmount, 1995)

——, *Kitchener's Army* (Staplehurst, Spellmount, 1989)

White, A., *The Men Who Made Fulham Football Club* (Stroud, Tempus, 2002)

Who Was Who 1897–2005 (London, A & C Black)

Wilson, H. and Hammerton, J., *The Great War, 13 vols*
(London, Amalgamated Press, 1914–1919)

Winter, D., *Death's Men* (London, Allen Lane, 1978)

Work of the Royal Engineers in the European War 1914–19: Military Mining (Chatham, Institute of Royal Engineers, 1922)

Wyrall, E., *The 17th (S) Battalion Royal Fusiliers 1914–1919* (London, Methuen, 1930)

——, *The Diehards in the Great War* (London, Harrison & Sons, 1926)

——, *The History of the Second Division 1914–1918*
(London, Nelson, 1921)

——, *The History of the King's Regiment (Liverpool) 1914–1919*
(London, Arnold, 1928)

Zipfel, E. and Albrecht, O., *Geschichte des Infanterie-Regiments Bremen (1. Hanseatisches) nr. 75,* (Bremen, H.M. Hauschild GmbH, 1934)

INDEX

405

411